This book may be kept

The Teaching of
Speech

PRENTICE-HALL EDUCATION SERIES
Dr. Harold S. Spears, Editor

ANDREW THOMAS WEAVER, *University of Wisconsin*

GLADYS LOUISE BORCHERS, *University of Wisconsin*

DONALD KLIESE SMITH, *University of Minnesota*

The Teaching of Speech

A TEXTBOOK
FOR COLLEGE COURSES IN
SPEECH EDUCATION

1952   New York   PRENTICE-HALL, INC.

Preface

SPEECH teachers and students preparing to teach speech, in seeking practical suggestions about what to teach and how to teach it, quite properly ask a bewildering variety of questions about their profession. They want to know how, and to what purpose, successful teachers in the field have organized, motivated, conducted, and evaluated their classroom experiences. They want to understand the place of speech education in the curriculum, grasp speech education goals and their relationships to the general purposes of education, and learn of effective integrations of speech with other school subjects.

This book is designed to offer helpful solutions to some of these urgent problems by (1) presenting speech training as an integral factor in the total educational enterprise, (2) analyzing in detail the speech teacher's task, and (3) showing how successful speech teachers are fulfilling their functions.

Part I presents the speech discipline in its historical and educational setting and explains why this discipline has emerged today as a vital element in the training of all students: The normal, the handicapped, and the talented. The teaching and learning of speech is shown, too, to be an important component of any curriculum, whether it is organized under a progressive or a conservative philosophy of education. Part II focuses on specific, practical, and tested methods for the direct improvement of the student's basic speech habits. Part III describes in detail nine useful forms of speaking activity, indicating how each may be taught, from initial motivation to final performance. Part IV sets forth the theory and techniques of criticism and evaluation which are prerequisite to maximum student improvement.

v

Included in these four sections are carefully organized exercises, tests, check lists, diagrams, poems, prose readings, and selections from speeches and plays, and appended to each chapter is a short working bibliography of available references. The material is arranged in such a way that the various parts of the book may be used in whatever order serves a particular situation best: If the reader desires first a basic understanding of educational backgrounds, he may start with Part I; or, if his main concern is with specific classroom procedures, for example, or a specific form of speaking, he may turn immediately to the chapters most appropriate to these topics.

The responsibilities of teaching speech should not be undertaken lightly. Perforce, every speech teacher deals directly with vital and intimate aspects of his students' behavior and lives, and he owes to his classes the painstakingly careful counsel and guidance which can result only from an earnest and thoughtful consideration of the many intensely personal matters involved in speech.

This book does not presume to provide final and definitive answers to all the problems which the speech teacher will face; rather, its aim is to help teachers discover more fruitful and constructive methods of attack upon the many difficulties and questions with which they will be confronted from day to day.

Madison, Wisconsin   ANDREW THOMAS WEAVER
                                                        GLADYS LOUISE BORCHERS
                                                        DONALD KLIESE SMITH

Table of Contents

PART I

The Place of Speech in Education

CHAPTER 1

Speech Education and the Needs of School Children

INTRODUCTION

A BOOK on the teaching of speech is justified only if we accept two assumptions concerning the nature of speech and education: First, that speech can be taught, and, second, that it ought to be taught as a part of the curriculum of our schools. Both of these assumptions have been challenged upon occasion, and consequently have figured in controversy dating back as far as the origin of formal theory concerning the nature of speech and its place in education. However, the assumption that speech can be taught seems today to have passed beyond the area of controversy.

SPEECH CAN BE TAUGHT

Speech Is Learned Behavior

Since we have come to understand more clearly the nature of speech, there has been little reason to question the belief that the speech behavior of any individual can be modified by appropriate learning activities directed by an efficient teacher. Speech is an aspect of human behavior, and it is _learned_ behavior in the same sense that handwriting, spelling, or table manners are learned behavior—even though skills in speaking may be somewhat more complex. The simple fact is that not only can speech be taught, but actually speech has been taught to everyone. Each of us adheres to a particular complex of speech habits, attitudes, and generalized abilities by reason of the nature of our environment and experiences from early childhood. This complex is considerably developed in any child by the time he reaches school age, but his speech patterns when he enters school are no more fixed for all time than are his physical characteristics. His speech behavior, like his physical growth, will be subject to constant change and modification as he proceeds with the universal task of growing up, and it will be subject to change and modification influenced greatly by the sort of experiences he encounters. In a very real sense all schools teach speech in one way or another; they may teach speech by taking certain positive steps to help children speak more effectively, or they may teach it by ignoring their role in the shaping of speech habits and, thus, by this neglect share in the fixing of inadequate and ineffective patterns of speaking acquired early and later crystallized by the child.[1]

If we agree here that speech can be taught, there remains the question of whether or not this complex skill can be taught within the limits of the time and other resources available to the classroom teacher. The question is a vital one. Certain characteristics of speech are recognizably difficult to alter; certain habits seem to persist stubbornly in the face of long and arduous effort to modify them. Consequently, teachers of speech have asked repeatedly: What can be taught within the limitations of the curriculum? The results of the considerable body of research along this line indicate that teachers of speech are generally successful in modifying the speaking behavior of their students in ways which can be measured or observed with reasonable objectivity.

Results of Experiments Evaluating Speech Instruction

Experiments have shown that high school students, after taking fundamental courses in speech, are able to speak more acceptably,

---

[1] Elise Hahn, "Analysis of Speech of First Grade Children," Quarterly Journal of Speech (October, 1948), 34: 361–366. In her study of first grade children, Mrs. Hahn observes "that all the types of speakers observable in college speech classes—the garrulous, the over-assertive, the shy, the poised, and the enthusiastic—have easily recognizable counterparts in the first grade. One can only conclude that the individual manner of speaking becomes organized at an early date and that the school system at present only permits the same habits to continue into adulthood."

not only to their teachers, but also to boards of judges representing a wide variety of adult occupations—and that these results are attainable by different teachers in different high schools.[2] Not enough is known about personality to say with assurance that the changes resultant from speech training are inevitably good, but the general trend of personality changes resulting from speech training seems to be in the direction of more satisfactory social adjustment.[3] Few would question the efficiency of speech training in reducing social fears, including fear of the speaking situation.

There is evidence, too, that the specific skills involved in the complex act of speech can be changed as a result of classroom speech training. Individuals can be helped to communicate their feelings more effectively through the use of visible action; they can be taught to use movement and gesture more meaningfully; and they can be helped to improve vocal quality and to use more appropriate volume, rate, pitch, and inflectional patterns. They can be trained in the use of language particularly suitable to effective speaking. Beyond the direct evidence that speech instruction affects the observable aspects of speech behavior, there is evidence that it also affects those inner attitudes which are related to speaking performance.

Finally, there is an increasing body of evidence that certain types of speech training result in improvement in the generalized skill of critical thinking—at least to the extent that such skill can be measured by existing tests.[4] This finding, of course, seems consistent with our understanding of the essentially verbal nature of thought itself.

---

[2] G. L. Borchers, "Direct and Indirect Methods of Instruction in Speech," J. of Ed. Research, March, 1936, p. 512; Ruth Dieckhoff, "An Experiment in Methods of Instruction in Speech," (M. A. Thesis, U. of W., 1939).

[3] For a brief summary of research pertinent to the effects of speech training on various aspects and speaking, and on personality, see A. T. Weaver, G. L. Borchers, and G. G. Eye, "What Speech Can Contribute to High School Education," *Bulletin of Nat. Assoc. of Sec. School Principals* (November, 1945), 133: 9–18. For an extensive summary of research pertinent to all the effects of training, see Howard Gilkinson, *Outlines of Research in General Speech.* Minneapolis: Burgess Publishing Co., 1948, pp. 32–41, Bibliography.

[4] W. S. Howell, "The Effects of High School Debating on Critical Thinking." (Ph.D. Thesis, University of Wisconsin, 1942); W. Brembeck, "The Effects of a Course in Argumentation on Critical Thinking." (Ph.D. Thesis, University of Wisconsin, 1947).

In surveying the widespread evidence of the value of speech education, it would be easy to grow lyrical about the place of speech in education. A word of caution is necessary: Diversity of available instructional materials, methods, and objectives makes inevitable diversity of results. The intent of this brief survey of the results of speech training is not to picture speech education as a kind of educational "snake oil." Speech teachers, like other teachers, need to avoid the tendency to define the objectives of their work in terms of *all* the objectives possible to education. They need to remember Whitehead's injunctions about the business of education —that schools, instead of trying to teach too many things, ought to try to teach a limited number of selected things well. The wealth of research concerning the outcomes of speech training does not constitute a statement of the outcomes possible to any one course in speech, but it does serve to underline one simple point—that speech courses do get results—tangible, measurable results, consistent with the teacher's goals and methods.

SPEECH OUGHT TO BE TAUGHT IN THE SECONDARY SCHOOL

In recent years, the high school curriculum has become increasingly a battleground in which a variety of disciplines have competed for a share of the limited time available. The fact that speech education, or any other skill or body of information, *can* be taught does not assure its inclusion in this curriculum. Many things can be taught. The point is: Which of them should be taught? Before deciding how, or to what extent, secondary schools should concern themselves with speech, it is important to ask: (a) What is meant by speech education? and (b) What relevance has such education to the general objectives of secondary education?

It is apparent that not all persons who call themselves teachers of speech seek the same sorts of goals, or understand the field of speech in the same sense. Everett L. Hunt observes of rhetoric that "in its protean forms it is at home in institutions of salesmanship, in seminaries of charm and personality, in the psychology of advertising, in propaganda machines that wage hot and cold wars, in defense of intolerance, racial hatred and special privilege, or in utopian appeals for will-of-the-wisp ideals that ignore the realities of human nature." [5]

A variety of classroom activities, extending from drill in the proper intonation of the word "idea" to the study of efficient ways of discovering and structuring valid ideas, are all identified as speech education. Moreover, some speech teachers are occupied almost exclusively with one or the other segment of such activities. As a result, it is inevitable that critics both within and outside the field of speech should have varying views of the significance of speech to education generally. The problem is not new. Plato criticized the speech teachers of his day on philosophic grounds, and then proceeded to define his own system of speech education. In our day, speech teachers are often divided on fundamental questions as to how speech training ought to be conducted, and what it ought to include.

In the light of this existing controversy it would seem wise to reserve a decision on the proposition that speech ought to be taught in our high schools until the nature of the speech education in question has been defined. The prime purpose here is just that—to define, by an examination of history, a study of contemporary trends and practices, and a detailing of classroom objectives, activities, and procedures, the nature of speech education as it is understood by the authors. The problem may be clarified for future discussion, however, by an introductory statement of the general nature of speech education, and the relationship of such education to the objectives of the high school.

The Nature of Speech Education [6]

The casual observer of educational trends may find it curious that we have spoken thus far only of speech rather than of public speak-

---

[5] E. L. Hunt, "Rhetoric and General Education," *Quarterly Journal of Speech* (October, 1949), 35: 277.

[6] The early chapters of this book talk about speech education largely in terms of the education of the speaker. Historically, this has been the emphasis given to speech training, and most instructional practice has been directed toward the single objective of improving the speaking skills of students. However, we view *listening* as an important feature of every speaking situation, and the development of listening skill as an integral aspect of the program in speech education; *speech education* should include instruction in both *speaking* and *listening*.

ing, or drama, or debating, or any of the other particular forms of speaking. This distinction is of considerable importance in explaining the nature of the concern of the speech teacher. It places the emphasis on speech for everyday private communication for everyone instead of on public performance for a selected few.

Fundamentally, the teacher of speech has made three rather simple observations about speaking in our society. First, speaking is an extraordinarily ubiquitous activity. Research has confirmed the common sense observation that about 90% of the language activity of most people takes the form of speaking or listening. The fact that a child entering school may be talking to the extent of 30,000 words a day before he has written half a dozen words, is only a prophecy of the condition that will prevail throughout most of his life. Teachers may inhibit the spoken output and increase the written output to some extent—may even enshrine "freedom *from* speech" as a civil right for teachers to parallel "freedom *of* speech" —but basically the children with whom they work are destined to continue to use language primarily as speakers or listeners.

Second, this extraordinarily common activity is also vitally important to both individual and society. The child who wants a new toy, the statesman who wants a new (or old) form of medical care, the boy meeting girl, the housewife shopping for groceries, and leaders seeking by discussion to attain wisdom in policy with regard to a hydrogen bomb, all have a common concern with the skills of speaking. While it is not possible, or just, to place various forms of human activity in a hierarchy of importance, it is also impossible to deny that speaking and listening are among the most important forms of human activity.

Third, speech, this common activity of such signal importance, is used in an almost bewildering variety of forms and for an almost infinite number of distinctive purposes. Conversation, a child's dramatic play, a radio discussion, a sermon, a congressional debate, or a club meeting, all involve speaking and listening: They make common use of audible and visible symbols; they seek the co-operation of listeners, and they have form and purpose.

The three foregoing observations about speech are easily made, but within them lie hard facts which have shaped our conception of speech education. In essence this conception is that, as speech teachers we are concerned with speech for all people. We want to help not merely the handicapped child who cannot articulate successfully the sounds of his own language, and not merely the neophyte leader whose future is closely linked with skill in persuasive speaking technique; we want every child to reach his individual potentialities as a speaker. We want to find ways of organizing and directing activities in the school which will have the greatest commonality of use, the greatest possibility for giving to each child greater effectiveness in developing skills and understandings of the multiform ways in which he will use speech throughout his life. To these common skills and understandings we want to add some particular skills in handling the forms of speaking most useful in our society.

In this concern with the needs of students we are fully aware that the sort of speaking which promotes understanding rather than confusion among people, and which stresses effective problem-solving rather than the exploitation of one man by another, is going to prove most useful to the greatest number of students. We see speaking skill not merely as a means by which people compete successfully with their fellow men, but, more properly, as a means by which people live together more effectively and harmoniously.

It is important, in a brief statement of the nature of speech education, to emphasize the breadth of view with which the successful speech teacher necessarily approaches his job. Few would contend that speech education as taught today succeeds in every respect in achieving the generalized types of skills and understandings most useful to all students. But it is to this generalized goal that the activities of speech teachers are directed. Within the diversity of method and activity practiced by speech teachers there is a growing core of recognition that speech education is larger than training in any single form of speaking, that it has as its focus the common stake of all people in speaking effectively, that it finds this commonality in a central concern with all matters which touch upon the use and interpretation of the audible and visible symbols of speaking, and that it sees speech in the social setting as a means of social adaptation and an instrumentality, part fact, part promise, of social co-operation.[7]

---

[7] A. T. Weaver, "The Case for Speech," *Quarterly Journal of Speech* (April, 1939), 25: 185.

Speaking Skill Is Needed by Every Person

There are many frames of reference within which one might consider the relationship of a particular educational discipline, such as speech, to the purposes of the American high school. Perhaps the simplest method of carrying on such a discussion is to raise the question of the relationship of speech to the needs of boys and girls, and the complementary question of the relationship of speech to the needs of a democratic society. Despite the persistent controversy which surrounds the content, methods, and purposes of the secondary school curriculum, there is a genuine center of agreement in this country that education in a democracy should enable boys and girls to live more effective, more satisfying, and more useful lives, and should strengthen the better characteristics of the society within which these boys and girls will live and work. This assumption that education should serve the welfare of both the individual and society is fundamental to our concept of the school curriculum. It has been evident in nearly all the classic statements and restatements of the purposes of secondary education.[8] A half century ago Herbert Spencer defined education as preparation for (1) self-preservation, (2) rearing and disciplining of offspring, (3) economic life, (4) social and political relationships, and (5) leisure. This is not greatly different in essence from the more recent statement of the Educational Policies Commission of the four basic objectives of (1) self-realization, (2) human relationships, (3) economic efficiency, and (4) civic responsibility. Both recognize the dual responsibility of the schools to the individual and to the state.[9]

Leaving for the moment the question of how speech training strengthens a democratic society, let us first examine the ways in which speech serves the lives of boys and girls. Our educational literature abounds in reports of elaborate investigations made to determine pupils' needs.[10] In general these investigations take two forms: (a) Those concerned with the prerequisites for desirable

---

[8] Harl Douglass, *The High School Curriculum*. New York: The Ronald Press, 1947, p. 30.

[9] For a further discussion of the nature and function of the high school curriculum, see Douglass, pp. 24–48.

[10] See D. A. Prescott, *Emotions and the Education Process*, Howard Bell, *Youth Tell Their Story*. Washington, D. C.: American Council in Education, 1938.

personality development in the individual, and (b) those concerned with the types of problems which young people encounter in meeting the demands of society. It is worth while to ask just how speech affects the fulfillment of student needs in these two areas.

Effective Speaking as a Prerequisite to Desirable Personality Development

The close relationship between speech and personality has attracted the attention of a wide variety of scholars. The casual way in which everyday judgments of personality are based largely upon the speech behavior of the person being judged has long suggested to psychologists that the scientific study of speech behavior might be a key to the identification of personality traits or types.[11]

Speech teachers, who need to understand the sources of the behavior they seek to modify, and who need to understand the implications of any modification they may succeed in effecting, are of necessity interested in the sort of study of speech carried on by psychologists, as well as similar work by scholars in their own field. More directly, perhaps, they are interested in the way in which the presence or absence of certain skills of speaking serve not only to *represent* personality, but serve also to *shape* personality. Specifically, they have in mind the fact that retarded or inadequate speech skills may not only constitute an immediate practical handicap to an individual, but also serve to distort his developing personality. As a child grows from early absorption with self and immediate environment into an increasingly social being, the adequacy of his adjustment to the social world will depend in large measure upon his ability to communicate freely and efficiently with other people. The so-called "well adjusted" adult, dear to the heart of the newspaper psychologist, is ordinarily one capable of easy and effective communication with other people. Moreover, he is usually one who has had a history of reasonably successful social experience, a history in which childhood and adolescent skills in speaking must of necessity have played an important role.

It is not difficult to observe the interaction of defective speaking skills and personality problems. Such observation is most easily

---

[11] A good review of the attention given speech by psychologists may be found in Sanford, "Speech and Personality," *Psychological Bulletin* (1942) 39, 811–848.

made concerning persons with severe speech defects, such as stuttering. It is commonplace for us to say of such persons that their greatest handicap is often not their speech defect per se, but the variety of anti-social personality traits they have acquired in conjunction with and in consequence of the speech defect. The observations that apply to the severely handicapped also hold true, though to a lesser degree, for children with minor inefficiencies in speaking. Teachers have long observed with sympathy the difficulties of children who, by their speech habits, cut themselves off from membership in, or the approval of, their own social group. There are many kinds of speaking difficulties that may lead to some degree of social isolation for a child, which will handicap the child's development as a happy, useful person.

The observations of teachers about the importance of speaking skill to the personality development of children has been interestingly confirmed by observers in other fields. Studying troublesome and ill-adjusted workers in Australia, Elton Mayo concluded that four basic causal conditions were present: (1) "These men had no friends except at the propagandist level;" (2) "They had no capacity for conversation;" (3) "All action, like social relationship, was for them emergency action;" and (4) "They regarded the world as a hostile place." [12] From both his own studies and those of Dr. Pierre Janet in clinical research, Mayo concludes that all such studies "lead to observation of the fact that those individuals usually described as psychoneurotic (though apparently free from any organic pathology) are unable to communicate easily and intimately with other persons." [13]

Does one develop adequate speech in consequence of adequate personality development, or does one develop an adequate personality in consequence of effective speech? It is not necessary, fortunately, to labor this question. The important fact is that personality and speech behavior are intimately associated and in constant interaction. The school system interested in meeting the needs of

---

[12] Elton Mayo, *The Social Problems of an Industrial Civilization.* Andover, Mass.: The Andover Press, 1945, p. 26. Marie Hochmuth develops the significance of this work to speech education in "Speech and Society." *Bulletin of Nat. Association of Sec. School Principals* (January, 1948), Vol.: 32, 151.

[13] *Ibid.,* p. 22.

children will try to help children in as many ways as possible. One obvious and important way to help them is to train them to speak more effectively. The consequence of such assistance may be not only to help children live more comfortably and effectively at the moment, but also to assist them in growing into successful adult relations with their fellow men.

Effective Speech Helps in Meeting the Demands of Society

The scientist in his laboratory is always chary about judging the personality of others. Outside his laboratory he is apt to join the rest of us in the universal and practical job of judging constantly the temperament and capabilities of his fellow men. It is easy to observe that most of us are overly hasty in our judgments of others; that we confuse the superficial with the substantial, the apparent with the real, and that the bases of our judgments are often obscure and illogical. Like some of our ancestors who were unable to see the greatness of an Abraham Lincoln beneath homespun and homeliness, we miss the real worth of persons who impress us badly on first acquaintance. It is difficult to see any easy escape from this situation. The business of the world demands evaluation of people. Men are hired and fired, marriages arranged and sometimes disarranged, friends won or lost, credit extended or withheld, and leaders appointed or rejected upon the basis of judgments of personality, temperament, and capabilities. Each of us can be aided to some extent in the work of discovering the heart of gold beneath the rough exterior and the noble soul within the unkempt body; but none of us can be spared the necessity of making innumerable judgments of other people upon more or less limited evidence. And we cannot escape the fact that we are being constantly judged by others upon equally inadequate grounds.

That the speech of the individual is significant in this business of judging and being judged is a commonplace; it is the most important aspect of a person's behavior available for our observation. The fact that too few people reveal themselves completely and do justice to their intrinsic qualities of character and intellect in their speech, is one of the misfortunes which blocks our social machinery. The complication is increased by the fact that some persons of limited

good will and questionable good sense are rather successful in caus-
ing others to overestimate them by reason of their proficiency in
certain aspects of speaking.

Since it is a fact that we judge and are judged on the basis of
speech behavior, each of us needs to seek proficiency in speech to
meet one of the demands placed on us by the conditions of social
living. If we apply for a job, we must understand that our speech
influences significantly the outcome of our job interview. If we
would become leaders, we must develop the ability to give others
confidence in our inner sincerity and our clarity of purpose. If we
would work in harmony with other people, we must control our
own speech in terms of our understanding of the purposes of our
fellow men. Instead of bemoaning the fact that we are being mis-
judged by other people we should seek to improve our speech to
the point at which we can reveal our real worth to other persons.

From all this one may conclude that if it is possible to view speech
skill as a prerequisite of desirable personality development, it is
equally possible to view it as one of the tools needed by the individual in meeting the demands of society. The relation of speaking
skill to success in "getting along" in the world is almost too obvious
to need elaboration. Inasmuch as speech teachers ever since the
time of Quintilian have been concerned with the practical needs of
men, and because speech bears such a significant relationship to the
matter of vocational success, a brief view of this particular aspect
of speech training will be of value here.

Speech and Vocational Success

Many vocations in our society place a premium upon special competence in speaking, and often emphasize a particular form of
speaking. Lawyers, teachers, salesmen, doctors, businessmen, politicians, foremen, and a variety of other occupational groups recognize
the relevance of speaking skill to achievement in their particular
jobs. Less obvious, but perhaps even more important, is the fact
that studies of job failures in all walks of life invariably indicate
that men fail in their various vocations not so much because of inability in particular industrial or occupational skills as because of
their failure in the skill of getting along with their fellow men. In
short, a broad view of skills of communication shows them to be
the basis of satisfactory vocational achievement in virtually the

whole sweep of economic life. Research in this area confirms common sense observation. So extensive is the recognition in this country of the vocational importance of speaking skill, and so widespread is the recognition by adults of the practical, personal handicap of speech deficiencies, that our own day has seen a great increase of speech training for adult groups. The concepts of the speech training being given by toastmaster's clubs, Carnegie courses, university extension courses, rural life discussion groups, and public speaking courses for labor leaders, business leaders, or army officers are as varied as the titles under which the work is conducted; they all possess in common, however, which reflect, in some measure, the need felt by multitudes of adults for better speech skills to help them in the business of making a living.

Many men need special skills in public speaking, debating, radio speaking, interviewing, and parliamentary leadership. Though specialized speech activities have a wide market in our society, a view of speech in a broader sense indicates clearly that none of us can meet personally the demands of our society without a considerable measure of skill in speech; it is an indispensable instrument of social adaptation and co-operative living. Our success in living and in making a living is inextricably linked to the manner and substance of our speech.

Speech and the Needs of a Democratic Society

Consideration of its relevance to the needs of children is one of the ways of testing the claims of any discipline to a place in the high school curriculum. There is another and equally significant way of viewing the curriculum. Schools carry a unique measure of social responsibility. In our society the system of free public education has been viewed as at once the bulwark and the hope of democracy. It is therefore inevitable that in evaluating the place of speech education in the school curriculum we should determine the relevance of such education to the needs and purposes of our society. In making such inquiry one ought to recognize that ideally the purposes of society and the needs of individuals are mutually supporting rather than in conflict. At least such is the hope, and, in some measure, the achievement of democratic society. However, one also ought to recognize that areas of conflict do exist, and that the needs of children, at least as they are pictured by children, do not always harmonize perfectly with the demands of the social order in which they live. These areas of conflict provide speech teachers with some of their most perplexing problems. Should children be helped to speak in such a way as to "get on" personally in the society in which they live, or should they be helped to speak in ways most productive of social good for the greatest number of people? Ideally we should hope that both goals can be achieved.

It is apparent that not all men who have achieved personal goals with speech, have acted for the better interests of society. An Adolf Hitler or a Gerald L. K. Smith, who speaks for the purpose of confusing, exploiting, or misleading his fellow men, has been the sort of spectacle that has stimulated periodic attacks upon rhetoric. Interestingly enough, such attacks are usually successful in direct proportion to the rhetorical skill of those making the attacks, a circumstance which serves to underline the further obvious fact that society could not banish rhetoric even if it chose. Societies do not and cannot exist apart from modes of communication, and a society which does not concern itself with the ways in which its members speak and the purposes for which they speak is neglecting a process which will either strengthen and develop that society, or weaken and destroy it.

Modern societies in which political power has been concentrated in the hands of a few, like twentieth-century dictatorships, have recognized to a unique extent their dependence upon speaking. Such societies have grown and sought to preserve themselves upon a basis of control over channels of communication by the few who would rule, and by the systematic and skillful use of various modes of communication, including speech, to exploit the bulk of society in the interests of these few. Machiavelli's Prince, Castiglione's Gentleman, and Hitler's youth leader were men of different sorts, but they were all men who counted speaking skill as one of the means of their leadership, however corrupt the ends of such leadership. George Orwell, in his novel, *Nineteen Eighty-Four*, shows how a totalitarian state sought to perpetuate itself by systematic manipulation of the language used by its people. The language of this state was called "Newspeak," and abounded with slogans or words which were in themselves contradictory, like "War is Peace," "Freedom is Slavery," or "Love is Hate." Such words as *crimstop, black-white,* and *doublethink* served to summarize the elaborate mental training given all children in order to make them "unwilling and unable to think too deeply on any subject whatever." [14]   The "Newspeak" of Orwell's imaginary totalitarian state, is only too reminiscent of the way in which dictatorships in our own day have used speech to confuse their subjects, to distort the capacity of persons to understand that which is real, and to think critically about the problems which they face.

Dictatorships have viewed speech as an instrument of exploitation. They have also viewed it as a skill to be cultivated in the few who are to hold power.   Democracy, in precisely the measure that it has diffused power among all the people, has required decision making and social action as parts of the responsibility of all men.   Thus, democratic society has developed an immense concern with the speaking and listening skills of all men.   The notable picture of the "seamless web" of democratic life, given us by David Lilienthal, becomes reality to the extent that men everywhere are able to communicate with one another, and to the extent that they are able to reach understanding through mutually-held-and-used skills and purposes in speaking.   This is not to suggest that all men in a democracy must speak with equal skill, or that all must be leaders, or that leaders are not needed.   It is to suggest that in a democracy the skills of leadership must be widely held and shared; that the minority which leads must regard as important the creative purposes of society as a whole; that there must exist the "just balance between talk to the voters, and talk among them"; [15] and that there needs to be the widest possible use of speech to broaden areas of understanding among men.   As Professor O'Neill observed more than twenty-five years ago, "Civilization itself consists largely in man's improvement in form, in technique, in knowing what to do with, how to treat, with what technique to handle the substance of the Universe. . . ." [16]   There are forms and techniques of speaking which serve democracy well, and for which democratic society should show special concern.   There are forms of communication

---

[14] George Orwell, *Nineteen Eighty-Four.*   New York: Harcourt, Brace & Co., 1949, p. 212.

[15] W. E. Utterback, "Political Significance of Group Discussion," *Annals of the Am. Acad. Pol. and Soc. Sci.* (March, 1947), p. 38.

[16] James M. O'Neill, "Speech Content and Course Content," *Quarterly Journal of Speech* (February, 1923), Vol. 9: 1, p. 144.

appropriate to democratic purposes, and we need the widest possible sharing of skills in the use of these forms, and the widest possible preference for these forms in our speaking and listening public.

What forms of speaking are appropriate to democracy? What skills need to be widely shared to foster understanding among men? Society cannot exist without communication, but what sort of communication will nourish our particular society? Questions of this sort are again a part of the burden of this entire book, but it may be possible at this point to make certain specific observations about speech in a democratic society.

It is apparent that democratic societies have developed certain forms of speaking consistent with their own ends. Of these forms, discussion and debate come most quickly to mind, and are perhaps most readily observed. Decision making in a democracy requires wide sharing of information, adequate presentation of alternative solutions to the problems of society, and orderly, commonly-held techniques for resolving conflicts among individuals and social groups, whether by the integration of group opinions, by compromise, or if need be, by majority rule. The philosophy and techniques of discussion and debate are appropriate to these requirements of democracy, and as a result these forms of speaking have flourished in our own nation. The immense amount of discussion and debating in this country is more a sign of the need of our society for such activity than an indication of the existence of widespread understanding of either the techniques or possibilities of such activity. Casual observation of radio debate and discussion will sustain the notion that much discussion in America is characterized by a sharing of prejudices rather than information, and much debate by an exchange of recriminations rather than argument. Democracy cannot exist without discussion and debate; it cannot prosper without the effective and productive use of such forms of speaking. This fact is of vital importance to American schools. As Ewbank and Auer observe, "Discussion and debate are the essential tools of democracy. The schools can and should, in classrooms and in forensic competitions, train future citizens in the proper use of these tools." [17]

---

[17] H. L. Ewbank, and J. J. Auer, "Decision Making: Discussion and Debate," *Bulletin of Nat. Assoc. Sec. School Principals* (January, 1948), Vol. 32, p. 49.

There are other less apparent, but equally significant relations between democratic society and particular techniques of speaking. The disparity between the American ideal of an "informed electorate," and the evidence provided by public polling groups as to the actual status of the electorate's information has presented our country with a continuing and fundamental crisis. "People generally," we say, "need to know a great deal about the complex problems which confront them." "People generally," the pollsters tell us with monotonous regularity, "know singularly little about these problems." This crisis is not new, but it takes on increasing urgency in a world making decisions on such literally explosive issues as those surrounding the creation and use of a hydrogen bomb. In consequence of this crisis, we have witnessed in the last few years a remarkable exodus of scientists from the laboratory to the public platform; not long ago they subscribed generally to the belief that their responsibilities were for the discovery of facts, not for their dissemination or popularization. Now, suddenly, it seems immensely important that men who have knowledge and who have thought deeply be able to communicate their knowledge and the product of their thinking. It is clear that our society requires not only that *some* men be informed concerning problems of immense complexity, but also that *all* men share to some extent in this knowledge. In such circumstances our society strongly needs "good men skilled in speaking," and men whose special information and understanding is coupled with the rhetorical skill needed to transmit, disseminate, and popularize their specialized information and understanding.

There are immense, unanswered problems about the sort of speaking and speech training most appropriate to the needs of our democratic society. In general we observe that speech is the essential instrument by which social groups secure co-operation, but we also realize that some speaking is divisive and destructive in its social impact. Some speech teachers have sought to set up complex normative standards for *good* speaking, to get scientific bases for approving the sort of speaking which unifies, informs, and promotes understanding, and for condemning that which divides or misinforms. As we shall indicate more fully later in this book, the formation and application of such standards of "good" speech is a task which challenges the teacher's art to the utmost and which requires the finest sort of teachers and teaching. It is also a task in which our democratic society has an immense stake.   The easy optimism with which many of our schools have neglected the speaking of their students is scarcely defensible in view of the social consequences at issue.   It is the sort of optimism composed of diverse, and often unstated attitudes—"that children already know how to speak well enough when they come to school," or "that speech comes natural to people, and can't be taught."   These attitudes represent tragic misunderstandings.   The optimism they breed is justified neither by the state of our world nor the needs of our society.   As Dr. Hochmuth observes, "Speech is a means to an end.   It must be cultivated as a means for bringing stability in human relations and as a tool for helping to secure peace in our time.   This will not be done by English teachers or speech teachers who emphasize only the accuracies of language or the logic of conclusions.   It must be done by people who recognize the psychological, sociological and political implications of talk. . . .   Until the schools give more attention to the development of social competence than has ever been given in the history of our country, there can be little hope for finding these personal disciplines that are necessary for cooperative behavior in an industrial society, a democratic nation, and a world order." [18]

SUMMARY

We have tried to establish two propositions in this chapter—(1) that speech can be taught, and (2) that it ought to be taught.   Most people today, including the majority of educators, concede these points, yet the provisions made in many schools for helping children with their speech are often haphazard.

In showing that speech ought to be taught, we have defined broadly the field of concern to speech teachers, and have suggested the importance of such a discipline in meeting the needs of children and the needs of the democratic society in which we live.   Such an elaboration of the importance of speech was not undertaken as a case of special pleading, not as a polemic in behalf of a single educational enterprise.   Rather, it was undertaken with the belief that speech teachers capable of doing their job need to understand the precise way in which their work is important.   It is possible that the singular neglect of speech in some of our secondary schools has

---

[18] Marie Hochmuth, "Speech and Society," *op. cit.,* p. 33.

been in part a responsibility of those teachers of speech and English whose concept of their own job has been limited or defective.

In defining speech broadly we recognize that we are discussing a form of human behavior which is nourished and shaped not only by the speech teacher, but by the whole of a child's education, the totality of his experiences at home, in school, and in society. In so viewing speech we recognize the fact that practically everyone will learn some form of speech that will be adequate to some degree; but we also stress the special contribution of the teacher particularly competent in understanding and directing speaking activity, and the teacher who is given time to work with boys and girls directly in improving their speech.

We hold that children learn the important skills of social adaptation not merely from reading about them, but primarily by working with people, speaking with them, listening to them, and observing their behavior—and that it is this type of activity which the speech class can provide under rational, purposive supervision. We hold that practical ability in solving problems, judging values, and discriminating among ideas in our society is well learned only when students actually practice these activities as they will use them throughout life in the capacity of speakers and listeners. In short, we maintain that speech training makes a legitimate and major contribution to the processes of education generally, and that the methods and materials of the speech class are essential to the attainment of the basic purposes for which schools exist in a democracy. We shall proceed to examine these methods and materials in detail.

SELECTED BIBLIOGRAPHY

"A Program of Speech Education" (recommended by the Speech Association of America to the North Central Association), *Quarterly Journal of Speech* (October, 1951), 37: 347–358.

Backus, Ollie, *Speech in Education*. New York: Longmans Green & Co., 1943, Introduction and Chapter 1.

Hochmuth, Marie, "Speech and Society," *Bulletin of the National Association of Secondary School Principals* (January, 1948), 32: 151, pp. 17–33.

Knower, Franklin H., "Speech Education for all American Youth," *Bulletin of the National Association of Secondary School Principals* (January, 1948), 32: 151, pp. 11–16.

N. E. A. Educational Policies Commission: *Education For All American Youth*. Washington, D. C., 1944, 89–100, 134–136, 148.

N. E. A. Educational Policies Commission: *The Purposes of Education in American Democracy*. Washington, D. C., 1938, 39–50.

Weaver, Andrew T., Glen G. Eye, and Gladys L. Borchers, "What Speech Can Contribute to High School Education," *Bulletin of the National Association of Secondary School Principals* (November, 1945), 29: 133, pp. 9–18.

CHAPTER 2

The Evolution of the Speech Program

S PEECH education is more extensive in the United States than anywhere else in the world. Not only is there more direct speech teaching in our elementary schools, high schools, colleges, and universities; not only are more undergraduate and graduate speech degrees granted; but also in the United States at present the concept "speech" has a broader and a distinctly new-world connotation.

Like many things American, our speech education was patterned at first after European models. The plans, the texts, and the training of the teachers followed English practices. Speech education in England, in turn, had been influenced by the theories of Medieval priests who had received their inspiration from Rome and Greece, and those sources had been influenced by much earlier writers in Egypt.

If we were to graph the emphasis given speech training throughout history, we would note marked variation in various periods. But it is clear that one of the high points would be in the twentieth century and in the United States. The curve begins about 3000 years before Christ, and turns most sharply upward from 500 B.C. to 100 A.D. and again from 1800 to 1950. It represents a longer heritage than most disciplines can boast.

THE ANTIQUITY OF SPEECH EDUCATION

Egyptian Records of Speech Teaching

It is not difficult to understand that the importance of speech as a means of controlling society was recognized long before the beginning of the 5000 years in our suggested diagram. The first human associations brought the need for some kind of talk. In this text, however, we are concerned mainly with formal instruction in speech, and the first records of this teaching are found in the oldest book in the world, variously dated 3200 to 2000 B.C.

In 1847 the National Library of Paris received for its collection the famous Prisse Papyrus, so named because it was presented to the library by M. Prisse D'Avennes, an early French archaeologist whose assistant in excavating an Egyptian tomb uncovered this interesting relic of the ancient past. The papyrus is also known as *The Instruction of Ptah-ho-tep and the Instruction of Kegemni.*

When an Egyptian felt that he was coming to the end of his life he made his will and left his descendants both property and advice. The advice was usually considered more important and significant than the property, because the advice was the product of a lifetime of experience which was being passed on to the eldest son as a guide for his future. Such advice varied widely. Certain types of officials left suggestions of a political character, and counselors to kings bequeathed to their heirs the secrets of successful court conduct.

The earliest book which has come down to us was designed to prepare a young man to become the governor of a city and a counselor to a king. The first section was for the instruction of Kegemni when he was made governor of his city and vizier; the second section was for the instruction of the son, Ptah-ho-tep, by his father. Both sections are compilations of maxims, comments, and observations on behavior in a variety of situations, made by men in their old age. The senior Ptah-ho-tep was a vizier under the King Isosi of the V Dynasty (2500 B.C.) of the old kingdom of Upper and Lower Egypt. There is no way of knowing for sure that the advice recorded on the second part of the papyrus was really spoken or written by the senior Ptah-ho-tep as the Egyptians had a custom of signing the name of an important personage to the compositions of lesser folk.

For people in general the most significant point about the papyrus is that it is the ancestor of all books. The Egyptians spoke of their papyrus rolls as books; in fact, the Egyptian symbols for book appear in the papyrus of Kegemni, whose instructions precede those of Ptah-ho-tep, and Battiscombe Gunn entitles his translation of the papyrus, *The Instruction of Ptah-ho-tep and the Instruction of*

Kegemni: The Oldest Books in the World.[1] This papyrus is a roll wound around sticks. The material of the roll is a thin sheet made by cutting longitudinal strips of the pith of the papyrus plant, placed crosswise in several layers, then soaked with water and pressed into a smooth surface. The Prisse Papyrus, when spread out flat, measures twenty-three feet, seven inches in length, and five and seven-eight inches in width. In eighteen vertical columns printed with black and red ink is the advice which a father considered of greatest importance and wished to pass on to his son. About half of these precepts concern themselves with how to acquire fair speech, "more rare than the emerald that is found by slave maidens on the pebbles."

In many particulars, Ptah-ho-tep's conception of speech was surprisingly modern and American; he thought of it as a means of controlling society. A little imagination can help to classify his precepts under the same captions which Charles Henry Woolbert suggested in his *Fundamentals of Speech.* "A man speaking is four things," said Woolbert, "all of them needed in revealing his mind to others. First, he is a will, an intention, a meaning which he wishes others to have, a thought; second, he is a user of language, molding thought and feeling into words; third, he is a thing to be heard, carrying his purpose and words to others through voice; and last, he is a thing to be seen, shown to the sight, a being of action, to be noted and read through the eye."[2]

Ptah-ho-tep stresses the first element, subject matter, and he is concerned with ethics in dealing with it. "If thou find an arguer talking, thy fellow, one that is within thy reach, keep not silence when he saith ought that is evil; so shalt thou be wiser than he. Great will be the applause on the part of the listeners, and thy name shall be good in the knowledge of princes."[3] Ptah-ho-tep showed further how a feeble debater with worthless subject matter can best be left to refute himself. "If thou find an arguer talking, a poor man,

---

[1] Translated from the Egyptian with an introduction and appendix by Battiscombe Gunn, London: John Murray, Albemarle Street, W., 1918.

[2] Charles Henry Woolbert, *Fundamentals of Speech.* New York: Harper & Brothers, 1920, p. 3.

[3] Battiscombe Gunn, *The Instruction of Ptah-ho-tep and the Instruction of Kegemni: The Oldest Books in the World—Translated from the Egyptian.* London: John Murray, Albemarle Street, W., 1918, and quoted in Charles Herbert Sylvester, *The Writings of Mankind.* Vol. 2. Chicago: Bellows Reeve Company, 1924, p. 748.

that is to say, not thine equal, be not scornful toward him because he is lowly. Let him alone; then shall he confound himself, question him not to please thine heart, neither pour out thy wrath upon him that is before thee, it is shameful to confuse a mean mind." [4]

Maxim XXIII, which E. A. Wallace Budge translated, "Speak only when thou has full knowledge; words are weighty things," [5] is a consideration of the elements of both knowledge and language. Ptah-ho-tep includes language also when he says, "If thou be powerful, make thyself to be honored for knowledge and for gentleness. Speak with authority, that is, not as if following injunctions, for he that is humble (when highly placed) falleth into errors." [6] Ptah-ho-tep sees the importance of language, attitude, voice, and action when he says, "Be not silent, but beware of interruptions and of answering words with heat. Put it far from thee; control thyself. The wrathful heart speaketh fiery words; it darteth out of the man of peace that approacheth, stopping his path. . . . He that obeyeth his heart shall command." [7] Gunn adds that Ptah-ho-tep recommends "speaking with authority." [8]

Continuing with Woolbert's classification we see that Ptah-ho-tep warns against a loud, noisy voice and recommends calmness and control.[9]

Like Woolbert, Ptah-ho-tep realizes that the speaker is something to be seen as well as heard. For him bodily action in communication is worthy of direct consideration. "If thou find an arguer talking, one that is well disposed and wiser than thou, let thine arms fall, bend thy back, be not angry with him if he agree not with thee. Refrain from speaking evilly; oppose him not at any time when he speaketh;" [10] and "Repeat not extravagant speech, neither

---

[4] *Ibid.*

[5] Wallace Budge summarizing, The Precepts of Ptah-ho-tep in *The Teaching of Ámen-Em-ápt*—The Egyptian hieroglyphic text and an English translation with translations of the Moral and Religious Teachings of Egyptian Kings and officials illustrating the development of religious Philosophy in Egypt during a period of about 2000 years, by Sir E. A. Wallace Budge, Litt. D.D. Litt., sometime keeper of the Assyrian and Egyptian Antiquities in the British Museum, London: Martin Hopkinsen and Company Ltd., 14 Henrietta Street, Covent Garden, 1924.

[6] Gunn, in Sylvester, *op. cit.*, p. 752.

[7] *Ibid.*

[8] *Ibid.*

[9] *Ibid.*

[10] *Ibid.*, p. 748.

listen thereto: for it is the utterance of a body heated by wrath, when such speech is repeated to thee hearken not thereto but look to the ground." [11]

Not only does Ptah-ho-tep have a modern point of view in analyzing speech into its elements, but his recognition of the audience as an integral part of the speech process is in agreement with the tenets of modern speech education. Ptah-ho-tep thinks of speech as a means of controlling society. He evaluates the speech process in terms of its effect on people; "If he address thee as one ignorant of the matter thine humbleness shall bear away his contentions." [12] He admonishes his son to adapt his techniques to different audiences. He predicts certain specific reactions to various manifestations of emotions, and sees the importance of ethics in getting the desired responses.

Other Egyptians emphasize the value of speech. One writes to his son and advises him to make himself a craftsman in speech. He points out that in that way he can gain the upper hand. He concludes with some such statement as: "The tongue of man is his weapon and speech is mightier than fighting."

Greek Culture and the Teaching of Speech

In the light of the advice to Marika-Ra and Ptah-ho-tep it is reasonable to wonder how complete a philosophy of speech may lie buried in the tombs of Egypt. It well may be that the Greeks were not the first to formulate rhetorical theory.

Homer recognizes the importance of speech

One hundred years after Ptah-ho-tep and almost 1000 years before Christ, in the *Iliad* and the *Odyssey*, Homer shows that he is cognizant of the principles of effective speech. Homer apparently thinks of speech as a means of controlling society; he is extremely sensitive to speaker-audience relationships; he knows the importance of prestige in getting listeners into a receptive mood; and he knows the role of experience in gaining audience understanding.

The following quotations show that like other authorities Homer

---

[11] *Ibid.*, p. 752.
[12] *Ibid.*

stresses subject matter, oral language, voice, and action in describing speech:

"Penelope said, 'Dear Stranger, among all the great travellers received in this house, never has one in speech given proof of such grateful discretion or juster insight than yourself.'" [13]

"Because we have had many way-worn strangers here; but never have seen such likeness as yours, I say, to Odysseus, in shape and feet and voice." [14]

"Her audience approved her." [15]

"Jalthybius whose voice was like that of a God." [16]

"Words quickened in them a longing to weep." [17]

"Wherefore he began in soft wheedling phrases." [18]

"At last there sounded the voice of manful old Echeneus, an elder Phoenician who excelled in speaking." [19]

"All men applauded the speech." [20]

"After all men were assembled in their places, Alcinous lifted up his voice." [21]

Whether Homer had developed his concepts of speech through unconscious imitation or direct teaching is not known, but it must be observed that as a result of some kind of learning he had mastered the technique of effective talk: He knew how to gather and arrange material, select appropriate words and sentences, and direct the delivery to audiences with voice and action which brought the desired responses.

Zeno of Elea, a first teacher of speech

Toward the beginning of the fifth century B.C., Zeno of Elea invented "dialectic," a method of disputation, which was indirect in nature, with the purpose of discovering truth rather than winning decisions. Zeno the Eleatic became the teacher of Pericles, who

---

[13] *The Odyssey of Homer* (translated by T. E. Shaw), New York: Oxford University Press, 1947, p. 264.

[14] *Ibid.*, p. 265.

[15] *Ibid.*, p. 38.

[16] *The Iliad of Homer* (translated by Samuel Butler), New York: Walter J. Black, 1942, p. 303.

[17] *Odyssey, op. cit.*, p. 49.

[18] *Ibid.*, p. 88.

[19] *Ibid.*, p. 98.

[20] *Ibid.*, p. 100.

[21] *Ibid.*, p. 104.

lived from 490 to 429 B.C. Since history records that Pericles' training in every area was under the most able teachers, it is safe to place his teacher of dialectic among the foremost teachers of speech in Athens. There is no record of the methods used by Zeno of Elea but there is a record of the results attained. His pupil Pericles comes down in history as an orator whose eloquence held both foe and friend spellbound.

Pericles lived in Greece when the popular assembly was very powerful. Citizens had to plead their own cases, and decisions were made by juries rather than judges. Pericles, the most accomplished statesman of his time, was conspicuous not only for his eloquence but also for his support of drama. He advocated and practiced speech of high quality, and he tried to make drama accessible to all of the people. The orations attributed to Pericles may not have been delivered exactly as they have been transmitted to us, but there is little doubt that his speech was effective in controlling and directing civic action.

Corax records methods for speech improvement

During the time of Pericles, Corax, a famous teacher, prepared a well organized system of suggestions for effective speaking. In 466 B.C. tyranny was overthrown and a democracy was established in Syracuse. As a result of this change in government, a good many citizens returned from exile to reclaim their property which had been appropriated by tyrants for their own use or as gifts for their court favorites. Some of these claims went back many years, and records were missing or inaccurate. It was therefore important to have all available documentary support for claims presented in effective order and form, and to make up for lack of evidence by sound reasoning. The need for speaking skill was real; with it, the property might be regained or, without it, the possessions might be permanently lost. Most individual claimants pleaded their own cases and, in doing this, many needed guidance. Corax of Syracuse grasped the opportunity and became a teacher of speech. He prepared himself to give professional advice, and became the formulator of the first organized principles and theories of effective speaking. He prepared a speech text: He developed rules for the arrangement of material; he told how to begin a speech and how to proceed through the narration, the argument, and the subsidiary remarks, to the conclusion or peroration; he suggested means of persuading an audience when the speaker is not equipped with all of the facts, but when reasonable conclusions can be drawn from available facts; and he illustrated probability (which became the heart of persuasive speaking), pointing out, for example, that it is not likely a puny man would assault a stronger man. The idea of probable results developing from a set of circumstances became "the great weapon" of the earliest Greeks, and today is a common method in persuasion.

Tisias follows the example of Corax

The name of Tisias, another Sicilian, is linked with that of Corax, because he was the pupil of Corax. He also saw the importance of rhetoric as a practical art, and he developed more fully the points of views introduced by his teacher.

Frequently it is difficult for students in the twentieth century to appreciate the significance for speech of that first step away from argument based entirely on facts and clear relationships between those facts to argument from probability, when few facts were present and when relationships were questionable. The techniques of the speaker who secured property for himself or his client when records of ownership were lost or ambiguous, and when circumstances were dubious and witnesses contradictory, required an understanding of human nature and skill in managing subject matter, language, voice, and action. This shift in the nature of argument was something akin to that great transition when man substituted words for things. Today such suggestions as those of Corax and Tisias are included in every speech textbook and taken for granted; these early discoverers are seldom given the credit due them.

The sophists—teachers of speech

For about one hundred years, near the middle of the fifth century B.C., liberal education was directed by a group of teachers known as sophists. They were interested in preparing students for civic life. Their main emphasis was on immediate practical needs. They were concerned more with success in life than in the pursuit of knowledge. They were at variance with the philosophers who taught truth, wisdom, and excellence per se.

Since the ability to speak effectively was an important qualification for success in life, particularly in Greece, many of the sophists were in demand as teachers of rhetoric, disputation, or speech. Schools of speaking were established and it is not difficult to understand why some were of higher quality than others. In many cases the criterion which determined the popularity of a school was the number of its students who were successful in their speaking activities. Clients came with cases of questionable merit, and teachers were tempted to recommend the use of false evidence and trickery designed to win decisions. These methods reflected unfavorably on the whole discipline of speech, and there developed in Greece a debate in which many philosophers opposed rhetorical training on the grounds that in order to be successful, orators had to be unethical. Plato attacked the evils of superficial knowledge and audience deception which he found in the rhetoric of his day. In three of his dialogues, the *Gorgias*, the *Phaedrus*, and the *Republic*, he developed a critical point of view about rhetoric which has been held by many philosophers down to the present day.

Plato was answered by teachers who insisted that speech was an essential skill in society, and that the most successful speech training was the most ethical. The debate had some of the characteristics of the conflicting points of view of such modern educators as Dewey and Kilpatrick, progressive school leaders, who advocate training for present needs, as contrasted with so-called "essentialists," who advocate knowledge per se.

Protagoras, Gorgias of Leontini, and Isocrates

Among the fifth century B.C. contributors to an organized method for increasing the effectiveness of speakers were Protagoras (481–411), Gorgias of Leontini (485–380, forty years after Corax and Tisias), and Isocrates (436–338, another forty years later).

Protagoras is known as the father of debate. He was the first to take the name of sophist and to teach and lecture for pay. He taught the importance of weighing both sides of a question. All of his works are lost, but Plato in his dialogues gives him a distinctive style and philosophy which are assumed to be accurate, and has him emphasize the importance of preparing men for citizenship.

Gorgias did not wish to be called a sophist. He preferred to be known as a rhetorician, but he was a teacher in the period when all teachers were called sophists. Gorgias lived in Leontini, Sicily, and in 427 B.C. headed an embassy which came to Athens to solicit help against Syracuse. Gorgias was so well received in Athens that he established his residence and remained there, supporting himself by teaching. He was in advanced years when he came, and he had a well-formulated philosophy of rhetoric and oratory based on long experience. His major interest was language. His style was elegant and abounded in figures of speech. At times he was criticized for superficiality. According to some authorities his orations were empty, but he deserves credit for bringing rhetoric from Sicily to Greece and for recognizing the possibilities of persuasion in the clever manipulation of words and sentences.

Isocrates is remembered as a celebrated Greek teacher of speech and yet he himself was not an effective speaker. He was called by Cicero "the father of eloquence," and R. C. Jebb believes that his rhetorical teachings are greater than those of Aristotle. Isocrates exerted great influence in Greece during the almost 100 years of his lifetime. He established a school which drew pupils from the entire Greek-speaking world. There is a tradition that in a very famous eulogy contest every contestant was trained by Isocrates. He appears to have thought of speech as a part of a broad general culture and his methods had a double emphasis—consideration for rhetorical composition, and training for Greek citizenship. It is true that Isocrates was known as a sophist and that he wrote speeches for pay, but his real interest was in teaching, and the label of "political philosopher" was much more to his liking than that of sophist, which in some areas carried the connotation of superficial preparation. He was evidently a teacher with techniques far ahead of his contemporaries. The principle of individual differences was a part of his philosophy, and he took great pains to make the speech fit the speaker.

For students of education, and especially speech education, it is important to evaluate the sophists as a part of a long and interesting heritage, beginning in Egypt and continuing to the present time. The sophists introduced and emphasized speech training. They also turned the aims of education to preparation for useful citizenship. It is true that they were criticized for teaching for pay, for aiming at winning decisions, and for directing attention away from knowledge to civic living. But time has minimized the danger of losing independence of thought and action when accepting salaries; it has differentiated ethical and unethical means of winning decisions; and it has vindicated training for citizenship as fundamental in education. That the sophists gave speech a place of distinction in education has never been questioned, and therefore, in a consideration of trends in speech education, the contributions of some of the sophists is distinctly on the positive rather than the negative side. Protagoras, Gorgias, and Isocrates gave us the beginnings of debate, the beginnings of artistic if extravagant prose, and the linking of oratorical ability and democratic statesmanship. Though all three men recognized speech as an indispensable skill, Isocrates is the most worthy of careful study.

Authorities agree that speech is learned

Because speech is so important in the lives of human beings, and is developed and possessed so universally, some people hold the belief that it is not learned but rather inherited by all human beings. Statements like "Everyone talks," "Speech is natural," "Anyone intuitively knows how to speak," are sometimes still heard today. They are heard less frequently now than they once were, however, and the point of view that speech can be learned or improved by following rules and suggestions is generally accepted. One of the greatest contributions which the speech teachers of the fifth and fourth centuries B.C. made was to insist that there was no such thing as unlearned oratory. They contended that speech was not an inherited faculty. They added that there were rules and principles which, if followed, would insure to any individual a certain degree of success in controlling listeners. In supporting these conclusions, they aimed at certain standards of excellence and tried to provide criteria for appraising orations.

The Ten Attic Orators

The Ten Attic Orators, so labeled because of their general agreement regarding the philosophy of speech teaching and speech performance, lived in Attica during the fifth and fourth centuries B.C. Their common emphasis was that the *idea* in speech is more important than the *delivery* of it. They were concerned first with thought and second with language, and therefore discouraged the use of flowery figures of language which call attention to themselves rather than to the thought involved. They recognized the need for adjusting techniques to different audiences and for using "grand," "plain," and "middle" styles suitable to the speaker, the audience, and the occasion; they distinguished between deliberative speeches and forensic speeches; and they made more specific and objective many suggestions which had been vague and latent.

The names of the Ten Attic Orators are worth remembering: Antiphon, Lysias, Andocides, Deinarchus, Isaeus, Lycurgus, Hyperides, Aeschines, Demosthenes, and Isocrates. Of the ten, the names of Isocrates and Demosthenes are most familiar. We have already considered Isocrates' prominence as a speech teacher. Demosthenes, in addition to contributing to the philosophy of speech teaching, was able to exemplify what he taught. His glory is that for the interests of Athens and of Greece he demonstrated through effective speech how a nation could be brought to a better life. The others of the Ten Attic Orators, too, were professional speech writers and teachers who established methods which provided the foundation for much speech teaching which followed.

The Rhetoric of Aristotle

Thonssen and Baird wrote in 1948: "Aristotle is perhaps the most highly esteemed figure in ancient rhetoric. . . . The *Rhetoric* is generally considered the most important single work in the literature of speech-craft." [22] Aristotle brought together in systematic, well-organized form all that was significant in speech education up to his time. Without doubt the high quality of his treatise was partially due to the fact that it was the result of a lifetime of thought and experience.

When Aristotle was seventeen he came to work under Plato who was then sixty-one and the head of an Academy. For twenty years Aristotle stayed in the fellowship, first as student and later as a teacher.

After the death of Plato, Aristotle left the Academy and, with three other pupils of Plato, set up a school in Assus. Among his pupils was Hermias, the tyrant of a town to the southeast of Assus. Aristotle married the adopted daughter of Hermias, and, through this connection, was invited by Philip of Macedon to come to Pella and take as his pupil the young Alexander. Aristotle accepted the in-

---

[22] Lester Thonssen and A. Craig Baird, *Speech Criticism*. New York: Ronald Press Company, 1948, p. 57.

vitation and remained at Pella for seven years, until Alexander turned his interests to the east in an attempt to unite the Greeks and the Persians. At that time, Aristotle set up his own school which came to be known as the Peripatetic School because of the habit which teachers and students had of discussing problems as they walked about in the garden. The organization of the school was something like that of a present-day college, with buildings, equipment, a faculty and a variety of courses. It is believed that much of the material of Aristotle's *Rhetoric* was delivered as lectures in the Lyceum in this later period of his life.

The *Rhetoric* is divided into three books: I is concerned with the speaker, II with the audience, and III with the speech. Many present-day authorities regard Aristotle's insistence on worth-while content as his greatest contribution to speech theory, but his explanation of audience control is of equal importance in a mature philosophy of speech education. The process by which individuals stir up meanings in other individuals was to Aristotle central in understanding speech. For him there was no speech without an audience, and in order to get the desired response from that audience the speaker had to understand himself and his abilities, his audience and how to move them, and how to construct an appropriate speech. Aristotle considered the speaker and the speech in the light of the audience. He observed that popular audiences are moved by the character of the speaker who addresses them and by the emotions which are aroused by his speech, as well as by the soundness of his reasoning. He saw that effective speakers must be able to use all of the kinds of proof which actually work with audiences. Aristotle accepted man as an emotional as well as a logical creature, and showed in detail how to deal with emotions. He did not suggest that the speaker try to *change* human nature, but rather that he attempt to *control* human nature. From the standpoint of both the speaker and the audience Aristotle made a scientific study of human nature, not as some said it should be, but as he saw that it was.

Aristotle brought a more comprehensive understanding to speech teaching than had many of his predecessors. Some of the other teachers looked upon speech as simply a "bag of tricks" by which audiences were to be fooled, but Aristotle insisted that careful investigation, sound subject matter, a knowledge of logical forms, and a working grasp of audience psychology made for the most effective speaking. Other teachers in Aristotle's day went to the opposite extreme. They thought that the truth could always be reached by adherence to cold, logical argument, and recommended that a speech be formulated in complete logical statements, called syllogisms. Aristotle showed how arguments before audiences, on issues of probability, seldom took the form of logical syllogisms. He discussed the deliberative speaking in government, the forensic speaking in the courts, and ceremonial, or epideictic speaking, and showed how each type of speaking took on characteristics determined by its purpose and its audience. In this way he made it clear that while rhetoric was related to logic, it also had its own special and necessary nature.

In Book III, dealing with the speech itself, Aristotle concentrated on organization, language, and delivery. He distinguished between language for writing and language for speaking, and gave some attention to both voice and action in delivery. Sometimes his *Rhetoric* is used as a text in present-day colleges. It is surprisingly up-to-date in its philosophy and in its suggestions for securing effectiveness in speech performance.

In spite of a thorough understanding of speech theory, Artistotle was not himself a distinguished speaker, and he did not produce as many successful orators as did Isocrates. Most critics believe that the time in which he lived was less opportune for speech making. At any rate, he seems to have been more successful in setting down principles than in helping others to make practical and immediate use of those principles.

"On Literary Criticism" and "On the Sublime"

Several hundred years after Aristotle two significant treatises appeared which still retain their importance today. They concentrated on one step of the five in speech preparation, namely, *elocutio* or style, the selection and arrangement of words and sentences. "On Literary Criticism" was written by Dionysius Halicarnassensis, better known as Dionysius of Halicarnassus, historian and teacher of rhetoric in the reign of Augustus from 27 B.C. to 14 A.D. "On the Sublime" has been attributed to Longinus Cassius, but was more probably either the work of Dionysius or of some author who lived earlier than Longinus, who was born 213 A.D. and died in 273 A.D. Both of these compositions emphasize the selection, arrangement, and relationships of words and phrases to material, including imagery, rhythm, and moral idealism, and both are helpful and inspirational even in the twentieth century.

Speech in Roman Education

Cicero and the functional approach

The practice of skills in meaningful situations, accompanied by an understanding of theory, is a generally accepted law of speech improvement. A classic example of this point of view is found in Rome more than 200 years after Aristotle. The Romans were a practical people, and it is to them that we turn for the beginnings of a marked emphasis on a functional approach to speech.

The Roman orator, Cicero, concerned himself with immediate needs and taught speech for immediate use. He was himself an extremely effective speaker and represented rhetorical art at its best. Although he added little to the theories of the teachers who had preceded him, he did make those theories and philosophies understandable and acceptable to his contemporaries. Cicero was aware of the criticism which had been made of speakers and teachers, especially during the period of the sophists. He recognized that there was some foundation for the reputation which they had gained for using poor subject matter. He had respect for the philosophers led by Plato who were the severest critics of rhetoric. He agreed with them, in general, and in the first part of his treatise, *De Oratore*, he advocated a thorough general education as prerequisite to good speaking. He prepared his book in the form of a dialogue in which celebrated orators presented differing points of view. Cicero's own ideas were assigned to Crassus, and the opinions of other critics and advocates to Antonius and six minor characters. Crassus advocated universal knowledge and the ability to speak on all subjects at all times. Antonius was willing to accept that as an ideal, but pointed out that a speaker with less knowledge might make up for his weakness by superior ability in the other elements of speech, namely, language, voice, and action. Time has not settled the controversy. Every speech teacher is called upon to meet the problems of inadequate subject matter, as well as of ineffective language, action, and voice, and the arguments presented by Cicero are still useful.

While the classical division of all speech preparation into five processes cannot be said to have originated with Cicero, he did state it with exceptional clarity. According to him the following steps are necessary in preparing for any kind of speech: First, *inventio*, a survey of all related materials; second, *dispositio*, planning the speech in all of its parts; third, *elocutio* or language, the study of words and composition; fourth, *memoria*, the ability to gain command of all material; and, fifth, *pronuntiatio*, or delivery, the use of the voice and body to stir up meanings in the audience. Save for a decreasing emphasis on *memoria*, the five steps are as useful today as they were in 100 B.C.

Cicero's clarification of *dispositio*, or planning, has continued to be a part of our teaching equipment. He preserved the divisions of *exordium*, or introduction; *narration*, or facts of the subject; *proof*, or the establishment of the facts; and the *peroration*, or conclusion, of the speech. These—like the subdivision of *elocutio* into plain, moderate, and grand styles; and the essentials of *elocutio* into correctness, clearness, and appropriateness—originated with Isocrates and the Attic orators, but Cicero stated them more clearly for posterity.

In a sense Cicero did for Rome what Aristotle did for Greece, but his work was less scholarly and more popular in nature; it appealed to a broader and less discriminating public.

Quintilian—public school teacher of speech

In Rome during the first century after Christ, the increase of governmental control reduced the need for functional speech training. In spite of this, a writer appeared who understood the Greek tradition, and who tried in one treatise to record and save all that had preceded him, on speech education. Quintilian's *Institutio Oratoria* was not a text for students but rather a methods manual for teachers. The work was in the form of twelve books, and in content covered the education of the perfect orator.

Quintilian was born in Spain in approximately 45 A.D. His father was a rhetorician who practiced in Rome, and, because of this fact, sent his son to Rome to be educated. After completing his education, Quintilian returned to Spain, but later was recalled to Rome to teach rhetoric. He was paid by the State, and should be remembered as the first speech teacher in a public school. For twenty years he continued to educate both men and women students, among them Pliny the Younger and other important personages of the time. When Quintilian retired he devoted his time and effort to the *Institutio Oratoria,* a book on Pedagogy, dated about 95 A.D.

In this most famous of all books on methods of teaching speech, Quintilian made use of all that had been advocated by his predecessors in both Greece and Rome. His aim was to help teachers to train the perfect orator, and his individual contributions fell into two categories—aids for the general educator, and aids for the speech educator.

Quintilian re-emphasized Aristotle's and Cicero's recommendations for thorough training in all types of subject matter, but expanded the conception to what might now be called a background in general, liberal education. He went beyond knowledge of subject matter to training for living, and insisted on thorough preparation for every phase of the good life.

He urged attention to teaching in early childhood and advocated training nurses and both fathers and mothers for the sake of the child. He taught that the child should be trained in speech from the moment of his birth: "Do not allow the boy to become accustomed even in infancy to a style of speech which he will subsequently have to unlearn." [23]

Quintilian believed in the integration of various fields of knowledge. He saw relationships among all subjects and was persuaded that knowledge in a given area could not be mastered successfully if separated from other areas. He saw the need to concentrate on the improvement of skills and habits, but he recommended the fixing of the skills and habits in real life situations. He not only attempted to integrate all areas within the school, but also went outside the school into the community for applications of his teaching.

Quintilian pointed out the individual needs and abilities of students, and recommended that each person be treated in the manner which would best make use of his talents and aptitudes. Thus the principle of individual differences functioned significantly in his philosophy.

It is generally agreed that the qualities of kindness, tolerance, and understanding are especially important characteristics of the successful teacher of speech. Speech education is so personal that only

---

[23] Quintilian, *The Institutio Oratoria,* Book I. (English translation by H. E. Butler). New York: G. P. Putnam's Sons, 1920, p. 23.

those teachers adjusted to student personalities will be successful. Quintilian reveals himself in his book as an ideal teacher of speech. He believed in improving speech skills by direct teaching. On the one hand he concentrated on language, pronunciation, action, and voice, and on the other, provided opportunities to use these improved skills in public speaking, reading, story telling, oratory, debate, discussion and everyday conversation. Recent scientific studies have established the wisdom of his procedures.

Above all else, Quintilian's method of teaching speech is remembered because of his insistence on high ethical standards. "The first essential for such an one is that he be a good man, and consequently we demand of him not merely the possession of exceptional gifts of speech, but all the excellence of character as well." [24] Quintilian's definition of the perfect orator is worth noting. Not, the *man* trained in good speaking, but "the *good man* trained in speaking."

Quintilian's treatise on the education of the speaker is the most exhaustive in all classical literature. He preserved for posterity practically all that was worth while in what had preceded his period, set in a point of view directed toward the child rather than toward the subject matter. He began with the parent and the new-born baby and ended with the trained and experienced orator in old age. He was the first speech teacher to concentrate primarily on the student.

The history of speech teaching reveals a direct correlation between the amount and kind of speech education and the contemporary need for trained speakers. The people in Quintilian's time had little use for discussion and public speaking. They had no vote. They exerted no power in government. Of the three kinds of oratory, deliberative, forensic, and epideictic or occasional, only the third was participated in by the people. It was in this area that training was most highly motivated, and commemorative orations, speeches of welcome, farewell, and dedication, and eulogies received marked attention from Quintilian in his school. With this training Quintilian attempted to revive interest in deliberative and forensic oratory by setting up contests in those areas in order to make the situations as real as possible. However, such makeshift practices

---

[24] *Ibid.*, p. 9.

did not stem the tide. Sonorous tones, emotional appeals, graceful gestures, and flowery language became the fashion, and the thought was often neglected. The period came to be known as the second sophistic era because many of the adverse criticisms of the early sophists could also be made of teachers in this period. Once more the speaker was satisfied to emphasize *himself* rather than the *truth* which he wished to communicate.

When we say that Quintilian was the first teacher to be concerned with boys and girls rather than subject matter, we do not mean that Quintilian emphasized the speaker rather than the truth. We mean that for him the whole value of speech training was determined by its effects upon the speaker. Quintilian approved many of the ideals of Isocrates, Aristotle, and Cicero, but his primary aim was to produce the perfect speaker. He was less concerned with what happened to government than with what happened to his pupils, although his philosophy did not allow him to label his teaching a success unless his students became useful citizens contributing to the society in which they lived.

There are records then which show that, 3000 years before Christ, rules and suggestions for teaching speech had begun to evolve. They started in Egypt with a recognition of the importance of effective communication, with a consideration of the four elements of speech, and suggestions for the improvement of each. These suggestions were followed by Homer in his *Iliad* and his *Odyssey*, formulated into a method of teaching by Zeno of Elea and recorded in a manual by Corax who, with Tisias, described the first formal organization for a speech, with the explanation of probability. In the fifth century, the sophists stressed the use of speech in civic living, and the most effective of these teachers recognized that speech is a learned rather than an inherited art, used always in order to gain response from others. The Attic Orators emphasized the urgent need for adaptation to audience, speaker, and occasion. They weighed the problem of form versus substance, or content, and concluded that in good speaking the thought should overshadow language and delivery. Protagoras clarified the need to consider both sides of controversies in the settlement of civic problems. Gorgias saw the possibility of persuasion through the elaboration of language; his interest was mainly in figures of speech. Isocrates refined language and made appeals and techniques less obvious. He applied all speech to life situations, and he and his pupils became a real force in the civic community. Demosthenes demonstrated effective speaking and exemplified the best teaching of the time. Content and speaker-audience relationship were emphasized and explained in Aristotle's *Rhetoric*. The elements of speech were defined, and the idea of adaptation to a speaking situation was introduced. Cicero defended the need for worth-while subject matter, stated clearly and expanded the steps in speech preparation, redirected attention to the divisions of a speech, and demonstrated how speech could be made to function in the conduct of public affairs.

For the teacher of speech today, Quintilian's progressive point of view, with its emphasis on education in general, the importance of forming habits early, the need for fixing improved habits in real situations, speech as essential to civic living, and high character as the foundation of all good speaking, is more important than the fact that Quintilian brought together in clear form the contributions of the important thinkers who had preceded him. He did more than edit the ideas of the authorities in speech education; he was perhaps the greatest speech *teacher* the world has ever known.

The Middle Ages and St. Augustine

From the time of Quintilian to 1500 A.D. interest in speech teaching was kept alive mainly by the church fathers in the monasteries of southern and western Europe.

St. Augustine's *De Doctrina Christiana* or *On Christian Doctrine* is of particular interest to us because it was in reality a book on pedagogy. Like the writers who have been surveyed before him, St. Augustine attempted to revitalize the best of the teachings of Cicero, Quintilian, and the Greeks. He tried to discourage the sophistic doctrine of display and artificiality so prevalent in his time. The classical controversy of subject and truth versus speaker and delivery was still prominent.

Imitation recommended

In searching for a new solution to this old problem of form versus content, St. Augustine recommended imitation. He believed that a student who never analyzed delivery but emulated a successful speaker would be more likely to think the thought as he uttered it and minimize the techniques of delivery, than would a student who studied his own delivery and attempted to improve it directly.

Reading emphasized

St. Augustine is also remembered for introducing reading into speech training. He believed that in order to read the Scriptures effectively it was important first to have the full meaning. In both reading and speaking St. Augustine was guided by audience response, and, in addition to the contributions of earlier rhetoricians, he introduced symbolism as an important technique of persuasion. He examined bodily action to determine the nature of his own performance and in his writings taught others to do the same. He was a typical, yet an outstanding representative of the medieval period. Other religious leaders made minor contributions, but none developed a more original point of view than did St. Augustine. The most that can be said for the period from 100 to 1500 A.D. is that the church fathers with St. Augustine as the leader, by careful hand copying, and exemplification in preaching saved for posterity much that was worth while in the teaching of the ancient Greeks and Romans.

THE TEACHING OF SPEECH COMES TO ENGLAND

The development of speech theory and training in England, from the sixteenth to the nineteenth centuries, is a story of particular interest to American teachers of speech, since it was from England that America was to adopt its earliest educational practices. Moreover, developments in England during these centuries highlighted one of the problems which has always confronted teachers of speech. This is the problem of whether speech is to be taught as a broad educational discipline, embracing concern for the subject matter of speech as well as its forms and delivery, or as a narrow discipline concentrating on some special aspects of speaking skill.

Classical rhetoric, as envisioned by Aristotle, Cicero, and Quintilian, had been a broad discipline, dealing with discovering and arranging subject matter, as well as with using language, and memorizing and delivering speeches. It had studied the art of the speaker as related to his purpose, his audience, and his subject matter. By the end of medieval times, however, a tendency had developed to organize the study of language skills into several related, but separate and specialized types.

The Growth of Specialized Areas of Study in Language

The work of the celebrated French educator, Peter Ramus, during the sixteenth century illustrates the movement by which the study of rhetoric was divided into several limited and specialized areas. Moreover, Ramus' theories had great influence on the teaching of rhetoric both in England and on the continent, and in America, for more than a century following his work. Ramus was interested in dividing education into diverse branches of study, each of which would have its own special province, and none of which would overlap any other. He was distressed by the fact that classical treatments of rhetoric and logic seemed to overlap at many points. For example, both the logicians and the rhetoricians were interested in discovering and organizing ideas. Ramus' theory was that the teaching of the discovery and arrangement of ideas should be assigned to the teacher of *logic*, or *dialectic* as he called it, while the teacher of rhetoric should attend only to instruction in putting ideas into effective and ornamental language, and instruction in delivery. The third of the language studies, *Grammar*, was to deal with etymology and syntax. Ramus' *Dialectique*, written in 1555, covered the portion of the curriculum he had assigned to this discipline. Audomarus Taleus, a friend of Ramus', wrote a *Rhetoric* limited to the study of *style*, or tropes and figures of speech, and *delivery*, including voice and gesture. Both Ramus' and Taleus' works were translated into English, and for more than a hundred years they furnished the dominant theories under which instruction in dialectic and rhetoric was conducted in England.

Although Ramus emphasized the close relationships which should be maintained between dialectic and rhetoric, it was perhaps inevitable that his successors and contemporaries similarly interested in specialization should have developed increasingly narrow and specialized interests.

The Emphasis on Style

One specialized branch of instruction in the use of language which developed in England was preoccupied with the study of words, sentences, and figures of speech. In the sixteenth and seventeenth centuries more than a dozen English texts were published which dealt with rhetoric only as an art of ornamenting ideas by putting them into fine language, abounding in figures of speech. If we look today into such works as Richard Sherry's "*Treatise of Schemes and Tropes*," published in 1550, or Henry Peacham's "*Garden of Eloquence*," published in 1577, we can observe how these writers seem to have lost all feeling for speech as a practical art concerned with controlling the behavior of an audience, and to look upon it as an exhibitionary art. The results of the teaching based on this narrow view of rhetoric seem to have been extremely unsatisfactory. At least by 1667, the Royal Society of London, a scholarly association, was angrily denouncing the teaching of this sort of rhetoric, which seemed so useless in meeting the need for speech as a means of reporting and discussing the activities of scientists.

The Emphasis on Delivery

By the seventeenth century, another group of English scholars had become concerned over the lack of attention to speech delivery in English education. They wrote books devoted to the study of pronunciation, voice, and bodily action. Among their early publications were Robert Robinson's *Art of Pronunciation* (1617), John Bishver's *Chirologia* and *Chironomia* (1644), Gilbert Austin's *Chironomia* (1806), and Albert Bacon's *Manual of Gesture* (1872).

There followed in England a period in which John Walker, Thomas Sheridan, James Burgh, and Joshua Steele led a movement to give delivery primary emphasis, and the concept of "speech" was expanded to include reading and acting as well as public speaking. These men called their discipline "elocution," and the elocutionary movement which grew up in the eighteenth and nineteenth centuries was to exert great influence over the teaching of speech in England and America. It is interesting to remember that in ancient rhetoric the term elocution had been applied to the study of language style, but that a switch in terminology in the eighteenth century in England attached it to the study of speech delivery.

Not all of the elocutionists approached the study of delivery from the same viewpoint. Sheridan's *Lectures in Elocution* (1763) and Walker's *Elements of Elocution* (1781) presented two opposing methods of training in speech delivery. Sheridan advocated a natural method of delivery, and Walker a mechanical method. Sheridan warned against artificiality and affectation, and recommended sincerity, naturalness, and spontaneity. Walker, on the other hand, worked out a detailed system of rules for pronunciation, accent, inflection, movement, emphasis, variety, and ease. Both schools of thought had their followers in the nineteenth century. Many teachers of elocution became narrow specialists in speech delivery, and by the end of the nineteenth century the whole elocutionary movement was being vigorously criticized for promoting artificiality and display. We should remember, however, that the British and American teachers of elocution were often men of broad intellectual interests, who taught reading, acting, and public speaking, and who attempted some scientific study of speech. Their work contributed significantly to the development of modern speech education.

"Classical" Rhetorics Appear in England

It should not be thought that the development of specialized interests in speech education resulted in the complete disappearance in England of teaching which treated rhetoric as a broad discipline, embracing the discovery and arrangement of subject matter as well as style and delivery. As early as 1530, Leonard Cox published a book called *Arte and Crafte of Rhetoryke*, which contained many of the ideas of the classical rhetorics of Greece and Rome. In 1553, Thomas Wilson published a more comprehensive book called the *Arte of Rhetorique*, which covered much of the same ground that Aristotle, Cicero, and Quintilian had treated. Wilson's book was popular, and went through eight editions in thirty years, but it was overshadowed by the works of Ramus and Taleus when these books came to England.

In the seventeenth century Francis Bacon revived much of the Aristotilean concept of rhetoric as a broad study, and made some original contributions to rhetorical theory. Bacon emphasized the importance of audience adaptation and, better than his predecessors, saw the importance of everyday speech in the affairs of men. Bacon wrote no single text in rhetoric which could be used by teachers of speech.

In the eighteenth and nineteenth centuries, however, there appeared in England three texts which were widely used in both England and America, and which stressed a comprehensive theory of speech as opposed to a narrowly specialized one. In 1776, George Campbell's *The Philosophy of Rhetoric* appeared. It contained an interesting classification of speech purposes in terms of the psychology of Campbell's day, which viewed the human mind as divided into faculties, e.g., the faculty of knowing and the faculty of feeling. Speech purposes were set by the speaker's decision to appeal to a particular faculty in his listeners. Hugh Blair, a professor of Rhetoric and Belles Lettres in Edinburgh University, published his *Lectures On Rhetoric* in 1783. This work became immensely popular in both Britain and America. Blair drew heavily upon Greek and Roman authorities such as Isocrates, Lysias, Demosthenes, and Cicero for his examples and ideas. His work emphasized not only speech making but also literary criticism, and he has been called the father of the study of English Literature.

Richard Whateley's *Rhetoric*, published in 1828, was perhaps the last important English text which followed closely the definitions given to rhetoric by Aristotle, Cicero, and Quintilian. Archbishop Whateley sought to analyze the laws of moral evidence and persuasion. He classified many concepts in argumentation, including probability, sign, example, analogy, and fallacy. He thought that the best speech was the most ethical, and emphasized how training in rhetoric made one a better listener as well as a better speaker. The person trained in rhetorical techniques, Whateley believed, would not be easily misled by a dishonest speaker who used these techniques.

Although it is easy to read into history one's own beliefs about how speech should be taught, it may be that the experiences of the English teachers of rhetoric from the sixteenth to the twentieth centuries provide some genuine lessons for modern speech instruction. At least some speech teachers believe that British experience warns us to view speaking as a complex human activity, which must be closely related to liberal education generally, and which includes skills in finding and organizing subject matter, in using language, and in presentation. It would seem that teachers of language who have become preoccupied with a narrow aspect of speaking, whether the aspect be style or delivery, have often forgotten the fundamental uses to which speech is put in real life, and the variety of ways in which people become effective speakers.

SPEECH TRAINING COMES TO THE NEW WORLD

After having passed from Egypt to Greece, to Rome, to Europe, and to England, the path of speech training turned to the United States.

Rhetoric and Oratory at Harvard

In 1636, when Harvard College was established mainly for the training of ministers and lawyers, speech was a part of the curriculum. The emphasis was on oratory and public address, and the training consisted largely of memorized declamations delivered in classical languages. The entire program was transplanted from England; the texts and references were English. It was to be more than 150 years before America would publish her own text and reference books and adapt her regimen of training to her own peculiar needs.

The Introduction of Drama

Between 1680 and 1800 an interest in Educational Drama sprang up. It was a daring innovation in American colleges. The first college-sponsored dramatic production took place at Harvard in 1680, followed in 1690 by a production of *Gustavus Vasa*. Regular dramatic productions have taken place at Harvard ever since 1758. William and Mary entered the educational theater in 1702, presenting *Pastoral Colloquy*, with the governor of Virginia in attendance. In 1735 William and Mary produced a play with an entirely student cast. In 1760 Princeton produced a dialog called *Ode to Peace;* in 1761, *Military Glory of Great Britain;* and in 1765, *Liberty*. In 1799 *The Busy Body* and *Love á la Mode* were presented by the students of Transylvania University at Lexington, Kentucky. Without doubt, an examination of college records would reveal that all over the United States in the eighteenth century there was a growing interest in educational theater.

Academic Recognition

Academic recognition has been very important in the history of speech education in America. This was given to rhetoric and oratory before it was granted to any other area of the speech field. In the eighteenth century, rhetoric was made a part of the curriculum at William and Mary, Princeton, and Pennsylvania. William and Mary listed it in the first published curriculum in 1729. Evidently the interest continued, for fifty years later there were still records of the presentation of original orations. The University of Pennsylvania appointed a professor of oratory in 1753, and in the same year Princeton listed rhetoric in its curriculum. These records indicate a widespread and expanding respect for speech training.

Speech Required for Graduation

Another distinctive development of the eighteenth century was the beginning of required work in speech. The requirement at Princeton of the formal study of rhetoric for all sophomores in 1760, and of public speaking for all seniors in 1764, indicated the recognition of a general need for speech training which was distinctively American. In the same century, Harvard required all seniors to take courses in logic, and all freshmen, courses in rhetoric and elocution. These developments doubtless were typical of the trend of the times.

Textbooks Published in America

The publication of textbooks on speech started in America in the eighteenth century, first by the reprint in Philadelphia of Burgh's *Art of Speaking*, and later, in 1791, by Caleb Bingham's *Columbian Orator*, the first college speech text by an American author. America really had begun to recognize her peculiar speech problems and to attempt to do something about them.

General Expansion

The connection between the events of the day and college speech training was indicated as early as 1780 by mock trials such as the one held at William and Mary during that year.

The nineteenth century brought new expansions and additions. There was an increasing number of professorships in the field of rhetoric. John Quincy Adams was appointed professor of rhetoric at Harvard in 1805, and rhetoric and elocution continued to be taught at Princeton and Pennsylvania.

The interest in drama also became more firmly established. In 1866, Brown University established a drama club and, in 1876, the *Triangle Drama Club* was organized at Princeton.

Then quite suddenly a flood of books on various phases of speech began to come from American authors. Here was the unmistakable evidence that America was different, and that her speech training had to be developed *by* her own people *for* her own people. These nineteenth century American publications started in 1805 with the *Lectures* of John Quincy Adams, and included *The American Orator*, by Increase Cook (1812), *The Analysis of Vocal Inflection*, by Ebenezer Porter (1824), *The Philosophy of the Human Voice*, by James Rush (1827), *The Elocutionist*, by Jonathan Porter (1829), *The Grammar of Elocution*, by J. Barber (1830), *The Rhetorical Reader*, by Ebenezer Porter (1843), *Practical Elocution*, by Andrew Comstock (1837), *Orthophony or Voice Culture*, by James Murdock and William Russell (1845), *Practical Elements of Elocution*, by Robert J. Fulton and Thomas C. Trueblood (1893), and *The Art of Reading and Speaking*, by James Fleming (1896).

The Introduction of Speech Science

No book in the foregoing list was of greater significance than the *Philosophy of the Human Voice* by James Rush, which signaled the beginning of the scientific approach to speech teaching in America. It introduced a treatment of individual differences in speech which was to have great influence on training in every one of the elements of speech. The idea that the speech of an individual was dependent on his peculiar physical equipment was the forerunner of the point of view that the teacher should not recommend "a low voice" or "a high voice," "a powerful gesture" or "a graceful movement," "language with motor images" or "words of kinesthetic power." The teacher examined the *student*, he noted the inherited physical equipment and the background of experiences, and out of these he attempted to develop the speaker. Such a point of view held that the kind of voice should be determined by the size and shape of the vocal mechanism; language sounds, by the formation of the mouth and the occlusion of the teeth; visible actions by the total physical structure of the body; and language forms and subject matter, by background and experience. The beginning which Rush made was eventually to lead teachers of speech to a very careful examination of the individual physical and psychological needs of students.

AMERICAN SPEECH TRAINING ADAPTED
TO AMERICAN NEEDS

Inadequate Home Training Recognized

The nineteenth century also brought more required work in speech. This trend grew out of situations and conditions peculiar to America. The belief that many students came from homes where they had had no opportunity to learn the "King's English" was distinctively American. Princeton, Harvard, Yale, Pennsylvania, and William and Mary increased their requirements in rhetoric for all students.

Introduction of the Speech Contest

Inter-society and inter-school speaking contests started in this period and have persisted over the years, despite scattered criticisms and protests leveled against them. Originally they represented an effort to make speech training more vital. They carried the student beyond his society and his school into real life situations: In 1847 the University of Pennsylvania held a public debate; the students at William and Mary petitioned for a debating society in 1852; Princeton gave prizes for extemporaneous speaking, debate, and oratory in 1877; and Rockford College held an inter-collegiate debate in 1883, as did Cornell and Pennsylvania in 1897.

Speech Training Moves to Lower Schools

To follow significant speech-education trends in the United States it is not enough to look at developments in the colleges. In comparison with the large numbers enrolled in the common schools, relatively few attended college. Late in the eighteenth century and early in the nineteenth, speech training began to be incorporatd in elementary and secondary education. The trends at the lower level followed somewhat the same pattern as those at the college level. The first influence was British, and the texts used were imported from England. Furthermore, they were designed for adults rather than for children, but speech was not the only area where the needs of the child were not recognized as different from those of the adult. Thomas Sheridan's *A Course of Lectures on Elocution* and *Lectures on the Art of Reading*, William Enfield's *The Speaker*, and John

Walker's *Elements of Elocution* were used extensively in training children and adolescents in the late eighteenth century.

Casual Observation Suggests Methods

The two hundred-year period from 1700 to 1900 might be labeled a trial-and-error time for speech training in the lower schools. Doubtless, most clearly defined principles of education are the result at first of casual observation and random ventures which are later proved or disproved scientifically. Erickson presents the best review of speech training in these two centuries through a critical estimate of the textbooks used in the lower schools. She analyzed more than one hundred and fifty books, and from the first one, *The Young Gentleman's and Lady's Assistant* by Donald Fraser, published in 1791, to the last one, *Choice Readings* by Robert I. Fulton and Thomas Clarkson Trueblood, published in 1884, she finds certain common characteristics. First, literary selections make up a large part of many of the books which give most attention to content. Second, although all of the other elements of speech are considered at some time, voice, language, and pronunciation receive more attention than bodily action and attitude. Third, the careful observer can see in these texts the forerunners of practically all the developments in speech education which have come later.

In many instances the literary material is selected because of its moral quality. The importance of ethics in education and in speech development is considered fundamental. In the last part of the period more attention is given to child interest, and, finally, some distinctions are made among different age levels. Methods for insuring that the reader will get the meanings before attempting to give those meanings to others are beginning to appear in the textbooks, and students are being encouraged to concentrate on the thought during the actual reading or speaking rather than on techniques of delivery.

The relationship between thought and language is explained in these early books and some differences between language for speaking and language for writing are made clear. Specific rules and suggestions, as well as models to be studied, are recommended in teaching the use of appropriate language.

Dr. Erickson finds in these books some detailed analyses of voice. The elements of rate, pitch, force, and quality are all given space, as well as the subdivision of quality into natural, falsetto, whispering, and orotund. Finally, these elements are considered from the standpoint of their effect on listeners. The need to be heard, the need to be expressive, and the need to make a favorable impression are the major criteria of evaluation.

While most authors merely recommend practice as the solution of voice difficulties, others lay out specific methods for improvement. They stress the relation between voice and general health and the need for time and patience in changing habits. Ear training is made a part of the process of developing an individual's best pitch and breathing which will result in a voice strong enough to be heard easily. Students are warned against using unpleasant pitch patterns. A middle rather than an optimum pitch is suggested, and vocal variety is considered an advantage. However, the relationship between variety and attention is not made clear. Many authorities teach that habits are formed most readily in situations which are of importance and interest to the student.

During this early American period the improvement of pronunciation was a part of the speech training in the lower schools. In some schools there was a teaching trend toward over-precision in articulation and, in many, there was an unjustified faith in the teacher as a model. But the point of view that the best pronunciation is that which is used by the cultured people in a community and which does not attract attention to itself was quite generally accepted, as it is today.

Bodily action, while definitely treated in the speech texts of the eighteenth and nineteenth centuries, was not emphasized as much as thought, language, voice, and pronunciation. Authors saw a relationship between thought and action, and voice and action, and they made much of the importance of total physical activity. McGuffey encouraged freedom and poise, and Russell asserted that if a speaker concentrated on the thought his body would respond and express the idea. Some books included detailed pictures of various expressions of emotions.

In these books there was a hint that attitude was related to the communicative process. Some authors pointed out that the speaker's frame of mind affected the impression made in speaking. "Work for a dignified attitude," was the advice of one authority.

Speaking, reading, and debating were all used for speech practice in the lower schools much as they were in colleges.

During this period not only the gifted and average, but the handi-

capped in speech were given attention. Increase Cook in his introduction to *The American Orator* recommended some special helps
for the severely handicapped. Other books gave suggestions for
dealing with lispers, stutterers, and other speech-handicapped individuals.

In spite of the growing concern about the elements, speech training in the eighteenth and nineteenth centuries in the main was
focused upon the total process of speaking rather than its parts.

The Establishment of Special Schools

During the last years of the nineteenth century and the first years
of the twentieth, there were some outstanding teachers who established speech schools. Samuel Silas Curry at his *School of Expression* in Boston trained many able teachers and published half a dozen
books. The heart of his doctrine was unity in speech through the
co-ordination of mind, voice, and body. Charles Wesley Emerson,
founder and head of the *Emerson School of Oratory*, exemplified
what he taught, and believed that through high character and an
application of the principles of evolution the individual would achieve
power in speech. Robert McLean Cumnock opened his *School of
Oratory* at Northwestern University in 1878. The heart of his
philosophy was adaptation. He considered his audience and his
materials and made each speaking situation a special problem.
Though he wrote no textbook, his *Choice Readings* has gone through
three editions and is still popular.

Influential Speech Centers Shift to Midwest

The twentieth century shifted the center of speech teaching from
the Atlantic seaboard to the Middle West, and the general emphasis
was placed on speech training for everybody. Fundamental courses
in both speaking and reading were added to the curricula of colleges and universities.

Emphasis on Speech Psychology

Walter Will Scott published *The Psychology of Public Speaking*
in 1907; the University of Wisconsin instituted a course in the
Psychology of Speech in 1916; and Charles Henry Woolbert earned
a Ph.D. in Psychology at Harvard in 1918 and made use of modern
psychology as a basis for his teaching of speech. These develop-

ments turned the attention of speech teachers to human behavior and its manifestations in the audience and the speaker. A thorough understanding of how to influence people came to be generally accepted as fundamental in the training of the speech teacher and the speech student.

A National Association of Speech Teachers Organized

In 1915 speech teachers in many universities and colleges felt the need for the exchange of ideas and more professional co-operation. Seventeen individual teachers met in Chicago and organized a national association, which has come to be known as the Speech Association of America and now has a membership of over 5000. These founders believed that speech proficiency was essential to effective American citizenship, and they envisioned new ramifications in the field of speech education. Their goal was unified departments of speech with areas devoted to Rhetoric and Public Address, Reading and Interpretation, Discussion and Debate, Dramatic Literature and Production, Speech Psychology and Voice Science, Teacher Training for Elementary and Secondary Schools and Colleges, and Speech Correction and Pathology. Fifteen years after the founding of the Association a survey showed that there were 2,083 courses in college speech, under 694 titles. The years have brought new titles such as Choral Speaking, Radio, Television, and the like, and by 1950 few reputable colleges or universities were without a program of speech education.

The field of speech education has become so extensive and so diversified that professional workers are now organized on regional and special-interest bases. There are many state associations and there are Eastern, Southern, Central, and Western Associations. There is an American Educational Theatre Association and there is an American Speech and Hearing Association. All of the regional groups publish journals, as do many of the state groups. The specialized groups have their publications, and the parent national organization publishes *The Quarterly Journal of Speech*, *The Speech Teacher*, and *Speech Monographs*. Taken all together, there is an impressive and constantly growing body of professional literature available to the student of speech training.

Graduate Degrees

Graduate schools offered the Master's and Doctor's degrees in speech, and since granting of the first Master's in 1902 and the first Doctor's in 1921, 7,530 Master's and 621 Doctorates have been granted. Research has added and will continue to add to the understanding of speech theory.

Professional schools began to make speech a requirement for graduation and now, in many colleges, engineers, lawyers, teachers, farmers, and businessmen are required to show speech proficiency before they are graduated or recommended for positions.

Speech Adapted to Community Needs

In North Dakota, North Carolina, Utah, Louisiana, Missouri, Wisconsin, and many other states, speech education, especially in drama and discussion, has been extended to the citizens in rural and urban communities.

From the colleges, interest in speech training moved first to the high schools and then to the elementary schools. Speech education has been brought to boys and girls in many different ways, until now it is a rare exception to find any principal or school superintendent who does not list effective talk high on the list of the essentials for effective living. The school organization varies with localities, staff, and equipment, from a separate teacher and separate courses for each speech activity to the classroom teacher who is responsible for all phases of education. The aim everywhere is to take care of the handicapped, the average, and the gifted, and to help each individual make maximum progress.

SPEECH TRAINING IN OTHER COUNTRIES

During the twentieth century, when the expansion in speech education was so marked in the United States, similar developments took place in Europe. However, an overview taken in 1939, before the Second World War, showed that nowhere in Europe had speech education developed and been recognized as essential for citizenship as it had in America. In Germany attention was given to speech correction in special schools and in clinics, the universities had scattered courses in direct address, choric speaking, reading and phonetics, and, below the college level, boys and girls were given some opportunities to talk—but with little direction. In France there were some re-education centers for the handicapped, and drama, reading, choric speaking, and phonetics were given some consideration in the colleges. In Denmark therapy for the handicapped was well organized in special institutions for the most difficult cases, in designated school buildings for the less handicapped, and in the regular classrooms for the least handicapped; but, except for training in phonetics, the average and the gifted received little consideration at any level. England's boys and girls were gaining appreciation of poetry through choric speaking, advanced work in phonetics was carried on at the University of London, and a national organization for speech improvement gave promise of higher standards for all teachers. Switzerland had the beginnings of training in public speaking, reading, and phonetics, in her universities. She had a number of special schools for the handicapped and in her public schools she was aware of the relationship between democratic citizenship and effective speech.

PRESENT STATUS

Despite the fact that centuries of experience have gone into the development of speech education, it may be that in twentieth-century United States the theories and methods of speech instruction will undergo their most extensive modifications. Educational theory itself is passing through great changes in this century. Modern philosophies of education, and research in the learning process generally and in speech training specifically are affecting the methods and content of contemporary speech education. All of the twenty-two chapters of this text are designed to help prospective teachers understand the present status of speech teaching in the United States.

SELECTED BIBLIOGRAPHY

Brandenburg, Earnest, "Quintilian and the Good Orator," *Quarterly Journal of Speech* (February, 1948), 34: 23–30.

Cicero, *De Oratore*. (J. S. Watson, ed.) Philadelphia: David McKay, 1899.

Cooper, Lane (ed.), *Theories of Style*. New York: The Macmillan Company, 1907.

Gray, Giles W., "The Precepts of Kagemni and Pah-Hotep," *Quarterly Journal of Speech* (December, 1946), 32: 446–454.

Hudson, Hoyt H., "The Tradition of Our Subject," *Quarterly Journal of Speech* (June, 1931), 17: 320–329.

Hunt, Everett Lee, "Plato and Aristotle on Rhetoric and Rhetoricians," in *Studies in Rhetoric and Public Speaking*. New York: The Century Company, 1925, pp. 3–60.

Jebb, R. C., *The Attic Orators*. Cambridge: J. E. Sandys, 1909.

Parrish, W. M., "The Tradition of Rhetoric," *Quarterly Journal of Speech* (December, 1947), 33: 464–468.

Quintilian, *Institutio Oratoria*. (H. E. Butler, trans.) 4 vols. New York: G. B. Putnam's Sons, 1920.

Roberts, Rhys (ed.), *The Rhetoric of Aristotle*. Oxford: The Clarendon Press, 1924.

Ryan, J. P., "Quintilian's Message," *Quarterly Journal of Speech* (April, 1929), 15: 171–180.

Smith, Bromley, "Corax and Probability," *Quarterly Journal of Speech* (February, 1921), 7: 13–42.

————, "Gorgias: A Study of Oratorical Style," *Quarterly Journal of Speech* (November, 1921), 7: 335–359.

————, "The Father of Debate: Protagoras of Abdera," *Quarterly Journal of Speech* (March, 1918), 4: 196–215.

Sylvester, Charles H., *The Writings of Mankind*. Vol. II (20 vols.) Chicago: Bellows Reeve Company, 1924.

Thonsson, Lester, and A. Craig Baird, *Speech Criticism*. New York: The Ronald Press, 1948.

Wagner, Russell H., "The Rhetorical Theory of Isocrates," *Quarterly Journal of Speech* (November, 1922), 8: 323–336.

Whateley, Richard, *The Elements of Rhetoric*. New York: Sheldon and Co., 1871.

CHAPTER 3

The Scope and Purpose of the High School Curriculum

INTRODUCTION

W HAT is a teacher of speech? One way of answering this question would be to observe the work done by speech teachers in the school program. But observation of the work of speech teachers may prove confusing. Many persons who call themselves speech teachers carry out widely differing sorts of teaching functions. One teacher of speech may have as his total responsibility the directing of plays; another may coach debating; a third may teach an elective course in public speaking or dramatics; and yet another may give a required course titled *speech fundamentals*. Few high schools with a "speech program" have the same, or even superficially similar, curricular offerings and practices.

The dissimilar speech offerings of various high schools are reasonable illustrations of the fact that every high school ought to organize its speech instruction in ways appropriate to the needs of its own students and its own community. To some extent this dissimilarity is also a reflection of the fact that few schools are organized to give speech instruction suitable to the needs of all their students. Their programs reach specific groups of students in particular ways, and, accordingly, these programs develop peculiarities of emphasis.

It is desirable that the prospective speech teacher be aware of the full extent of the high school speech program, not as it is represented in the offering of any one school, but as it has been exemplified in the purposes and programs set forth by a variety of schools. Such an awareness will acquaint the teacher with the multiplicity of jobs speech teachers are called upon to perform in different schools. It will also enable him to evaluate the adequacy of the speech offering in any particular high school by seeing how well that program is designed to serve the general ends of speech education. Accordingly, this chapter will examine the general scope and purposes of speech instruction in the high school curriculum. This examination will include five related considerations:

1. The scope of the high school speech curriculum as it now exists.
2. The causes for erratic, and sometimes negligent, planning for speech instruction in the high school.
3. The rationale of a speech program adequate to the needs of all high school students.
4. The goals which will be sought by an adequate speech program.
5. Persistent problems in planning the speech curriculum.

THE SCOPE OF THE SPEECH CURRICULUM

Three aspects of the secondary school speech curriculum may be distinguished: (a) The program of co-curricular speech activities; (b) the program of curricular instruction, including speech courses and speech instruction as a part of other courses; and (c) the program of clinical services for students with severe speech handicaps. Separate consideration of these three aspects will serve to indicate the extent of the activities identified with the work of speech teachers in the American high school. It will also reveal certain interesting facts about the status of speech instruction in many secondary schools.

The Program of Co-Curricular Speech Activities

We have chosen to consider first the co-curricular program, since more high schools give speech instruction to high school students through co-curricular activities than in any other way. This fact may not represent the wish of speech teachers; it may not even be desirable, but it is true of the present-day secondary school. We have chosen to call these activities co-curricular, rather than extra-curricular, simply to emphasize two points: (a) That in many schools speech activities are a substantial and significant avenue of speech improvement for large numbers of students, and (b) that in many schools speech activities are not something "added to" a curricular program in speech instruction, but are instead the primary way in which speech training appears.

Common Activities

In the co-curricular programs of different schools the following activities are common:

1. *Drama:* Play readings, all-school plays, class plays, operettas, one-act plays, play contests, and festivals.

2. *Contest speaking and reading:* Interscholastic contests in interpretation of literature (declamation and reading), extemporaneous speaking, oratorical declamation, and original oratory.

3. *Debate:* Intramural and interscholastic competition in debating propositions selected by state or national debating associations.

4. *Discussion:* School and inter-school forums; interscholastic discussion contests.

5. *Speech clubs:* Drama clubs, debate clubs, radio workshops, and the like. Such clubs may support or extend school and interscholastic work in particular types of speaking, may be social groups formed by students with common interests, or, as in the case of radio workshops, may foster a student interest group around a "newer" center of student interest and activity.

6. *Community speaking enterprises:* (a) Speaker's bureaus organized to get student speakers before adult groups in the community or before student audiences in other schools, and (b) school radio programs, filling regularly allotted time on local radio stations.

7. *Other student activities of which speech training is a concomitant aspect:* School assembly programs, student councils, class groups, and the like, are organized for purposes other than the giving of speech training. However, the value of such activities to the speech development of certain students in such skills as public speaking, parliamentary procedure, discussion leadership, and the like, is apparent and is often noted as one of the educational values of these activities.

When one reflects that speech-trained teachers are often called upon to direct any one, or even several of these activities, emphasis is added to our observation that the job of teaching speech appears to be one of bewildering variety.

The place of co-curricular speech activities in the school program:

1. *The "activity movement" is an old, persistent, and distinctive phenomenon of the American high school.* Since 1900, most schools of any size have developed elaborate activity programs in athletics, music, speech, journalism, and "student interest" groups, ranging from chess enthusiasts to camera fans. Many school administrators and parents believe strongly in the educational value of such programs, and efforts are often made to get every student in school into some type of activity. Not all teachers or school administrators have viewed the expansion of school activities approvingly; inevitably tensions have developed between curricular and co-curricular aspects of the educational program, and speech teachers are not infrequently involved in these tensions. It is sufficient for our purpose here to note that since 1900 there has been a general trend toward the expansion of school activities, including speech activities, in the secondary school program.

However, it is well to recall that speech activities antedate the general activity movement in the American high school, and that they were an established feature of the secondary school program long before the appearance of any general activity movement. Speech activities were not developed, moreover, as a kind of frosting on the educational cake, nor did they arise from any vague notion of the desirability of "keeping young people busy." They were established deliberately in recognition of the specific importance of speaking skill in a sound education. Thus, while today the speech activities of a high school are apt to be only part of a larger activity program, these activities are in some ways unique in that they were developed prior to the general activity movement and have an educational goal that has been from the first relatively specific and clearly defined—improved speaking skill.

2. *The co-curricular program in speech will generally reach only a small percentage of the students in any school.* Moreover, even though greater numbers of high school students are taking part in speech activities today than at any time in history, these numbers represent a smaller percentage of the total school enrollment. A secondary school in 1870, with only a handful of students, could readily organize supervised speaking activities for all. In colleges of the same period the college president sometimes gave personal instruction in oratory to all of the students. But the tremendous ex-

pansion of school enrollments in this country has had profound effects on the school curriculum, one of which has been to reduce sharply the percentage of students participating in supervised speaking activities, as well as to change the whole basis for organizing and directing such activities. Today co-curricular speech activities are seldom considered in relation to the speech needs of all students but are, instead, thought of as providing training for a small segment of the student body, usually a group possessing *exceptional abilities or interests* in speech. For this reason, a high school may maintain a debate squad to give valuable intensive training to a small number of students with unusual academic ability or leadership potential. The debate squad is not considered the medium for giving all the students of the school instruction in argumentation, critical thinking, and persuasive speaking.

There are exceptions to the general description we have given of speech activities in the curriculum. Many schools, convinced of the value of speech activities, and perhaps lacking an adequate curricular program in speech, try to broaden the base upon which their speech activities are conducted. A few schools still send all their students into some form of co-curricular speaking activity. Moreover, a few schools on occasion use speaking activities to aid students with serious speech handicaps, and not merely to provide opportunities for superior speakers. But in general, co-curricular activities reach a limited percentage of any school population, and they are concentrated on students with exceptional abilities and/or interests.

3. *Many schools have devolved to speech activities important purposes other than helping students to achieve better speech.* Class plays, for example, are often ventures in "money raising." Administrators often view school plays, radio programs, and speaker's bureaus as important means of promoting public relations. These functions are worthy enough. Sometimes they harmonize well with the goal of speech instruction, but at other times they interfere with the optimum contribution of an activity to speech training. Thus the junior class play selected exclusively in terms of its box-office appeal may not be the one best suited to the development of the students who work in the play. Or if debate teams are supposed to serve the primary function of bringing glory to their high school, the number of students participating in the debates may be re-

stricted out of all proportion to the number of students interested and capable. The fact that speech activities often must serve a variety of functions contributes to the situation described in our next observation.

4. *Co-curricular speech activities are an unstable basis for speech instruction.* This instability is evidenced in many ways. The number and type of activities, and the number of students taking part in them, varies almost fantastically from school to school. Thus a high school of 900 students may have 200 students taking part in one or more speaking activities. A nearby high school with 1500 students may have fewer than 100. One high school may offer its students training in drama, debate, radio, and public speaking, while a neighboring high school may present a junior class play as its only speech activity. Within the same school the nature of the co-curricular offering may change rapidly, indicating that it depends upon the energies and enthusiasms of particular teachers, and lacks the continuity which ought to be assured to a planned program, having an important and distinctive educational function.

The Program of Curricular Speech Instruction

One might suppose that co-curricular activities in schools would represent logical extensions of certain courses, or types of instruction, in the regular school curriculum. The reverse has often been the case, and many types of study have found their way into the school curriculum only after the value of their educational objectives had been established by the growth of co-curricular activities. School athletic programs flourished before physical education classes were established and required; plays were produced by student groups before drama courses appeared; school newspapers and annuals preceded courses in journalism; and interscholastic debate flourished before courses in argumentation and debate were introduced into the curriculum.

The reasons for this movement from the co-curriculum to the curriculum are apparent enough. Teachers have argued that significant educational purposes ought not to be left to a limited and unstable co-curricular program; that if an activity has educational value, participation in that activity is worthy of school credit; and that the co-curricular program usually reaches only particularly gifted students and leaves without help those most in need of it.

Speech courses as electives

In general, the greatest pressure for curricular as well as co-curricular instruction in speech has arisen from the last of these reasons. Speech instruction increasingly has come to be regarded as a responsibility of the school to all of its students, and a responsibility to be met only by organized, credit-bearing course work.

The paradoxical fact that the fundamental aspect of the speech program—course work or curricular instruction—has developed later than the activity program, may help to account for the variety of ways in which speech instruction has been put into the curriculum of many schools. Most commonly, high school courses in speech have entered the curriculum as elective courses in public speaking, drama, debate, or speech fundamentals at the eleventh or twelfth grade levels. Since many high schools provide for a range of elective courses in the upper senior high school, such courses have been included in the curriculum without greatly increasing competition for school time, particularly in the larger high schools.

It should be noted that elective courses in speech at the upper senior high school level have made but little progress in the direction of providing speech instruction for all high school students. Like activity programs, such electives have served only a fraction of the student population, although they have served this fraction in a more systematic manner than has the co-curricular program. Often elective courses have reached the fraction of students with special abilities or interests in speech, although in some schools these courses have been set up for the needs of students with speech deficiencies. In others, regrettably, speech electives have been used to fill out the programs of students considered incapable of taking electives in mathematics, science, or foreign languages, or of students who have developed an unusual antagonism to courses in literature.

Required speech courses

More recent than the upper-level elective courses is the move toward required work in speech fundamentals. Such required courses have been instituted as a direct solution to the problem of "speech training for all students." Usually they have appeared as semester or year courses. In different schools such courses have been organized at the seventh, ninth, and tenth grade levels. Sometimes these courses have been assigned a portion of the curricular time previously occupied by required work in English, since it is often assumed that English should embrace the objectives of speech training.'

Another answer to the demand for training in speech fundamentals for all students has been the inclusion of speech training as a portion of integrated or correlated courses covering areas of skill or subject matter broader than speech. Many schools have viewed the required course work in English as including instruction in speech fundamentals. Recently there has been a move toward a change in the title of English courses to communication or language arts, to indicate that speech objectives have been included. Speech also has been correlated with social studies, or with courses for guidance or orientation purposes. More recently a number of schools have set aside larger blocks of curricular time, usually at the seventh, eighth, and ninth grade levels for programs variously referred to as "core curriculum," or "common learnings." Such programs have ordinarily replaced traditional instruction in English and have taken over the responsibility of giving students training in the communication skills of speaking, writing, reading, and listening. This is not the full extent of many "common learnings" programs, which are based upon a considerable theory as to the way in which learning can best be promoted in the high school curriculum, but it is enough for our purposes here to observe that such programs do sometimes in theory include the usual objectives of speech training.

The Place of Curricular Instruction in the School Program

1. *Late development of curricular work.* In general, activity programs in speech, and elective courses in speech, have preceded the establishment of programs of instruction designed to reach all students. This is true even though the validity of the goal of speech instruction for all students has long been acknowledged. Most investigations of the current status of high school speech instruction indicate that despite progress in the development of curricular instruction, many high schools still provide only nominally, or not at all, for an all-inclusive program of speech instruction.[1] The speech

---

[1] *Speech Education in Ohio.* A Research Survey of Speech Education in Ohio Schools for the Year of 1948–49. Conducted by Franklin H. Knower, Dept. of Speech, Ohio State University, Columbus, 10, Ohio. (Mimeographed).

curriculum seems to be weakest at the point where it logically should be strongest—the provision of basic instruction for all.

2. *Wide variation of courses from school to school.* Speech training may appear in fundamentals courses, or in specialized courses in drama, public speaking, or any of a number of other forms of speaking. It may appear in required courses, in elective courses, or in both; or as a part of larger areas of the curriculum. It may appear in any one, or several of a number of high school grades. In very general terms, required instruction and instruction in speech fundamentals have tended to appear at earlier grade levels, while elective courses and instruction in specialized aspects of speaking have appeared at the upper senior high school level.

3. *Marked differences between speech courses and integrated courses including speech.* A sharp division of curricular practice has developed between schools offering separate courses in speech fundamentals, and those in which such instruction is treated as an aspect of other courses embracing a wider range of purposes variously called English, language arts, communication, or common learnings and core curriculum programs. The significance of this division of practice will be examined at greater length later in this chapter.

The Clinical Services Program for the Handicapped

About one out of every ten school children has a problem which seriously handicaps him in his use of speech. Many have problems calling for clinical attention. That is to say, the child exhibits an abnormality in his speaking which by reason of its complexity or its nature will not ordinarily yield to improvement from classroom instruction. For example, children who stutter, or those who are unable to produce certain specific speech sounds have the best chance to improve if they get the individual help of a speech correctionist trained in the diagnosis and treatment of serious speaking disorders.

We shall not at this point become involved in the problem of identifying all the types of speech disorders which ought to receive clinical attention. But we do wish to point out the existence of a group of students whose speech problems are of such a nature that their needs are not adequately met by either organized curricular instruction in speech, or by a program of co-curricular speech activities. It is an awareness of the needs of this group of students which has accounted for the organization of clinical speech services in many school systems.

Such clinical services, where available, are manifestly a part of the school program of speech instruction. Yet only infrequently is the same teacher responsible for classroom speech instruction and work in speech correction. Larger school systems often provide speech correction services as a part of a broader program of special services for all sorts of handicapped children. In such systems it is more common to find the speech correctionist doing such tasks as psychological testing or clinical work in remedial reading as a part of his job, than it is to find him teaching a course in speech. Smaller high schools usually do not offer clinical aid to students with severe speech handicaps; they get only occasional help from traveling clinics which may be sent out by state universities, or state Boards of Education.

It is not our view that all speech teachers should necessarily be thoroughly qualified to handle severe speech disorders, but it is our belief that the classroom speech teacher is of necessity more closely concerned than are other teachers with the needs of the speech handicapped child. Therefore she should have the capacity to identify these handicapped children, to give parents and other teachers some insight into their special needs, and to assist in the establishment of co-operation between the regular school curriculum and whatever facilities for aid to the handicapped are available.

This text examines the problems of teaching speech primarily from the standpoint of the classroom teacher of speech and the director of speech activities. In subsequent chapters we will indicate the types of problems the classroom teacher will encounter in the speech of children, and the methods for helping such students *within the framework of normal classroom instruction.* We will not, however, consider further the specialized work of the speech correctionist, or the sort of teaching procedures used in the clinical instruction of students with severe speech handicaps. Only teachers well trained in the diagnosis and treatment of students with severe disorders should attempt remedial work with such students. Unless the speech teacher has had such specialized training, she should seek either to refer the severely handicapped child to a teacher with such training, or to get advice from a speech correctionist. It is difficult, of course, to draw any hard and fast line between the sort of speech problems the classroom speech teacher ought to deal with personally, and the sort of problems for which she should obtain the assistance and advice of specialists. It is probably desirable that the teacher should err in the direction of caution by seeking help whenever she feels any reasonable doubt of her own competence to deal with the difficulty. Ordinarily such help is reasonably easy to get. To be sure, only a few high schools today have available the services of a trained speech correctionist, but in many states the Department of Education has developed a program of service for speech handicapped students. In other areas state universities maintain traveling clinics for the purpose of giving assistance to teachers and students in school systems without other clinical services. In some instances, the high school speech teacher may wish to write to an expert in the field of speech correction on the staff of a nearby college or university.

A SCHEMATIC OVERVIEW OF THE HIGH SCHOOL SPEECH CURRICULUM

It is now possible to observe a certain systematic relationship between the speech programs of high schools and the needs of various groups of school children. This may be done by examining the school program as it relates to the needs of (a) all students and (b) sub-groups of exceptional children.

THE PROGRAM OF SPEECH IMPROVEMENT FOR ALL STUDENTS
Curricular instruction in speech fundamentals, usually including one or more of the following:
1. A required course or courses in speech fundamentals.
2. Required units of speech fundamentals within other classes.
3. Instruction in speech fundamentals as an integrated part of the function of classes embracing broader objectives, as:
    a. English, language arts, or communication courses.
    b. Core curriculum or common learnings programs.

THE PROGRAM FOR STUDENTS WITH SUPERIOR INTERESTS OR SKILLS IN SPEAKING
1. Elective courses in speech, like public speaking, dramatics, debate and discussion, or radio speaking.
2. Co-curricular speech activities in dramatics, debate and discussion, individual speaking contests, community speaking programs, radio workshops, speaker's bureaus, assembly programs, and the like.

THE PROGRAM FOR STUDENTS WITH SPEECH HANDICAPS REQUIRING CLINICAL ATTENTION

  1. Speech surveys.
  2. Clinical services for diagnostic and remedial work with severely handicapped students.

This analysis of the speech curriculum should not be considered a rigid one into which all schools must fit. Many schools adapt the program to make provision for students in ways not consistent with this analysis. For example, although we have observed that elective courses in speech usually reach only a fraction of the student population, this is not true in all schools. Electives have flourished in some schools until they have been taken by most of the student body. Similarly, some schools have promoted widespread participation in speech activities as a substitute for extensive course work. These exceptions in no way invalidate the analysis we have made of the *usual* speech program.

The prospective teacher of speech in examining this analysis may well have been surprised by two phases of the speech curriculum: (a) The breadth and diversity of tasks performed by speech teachers, and (b) the peculiarly inverted order in which the speech curriculum has developed, making it weakest at the point at which it ought to be strongest. The program of speech improvement for all students logically ought to take precedence in the curriculum over explicit provision for superior or handicapped students. Obviously the program of "speech for all" includes something of value for both handicapped and superior students, which is not true of programs aimed particularly at these special groups. Yet adequate provision for speech improvement for all students probably is the exception rather than the rule in the American high school. Since we believe this situation manifestly undesirable, it may be well to ask why it has developed. Only as speech teachers can understand the reasons for the neglect of speech training, can they be in position to give useful advice for its improvement.

WHY DO SOME SCHOOLS FAIL TO PROVIDE SPEECH INSTRUCTION FOR ALL STUDENTS?

An interesting observation to be made about the neglect of speech education in the American high school is that it has not always been an error of intent. Educators, teachers, and parents seem to have "meant well" so far as the need of school children to speak effectively was concerned.

The period of expansion of the secondary school in America has come since 1900. This also has been the period of curricular reorganization. It would not be accurate, however, to say that speech was "organized out" of the curriculum. Nominally the high schools of forty years ago recognized the importance of speaking skill and accepted the view that schools shared with parents the responsibility of aiding students to develop such skills. However, for the most part, this nominally accepted responsibility was not translated into an actual program of instruction suited to the development of speaking skill. The failure was one of practice, not of intent; what actually took place was not that which was anticipated.

Nominal Versus Actual Responsibility

Some insight into the nominal status of speech instruction in the high school curriculum may be gained by examining the circumstances in which English became the most extensively required course in the high school curriculum. To do this, we will consider in broad terms certain significant changes which occurred in the secondary school curriculum between 1870 and 1920.

In 1870 a typical student in a secondary school did not have three or four years of a required course called English. Neither did he have course work in speech, public speaking, language arts, or communications. Nevertheless, a substantial portion of his school day was spent in studying the composition, structure, and literature of his native tongue. His curriculum included: English grammar, English rhetoric, English literature, logic, classics, elements of criticism, and composition. Daily, or at least each week, he had exercises in declamation, and he may have taken a course in elocution. In addition to such diverse studies of his own language, he most certainly studied Latin, Greek, or both, if he looked forward to law, medicine, or the ministry. In a sense, his curriculum was "language centered," although the universities of the period required only a minimum of study of the English language for entrance.

We need not examine here the adequacy or utility of this "language-centered" curriculum for the needs of either the student or his society. Suffice it to say that by 1870 this curriculum was already undergoing changes which ultimately caused it to be completely reorganized within another fifty years. Some of these changes were from pressures within the world of learning, where new academic disciplines and enormous new bodies of knowledge were creating demands that academic time be diverted to the natural and social sciences. Part of the pressures were from without, where the expanding concept of public education for all children was raising ever more strongly the important question of "who goes to high school and why?" By 1920 the diversity of titles under which courses had been taught dealing with the study of the English language, and with the reading and writing and speaking of English, had generally disappeared. Reorganization and consolidation, re-examination and elimination were the order of the period.

Again, in the broadest possible terms, the high school English course was the product of this period of reorganization and consolidation. In its inception it was an effort to integrate into a single course sequence previously diverse language disciplines. As Stout points out in his interesting study of the curriculum of high schools in the North Central states, English courses, which generally appeared after 1900, were a "judicious combination of grammar, literature, and composition (both oral and written)." Some idea of the scope of the responsibility accepted for the high school English course may be derived from an examination of a statement of the general nature of the English curriculum as it was envisioned by the Commission on Units and Curricula of the North Central Association of Secondary Schools and Colleges, in 1918:

The study of books of an informational or persuasive character should support the study of oral and written composition for utilitarian purposes; likewise the practice of literary or creative composition, of reading aloud, and of dramatizing should aid the appreciative reading of novels, dramas, essays and poems. The terms "composition" and "literature" are used to designate these two types of activities in this report, and they should represent separate units with equal credits in the high school.[2]

---

[2] Cited in John Elbert Stout, *The Development of High School Curricula in the North Central States from 1860–1918*. Chicago: University of Chicago Press, 1921.

It should not be thought that English courses suddenly appeared on the horizon and swept all courses in grammar, rhetoric, logic, and elocution out of the school curriculum, but it is apparent that the English courses developed as a part of a movement toward the consolidation of various disciplines in the uses of the English language. Declamation exercises and work in elocution persisted in many schools long after the appearance of English courses, and courses in public speaking began to appear in the high school curriculum after 1900 as a broader successor to these more specialized forms of speech training. It was the English courses, however, which became the required segment of the curriculum, carrying the objective of instruction for all students in speaking, along with a number of other significant purposes. So extensive was the burden placed upon the consolidated English course, and so diverse and complex were the skills and understandings which were to be combined in it, that certain phases of instruction inevitably received only nominal attention, while others were pursued with considerable vigor. For a number of reasons the elements of speech instruction were peculiarly vulnerable to neglect. Some of these reasons persist to the present day; some of them have all but disappeared.

Speech Instruction is Time Consuming, and
Requires Small Classes for Optimum Success

As high school enrollments have expanded, there have been heavy adverse pressures on types of course work requiring small classes and individual instruction. Classes with more than 25 students are apt to be somewhat ineffectual for speech instruction, since they sharply limit the opportunity of the individual student for practice and criticism. Moreover, speech instruction is relatively expensive because it requires time for individual attention. However, this is not a particularly significant factor in its neglect, since there is ample evidence that schools have been able to support those activities which are recognized as important, regardless of their cost.

Speech Instruction Lacked Sound Theoretical
Foundations in 1900

At a crucial period in the reorganization and consolidation in the high school curriculum, a theory of speech instruction suitable to the needs of all students was almost non-existent. The speech instruction being given in the high schools of that day was heavily concentrated on formal aspects of delivery, especially in the declamation of poetry or prose literature. Many teachers rightly challenged the utility of the training, and there was a general reaction against the value of instruction in elocution. The traditional theory of speech-making, as embracing all of the techniques requisite for effective speech, had been neglected in the college and university instruction of the day, and most teachers were unfamiliar with such a body of theory. The concept of a type of instruction which would be helpful to students not only in highly formal and specialized speaking functions, but also in the speech of everyday living, was still in the future. The narrow perspective with which speech instruction was viewed may be understood by examining the context within which the teaching of "oral English" was discussed in the early part of this century. At a meeting of the Illinois High School Conference in 1918, the President of the English section gave a talk on "Better Oral English." He said that he had translated "all the practical advice I have . . . into five very brief statements . . . These are: 1. Think of your lips. 2. Watch your consonants. 3. Sound your vowels. 4. Separate your syllables. 5. And above all, see to it that you make the proper impression upon anyone who may hear you."[3] Such advice might have simplified the organization of speech instruction in the English classroom, but it could not have resulted in speech improvement for very many students.

By 1918 a vigorous new concept of the nature and function of speech instruction was already in the making, but by the time it was generally available to teachers, custom to a considerable extent had structured the content and practices of English instruction.

Trained Speech Teachers Generally Unavailable in 1900

Through no fault of his own, the teacher who took over English instruction and assumed nominal responsibility for cultivating the speech skills of students, was for the most part untrained in speech. Only a limited and highly specialized form of speech training was available to him in many colleges and universities, and none at all in some. In 1800 university instruction in rhetoric had been directly concerned with the theory, and sometimes the prctice, of speech-

---

[3] *University of Illinois Bulletin XVI* (Nov. 18, 1918) 12: 175.

making, but by 1900 it had become almost wholly absorbed with written composition. Often it considered only that aspect of composition which had to do with language style. College course work in speech fundamentals was yet to be developed. Only a few hardy pioneers had thought much of the needs of students with speech handicaps. Plays were being given by college students, but course work to help prospective directors and teachers of drama was just beginning to find its way into the curriculum. Courses in public speaking were more generally available, but there was no assurance that they would be a part of the training of those going out to teach high school English.

The unavailability of English teachers with speech training continues to be a serious problem for those schools in which the English course still assumes responsibility for speech instruction. In this respect it is interesting to note a portion of a survey of speech instruction in Ohio, reporting the opinions of college professors of education:

Our 12th and 13th questions concern the relationships of the speech and English programs. We know that many think of these programs as working toward the same objectives. Eighty-six per cent of our interviewed professors say that high school English teachers are not adequately prepared to do a satisfactory job of speech instruction, 7 per cent say they are so prepared, and 7 per cent say that they don't know. Not one of these teachers said yes to the question: Is the high school English curriculum ordinarily so organized that the teacher has time to give an adequate amount of instruction in speech and accomplish all the other things expected of her as well? On the other hand 83 per cent said no to this question. Seventeen per cent say that the English teacher is ordinarily not interested in this problem.[4]

Development of Speech Programs Hampered by Faulty Assumptions

In the light of modern research into speech instruction, it is hard to believe that some of the earlier assumptions that were made ever were taken seriously. Yet these assumptions were made, and to some extent they are still held. Wherever found, they stand as a serious barrier to the development of curricular work in speech. Let us now examine some of these persistent assumptions.

1. It has been assumed that the study and practice of writing will insure the development of speaking skills. Such an assumption may

---

[4] *Speech Education in Ohio, op. cit.,* p. 50.

have served as a rationalization for the neglect of direct instruction in speaking for high school students. There are, of course, many particular skills and resources common to the effective practice of both speaking and writing: Vocabulary, skill in library research, skill in critical thinking, to mention a few. There are also many particular skills peculiar either to writing or speaking: Punctuation, skills of voice and action, skill in face-to-face social adjustment, for example. Repeated research has indicated that the totality of skill in speaking and skill in writing, as we can best evaluate them, are only slightly related to one another. A 1951 study by McCrery found a correlation of only +.35 between student grades in writing and their grades in speaking, and of only +.24 between student ratings of the speaking and ratings of the writing of their classmates. These combined correlations would give a student's performance in speaking only about a 4 per cent efficiency in forecasting his performance in writing.[5] This finding tends to corroborate the results of earlier research on the same issue.

This research would seem fairly conclusive evidence that one cannot now assume that the direct teaching of writing skills will indirectly produce speaking skill, or that a converse relationship exists. Of course, all teachers who are working to help students develop language skills, whether in speaking or in writing, will continue to be interested in establishing effective ways of teaching *generalized skills* useful to both speaking and writing. But there is no evidence that teaching limited to these generalized skills will by itself secure either effective speaking or effective writing.

2. It has been assumed that the practice of speaking will, in and of itself, assure improvement in speaking. Such an assumption would justify the neglect of direct speech instruction in the speech curriculum, as long as the school program offered students numerous opportunities for speaking.

This assumption was tested by research conducted by Borchers in 1936,[6] and by Dieckhoff in 1939.[7] In each case, improvement in

---

[5] L. L. McCrery, "An Experimental Study of Relationships Between Writing and Speaking Performance as Measured by College Grades and Standard Rating Scales," *Journal of Communication* (May, 1951), I: 40–44.

[6] G. L. Borchers, "Direct vs. Indirect Methods of Instruction in Speech," *Journal of Educational Research* (March, 1936), 512.

[7] Ruth Dieckhoff, "An Experiment in Methods of Instruction in Speech," (Master's Thesis, University of Wisconsin, 1939).

speech skills by students who received direct instruction in speech was compared with the improvement by students who had equal opportunity to participate in speaking activity, but who did not set specific speech improvement goals prior to their activity, or evaluate their activity in terms of speech skills. Improved speech was achieved only by direct instruction in speech.

3. It has been assumed that most people know how to speak "well enough." This assumption would justify either the provision of training in speech only for the minority of students who are conspicuously inferior in speaking ability, or perhaps the establishment of activities for those with superior skills.

It is true that students entering school already have considerable skill in speaking, but they have to be taught skills in reading and writing almost in their entirety. It is also true that students who have favorable speech environments in their homes or neighborhoods may acquire considerable proficiency in speaking as they mature. Their skill may exceed that developed by less favored contemporaries even with direct instruction in speaking.

However, only if one equates speech skill narrowly with certain specific standards of articulation or pronunciation, or even with such attitude complexes as social confidence, can it be assumed that most, or even many high school students know how to speak "well enough." The question immediately arises, "well enough" for what? A child may speak "well enough" for a child, but does this mean that he has acquired skills which will assure his maximum contribution to society as an adult? A student may speak "well enough," if we assume that he will never have need for greater proficiency in achieving vocational success, or in promoting successful relationships with other persons than he now has. In general, the assumption that a child speaks "well enough" makes no more sense than would the assumption that a child is educated "well enough." There is a practical limitation to the amount of direct speech instruction that can be given children, just as there is a practical limit to the amount of time students can devote directly to the business of getting an education, but it is usually the best educated who are the last to assume that they are educated "well enough."

It is our belief that many of the problems which have contributed to the neglect of curricular instruction in speech have been ameliorated during the last fifty years. Research has contributed positive knowledge about the nature of speech instruction and the conditions under which it can and should take place. The theoretical foundations of speech instruction have expanded enormously. Today we have available tested procedures for teaching fundamentals of speaking, skills suitable to the speech needs of all students. The results of these procedures are not as significant as most speech teachers would like them to be, and experimentation with new procedures will continue; but already there are available methods which bring substantial and measurable results. The rapid expansion of speech work in American colleges and universities has increased the supply of high school teachers trained in speech. The experiences of many high schools of different sizes and types have pointed to a variety of ways in which speech work can be incorporated into the curriculum, even in the midst of all the other pressures for curricular time.

If we are justified in believing that curricular instruction in speech improvement will be an expanding aspect of high school education, it may be expedient at this time to examine the basic considerations which ought to shape this program. These basic considerations can be clarified in three ways: (a) By examining the assumptions upon which an effective program of curricular instruction can be organized; (b) by examining the goals which such a program will seek to achieve; and (c) by examining persistent problems in curricular organization.

BASIC CONSIDERATIONS WHICH SHAPE THE SPEECH CURRICULUM

Assumptions Underlying Curricular Organizations of Speech Instruction

All secondary school students should receive instruction in speech

This assumption asserts that speech instruction ought to be a part of the education of all students and, therefore, should be required. This view, as we have already shown, is widely accepted, even though many schools have not translated their nominal acceptance into an actual program of instruction.

Speech instruction should begin as early as
possible in the student's schooling

For the secondary school speech instruction ought to begin in the seventh, ninth, or tenth grades, depending upon the organization of that school as a six year, four year, or three year sequence. The common practice of delaying speech instruction until the eleventh or twelfth years seems to be based on expediency rather than good sense. The speech development of a child is continuous, and each year finds him equipped with new potentialities and facing new problems. For example, the eighth and ninth grades are very important years as far as the speech development of many students is concerned. The onset of puberty confronts them with serious problems of social adjustment. In the eighth and ninth grades some students for the first time may find it difficult to talk easily in social or classroom groups. Without some continuity of practice and *skilled guidance* in speaking at this period, the child may develop habits of non-participation or withdrawal from the social situation. *Some* students do "grow out" of *some* of their speaking problems— *sometimes*. Just as often, without help, they transmute these problems into ineffective habits of speaking or negative attitudes toward speaking, which grow more fixed the longer they persist without remedial attention.

Teachers of speech at the upper high school and junior college levels, know that much of their teaching is directed toward the modification of ineffective habits or attitudes which their students have learned earlier in their schooling. Delayed speech instruction usually is wasteful speech instruction.

Provision should be made for some continuity
of speech instruction

The same motives that prompt the early placement of curricular speech instruction indicate the need for some provision for continuity of instruction. Too much curricular speech instruction, as it is now organized, is on a "one-shot" basis, profiting students in a certain state of readiness, but missing entirely students in differing states of readiness. Curricular instruction in speech should be organized to help students with their problems as they arise, to develop potentialities as the student matures, and to focus the continuing attention of the child upon his specific speech needs until he makes progress. Different schools have found different answers to the problems of continuity. In some schools specific units of speech have been incorporated into the English sequence in the seventh, eighth, ninth, and tenth grades. In other schools, where speech is integrated with other goals in the English or language arts sequence, the problem of continuity is taken care of, to the extent that the speech instruction is actually given. In still other schools, speech is taught as a separate course in the seventh grade and again in the ninth grade, but the speech teacher has time to observe the speaking activities of students in the eighth and tenth years, and to counsel these students in regard to the development of their speaking skills. Another answer has been provided by closer relationship between the speech teacher and other teachers in the school. By acquainting other teachers with the speech needs and goals of various students, as they develop from experiences in the speech class, the speech teacher solicits the help of other teachers in providing some continuity of attention to these needs.

Speech instruction should give guided experience in
all the aspects of speech common to speaking situations

Skills in using voice, action, and language, and in handling attitudes and purposes should be studied as they relate to total speech situations. Historically, the study of speech has suffered from too narrow concentration upon isolated, specific phases. To some teachers speech has meant the study of pronunciation and articulation; to others it has meant composing a story or an essay to be read aloud. Speech in actual life is a complex act in which the speaker may succeed or fail for any one of a variety of interrelated causes. A student may be ineffective in a speaking situation because his voice is too weak, because he is tense and fearful in his attitude toward other persons, because he mispronounces words, or because he makes assertions which provoke the antagonism of some of his listeners. Speech instruction, to be effective, must treat speech as a total act, and give students access to the study of all the factors which are a part of the communication process.

Speech instruction should stress the most useful forms of speaking

Speech instruction ought to give all students directed practice in and study of those forms of speaking which he will find most generally useful in his school life and in his adult life. These forms include informal and formal discussion, conversation and social forms, public speaking to inform and persuade, reading aloud, as in story telling, oral interpretation, and creative or formal dramatics. Most teachers would also include practice in parliamentary procedure.

Two types of skills may be distinguished as operating in almost every speaking situation. First, there are those generalized skills which may be useful to many on all occasions in which speech is used. A student with an expressive, pleasant, and flexible voice may be said to have acquired a skill which generally will be useful in any situation in which he uses speech, whether that situation involves conversation, public speaking, or acting in a play. Each speaking situation, however, also may require forms of speaking peculiar to that special occasion. Thus, a student with highly developed general skills in speaking may fail as a parliamentary leader if he lacks knowledge of the rules of parliamentary procedure. Or a group of "generally good" speakers may produce an ineffective public discussion because of inattention to conventional aspects of organizing and conducting discussion.

It is not always easy to tell whether an effective speaker has acquired generalized skills in speaking or merely a "bundle" of particular ways of behaving which he uses in particular speaking situations. Probably good speakers acquire their skills both in "bundles" associated with particular speech situations, and as generalized skills which they find useful in all situations.

Fundamental instruction in speech is especially concerned with the development of generalized skills useful in many situations. It recognizes, however, that students use speech in particular forms, and that they need not only generalized skills, but also particular skills in handling the specific forms useful in their daily living. It also recognizes that certain students may learn speaking only in terms of particular groups of skills, and stop short of acquiring any generally useful skills. Accordingly, adequate speech instruction should develop a variety of useful forms of speaking, both in the general skills which operate in all of these forms, and in the specific requirements of each form in the situations to which it is appropriate.

All instruction in speaking also should be instruction in listening

Listening is the reciprocal skill to speaking. The most useful speaking practice is that which includes all the dynamic elements of speech in real life situations. This means that the speaker has a real purpose or need to speak, that he has an audience, and that there is reciprocal stimulation between speaker and audience.

Too many teachers have complained that speech instruction is wasteful of school time, because one student speaks while twenty-five others do nothing. This complaint suggests that the speaking activity of the class in question is not being carried out under the most useful conditions. Instruction in speech is equally instruction in listening, and the activity of all members of a speaking situation, listeners as well as speakers, should become a part of the educative experience.

Conditions conducive to speech progress

Students make optimum progress in speech only when instruction observes certain conditions of need, understanding, improvement, and practice. In general, as reasonably defined by research, there are four conditions under which students make progress in speaking skill: (a) Students speak in terms of a real need; (b) students understand specifically their own needs as speakers; (c) students set definite speech improvement goals for themselves; and (d) students practice speech under competently managed criticism.

The implication of these conditions for the structure of the speech curriculum is clear. Students need some time in the curriculum to consider the nature of effective speaking and listening, to receive skilled help in analyzing their own needs and potentialities, and to define the ways in which they can go about improving their skills of speaking and listening. One of the practical problems in setting up an effective speech curriculum becomes that of clearly identifying the time and place for the attention to speech processes as such.

The Goal of Speech Instruction

Though one of the most general goals of speech instruction may be inferred from the foregoing assumptions basic to the speech curriculum, a specific statement of these goals may serve to define further the actual operation of speech instruction. These goals will be stated here in terms of the operational objectives of the teacher. All teacher goals need to be translated into the specific learnings sought by and for students, but these student outcomes will be reasonably implicit in the teacher goals.

GOALS OF THE SPEECH TEACHER

1. To make an early and continuing diagnosis of the speech needs and abilities of all students.

2. To help students gain as much insight as possible into the nature of their own speaking and listening abilities, and into their needs as speakers and listeners.

3. To provide all students with a variety of purposeful speaking and listening activities.

4. To help all students develop certain understandings basic to improved skill in speaking and listening, including:

    a. Understandings of the way various aspects of speech influence the effect of speech in actual social situations.

    b. Understandings of the characteristics of generally effective speaking and listening.

5. To help students acquire attitudes toward self and others in the speaking situation, useful to effective speaking and listening, as:

    a. A willingness to participate in speaking situations.

    b. A belief in the possibility of using speech to improve understanding between people.

    c. A willingness to accept the diversity of attitude and experience which sets the communicative problem between speaker and listeners; to talk to others partially on their own terms.

6. To help each student define specific improvement goals in terms of his own abilities and needs.

7. To help each student make optimum improvement in terms of the specific goals he has set for himself. These goals may be single or several.

8. To help each student to improve his use of certain specific forms of speaking, including:

    a. Conversation and social forms; interviewing.

    b. Informal and public discussion, and informal debate.

    c. Parliamentary procedure.

    d. Public speaking to inform or persuade others.
    e. Reading aloud.
    f. Recreating literary experience (story telling, interpretation of literature, creative and formal dramatics).
    9. To keep continuous check on the effectiveness of instruction by systematic evaluations of student improvement.

Some Problems in Organizing the Speech Curriculum

Should speech be taught in a class labeled "Speech?"

Should curricular instruction in speech be organized in separate speech classes or as a part of English, language arts, communication courses, or broader integrations of experience?

As a practical problem in curricular organization this question has generated much discussion among speech teachers, English teachers, and school administrators. From the internal standpoint of "effective speech instruction" the problem is probably not a fundamental one.

We believe that effective speech teaching will be most likely to take place when three conditions are met in the school curriculum: (a) A good teacher, trained in speech and interested in speech is, (b) given the responsibility, and (c) is allowed sufficient curricular time for aiding the speech improvement of students. This teacher may have this responsibility and this time in a class called speech, or he may have it in a course called English, language arts, communication, or common learnings. Thus, the fundamental curricular issue so far as effective speech instruction is concerned is not the problem of separate or integrated organization but the problem of providing a trained teacher with responsibility and time.

Arguments against the speech class

From the viewpoint of organizing a school curriculum as a whole, the problem of separate classes or integrated classes is much more fundamental. Both the proponents of integrated courses and of separate speech classes, can present important theoretical and practical arguments for their points of view. Following is a list of some of the advantages of organizing speech fundamentals within a sequence in English or language arts:

    1. English is universally established as a required part of the secondary school curriculum. If speech training is integrated with the

English program, it is assured of reaching every student and of providing some continuity to speech instruction.

2. Classes embracing broader areas of instruction may be able to provide situations in which students have more real need to speak and write and in which speaking and writing become functional in serving the broader purposes set by the class. It has been said that students "don't speak speech." This is not a particularly profound observation. Students can talk about speech, just as easily as they can talk about basketball. But it is true that most of the problems which challenge high school students, and for which they need speech, do not involve the study of speech per se. Integrated courses thus may help solve the problem of what students should talk about. There is some evidence that broadly integrated classes have been successful in teaching specific skills such as spelling, hand-writing, and arithmetic, but there is no specific research available providing any final proof of the efficiency of such classes in developing speaking skills.

3. Certain skills basic to both speaking and writing may be conveniently taught together, such as vocabulary, use of the library, standard English usage, critical thinking, and the like. Students may see interrelationships in communication arts which help them to learn faster.

Arguments in favor of the "Speech" class

Following are some of the advantages of organizing speech fundamentals as a separate class:

1. Separate speech classes increase the probability that skilled speech teachers will work with students. In point of fact, few teachers today are trained in or interested in teaching such diverse skills as speaking, reading, listening and writing—or in teaching these skills as they relate to the study of the civic and personal problems which may be considered in a core or common learnings class. In integrated classes, certain skills come to be treated incidentally, according to the special interests and capabilities of the teacher, or the directions set by particular outbursts of student energy.

2. All present evidence points to significant differences between speaking and writing skills, rather than to similarities.

3. Students should see their speaking skills as related to all aspects of the curriculum and of living outside the school. Speaking skills

should be made functional in the students' work in science, history, physical education, and social living, and the subject matter for speaking ought not be related to just the reading or the problems set by a defined area of integration within the curriculum.

It is probable that factors more complex than the single issue of "efficient speech instruction" will determine the way in which such instruction will be organized in particular schools. Small high schools, and most high schools are small, cannot have teachers specialized in every discipline or subject matter area. Schools will have to adjust their curricular structure to the numbers of their staff and other special conditions.

How may speech instruction be made functional for the child outside the speech classroom?

Teachers often disconsolately observe the capacity of their students to compartmentalize their behavior. Thus, students learn to prepare public speeches in an efficient way in the speech class and desert these methods entirely when confronted with the same sort of task in the science class. It is obvious that all students will do more speaking outside the speech classroom than they will do in it, and that one of the important problems is that of increasing the assurance that they will practice useful speech skills outside the speech classroom. A variety of answers have been developed for this problem of assuring the functional nature of speech training, all of which may contain some useful elements.

1. *Practice in terms of needs.* It is essential that all goal setting in the speech class, all practice of speaking skills, be done explicitly in terms of the needs of the students in their everyday living. Students must co-operate in setting the goals and standards of the class, and they must do so in terms of the realities of their everyday experience. Speech teachers can help students interpret their experiences outside the speech class, and lead them to see more clearly their own speech needs and potentialities. But, if the speech teacher attempts to set standards in the speech class which are not perceived as real or useful by the students, then the possibility of such training becoming functional is negligible.

2. *Work with other teachers.* Speech teachers need to work closely with other teachers. It is agreed that good oral reports ought to have discernible introductions, unified central propositions, and

conclusions of some sort. All teachers should make these forms matters of expectation in their classes. If no one but the speech teacher regards these points as important, then students will consider them important *only in the speech class.* In general, the goals set in the speech class must be acceptable to most members of the school community. It is a part of the function of the speech teacher to help other teachers to an understanding of these objectives, and to win their co-operation in teaching them.

3. *Observe speech in all school situations.* Follow-up, or visitation by speech teachers to observe the speaking of students in other classes may serve to set for students the pattern of making speech skills functional. Within limitations of time and of consent by other teachers, speech teachers ought to seek out opportunities to hear their students talk in other classes. They ought to use such visitation to refresh the students' memory of goals set for speech improvement and to gather data for helping them further.[8]

*How may speech teachers best co-operate
with school administrators?*

Teachers who develop great enthusiasm for the importance of their particular work are often able to inspire their students to greater and more lasting effort. But sometimes they inspire less fortunate feelings in school administrators! It may not be easy for the speech teacher to recognize the fact that there are many areas of skill and subject matter which have legitimate claims to a "share of the sunlight" in the school curriculum. For, like others, speech teachers are apt to see their own discipline as the "center" of the curriculum, the essential core of training around which all the rest of education revolves as satellites about a luminous planet. While it may not be easy for speech teachers to see themselves in perspective, it is possible, and it is necessary. The person best able to interpret for the teacher this factor of "perspective," this awareness of the needs and exigencies which control the operation of the entire school curriculum, is usually the school administrator. That, after all, is a part of his job, and, therefore, it is a task he is likely to perform better than anyone else.

---

[8] A description of the organization of such a follow-up program appears in the N.E.A. *Bulletin of the National Association of Secondary School Principals* (January, 1948) No. 151, 32: 157–165.

We have tried to make clear in this chapter the fact that all is not ideal with the state of speech instruction in many high schools, but we would urge teachers who believe in the need for speech training to approach each school intent upon doing the best possible job of helping students speak better *within* the framework of the routine and organization which has grown up in the particular school. The best way to improve the quality of speech instruction in a school, is to do a good job of teaching and not to *"sell"* administrators on the pressing need for sweeping reallocations of curricular time.

We have explored the issues which surround the speech curriculum in the modern American high school in some detail on the grounds that all speech teachers need to be in a position to give sound advice on curriculum practices in their own area of teaching, and that they need to understand the assumptions and goals which condition their work. But we have not explored the speech curriculum with the idea that all speech teachers ought to go forth to tell others how speech training must be organized. Parents, school administrators, teachers, and school children should share in building the curriculum of any given school. The speech teacher should recognize the legitimate functions of all persons connected with the school in the important task of curriculum-making.

SUMMARY

This chapter has surveyed broadly the high school speech curriculum. It has described the scope of activities associated with teaching speech, and the ways in which high schools have attempted to meet the needs of all their students for better speech. The insufficiency of many curricular programs for teaching speech has been observed, and the reasons for this insufficiency examined. The assumptions upon which a sound speech curriculum may be based have been described, and the goals of speech education have been set forth. However, the final issue of whether or not speech instruction is to be efficient will not be decided by external characteristics of the speech curriculum or by statements of goals; it will be decided by what takes place between teachers and students. It is to the internal workings of classroom instruction in speech that we now turn our attention.

SELECTED BIBLIOGRAPHY

Alberty, Harold B., *Reorganizing the High School Curriculum.* New York: The Macmillan Company, 1947.

Carpenter, George R., Franklin T. Baker, and Fred N. Scott, *The Teaching of English in the Elementary and the Secondary School.* New York: Longsmans, Green & Co., Inc., 1904, 37–66. (An account of the development of the English curriculum at the turn of the 20th century.)

Hatfield, W. W., *The Experience Curriculum in English.* National Council of Teachers of English. New York, 1935, 133–137, 159–184.

Hook, J. N., *The Teaching of High School English.* New York: The Ronald Press, 1950, 24–40.

Irwin, Charles E., "Thirty Years of Speech Training," *Chicago Schools Journal* (March–April, 1951), 32: 129–134.

Lindsley, Charles F., "Integers and Fractions: A Pedagogical Inquiry," *Western Speech* (March, 1951), 15: 5–10.

Miner, Adah, "The Role of Speech in the Language Arts Program," *College of Education Record* (December, 1950), 17: 25–27.

Pooley, R. C., and Robert D. Williams, *The Teaching of English in Wisconsin.* Madison: University of Wisconsin Press, 1948.

"The Role of Speech in the Secondary School," *Bulletin of the National Association of Secondary School Principals.* (November, 1945), 29: 133, 19–29; 51–65; 138–155. (A series of articles on the objectives of the speech program, speech defects, and speech programs in large and small high schools.)

Robinson, Karl F., *Teaching Speech in the Secondary School.* New York: Longmans, Green & Co., Inc., 1951, 3–35, 50–71.

Smith, Dora V., "The English Curriculum in Perspective," *College English* (March, 1946), 334–343.

————, "A Curriculum in the Language Arts for Life Today," *English Journal* (February, 1951), 40: 79–85.

"Speech Education for All American Youth," *Bulletin of the National Association of Secondary School Principals* (January, 1948), 32: 151, 133–135, 157–178. (A series of articles on speech correction, and on the relations of speech to the curriculum and school life.)

Wells, Charlotte, "Speech in the Full School Program," *Elementary English* (April, 1951), 28: 201–204.

CHAPTER 4

The Basic Pattern of Speech Instruction

INTRODUCTION

Can an activity organized and conducted as diversely as is the teaching of speech be described? Is there any general structure which defines the fundamental pattern of effective speech instruction wherever it is found? We believe that such a general description can be accomplished. We hold that effective speech teaching always incorporates certain specific and observable operations, and that if speech is being taught—either in a language-arts class or a speech fundamentals class, a common learnings program or in a one-room school—if speech really is being taught, these characteristic and basic features will be present.

EXAMPLES OF THREE TEACHING SITUATIONS

Examine the following brief descriptions of three diverse teaching situations in each of which speech is being taught.

Unit in Modern Drama in Language Arts Class

Teacher A is teaching a modern drama unit in a twelfth grade language arts class. His students have studied the problems involved in reading dramatic literature and have decided to read a group of modern plays, all of which deal in some way with a single theme. This class has selected the theme of *War*, and has raised the question, "Does drama give us insight into the nature, causes, and consequences of war?" The class has been divided into five groups, with each group reading a different play. Each group has been given the problem of reporting to the entire class on its experiences with the play assigned to it. This report is to give the class:

1. *An understanding of the nature of the play (perhaps, how it came to be written, if this is pertinent).*
2. *The reactions of the reading group to such questions as:*
   a. What is the author trying to say?
   b. Is it worth saying?
   c. Is it said effectively?
3. *What is the "flavor of the play" as discovered by a reading of some key scene?*

This report to the class involves the groups in a number of speech problems. Each group must decide the form in which the report should be given, and the "ways and means" available to make the report effective. The teacher works with each group in its consideration of "ways and means." As twelfth grade students, the members of this class have already studied such matters as making public speeches, organizing discussions, and play reading, but the teacher helps them recall their previous experiences in speaking which apply to an effective group report.

Each report is made the basis for a discussion by the entire class. The discussion centers on the points raised by the reporting group. However, if particularly effective planning or presentation is evident, the teacher opens the discussion of this effective speaking, and in some cases the class has suggestions for improvement to make to groups or individuals. Individuals and groups are then given time to state some specific goals for improving similar presentations in the future.

Preparation for "Honors" Assembly

Teacher B has been approached by the president of the student council, who has three speeches of presentation to make in an "honors" assembly. The teacher explores with the student the general nature of ceremonial speaking, and then examines with him the specific problems he faces, to see what *topics* may be available. He suggests that the student prepare an outline for each of three short talks and bring these outlines in for criticism. The talks thus prepared, after further help from the teacher, are given with reasonable success. After the assembly, the teacher finds informal occasion to commend the speaker on certain of the better points of his presentation. The student observes that some of his friends were unable to hear him in the back of the auditorium, and when the teacher asks him how he feels about this criticism he says, "I'll take care of it next time. I'll talk louder."

Speech Fundamentals at Ninth Grade Level

Teacher C is teaching a class in speech fundamentals at the ninth grade level. She has played recordings of somewhat stereotyped radio speakers or actors, and has asked the class to describe the persons they hear speaking. The students give rather complete descriptions of each of the speakers from their voices. They draw conclusions about each speaker's appearance, personality, and character, from his voice. They are asked if this freedom that they feel about these inferences has any importance to speakers, and they decide that it does. The question is raised as to the accuracy of such stereotyping. The students have many examples of speakers who do not "look the way they sound," or who "do not sound like the sort of people they really are." There are other persons they know whose voices seem to fit. After some discussion the class reaches two decisions about the meaning of all this for speakers and listeners:

1. *Speakers ought to try to develop their own voices as much as they can to reflect the meanings they want to get across to other people.*

2. *Listeners ought to be careful about judging people from their voices alone, and should examine carefully what some speakers have to say, before rejecting them because "I don't like their voices."*

The class decides to make voice recordings of each student. Readings are selected, and a discussion is held of the "ways and means" of preparing the readings so that they will be as effective as the speakers can make them. The readings are then recorded, and "play back" sessions held in small groups. The students talk about their vocal potentialities, and set specific goals for themselves, for improvement along lines that seem practical. The class plans some further activity in reading aloud, in which the emphasis will be on "practicing vocal skills." The students also discuss the application of these skills to the speaking they are doing at home and in other classes.

ACTIVITY, CRITICISM, GOAL SETTING, COMMON TO ALL

Each of the examples just cited involves speaking and teaching situations with widely different characteristics. Yet in each the common thread of speech instruction is present. It may be described in three fundamental operations, each of which may be analyzed further:

The Operation of *Activity*	1. The student confronts a situation in which he has need to speak. (He is stimulated or motivated to speak.)
	2. He considers "ways and means" of carrying out effectively the speaking which he proposes.
	3. He engages in speaking activity. The activity is a social one, involving speakers and listeners, purposes and means, speech content and form.
The Operation of *Criticism*	1. There is interaction between speaker and audience. This involves examination of the effectiveness of the speaking activity. It involves an effort to bring thoughtful conclusions out of the actual experiences of the social group.
The Operation of *Goal Setting*	1. Individuals and groups set further goals for themselves. Understandings of self and others, and of the speech process are used for setting improvement goals.

This, we believe, is the pattern of instruction within which speech is taught and learned. It is an inductive pattern which sees knowledge and skill growing out of the thoughtful examination of experience, in which theory grows out of practice and is used to control future practice. It is the learning pattern of life. It may remind some of Goethe's observation, "doing and thinking, doing and thinking,—that is all there is to life." In a broad sense, that is all there is to the teaching of any subject, including speech.

If our analysis of the nature of speech instruction is sound, a more detailed examination of the three basic operations should prove a valuable tool for the speech teacher. Once these operations are understood, the beginning teacher may set about planning the conduct of his teaching with the assurance that he is in truth planning to teach speech. Moreover, these three operations give the experienced teacher a continuous frame of reference within which to check the adequacy of his day-by-day instruction.

OPERATION 1: THE CHARACTERISTICS OF USEFUL SPEAKING ACTIVITY

It is likely that the speech teacher who spends much of his available class time in telling students how they ought to speak, does so with some profit to his own speaking skill. The teacher who lectured so forcefully on "the art of rhetoric" in the schools of a century ago doubtless refined his own understanding of speaking. Whether he affected materially the speaking practices of his students is at least suspect. The basis of speech improvement is the practice of speaking, and that means practice by the person seeking to improve, and not by the person seeking to help him. Therefore, the bulk of the school time available for speech instruction ought to be occupied by students engaged in the practice of speaking.

It is doubtful that any speech teacher seriously questions the primacy of student activity in a program of speech improvement. Nevertheless, there have been some powerful forces operative in our schools to restrict seriously the opportunity for students to practice speaking.

For one thing, students practicing speaking occupy a lot of class time, and, as school enrollments have grown, the economic pressures to reduce opportunity for individual practice in speaking have correspondingly increased. Types of learning which can be achieved, possibly, by mass instruction have an understandable fascination for administrators, hard pressed to stretch an inadequate budget, and for teachers who may face a total of from one to two hundred students, divided among five or six classes daily. There is no short cut for helping students to improve their speaking ability. The school which fails to provide practice in speaking for all of its students does not have a program of speech instruction for all of its students. And the so-called speech class which is so large, or so mismanaged that each student speaks only at infrequent intervals, may be subjecting the students to a form of frustration in which they are asked to speak often enough to make skill in speaking desirable, but not often enough to be able to acquire such skill. The plaint of students so instructed was well put more than a hundred years ago by a student of Columbia college, where the growing college enrollment (more than 140 students) had reduced opportunity for individual exercises in speech.

"This speechifying is a great bother," he wrote in his diary. "It does not come around often enough to do one any good, or to accustom one to it, but just often enough to be the greatest plague in the college. It is a complete nuisance."[1]

Speaking activity is not enough. To say that activity is the basis of speech instruction is not to say that practice alone is sufficient to assure improvement. If activity alone guaranteed speech improvement, most high school students would attain a relatively high level of speaking performance by reason of their repeated performances in the school corridors, and the neighboring drug store. Perhaps some do, but others seem only to develop persistent habits of little utility when carried outside the ritual of adolescent conversation. The sort of speaking activity sought by the teacher of speech has certain definite characteristics. We may study these as a basis for planning to teach speech, or as a means of checking on the adequacy of the speaking activity engaged in by our students.

Speaking Activity Should be Purposive

Useful speaking activity does not start with a teacher's prescription to "make a speech," or read a poem. Nor does it proceed from a teacher's invitation to "earn some extra credit in this class by making a report next Friday on the 'Life of Emily Dickinson.'" Such speaking is in a sense purposive, but only in a narrow, school-roomish sort of way, a way quite tenuously related to the purposes for which people use their speech in the important business of living. The first characteristics of the sort of speaking activity which is useful in teaching speech is that it is purposive in the sense that the student feels a real need to accomplish some purpose with an audience, or with an individual listener. To put it another way, students ought to speak because they feel a need more real than placating a teacher armed with innumerable assignments, or bolstering some grade book accounting system. In our daily living, the needs for which we

---

[1] Diary of G. T. Strong, Nov. 13, 1835. Cited in Helen Roach, "History of Speech Education at Columbia College" (1754–1940), (Ph.D. Thesis, 1947).

have to speak involve information we want to put into the minds of others, experiences we wish to share with them, ideas which we want to have accepted, or problems which we need help in solving. These are the audience-related purposes which ought to lie behind the speaking activities designed to teach speech.

But useful speaking activity ought to be purposeful in another sense, a sense that is only indirectly related to an audience. It ought to be purposeful in the sense that the speaker is seeking in some specific and orderly way to improve his speaking. Here the activity of learning speech breaks to some extent with the general speaking activities of life. Students do not make optimum improvement in speaking skill merely by participating in speaking activities, even when those activities are well motivated, and even when the student has every reason to wish to speak well. Students improve when they wish to modify their speaking behavior in specific ways which they can identify and understand, and when they can define the changes which they want to make, and the ways and means of securing these changes. It is a necessary condition of improvement in speech, that a student say honestly and sincerely, "I wish to speak better," or, "I have need to speak well." But even this is not an all-sufficient guarantee of improvement. To this "wish" must be added the specific knowledge of the particular aspects of speaking behavior which can be improved and the means open to the student for improving in these defined ways.

The following example will illustrate how students develop purposes: High school students in a speech class in the Laboratory School at the University of Hawaii planned together to interpret their "Paradise of the Pacific" to some students in a mainland high school. They decided to send pictures with a tape recording of talks, discussions, readings, and an original play, all prepared and presented by members of the class. The first time the students played back the tape, several said they did not like the way they sounded. The speech of each one was then analyzed and a program for improvement laid out. The students had two goals: First, to contribute to a satisfactory recording, and second, to improve personal speech habits.

Thus we may observe that there are two sorts of purposiveness which characterize the activity useful for speech instruction: First, *purposiveness with relation to a goal to be achieved with an audience,* a goal which the speaker sees and wants, and second, *purposiveness with relation to a goal of self-improvement,* a goal which the speaker also sees and wants. Obviously these two purposes are inter-related. A student should view a goal of self-improvement as instrumental to the communicative purposes of his speech; he is not learning to speak more audibly merely for the joy of speaking more audibly, but rather because such skill is helpful in gaining acceptance from other persons.

Yet students do not inevitably or readily hold both sorts of purposes in mind when engaging in classroom speaking activity, and in the absence of skillful direction from a speech teacher, either or both forms of purposiveness may be lacking in student speaking activity. Only when both are present do we avoid the dilemma of (a) the student who is fiercely motivated to speak, but has no program for self-improvement, and (b) the student who can recite faithfully his own shortcomings as a speaker, but perceives no pressing need to set about eliminating them.

Speaking Activity Should be Varied

A second major characteristic of useful speaking activity is that it should be varied in both purpose and form. Though variety of activity may be valued in any classroom for its own sake, as a foe of monotony, no such simple opportunism accounts fully for the importance of variety in classroom speaking activity. Such an accounting may be had, however, by considering the multitude of purposes for which man uses speech, and the multitude of forms of speaking which are common to our culture. While the threads of audible and visible symbolism tie all acts of speaking together, it is important that students see how these fundamental processes relate to the variety of speech forms and purposes.

A brief survey of the common purposes for which speech is used in our society, together with some of the common forms closely associated with these purposes may serve to illustrate the need for variety in the speaking activity of the classroom.[2]

1. *We speak to gather and share information.* Informal speech abounds in such purpose. Questions and answers, direction-seeking, in-

---

[2] There are many investigations of the purposes for which speech is used. One of the best is in Thomas Clark Pollock, *The Nature of Literature,* Princeton University Press, pp. 162–196.

struction-giving are a part of the speech of everyday life. The same purposes are found in the more formal speaking of the interview, and of the public speech instruction.

2. *We speak to secure co-operative solutions to problems.* Many types of problems are solved by group inquiry more readily and better than by individual inquiry. This is especially true when the solution to a problem is one which will affect the interests of a group of people, so that the solution agreed to must not only be a good one, but must also be accepted. The form of speech most closely associated with such co-operative speech activity is problem-solving discussion. Some groups conduct their discussion within the framework of parliamentary procedure.

3. *We speak to influence the opinions of others.* Freedom to hold and express opinions is one of our most cherished liberties. So is freedom to seek to persuade others to our own opinions. The speech of the salesman, the speaking of political life, pulpit speaking, are all concerned with advocating ideas, and with seeking to influence the opinions of others. Informal speech is full of effort to influence others. So is much public speaking. Debate, whether parliamentary or in the classroom, brings together opposing advocates under rules of fair procedure. Much public discussion seeks to influence the opinions of listeners in ways desired by the speakers.

4. *We speak to share experiences.* When we have had an experience which we have felt deeply, we often wish to share that experience with others. Sometimes we may do so with creative forms of writing, with the effort to create literature; sometimes we may do so with speech, attempting to evoke in another something of the complete experience we have had. Sometimes we use speech to re-create or to enhance the meanings which caused an author to write a play, a story, or a poem. When we take part in plays, or retell stories, or interpret orally prose or poetry, we are trying to share with others our experience with this literature. In conversation, or on the platform, speakers often try to share more completely their deeply-felt experiences with a listener.

5. *We speak to ease social tensions.* The speech of social conversation often has no purpose other than the easing of tensions. The other conventions of social form are usually aids to social living—they help us to know what to expect from other people, and to know their expectations of us.

Because all persons need speech for all of these varied purposes, and because different purposes affect the forms and qualities of efficient speech, it is apparent that the speaking activities of high school students need to be varied. They should be varied enough to give each student experience with speech directed toward the various purposes for which he needs, and will continue to need speech.

We have observed that the basic operation of speech instruction is *activity*. It must be activity, however, which reveals two major characteristics: (a) Purposiveness, in the sense that the speaker has an immediate need to speak to some audience for a specific purpose, and in the sense that the speaker has a goal of personal improvement in speaking, which he sees as instrumental to his need to speak well; and (b) Variety, in the sense that all students have directed experiences in using speech for the many purposes, and in the many forms which will serve their needs in everyday living.

OPERATION II: HELPFUL CRITICISM

A teacher of speech may do many things—from painting scenery for the junior class play, to providing leadership for the school convocation committee. But none of his activities is more crucial to the success of his speech instruction than his activity as a critic of speech, and as a stimulator and a leader of helpful criticism. He may properly feel that his most important job as a teacher is to listen to students' speaking, and then to help students make sound and useful interpretations of their speaking experiences.

The crucial nature of criticism in speech instruction may be understood if we consider carefully the way in which students form and modify their speaking behavior, as a result of speaking experiences. This is not to say that all of our speaking behavior is exclusively the product of experience, for obviously, to take only one illustration, our basic physiological and neurological equipment influences the way in which we speak. But it is to say that many of the important characteristics of our speech habits and adjustments are related to our past experiences in speaking. More specifically, our behavior is related to the interpretation we have placed on our experiences. Thus a student, at one point in his life, may talk to others on a subject of great personal importance to him. Perhaps, because he makes a poor choice of subject, or misjudges the occasion upon which he is speaking, he is ridiculed by his listeners. Thereafter he may avoid speaking of matters which have any real importance to him in public or semi-public situations. His public speaking may become noticeable for its general unimaginativeness, or lack of vigor. He may withdraw from the speaking situation and, perhaps, complain, "I can't think of things to say," or "I've never done anything worth talking about." Or he may take refuge in "clowning," deliberately creating the impression that he regards his own ideas as trivial.

Very possibly this student never realizes fully the relationships of the interpretation he had placed on an earlier speaking experience to his subsequent speaking behavior. For example, Frank Martin's talks in class were dull and boring. In an effort to find more meaningful material for this student, the teacher had a private talk with Frank. She discovered that his name was not Martin but Martini, that he was born in Italy, and that he had had many experiences the relating of which would have held his classmates spellbound. But to quote Frank, "I wouldn't let those kids know for a million dollars that I was born in Italy. They're not going to call me a dago."

The teacher helped with the preparation of a description of a storm at sea when Frank, more adventuresome than any other passenger, got on a sturdy chair and slid from side to side of the tilting water-soaked deck until the turbulent sea had calmed. The class applauded and asked him to tell them more. Frank had learned that there was more sound satisfaction in describing honest experiences than there was humiliation in having some ignorant person thoughtlessly call him a dago.

It is important to note how experiences affect our speaking behavior, according to the interpretation we place on those experiences. These effects may be good or bad, as judged by their effects upon the efficiency of our subsequent speaking. Speech instruction seeks to increase the likelihood that the effects of speaking experiences will be good; it does this by making these *directed* experiences. Efforts are made to place students in speaking situations in which they will experience some measure of success. They are then given assistance in interpreting their experiences intelligently; they speak in an environment of criticism regulated by the speech teacher. The teacher listens, comments, and directs comments, to the end that students may place useful interpretations on their own speaking experiences. Students are helped to see (1) that others value their speaking on occasion, (2) that their problems are shared by others, and (3) that there are specific ways in which they can become more effective.

It is true that not all speaking activity contributes to speech improvement; it is equally true that not all criticism is helpful to the student being criticized. Skillful conduct of criticism is an art, one of the highest professional arts that the speech teacher can attain. It requires judgment in knowing when to criticize and when to be silent, where to criticize, when and how much to praise or blame, and how rapidly and completely students may be led to an honest appraisal of their own speaking. Because of the complexity of this operation, Chapter 21 is devoted to a more thorough exploration of the management of criticism in the speech class.

OPERATION III: GOAL SETTING

One of the significant ends of speech criticism, as we have already implied, is increased insight on the part of the speaker into the specific ways and means open to him to improve his own speaking. This is also the basis upon which the student may establish the goals of self improvement which we have said must be present in useful speaking activity. Goal setting, then, is the operation mediating between criticism and activity—it is the end of helpful criticism and the beginning of purposive activity.

It is obvious that speech teachers must set goals for their teaching. The really significant operation of goal setting in the speech class, however, rests with the students themselves. Many of the activities of the speech class, therefore, are designed to increase the chance that each student will have for his own speech improvement specific, attainable goals which he accepts as important enough to warrant his efforts toward their achievement. The activities which enter into this operation of goal setting are of many sorts. Listing a few of them may serve to illustrate the manner in which the operation may be made effective in the speech class.

1. Students in Class A are discussing all of the ways in which they have observed people using speech. Discussion leads to a consideration of the common elements in all these situations, and it is observed that in every case speakers are attempting to get a response from listeners. Some students confess that they have never before thought of their own speech in this way.

2. A number of students in Class B have given informational talks. Informal tests reveal that little of the information presented has been grasped by anyone in the class. The purposes of informative speaking are discussed, and some specific ways of attaining these

purposes are listed on the board. The next students to give instructional talks are asked to try some of these ways of "making information stick," and to use tests to see if the suggested methods really work.

3. Students, after hearing recorded speeches by well-known speakers, ask, What characteristics have helped these people become effective speakers? Can we seek some of these characteristics in our own speech? Attainable goals are listed.

4. Students meet for "play back" sessions of some of their own speeches which have been recorded. Each recording is discussed. Each student writes down specific goals for improvement which he thinks he could attain in his next speech.

5. A student has given a talk, and one of his classmates observes, "He looks and sounds conceited." Other students indicate their agreement. The teacher "happens" to see the student after school and asks him to come in and talk over the speech. The student does so, and efforts are made to evaluate the causes and significance of the remarks by his classmates. The student is challenged to formulate his own statement of a goal for self improvement.

6. The teacher hands a student a note at the end of one of his talks, suggesting a specific goal for improvement in his next talk. Before the talk, the student is asked to state any goal of self improvement he has in mind. The teacher can judge whether or not his suggestion has been translated into a goal by the student.

These are a few illustrations of the operation of goal setting in the speech classroom. It is apparent that in each the emphasis has been on students identifying their own goals for improvement. The operation may be facilitated by group activities, but must ultimately rest upon an individual basis.

SUMMARY

Many of the subsequent chapters of this book will deal with the actual ways in which speech teachers set up activities, criticism, and goals as they go about the business of teaching speech. Speech teachers need to see these operations in continuous interplay, as the real structure of their work. The essence of speech teaching cannot be described either as an outline of subject matter, or as a series of teaching units. It must be perceived in a total way as the creation of an environment of directed experiences, within which students will have maximum opportunity to become more effective speakers. The entire process is indicated by the simple diagram below:

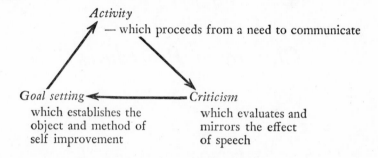

Activity
— which proceeds from a need to communicate

Goal setting ← *Criticism*

which establishes the   which evaluates and
object and method of   mirrors the effect
self improvement   of speech

SELECTED BIBLIOGRAPHY

Allport, G., *Personality*. New York: Henry Holt & Co., 1937, Ch. 7.

Bode, B. H., *How We Learn*. Boston: D. C. Heath & Company, 1940.

Dewey, John, *Experience and Education*. New York: The Macmillan Co., 1938.

Gates, Arthur I., Arthur T. Jersild, T. R. McConnell, and Robert C. Challman, *Educational Psychology*. New York: The Macmillan Co., 1949, Chs. 9, 10, 11, 12.

Judd, C. H., *Educational Psychology*. Boston: Houghton Mifflin Co., 1939, Ch. 12.

N.E.A. Educational Policies Commission: *Learning the Ways of Democracy*. Washington, 1940.

CHAPTER 5

Classroom Procedures

INTRODUCTION

A CERTAIN oft-quoted philosophic observation separates teachers from doers. Within limits such a division is defensible. A football coach need not necessarily be a good player, some persons with limited ability in creative writing have helped others to learn to write, and successful play directors are not always great actors. But in a wider sense, a skillful teacher of speech, or of any other discipline, is a skillful speaker. His speaking skill is of a particular sort. He may or may not be the most effective public speaker, or reader, or actor, or conversationalist in his community. But like all of these other speakers, he must be a person who has entered a social situation, for a certain purpose, and has said and done the things appropriate to the achievement of that purpose. In a special way, the speech teacher confronts the same sort of problems which all speakers must solve. He must be one who practices his own art.

For this reason, we suggest that teachers of speech approach the job of teaching in terms of the principles of their own art. To beginning teachers, who may have had considerable experience as speakers, this will clarify the way in which they can bring their past experiences to bear on solving the new problems of teaching. Experienced teachers may find it interesting to check their practices in teaching against the speech principles they advocate. Here are some statements which attempt to give a picture of the process of teaching as a special form of speaking.

GOOD TEACHERS ARE LIKE GOOD SPEAKERS IN THAT:

1. They *define and narrow their purposes.* They select purposes possible of achievement in the circumstances which they confront.
2. They *plan the "ways and means" of fulfilling their purposes.* They are manipulators of situations, seeking all available ways of accomplishing such worth-while goals as they have set.
3. They *remain flexible in outlook, in order to make the most of unanticipated opportunities which may arise.*
4. They *seek to make good first impressions, first impressions relevant to their long-term purposes.*
5. They *seek the active co-operation of all members of a social group.*
6. They *consider the influence of all aspects of a complex social situation on the possible achievement of their goals.* They study their students, their materials, and the circumstances under which they must teach.
7. They *understand that the better person one is, the better teacher he is likely to be.*
8. They *understand that teaching is seldom completely successful.* There are always degrees of success and failure in teaching.
9. They *understand that there are different roads to successful teaching.*
10. They *understand that skill is acquired by "doing and thinking," not by prolonged discussion of principles.*

If this view of the relationship of teaching to speaking is a valid one, a more detailed examination of each of these statements ought to tell us much about the job of the speech teacher. It ought to tell us about his goal-setting activities, his planning activities, the conduct of the "first days" of class, and some of his problems and hopes.

Good Teachers and Their Goals

Teachers, like public speakers, sometimes exhibit two sorts of temperamental excesses in setting up the purposes of their teaching. Some teachers are visionary, and state only the most world-shaking aims for their instruction. "My goal in teaching speech," they say, "is to build character," or "to pave the way for a better tomorrow," or "to give boys and girls a happier life." These grandiose claims serve no real purpose, for a teacher of any sort who did not have such aims would be of doubtful worth. Such statements tell us little about the specific sort of activity which actually would be appropriate to instruction in the speech class. They may suggest some of the goals of education, but they do not help much in terms of the goals of the Speech 10 class, held on Wednesday from 9:50 to 10:45. The type of teachers described above may be likened to the student speaker who states that his purpose in a five-minute talk is "to lead his audience to understand the causes and cures of war and other forms of international conflict." We may applaud the speaker's vision, but we still know very little about what he intends to accomplish in five minutes, and we might even guess that he does not know either!

Other teachers renounce visionary thinking completely. They may tend to set goals specific enough to be related to the activity of a single hour of teaching, but so narrow that they raise serious question as to whether the goal is worth seeking in the first place. A student reports an experience with one of his teachers who had developed a strong belief that the polite phrase, "thank you," was considerably more efficient than the more pretentious phrase, "thank you very much." This teacher set as his goal for fifty minutes of instruction the elimination of the latter phrase from the speech patterns of his students. He planned carefully, exerted his considerable personal charm in favor of "thank you," likened the more elaborate form to various effusive and offensive circumlocutions, and used oral drill, vari-colored chalk, and many illustrations to dramatize his point. Later in the school year, this teacher was very helpful to one of his students seeking a job. The student approached the teacher, motivated by genuine gratitude, only to be reduced to stumbling speechlessness by the sudden conflict between his feelings and the memory of the low status of effusiveness in the expression of appreciation! The moral of the story is that a teacher may be too specific on issues which have to be settled on broader principles.

Some teachers of speech seem to get real satisfaction from the achievement of narrow and specific goals, without raising the question of the relevance of these goals to the broad purposes of general education, or of specific speech instruction. They may be likened to the student who for four years, in the fifth, sixth, seventh, and eighth grades, addressed his classmates on "Types of Indian Arrowheads," displaying each year his own fine collection. By the end of the fourth year most of his audience knew as much about the collection as did the speaker, whose mission had been clearly accomplished, but certain cynics among his classmates began to grumble audibly about the use to which he was putting their time. Teachers, of course, will detect the fact that this student speaker had two purposes—the announced one about arrowheads, and the real one of impressing a succession of new teachers with the magnificence of his collection.

There is a reasonable compromise between these temperamental extremes. The goal-setting activity of the teacher ought to begin with a vision of the purposes of education generally. This goal-setting activity ought then to proceed to an understanding of the goals of speech specifically, as these goals are related to the over-all goals of education. The first four chapters of this book have concerned themselves extensively with these broader goals of speech instruction. But the teacher must proceed ultimately to concrete goals, relevant to these broader purposes, yet specific enough to fit (a) the real activity of the class period, and (b) the time and space limits of the classroom.

Most teachers, we suspect, do not narrow their goals sufficiently to make them very useful in the planning of classroom procedures. Here is an actual statement of the goals set by a speech teacher for the first two weeks of work with a class of tenth grade students in a speech fundamentals course:

1. To overcome fears of speaking.
2. To achieve freedom and ease in using bodily action for speaking before an audience.
3. To understand why it is important to speak effectively.
4. To understand the characteristics of effective speech.
—Just like that!

Now we may acknowledge that the teacher probably meant a good deal less than he said when he stated these goals, yet the very size of the burden he assumed when he made such statements is enough to frighten us, and it would doubtless frighten his class, if he let them in on the secrets of his planning.

Consider the first of these purposes. Undoubtedly students of speech are more anxious to gain confidence, or poise, than they are to secure any other result of speech training. The facts that this goal is so nearly universal among students, and is so avidly sought, are warning enough of the social fears faced by many students. One of the important end products of considerable periods of speech instruction is the mitigating, or relieving, of such fears *to some extent*. But it is not a goal which can be achieved totally under any conditions, let alone in two weeks of class work. And, of course, it may be that some speakers never really overcome their social fears so much as they learn to understand, reduce, and live more comfortably with these fears.

Here is another statement of a teacher's goals for the first two weeks of a class in speech for tenth grade students:

1. To help students feel that talking on many different subjects, and in many different ways, will be valued in this class.
2. To help the students get acquainted with one another, and to learn something of the interests and attitudes of their classmates.
3. To help students identify some of the ways in which speech has been useful to them in the past.
4. To help students identify some of the ways in which they are speaking, and the purposes for which they are speaking at present.
5. To help students identify some of the ways in which students have been able to learn to speak more effectively.

Such purposes represent only one approach to the teaching of speech, and certainly should not be considered the only or the optimum statement of goals in starting a speech class. Our point is simply that this teacher has stated goals which may be possible of achievement in the allotted time. Moreover, these goals are specific enough to give some indication of the sorts of activities which a class might use to achieve them.

Yet even these statements are still somewhat general, and would go through a further refining in the direction of concreteness if the teacher began to consider goals for a single, specific class period. We shall consider the matter of goals for a daily plan a little later, pausing here with the single observation that the goal-setting activity of the teacher must move through successive stages of concreteness until goals are ultimately conceived, or stated, which are possible of achievement in a specific time and place, and yet relevant to the broader purposes of speech instruction and education generally.

Goal setting involves both teacher and student

Teaching would be simpler if it were not for the fact that students learn only in terms of their own purposes. And sad to relate, the goals of teachers and the goals of their students are not always the same, and not infrequently may be diametrically opposed to one another. All communicative situations, of course, involve the same problem. Audiences tend to hear and remember the things that they want to hear and remember, often without too much reference to the intent or the language of those who address them: For example, in giving a speech, a university professor was moved to make some passing comments on domestic relationships. He said that certain types of conflict between husbands and wives are inevitable, but that he could not condone wife-beating because it is aesthetically unsound! Of course his remarks had no serious intent, but he was surprised to see a story in the newspaper the following morning under the headline, "Professor Advocates Wife-Beating." The purpose of a reporter who was looking for a story with reader appeal, had proved more significant than the actual purposes of the speaker.

We might examine the somewhat gloomy picture presented in many speech classes demonstrating a conflict between teacher and pupil purposes:

Teacher's purpose	*Pupil's purpose*
To help students to articulate distinctly.	"I want to articulate the way other students do. Who wants to be a sissy?"
To talk freely and easily before an audience.	"My face is broken out. I want people to look at me as little as possible."
To like my students and be liked by them.	"Adults, all of them, are my enemies."
To enjoy talking with others in this class.	"That bunch who sit over near the window don't like me, and I don't like them. What do I care about what they think about my speech?"
To be more effective in speaking.	"I want a passing grade."

Fortunately for teachers, most students, in most schools, concede the desirability of school and education. Moreover, fortunately for speech teachers, most students to some extent admit their need for effective speech, and are interested in acquiring skills in talking to and listening to other students. Some degree of antagonism, however, between the purposes of teachers and those of students is all but inevitable from the nature of adult-adolescent relationships; this is the conflict that speech teachers must acknowledge and work with.

Since pupil goals determine the actual nature of pupil activity, and since students learn only in terms of their own purposes, some educators emphasize the idea that students ought at least to participate in planning the goals for a course. Others would suggest that all the real learning goals must come exclusively from the student's awareness of his own needs, elicited with the help of a teacher. We think that good speech teachers very generally should be able to give students real help in setting the goals of their work in speech—help based on the fact that the teacher has thought long and carefully about the sort of purposes high school students ought to try to achieve in their speech, and which also are possible for them. But we also believe that the effective speech teacher seeks maximum co-operation and assistance from students in planning and stating purposes which are real and meaningful to them.

In short, a student will improve as a speaker only if he wants to improve. Furthermore, he will improve only if he sees his needs specifically, only if he has goals which are immediate and personal, and only if he is doing things which he sees to be relevant to his own purposes. The teacher cannot simply *talk* these purposes into his students, but he can raise the sort of questions for discussion and set up the sort of speaking experiences for his class, which will help students to set goals relevant to their improvement as speakers. Rasey puts it this way:

He (the teacher) is the scene shifter and stage manager—manipulating circumstances about the learner, turning full spotlights on some items, shrouding others in intriguing shadows. Teachers sometimes get mixed up as did Rostand's chanticleer. Roosters don't crow up the sun, whatever they think. They just announce it. Teachers do not educate. They are bystanders. It is experience that educates. We facilitate the learner's experiencing so that he becomes more skilled in living and learning.[1]

The foregoing points to goal setting for the speech class as a "combined operation," with teacher and pupil working together. We have not yet described the actual techniques of such joint operations, but we have pointed out that speech teachers must ask con-

---

[1] Rasey, M. I., *This is Teaching*. New York: Harper & Brothers, 1950, p. 5.

stantly not only "what are *my* goals?" but also "what are the goals *of my students?*"

Some teachers like to list separately the teacher goals and the student goals for a particular day's work. Thus a teacher may open a speech class with an informal discussion of "pets" or "hobbies." His own purpose may be diagnostic, "to learn something of the speech characteristics and needs of the students in this class," while he may also hold for his students the goal of "feeling that talking on a wide variety of interesting matters will be valued in this class." It is thus clear that teachers may hold goals for themselves which are somewhat different from the goals they set for their students, but no teacher, in advance of meeting with a particular class, can do more than guess at the goals individual students will want to set for themselves in speech improvement. Actual knowledge of the student's own purposes must be developed by observing the student, talking with him, and listening to him verbalize his own objectives.

Goal setting a continuous job in the speech class

Teachers set goals for themselves because they wish to operate efficiently and purposefully in their work. Their goals must ultimately be related to the broad purposes of education, but they also must be narrowed and made concrete in terms of the daily activity of a particular class, if they are to be useful to the teacher. Teachers aim to state goals possible of achievement. The teacher's goals are for the direction of the activity, but the teacher's ultimate concern is not with himself, but with the learning of his students. Since students learn not in terms of the purposes of teachers but in terms of their own wants and goals, the teacher must look upon the goal setting of a speech class as a "combined operation," teachers and students working together. It is a continuous job which requires constant appraisal, re-appraisal, and reflection. The teacher questions himself and his students in the continuing rhythm of self-aware, purposive activity: Where have we been? Where do we want to go? and, How do we get there?

Teacher planning for achievement of goals

Course outlines, unit plans, and lesson plans play somewhat the same part in the life of the teacher that speech outlines do in the life of the public speaker. All of us are aware that people with purposes to be achieved must plan, and that when these purposes are to be achieved within discreet boundaries of time and space, the pressures for efficient planning increase. We believe in foresight, in the calculation of events and their consequences. At the same time, we are aware that effective planning, whether by teachers or public speakers, is an internal process, reflecting the planner's capacity for visualizing, for giving structure to his ideas and purposes, and for anticipating the responses of others to events and circumstances. Planning is a mental activity of a complexity never fully represented in a speaker's outline or a teacher's lesson plan. It is an activity which may be performed almost effortlessly and almost without self-consciousness by some persons, usually persons of great experience in dealing with others. For most teachers it is an activity requiring almost painful concentration and frequent failure.

In very general terms, most beginning teachers, like inexperienced speakers, seem to profit from attention to the routines of careful planning. Course outlines, lesson plans, and unit plans when reduced to paper have the effect of pushing a teacher into conscious grappling with the diverse factors which must be taken into account in his teaching. It is also true, however, that a teacher's planning never reaches full maturity in the mechanical activity of "writing out plans." It reaches maturity when the teacher visualizes the unfolding of the activity in his class in its entirety, when he sees the repeated pattern of the speech class, a pattern of activity, criticism, and goal setting, as a whole.

From Course Outlines to Unit Plans to Lesson Plans

The planning of the teacher proceeds often from the general overview of an entire course to the specific plans for the conduct of a particular class period. We shall consider these successive stages of planning in terms of course outlines, unit plans, and lesson plans, without, however, suggesting that all teachers formally set forth such sequences of plans in the course of their preparation.

Course outlines

The traditional course outline in the secondary school was at one time an outline of subject matter. It attempted to set forth, in orderly fashion, a body of information, which was, in theory at least, to be transferred into the mind of some youthful scholar. Such outlines, of course, have very little relevance to the design of secondary school work in speech. Speech instruction at the secondary school level, as we have already indicated, is seldom thought of in terms of a specific set of facts and generalizations, although instruction in speech does not proceed without reference to facts and generalizations. Rather, it is thought of in terms of skills to be acquired, and the experiences of speaking, listening, observing, and reading which may aid in the acquisition of these skills. A course outline for speech instruction, is apt, therefore, to take a form somewhat different from an outline of subject matter about speech.

However, in circumstances where courses in speech fundamentals, public speaking, dramatics, and the like are taught separately in the high school curriculum, the teacher must of necessity develop certain rather clear concepts of the nature of each course as a whole. Certain elements inevitably seem appropriate to such course planning:

1. Statements of the goals (outcomes) to be sought by the course. These statements will ordinarily view the instructional goals of the course in some detail, and may separate them into skills, information, attitudes and generalizations.

2. An outline indicating the scope and nature of the activity to be included in the course. This outline may appear in several forms:

    a. *A listing of the speaking, listening, reading, and observing activities which will be generally followed by all students.*

    b. *A listing of certain units to be covered by the course, plus an indication of the general scope of activities to be included in each unit. Dividing course work into units has become a popular method of segmenting high school instruction, generally, and we shall shortly consider in greater detail the nature of the unit, and unit planning.*

3. An outline of methods to be followed in evaluating the outcomes of the course. This statement should be relevant to the statement of the goals of the course, and represent the thinking of the teacher as to how students and teachers are to appraise progress toward the various goals.

Sources of course plans

Eventually the speech teacher's courses grow out of his own experiences in teaching. They represent the experiences which seem to the teacher most appropriate to the needs of the students with whom he works; which seem to lead most efficiently to the accomplishment of the general ends of speech instruction, and of education;

and which seem most helpful in the teacher's school and community, and to society generally. But the beginning teacher who is told to build a speech course in terms of such principles as student need, social need, utility, and the like, has not been told very much. These are criteria for judging the worth of a course, but they do not describe, or define the sort of experiences which ought to make up a course. The beginning teacher needs definite specifications for course plans in speech, from which he can work with students to the eventual development of a course, which seems to be getting results. Where shall he get such proposals? Obvious sources include: (1) Textbooks, (2) professional publications, (3) suggestions from other teachers, and (4) analysis of the speaking activities of his students.

Textbooks. Teachers often look upon textbooks as materials to be used in connection with some established course of study. It is well to remember that many texts are in effect complete and detailed statements of the author's concept of a course. Usually the authors of texts incorporate into their books the products of their own teaching experience, as well as the products of thoughtful examination of the practices of teachers generally. Textbooks are probably more careful suggestions for courses of study than are the sort of outlines normally entitled "course of study."

There are some common objections to the use of texts as course outlines: Texts are often synthesized from the teaching materials of many different teachers, and they give not a picture of a unified "teachable" course, but rather a reference file of materials. The criticism has some validity, and teachers of speech courses will frequently find the materials in texts organized into convenient units from which they can select and re-order the materials that they want to use, or can find time for. Another objection is that texts cannot give a picture of a course adapted to the real needs and interests of a particular group of students, and that a teacher ought to teach his own course, not one set up for students in a different situation and perhaps a different section of the country. Again, the criticism has some validity. The slavish following of a text without reference to the actual situations in the particular class is absurd. It results in the form of teaching in which students know more about the geography of the Peloponnesian peninsula, than about that of their own state. A teacher using a speech text as the basis for his course, will need to think always in terms of the relationship of his own group of students to the activities, and units suggested by the text.

Professional publications. Reports of teachers, or groups of teachers, on their own speech courses, or on recommended course outlines, are a helpful source of ideas for teachers. Speech teachers ought to follow regularly *The Quarterly Journal of Speech* and *The Speech Teacher* for suggestions for course materials. For those teachers of speech working in drama, *The Educational Theatre Journal* is a similar "must." The *English Journal* contains frequent materials on speech courses, and speech activities in the English or language arts class, and certain issues of *The Bulletin of the National Association of Secondary School Principals* carry material on speech courses. Some of the articles listed below are representative of the sort of help offered by such professional journals in the preparation of courses of study.

1. "A Suggested Outline for a Course of Study in Dramatic Arts in The Secondary School," *Educational Theatre Journal* (March, 1950), II: 15–31.
2. "Speech Programs," *The Bulletin of the National Association of Secondary School Principals* (November, 1945), 29: 138–155.
3. Painter, Margaret, "Oral Emphasis in the English Class," *English Journal* (September, 1947), 36: 48.
4. Robinson, K. F., and John Keltner, "Suggested Units in Discussion and Debate," *Quarterly Journal of Speech* (October, 1946), 32: 385–390.

Other teachers. It has often been observed that beginning teachers tend to repeat both the basic educational concepts and the teaching procedures of their own teachers. "We teach as we have been taught." The influence may be a benign one if the beginner has had a fortunate experience with superior teachers, or it may be the reverse. One of the unfortunate products of this tendency on the part of teachers is that they often try to transfer without modification the teaching methods and materials of their most recent college courses into their high school classrooms.

Nevertheless, the beginning teacher, in designing course plans, has no source of help better than the advice of experienced workers in the same field. In a more personal and direct way, this is similar to the helps provided by the reviews of textbooks and professional publications, but it is a tribute to the power of speech that beginning teachers often feel more confidence in the personal recommendations of an experienced teacher, than in published views of experienced teachers.

Analysis of student activity. From the first, the speech teacher should become a careful analyst of the speaking activities of his students, and of their needs. Regardless of the assistance he may obtain in the construction of his course, from outside sources, the course, to be effective, must represent these activities and needs.

Teachers who ask their students, "What sort of speaking are you doing with which you need help?" are often pleased to find that the problems faced immediately by high school students are usually the same sort of problems they will face as adults. There is no real conflict between the child's immediate needs for speech and his needs as a future adult citizen. The speech course influenced by such analysis may often reflect decisions like the following:

"The seventh grade is going to study parliamentary procedure. These seventh-graders have a lot of business to conduct in their class meetings, and things haven't been going very well."

"These ninth-grade students are going to use panel discussion extensively in their social studies class. They have agreed with the social studies teacher that it will be helpful to study the 'how' of panel discussion in speech class. They may even work out some of the discussions to be given in social studies during the speech class."

"These seventh-graders said that they could talk to adults now over the telephone, or in stores, but that they didn't know how to talk to adults at social gatherings. They are planning a parent-student tea, to be held after school, and are going to study how to welcome parents, how to introduce themselves and others, and some of the things adults might be interested in talking about."

"The eleventh-grade students agree that it's difficult not to be persuaded by forceful speakers, even when these speakers don't have our best interests at heart. They want to study the 'propaganda' tricks of speakers so that they can resist them. As teacher, I pointed out that we need to start further back, and develop skill in making conclusions warranted by evidence in our own speaking—at least when we are pretending to make conclusions of the sort that ought to represent evidence. We are planning some talks and discussions in which we will examine carefully the relationship between the evidence presented by various speakers, and the 'truth claims' based upon this evidence."

Textbooks, professional publications, other teachers, and analysis of students' needs and activities are the sources that influence our concepts of a course of study in speech. The beginning teacher should seek such sources purposefully in working for the development of his whole speech program.

Unit plans

Many secondary school teachers of speech plan their instruction in terms of relatively separate segments which they call *units*. In a loose sense, a unit is simply a grouping together of a certain number of activities presumably "unified" by some theme, or topic, or problem, or relatively specific area of learning. The unit may also be considered a block of school work of sufficient magnitude to lead students to certain rather specific goals. In this way, the objectives of the unit become central, and the learning activities which it includes are simply a selection of activities appropriate and sufficient to attain the stated goals. We call these statements about units a loose definition simply to recognize the fact that the term *unit* has a rather specific meaning to some educators, involving both a method of teaching and a method of organizing, though it is used also to describe a variety of methods of organizing teaching materials by teachers generally.

It is interesting to observe the various bases used by different teachers in the organization of their work. Three rather separate bases for organizing units in speech seem to be apparent.

1. Some teachers organize units of study around aspects of the speaking process. They observe that the act of speaking, in all contexts, involves certain interrelated, but identifiably separate aspects. Thus the study of speech may be carried out through the study of such aspects as voice, bodily action, the speaker's language (his words and word groups), the speaker's attitudes, purposes, preparation habits, personal resources, and the like. Such units may be called "*process-centered*" units.

2. Some teachers organize units of study around identifiable "forms of speaking" (the reasonably identifiable forms in which speech appears in our society), like public speaking, discussion, debate, reading aloud, dramatic production, conversation, radio speaking, and the like. Such units may be called "*form-centered*" units.

3. Some teachers would regard the unit as the statement of "the

something which gives rise to a student need for speech." Thus a unit of study would grow around a problem, the solution of which would involve the need for speech, and therefore the study of speech. Such problems might range from simple intellectual problems about speech itself, like "What is speech?" "Why do people need to speak effectively?" or "How may people improve their speech?" to problems confronted by students outside the area of speech, but which require the use of speech in their solution, like "How shall we improve our assembly programs?" "How may personality be improved?" "Should our city build a swimming pool?" "How good are the movies?" "Who reads comic books and why?" and so forth. Such units may be called *"problem-centered"* units.

Possibly too much time is spent in debating the merits of various ways of establishing the theme or center of attention in units. Many teachers will argue for the "problem-centered" unit on the reasonable basis that speaking activity must rise out of a real need on the part of the student to communicate, and they will criticize "process-centered" units and "form-centered" units on the ground that they create speaking for its own sake, and therefore give the student no real stimulus to speak. The defenders of "process" and "form-centered" units will observe that "problem-centered" units often get students so interested in a problem that they devote only sporadic attention to the speaking processes involved in its solution; or that individual students do not get a well-balanced diet of speech experiences, but tend instead to participate repeatedly in the type of speaking in which they already have acquired certain skills. The defenders of "form-centered" units and "problem-centered" units may reserve a special bit of criticism for their colleagues who use "speech processes" as unit centers. They accuse these teachers of fragmenting speech unrealistically. They observe that speaking always appears as a unified act in a social situation, and that people organize their speaking behavior around purposes and the conventional forms which may be useful to the solution of these purposes, rather than around *parts* of an act which is never really divided into parts.

In some ways all of these criticisms are sound. They appear to be warnings against the misuse of particular ways of organizing speech instruction, rather than criticisms which invalidate totally any method of organization. That is to say, the teacher of speech, whatever the basis of organization he uses for his unit, needs to remember that:

1. Students learn to speak most readily from practice in situations in which they feel a real desire and need to speak.

2. Students should attend to the speech processes as such, in the job of defining specifically their own needs as speakers, and in setting personal goals for practice and improvement.

3. Students should examine each form of speaking with reference to all the characteristics of process and convention which go to make up effective use of that form.

4. Students need a well-balanced group of speech experiences, to gain skill in using speech in many ways and many situations.

Behind the formal organization of the unit, the good speech teacher will keep explicit the picture of the speech course as *activity*, *criticism*, and *goal setting*.

What goes into a unit plan?

The advantages of unit planning rest in the potential capacity of such a plan to describe and define a relatively complete act of teaching. By this we mean that all the essential activities of teaching and learning, including the setting of goals, the diagnosis of student needs or status, the carrying out of activities of various sorts, and the evaluation of progress, can appear in a unit plan. Teachers, however, will not always have time to plan all of their units on paper in complete form; they will not always organize unit plans for their own use in the same way in which they might set up a plan for the examination of another teacher; and they will not always work out the plan exactly as they intend, or as visualized by the students who may assist in the development of the units. Despite these reservations, nevertheless, it is still useful for teachers to examine with some care the various sorts of planning which need to be done in the preparation of a complete unit. We suggest that such a unit will include all, or nearly all, of the following materials:

1. A statement of the specific objectives to be sought in the unit, including the skills to be practiced and perhaps improved, the attitudes to be encouraged, the facts to be retained, and the generalizations or concepts which may be better understood.

2. A description of the speaking activities which will be developed, including consideration of why these activities will be needed, or how they are to be motivated.

3. A summary of the specific aspects of speaking and listening skill which will be emphasized for the group, in the planning, performance, and criticism of these activities.

4. A description of plans for evaluating student activity, including the various critical activities of the class, and plans for teacher appraisals.

5. A listing of reading, observing, and listening activities which may be developed in line with the unit purposes including appropriate visual aids, books, magazines, and the like.

6. Equipment or materials needed.

An illustrative unit

The unit which follows is intended simply to illustrate the general ways in which the items listed above may appear in the planning of a speech unit. Its length, degree of elaboration, and mode of statement are essentially unimportant, since these matters are governed by the circumstances under which units are prepared, e.g., whether they are prepared for a teacher's own edification or to delight his fellow teachers. This unit is presented in somewhat abbreviated form.

A UNIT IN CLASSROOM SPEECHES OF INFORMATION (Oral Reports)

Time: 10 days; class size: 25 students.
Objectives
1. To help students to improve in the use of the following skills:
    a. Organizing material for a specific purpose.
    b. Planning to get and hold the attention of an audience to accomplish their purpose.
    c. Planning to help the audience retain key information by visual aids, repetition, and vocal emphasis or verbal underlining.
    d. Using a clear, pleasant, direct mode of presentation.
    e. Determining the specific purpose of a speech which has been heard.
    f. Making notes of the key information of the speech.
2. To help students acquire the following information and understanding:
    a. Knowledge of the three parts of a speech of information.
    b. Knowledge of two of the primary functions of each part.
    c. Understanding of the sources of failure in students' reports.
    d. Understanding of the characteristics of superior reports.

3. To help students develop the following attitudes toward speaking:
   a. Willingness to prepare informational reports for other students.
   b. Willingness to listen courteously and attentively to fellow students.
   c. Desire to exercise care in the accurate statement of information and sources of information.

Activity Plan

1. Play a recording of two student classroom reports. Discuss:
   a. Where were these reports given?
   b. Why were they given?
   c. How well did they succeed?
   d. What were the strong and weak points in the reports?
2. Discuss the uses made of oral reports in various classes of the schools.
   a. What complaints do you have against the speakers?
   b. Against the listeners?
   c. What problems have you faced as a speaker; as a listener?
3. Develop a plan to study specific skills in preparing, presenting, and listening to classroom reports. Class aids in setting up subjects for a five-minute report from each member with such questions as:
   a. What information would you like some speaker to bring you?
   b. What information would you like to bring this class which you feel the members would find useful and interesting?
4. Discussion of procedures in preparation of reports. Reading about and discussion of these procedures should accompany the actual preparation of the reports, including provision for use of the library in gathering information.
   a. Narrowing to a specific purpose: Have students develop one-sentence summaries of their proposed talks.
   b. Gathering available information.
   c. Selecting key items of information, plus anecdotes or details for support and interest.
   d. Making a sentence outline of the key information to be presented.
   e. Planning an introduction and a conclusion.
   f. Planning to use visual aids if appropriate; planning to emphasize key points.
   g. Practicing delivery.
5. Presentation of reports, with note taking, discussion, and critical activities on part of class.
6. Further evaluative and goal-setting activity.

Summary of Specific Learnings to be Developed (See statement of objectives)

Plan for Critical Activities

1. For some speeches have listeners make one-sentence summaries of the speakers' purposes. Let each speaker compare these with his own statement, and report back on how well the class understood his central purpose.

2. For some speeches, have class take notes on key ideas. Have speaker evaluate his success in emphasis. Check notes for suggestions to students who fail as note takers.

3. Discuss evidences of good planning in speeches which provide positive illustrations; call for suggestions to other speakers, when judged advisable.

4. Prepare with a good speaker to give the class a test on his talk, and have him grade, and report on, the meaning of the results.

5. Make notes commenting on their progress to speakers who are working on specific, personal goals in speech improvement.

6. Hold discussion at end of reports. Characteristics of good reports: How may they be prepared? As a group, where are we strongest? Where weakest?

7. Give a short written quiz over information on parts of a report, functions of parts.

8. Evaluate students' attitude development.

Goal-Setting Activity

1. Have individuals try to set a specific goal for the preparation or presentation of their next oral report.

2. Discuss using the skills just practiced for reports in other classes.

3. Arrange to have students speaking to other classes bring back reports of their use of the skills they have practiced, and of the success of their speaking. (Joint planning with other teachers is advisable in this project.)

Equipment and Materials

1. Recording equipment.

2. Recordings of classroom reports for first discussion.

3. Films.

Readings and Outside Listening Activity

1. Read text, *Living Speech*, Chap. 5.

2. Library reading for material for reports.

3. Observe expository speaking on T.V. with discussion of uses of emphasis, visual aids, and the like.

Teacher References

1. Brink, Lauren, "Extemporaneous Speaking in the English Class," *English Journal* (November, 1947), 36: 474–477.

2. Crandell, S. Judson, "The Teaching of Public Speaking in High School," *Quarterly Journal of Speech* (December, 1942), 28.

3. Korey, Ruth A., "Improving Report Period," *Instructor* (March, 1948).

4. Olson, Helen F., "Speech for All," *English Journal* (April, 1951), 40: 204–209.

Daily lesson plans

The final step in the planning of the teacher involves a sort of day-to-day ordering of activities and materials. With careful unit planning, the daily planning of the teacher can be reduced to an informal accounting for progress after each day of teaching, and a planning of the following day's activity. The actual constituent parts of the daily plan include, on a less elaborate scale, most of the elements of the unit plan. One of the real values to the teacher of effective unit planning, however, is that it sets the framework and pattern of daily planning, while assuring to the teacher flexibility to adjust and alter plans in the actual developments of each day's teaching.

Teachers plan because they have specific ends to be attained, usually in limited periods of time. Their planning involves the development of concepts of the nature and scope of particular courses, and the more specific program of unit planning, where the actual unfolding of the class activity is visualized. Unit plans set the framework for the detailed plans for the day-to-day operation of the class. Routine planning which takes conscious account of the various matters which must be considered by the teacher doubtless contributes to the efficiency of teachers, and is particularly essential for beginning teachers. All effective planning, however, is ultimately dependent upon the capacity of the teacher to visualize the unfolding of a class; to anticipate the responses, problems, and opportunities which will develop; and to keep the class proceeding in an orderly, structured path toward identifiable objectives, while maintaining sufficient flexibility to accept the unexpected and bring it into harmony with the purposes of speech training.

IMPORTANCE OF TEACHER FLEXIBILITY

Some teachers, once they have decided what their students ought to learn, and how they ought to go about learning it, develop an almost pathological attachment to the meticulous carrying out of their plans. Such teachers are apt to regard as misfortunes student interests and activities which interrupt pre-set classroom plans. It is unfortunately true that the multitudinous activities and interests of high school students often delay or stop altogether a student's acquisition of certain important skills and understandings. A student preoccupied with an adolescent love affair is not likely to take much interest in the interpretation of literature, although literature does offer some possibilities for lovesick teen agers. The chief yell-leader may find it difficult to attend to "an interesting problem in critical thinking," especially on a football day.

While the chaotic nature of student interests and activities is an educational problem, it is also the source of many educational opportunities, particularly for teachers of speech. This is true because the greatest opportunity for teaching speech arises whenever a student feels a real need to speak well. Good speech teachers ought to be alert to those activities of students, outside the speech classroom, which involve speaking activity, and which therefore confront their students with genuine problems in speaking. These opportunities come often to alert speech teachers, simply because speaking is one of the most common activities of people everywhere, and at every age. The speech teacher may discover, with a little probing, that the students in his class are confronting such problems as:

1. Giving oral reports in other classes.

2. Taking part in a discussion group in Senior Problems Class.

3. Introducing the speaker at the next assembly.

4. Working in a club which has decided to put on a skit for the all-school carnival.

5. Taking part in radio programs sponsored by the school over a local radio station.

The list might be extended almost indefinitely.

Some speech teachers like to think of their classes as "workshops" or "bases of operations," from which students get immediate help in handling those speaking problems which they are meeting in their daily living. This point of view has real merit, although it does not define the extent to which the speech teacher should use the time of the speech class for the preparation of activities to be carried on outside the class. No exact solution of this problem is possible, but certain fundamental points of view held by speech teachers can be set forth:

1. Speech teachers ought to welcome the fact that their students have immediate speaking problems in situations outside the classroom.

2. Speech teachers ought to study, with the help of their students, the range and nature of these immediate problems, and keep always before the group the picture of "speaking jobs we are now confronting."

3. Speech teachers ought to plan their units with sufficient flexibility to permit the class to turn its efforts to "targets of opportunity."

4. Most important of all, speech teachers should lose no opportunity to establish the relevance of the work of the speech class to the problems of speakers in all situations. The interest of the teacher in the "out-of-class" speaking of his students, and his willingness to discuss these problems, helps to establish this relevance. His willingness to adjust the work of the class so that certain individuals can work directly on out-of-class problems will help to confirm this relevance.

Disorganized teachers are probably not very efficient in helping students to learn, but neither are teachers for whom order has become a fetish more venerable than the real needs of their students. Speech teachers can impart strength to their instruction by a readiness to incorporate the out-of-class speaking activities of their students into the structure of classroom interest and activity.

THE SPEECH TEACHER WILL SEEK ACTIVE
CO-OPERATION FROM SOCIAL GROUP

The habit possessed by many public speakers of starting a speech with a joke has resulted in a good many painful anecdotes and considerable forced laughter on the part of sympathetic audiences. Aside from the problem of such humorous mal-practice, however, speakers tell jokes usually for a very fundamental reason: They want to be liked by their audiences, and they want to show themselves as men of good will. They want these things because they know that most successful communication involves the establishment of rapport between speaker and listener; it involves the active co-operation of two or more people. Of course, speakers stir up responses in audiences even when this condition of rapport does not exist, and these responses involve communication, but the communication is often not of the kind and degree desired by the speaker.

Effective teaching involves this state of rapport within the social group of the classroom. Learning proceeds best when the group has attained some community of conscious purpose, and when individuals within the group have some degree of receptiveness to the ideas, actions, and talk of their fellow workers. Teachers often become aware of the disastrous effects of interpersonal conflicts on learning, conflicts between their purposes as teachers and the seemingly opposing purposes of their students. At some level, such conflicts are inevitable: Teachers are adults, and their students are not, and it is in the nature of society that young people should find themselves to some extent in revolt against the purposes and standards of their elders. When such conflicts result in widespread rejection of the teacher's purposes and standards by the students, however, then the sort of learning involved in speech instruction must, at the very least, come to a halt.

Unfortunately, some speech teachers encourage this sort of conflict by the very way in which they seek to impose their standards of speech on their students, and the way in which they set themselves up as critical adults discovering the incompetence of student speakers. Well-meaning speech teachers have sometimes ridiculed the diction of students, perhaps observing that elided forms of articulation, resulting in such expressions as "goin'" "dontcha," and "would've" are at once slovenly, vulgar, and representative of a low level of taste and culture. The high school student who finds the habits of his own social group so stigmatized by a comparative stranger, and who may find that the stigma extends to the speech of his parents, well may be moved to reject the teacher and his purposes in toto. In such circumstances effective speech can become associated in the minds of students with what may be thought of loosely as "the peculiar and obnoxious prejudices of my teacher, a person whom I do not wish to emulate." Students may not put their attitudes this way; in fact they probably will not put their attitudes into words at all, but the attitudes are none the less real.

Another form of conflict may develop in the speech class; it may be less apparent to the teacher, but just as destructive to learning.

This is conflict between students as individuals, or as members of sub-groups within the class; often they are brought into the class, without aid from the teacher. Such conflicts are particularly damaging to the speech class, in which social activity, involving speakers and listeners, and speaking and criticizing, constitutes the heart of instruction. We are not apt to get good speaking or effective learning from students who are deliberately shutting themselves off from the scrutiny of classmates whom they dislike or despise. Such a situation gives us listening and criticism which are at best worthless, and, at worst, destructive to the attitudes of openness toward the ideas of others so needed by young and inexperienced speakers. Rasey describes a class in which students were giving talks, and asking for criticisms or comments afterwards. Only one member of the class was responding to the speakers' request, a girl who repeatedly observed that the speakers did not "place their voices well," until finally even this critic was halted by the "disapproving silence of her classmates."

The problem of technique and procedure in creating conditions of co-operation within the group is an immense one, but one that has received extensive attention in the literature of speech. For this reason teachers of speech should be in a particularly good position to seek application of the principles of their own discipline to the conduct of their classes. We shall deal with only one aspect of the problem of "methods" here, an aspect which has to do with the relationship of adults and adolescents, an almost constant feature of most teaching situations.

Speech teachers, with good effect, can exhibit in their own attitudes toward *all* the students of their class the qualities of friendliness and openness which they seek to encourage in the relationships within the group. It is difficult for students to hold persistent antagonisms to teachers who manifestly and genuinely like them. Moreover, it is difficult for them to escape seeing the significance to speaking and listening of the attitudes of a teacher who sincerely values the speaking and thinking of students with their varying interests, points of view, abilities, and personal characteristics. We do not mean that a good teacher has to be "one of the gang." A teacher who identifies himself completely with adolescents, who never enjoys the blessed relief of being free from the peculiarities of their attitudes, conversations, and enthusiasms, is probably no real

•

teacher. But good teachers must "bear with students gladly," and that means all students, from those who are readily liked to those who try one's patience sorely. Experienced teachers will observe that it is difficult at times to follow this injunction. We have some students who are sick in mind and spirit, and who are at war with society, and perhaps with themselves. A teacher tells of a class to which he found it impossible to turn his back, since fights, often with knives, would break out when surveillance by the teacher was relaxed for even a few seconds. Fortunately, groups of this sort are rare. The needs of children of this extreme type extend beyond the immediate reach of classroom instruction. More frequently, we have students who are simply ill-mannered and offensive. A teacher should be imbued with the belief that all persons have real worth and that a teacher should bring out this worth. It is well to remember that, by and large, it may be easier for teachers to like their students, than for students to like their teachers. Highet writes tellingly of this:

> It is easy to like the young because they are young. They have no faults except the very ones they are asking you to eradicate: ignorance, shallowness, and inexperience. The really hateful faults are those which we grown men and women have. Some of these grow on us like diseases, others we build up and cherish as though they were virtues. Ingrained conceit, calculated cruelty, deep rooted cowardice, slobbering greed, vulgar self-satisfaction, puffy laziness of mind and body—these and other real sins result from years, decades of careful cultivation. They show on our faces, they ring harsh or hollow in our voices, they have become bone of our bone, and flesh of our flesh. The young do not sin in those ways. Heaven knows they are infuriatingly lazy and unbelievably stupid and sometimes detestably cruel—but not for long, not all at once, and not (like grown ups) as a matter of habit or policy. They are trying to be energetic and wise and kind. When you remember this, it is difficult not to like them.[2]

IMPORTANCE OF CONSIDERING ALL ASPECTS OF COMPLEX SOCIAL SITUATIONS

Students of speech have long recognized the fact that the success of a speaker is contingent upon all aspects of the situation in which he talks—who he is, what he says, the circumstances of time

---

[2] Highet, Gilbert, *The Art of Teaching*, 1st ed. New York: Alfred A. Knopf, Inc., 1950, p. 27.

and place under which he speaks, and the nature of the persons addressed. The meaning of that which is said is not intrinsic within the words of the speaker, alone, but exists as the product of all aspects of the situation within which the words are spoken. All persons can find interesting examples of this fact in their experience, or in their study of other persons. Adolf Hitler, for example, seems to have exerted a powerful influence over immense audiences during his ascendancy in Germany after 1932. Some of his speeches which have been recorded for us seem to be tirades of unbridled passion as we listen to them today, and we wonder how such a man could have been accepted as a great leader by millions of people. Yet if we try to reconstruct the setting in which he talked, we may understand his effectiveness.

Good speakers are frequently careful students of the various interacting forces which constitute the circumstances in which they speak. And, similarly, good teachers must be students of all aspects of the classroom situation which they confront, and they must, as far as possible, take control over these circumstances, to the end of more effective teaching. Of these circumstances, the problems of inter-personal relationships within the classroom loom very large. The following important considerations affecting every speech class should be studied by the teacher.

1. *The teacher needs to study carefully the nature of his students,* including their characteristics as adolescents and their particular attitudes toward various types of speaking. These attitudes toward speech vary widely from group to group and community to community, and no teacher can safely generalize about "how high school students look at Speech." In some schools, for example, taking part in plays is an activity with high prestige for all students. In other schools it may be regarded as an activity for "girls and sissies." In some schools, students may consider it an honor to preside over assembly programs, while in others the same activity may be regarded scornfully as a job for a few students who are always trying to please the principal. Students who have had traumatic previous experiences with speaking in classrooms may regard "giving a speech" as the worst of punishments, while others may come to the classroom with a background of pleasant experiences in speech making. A teacher tells of a school in which the idea had become established among the high school students that "most students are unable to

stand up before the class and give a talk. Only a few specially gifted students can do this, while the rest of us always remain seated when we speak." In other schools, speech making is accepted as a routine activity for all students.

Obviously, these particular attitudes are important to the conduct of speech training. Initially they are matters to be observed and taken into account by the teacher in the conduct of the class, but in the long run they are matters over which the teacher will seek to exercise some influence. A drama teacher entering a school in which she found few boys taking part in plays, developed a long-range approach to the problem. She set herself patiently and carefully to the task of getting a few members of the football team, who had potential acting talent and, like all students, a basic interest in imaginative activity of dramatics, into some of the school plays. These boys had high prestige with other boys in the school, and their participation broke the log jam of silent prejudice against plays. A debate coach found that the willing co-operation of a local newspaper editor in giving more publicity to debate had the effect of stimulating student interest in that activity. Students generally value those activities which seem to be prized by the adult world. The point is illustrated by an incident that occurred in one of the larger Colorado high schools. A teacher reports that "the big boys" were not interested in speech. One of the leaders made his first significant class speech during a discussion of water rights for the community. Later a prominent citizen commended the teacher on the fine contribution of one of her students at a meeting to consider the problem of securing water for Colorado crops. "He was more persuasive than any other speaker and changed the vote," the man said. The teacher waited eagerly for her student (who had failed to see the importance of speech) to report. After a few days the boy explained to the class that, at a meeting where citizens were about to vote, he had presented arguments which his father and uncle had expressed repeatedly in private. His talk had affected opinion and action, and from then on he brought to the speech class enthusiasm and industry.

2. *The teacher needs to study carefully the problem of class size.* There are certain obvious limitations to the amount and quality of speech instruction which can be carried on in a class of 30 or 40 students. It is quite possible that swelling school enrollments have af-

fected speech instruction more adversely than instruction in any other school discipline. This is not to say that the teacher confronted with an oversized class should throw up his hands and announce, "I can teach nothing!" But it is to stress the fact that speech teachers ought to move purposefully to create understanding by administrators and the public of the conditions necessary for efficient instruction in their field.

The optimum size for speech classes is not known, but the experience of speech teachers gives a reasonable indication of desirable size. In general, classes ranging from 15 students to 25 students probably provide the best opportunity for effective learning. Classes with more than 25 students sharply reduce the frequency of speaking possible for any one student, and classes with fewer than 15 students reduce the opportunities for stimulating speaker-audience relationships, and restrict the variety of opinion, ability, and attitude which provides much of the excitement of a good speech class. The figures 25 and 15 have no rigid significance; a speech class does not become a difficult problem the minute it has 26 or 14 students.

3. *The teacher needs to study carefully the nature of the classroom environment.* It is probably easier to give students enjoyable and successful speaking experiences in classrooms which have (a) reasonably good acoustic characteristics, (b) freedom from persistent outside noises, and (c) pleasant, comfortable surroundings for speaker and audience. If choices can be made, it is perhaps better that the speech class be located in a room away from a noisy avenue. However, it is well that speech teachers avoid going into competition with their fellow teachers for the best facilities of the school. Moreover, to speak over noises may be a challenge.

Certain types of arrangement and equipment are conducive to speech instruction. A classroom with movable chairs and tables is desirable, since small group preparation with several groups operating simultaneously is a frequent occurrence in a speech class. A reading stand is usable, although speech teachers would do well to encourage students to be free either to use or get along without such a stand in their speaking and reading. A stage, or raised platform is helpful for public speaking, play reading, and dramatic productions.

Newer schools may begin to develop classrooms specially constructed to give the speech teacher maximum opportunity to provide for individual preparation or practice by a number of students, without the confusion attendant upon using a number of rooms in the school building, or carrying on many different activities in one room. The diagram opposite illustrates one such "ideal" arrangement. The radio "studio," control room, and practice rooms are observable from the class through glass partitions, but provide soundproof facilities for individuals or small groups.

A word of caution may be desirable at this point. Facilities such as those pictured here will not become general in the foreseeable future. Moreover, the lack of them is no insuperable handicap to effective teaching by an imaginative teacher. Neither Mark Hopkins' log, nor a broom closet would make a very desirable speech classroom, but almost any other sort of arrangement can be put to good use by a teacher with students who are interested in improving speech. Good lights, adequate ventilation, attractive bulletin boards, and cheerfully painted walls all make teaching easier and learning more pleasant.

RELATION OF FIRST IMPRESSIONS TO LONG-TERM PURPOSES

A teacher reports an experience with one of her students who had thought carefully about the need for getting an audience's full and complete attention during the introduction to a speech. The next time he had a talk to give the class, this seventh-grade scholar walked before the group, drew a cap pistol from his pocket, fired several "shots" into the air, replaced the cap pistol, drew some notes from his pocket, and announced, "My topic for today is 'the value of stamp collecting.'" This student had learned something about speech making, but his learning had stopped a little short of useful practice. He had discerned the value of startling activity in getting the undivided attention of an audience, but he had not raised and answered for himself the equally significant question, "attention to what?"

Clearly, the first days of the speech class are exceedingly important, important not only because they should please and excite students, but also because they should bring rapid progress in orienting students to the purposes and patterns of speech instruction. The speech teacher approaches his class from the first day with certain definite and important ends in view, some of which follow:

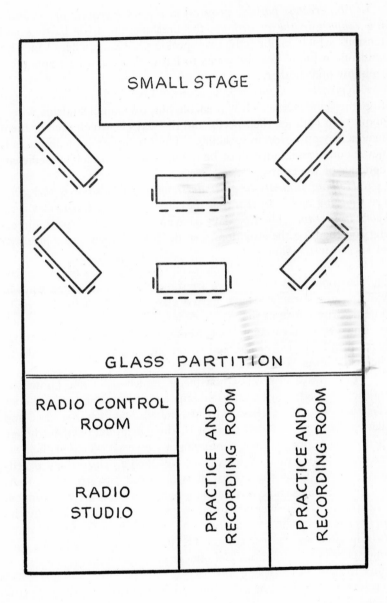

1. *The greatest possible progress in the slow process of establishing rapport in the classroom*—the breaking down of barriers and tensions which inhibit effective speaking. The teacher wants his students to know him, he wants to know them, and he wants them to know one another.

2. *Knowing students as individuals.* The teacher wants to begin to gather evidence which will enable him to counsel students wisely about their abilities, their needs, and the ways in which each of them may achieve progress in speaking. The teacher's job of diagnosis is never completed, but it must be quickly begun to facilitate efficient conduct of the course.

3. *Helping students to an understanding of what it is that they are studying and what it is that they are seeking to learn from their work in speech.* The first days have an orientation purpose, directing and focusing the attention of students on the particular purposes of speech instruction.

How do speech teachers demonstrate such purposes in their opening classroom activities? Here are some descriptions of the ways in which various teachers have started classes in speech fundamentals. The descriptions omit the necessary attention of the teacher to such routine matters as carrying the textbook and notebook to class, bringing a pre-sharpened pencil, and so on, and direct attention only to the major initial activities of the class.

a. This was a class in which many students did not know one another. The teacher used a combination of introductions and conversation to start the class. He introduced himself to the class, and then students were asked to turn to their neighbors and introduce themselves to one another, continuing a conversation about their interests until such time as the teacher indicated a halt to the proceedings. Upon signal, the groups of two moved into groups of four, and introductions and conversation around the circle were continued. The groups of four were enlarged to groups of eight, and finally the total class of about 16 students moved into a circle for informal introductions and conversation. The question was raised as to why time spent in introductions and conversation would help students in more formal talks to the group.

b. After a short informal conversation, the teacher asked his students if they thought animals knew how to speak. A lively argument developed. The teacher finally elicited the decision that the argument could not be settled unless the class knew (a) what they meant by speaking, and (b) more about the ways in which animals communicate. The teacher cited some library references on the communicative actions of various animals and birds, and some students volunteered to look these up. Other students said that they had interesting experiences with their own pets to report. All students were to read what the text had to say about the definition of speech. The class was ready to begin some speaking and reading activity, and to discover something of the nature and meaning of the process of speaking.

c. The class was asked whether or not it was important to be able to speak effectively. After a discussion, they suggested that it might be well to get the opinions of adults on the matter. It was agreed that each student would interview three adults on the importance of speech. Discussion followed on the ways in which an interview should be arranged and carried out. Textbook reading on this problem was assigned. The class agreed as to certain general questions which ought to be raised in each interview. The class discussed some important considerations in preparing reports for the class on the products of the interviews. They agreed upon the desirability of interviewing people in a wide variety of occupations, and various members undertook to interview specific types of people. The class appointed a committee to tabulate the data from all the reports. These plans occupied the periods before the actual beginning of the first reports by members of the class.

There are many other ways of opening the speech class: phonograph records of some interesting speakers, motion pictures of speech subjects, discussions of "speakers I have enjoyed hearing," the old reliable group discussion of "summer vacations," or the impromptu talk—"introducing myself." This last-named activity may easily be overworked. A speech teacher reports asking his students to introduce themselves at the first meeting of a class, on the fourth period of the school day. One of the students protested, "Do we have to do that again? We've already introduced ourselves three times today."

Planning for Early Progress on the Diagnosis of Student Needs and Abilities

The diagnostic responsibilities of the speech teacher can be discharged satisfactorily only with considerable difficulty. No test, or series of tests will indicate precisely the speech needs and abilities of the students in a particular class. The speaking of each student is to be evaluated by the teacher only after careful study of all available data concerning him, coupled with painstaking observation of his speaking habits in a variety of situations. The speech teacher cannot say, "I will analyze the needs of my students during the first week." But, because diagnosis is an important, difficult, and continuing job, he must turn his attention to the task from the very first day of class. Certain suggestions may facilitate this diagnosis:

1. *The teacher should begin at once to observe carefully the speech behavior and attitudes of his students,* both in speech class and in all other situations into which the teacher may follow them. He should try to see whether or not the behavior he observes is general for the student, or restricted perhaps to the classroom, or even to the speech classroom.

2. *The speech teacher often can secure valuable information about the speech of a student from other teachers* who have known him for a long time.

3. *Data in the office files on each student may be very helpful to the speech teacher.* Scores on standardized intelligence tests or aptitude tests, interest inventories, personality or social adjustment tests, reading tests, and school records may all give the teacher insight into a particular student's speaking habits and problems.

4. *Most speech teachers think it important to help their students develop insight into why they speak as they do.* They may ask students to write autobiographies, emphasizing the recall of types of information which account for aspects of their speech behavior and their attitudes toward speaking, or they may carry on class discussions in which students will attempt to show an understanding of their own ways of speaking.

5. *Many teachers plan early in the course to:*

    a. *Make a recording of each student's speaking,* so that in individual or small group play back sessions both the teacher and the students can share in diagnostic procedures.

    b. *Have students fill out an interview or questionnaire form,* with answers of particular significance to the speech teacher in his attempt to evaluate the student's speech.

    c. *Set up a record system on file cards,* so that the data about each student—observations about his needs, abilities, and progress, and records of his speaking activities—can be kept neatly.

The following is a sample of an interview form which has been used successfully by a teacher of speech fundamentals, but is not recommended as the only form that teachers should use. Teachers ought to devise their own questionnaires, asking only for that information which they actually will use, or which they think is directly relevant to their teaching goals.

SPEECH ANALYSIS INTERVIEW

(The interviewer should learn the material included in the interview and fill in the blanks at the conclusion of the interview. It is not necessary to follow the order of procedure given in the interview. Every effort should be made to put the student being interviewed at ease, and to approach the gathering of information in an informal manner.)

Date_____

Name_____ Grade_____ Age_____

Father's name_____ Home address_____

Test Scores

Name of test	*Date Given*	*Score*

Personal and Family History

Where were you born?_____ When?_____ Have you travelled in this state?_____ Where?_____ Outside of the state?_____ Where?_____ Where was your father born?_____ Your mother?_____ What is your father's occupation?_____ His nationality?_____ Your mother's nationality?_____ Have you lived with anyone besides your parents?_____ If so, specify_____ Do you like school?_____ Why or why not?_____ What courses do you like most?_____ Least?_____ Do you have any hobbies?_____ What are they?_____ Do you like sports?_____ Which ones?_____ Do you participate?_____ Do you like reading?___ What type?_____ Movies?_____ What type?_____ Do you have any other spare time activities?_____ Do you earn any money?_____ How?_____ Do you have any plans for an occupation?_____ Have you had any serious illnesses?_____ Specify_____

Speech Adjustment

Have you had any previous speech work in school?_____ If so, what?
_____ Any speech work outside of school?_____ If so,
what?_____ Do you think it is important to speak well?
_____ How important?_____ Do you like to speak to
an audience?_____ To talk to your friends?_____ To talk to strangers?_____ Are you nervous when talking to other people?_____ When
speaking before an audience?_____ If you are nervous, describe how you
feel_____ Would you rather tell
about an experience or write about it?_____ Do you dislike being
criticized for your speaking?_____ Has anyone ever made fun of your
speaking?_____ Do you remember any criticism anyone
ever made of your speaking?_____ Of your writing?_____
_____ Have you ever received special help with your speaking?_____ What help?_____ Can you speak as well when
standing as when sitting?_____ Do you go to many parties?_____ Do you
like parties?_____ Would you like to be a club president?_____ The
chairman of a committee?_____A cheer leader?_____ Put on an assembly?_____ Be in a play?_____

ANALYSIS CHART

General Impressions

                                        List general observations and
                                        comments

Projection of personality_____
Impression of poise and ease_____
Voice control and flexibility_____
Pitch variation_____
Variety of force_____
Variations in rate_____
Tempo (Fast, Slow, Good)

Reading

Pronunciation_____
Intonation _____
Recreation _____

Speaking

Conversational manner_____
Grammatical usages_____
Vocabulary and work choice_____
Sentence structure_____
Fluency (jerky, good, smooth)

Phonation

Quality of the voice

Weak	_____	Thin	_____
Harsh	_____	Metallic	_____
Nasal	_____	Denasal	_____
Breathy	_____	Muffled	_____
Clear	_____	Pleasant	_____
Rich	_____	Resonant	_____

Pitch: High, Low, Well-adjusted,
      Rising Inflections

Duration: Staccato, Normal, Drawl

Intensity: Weak, Overloud, Good

The diagnostic function of speech instruction may be correlated readily and advantageously with the program of speech correction in those schools in which clinical assistance is available to those handicapped in speech. The classroom teacher of speech should be alert to the possibilities of using the services of a speech therapist and of reciprocating by providing help for the correctionist.

Rapport, diagnosis, and orientation are the central goals which determine the initial activities of speech instruction. Like the introduction to a speech, the first days of speech instruction should not be planned until the teacher has a clear vision of the unfolding of the course as a whole; then they should be planned carefully and imaginatively. A good beginning may not be half the battle, but no one has ever been able to detect any particular merit to a poor beginning, either for a speech or for a course in speech.

THE PERSONAL EQUATION IN TEACHING

Aristotle may have been the first writer on speech to emphasize the manner in which impressions of a speaker's character, his honesty and sincerity or the lack of such qualities, influence the effectiveness of his speech. No speaker ever can separate what he *is*, or *seems to be*, from what he says. Similarly, a great deal of the effectiveness of teaching depends upon what sort of person the teacher is. We have no intention of attempting to discuss here the entire subject of the speaker's character and personality, but there is one consideration peculiarly important to speech teachers in this connection.   If they are to be effective in their work, speech teachers must be persons of broad interests and education.   This is true simply because speech is intimately related to all of the intellectual and artistic pursuits of people.   Students do not speak very much about speech.   The subjects of their talk range from model airplanes, to problems of personal and ethical behavior, to citizenship and public affairs.   Moreover, as we have observed again and again, it is absolutely essential to the development of the high school student's speaking skills that he see speech always as a purposeful, realistic act, relevant to all aspects of life.

We are not suggesting that speech teachers must be "universal experts" versed in all knowledge.   The expertness of the speech teacher is, and ought to be, subject to the reasonable limitations which affect all other educated persons; it should be expertness only in the processes of speaking.   But the interests of the speech teacher and his receptiveness to the interests and concerns of all sorts of students cannot be limited.   Speech teachers simply cannot afford the luxury of saying "I have no interest in politics," or in sports, pets, ethics, literature, science, or any of the other matters in connection with which high school students have need for speech.

Speech teachers are often concerned with the issue of making speech instruction function outside the speech classroom, and making it relevant to the daily living of students.   Gilbert Highet has well stated the case for believing that a good deal of the effectiveness of instruction and its vitality in the lives of students, goes directly back to the issue of "what kind of person the teacher is." He discusses the problem of making classroom instruction relevant to the world in these words:

The best way to do it is for the teacher to make himself relevant. Nine thousand times more pupils have learned a difficult subject well because they felt the teacher's vitality and energy proved its value rather than because they chose the subject for its own sake. If a youth, sizing up the professor of medieval history, decides that he is a tremendous expert in the history of the middle ages and a deadly bore in everything else, he is apt to conclude that medieval history makes a man a deadly bore. If on the other hand he finds that the man is filled with lively interest in the contemporary world, that he actually knows more about it because, through his training, he understands it better, that the practice of intellectual life, so far from making him vague and remote, has made him wise and competent, the youth will conclude without further evidence that medieval history is a valuable interest. A good teacher is an interesting man or woman.[3]

WHAT IS SUCCESS IN TEACHING?

Does perfect communication ever occur between a speaker and a listener? Rarely. Most speakers achieve at best only relatively successful control over the meanings their speech stirs up in others, and various degrees of failure in communication are a common phenomenon of daily living. "You misunderstood me," "What I meant to say," "I thought you said—," "How many times must I tell you—," all these and a hundred other phrases are the daily indicators of our frailties in communication.

This fact is important to the teacher because it indicates the context of expectation and hope within which he practices his art. Properly understood, it frees the normally effective teacher from feelings of guilt as he observes the partial or complete failure of some of his students to improve as speakers. It also frees him from the stultifying vanity of supposing that his teaching procedures are perfect. The speech teacher who is so unobservant as to believe that he is benefiting all of his students maximally, has stopped developing as a teacher. It is well enough for teachers to reach beyond their grasp, but, in the interests of a healthy, pleasant professional life, it is also well that they recognize the inevitable limitations laid upon the learning of students.

DIFFERENT ROADS TO SUCCESS IN TEACHING

Discussions of the attributes of effective speaking are apt to result in an idealized picture of the person who can succeed in speaking. Contemplation of this abstract paragon may discourage the average student of speech, who finds himself deficient in many respects, while an examination of the flesh-and-blood people who actually have been successful in speech may serve to encourage him. The examination of real speakers calls attention to the great variety who succeed; to Lincoln who was successful despite a rather "thin and reedy" voice; and to Emerson who was successful despite a rather cold, formal relationship with his audience. There is good reason to believe that people often succeed as speakers because of some

---

[3] Highet, *op. cit.*, p. 56.

particular strength that they possess, rather than because of the absence of defects.

Similarly, an examination of successful teachers reveals the interesting fact that persons of widely varying temperaments and talents succeed. Perhaps the greatest misfortune which could befall high school students would be to have all their teachers cut from one piece of cloth. One of the real values of education is that it brings students into relationship with a variety of teachers, each of whom is in some sense unique, each of whom makes some special contribution, and each of whom may touch with particular effectiveness the lives of certain individuals.

Naturally, we do not mean to say that all teachers are equally effective, that a teacher with a quick and uncontrolled temper is as useful as one with control, or that a passive and introverted teacher is as useful as one with vitality and real interest in people. But we do mean that teachers with a wide range of differences in temperament and ability achieve significant success.

In the final analysis, each teacher will succeed in ratio to his understanding and application of the principles of effective instruction, generally, and also to his understanding of himself. Each teacher must bring himself into a vital, and a necessarily unique relationship with his students, and with the purposes of his particular discipline.

ACTION VS. DISCUSSION OF PRINCIPLES
IN ACQUIRING TEACHING SKILL

At this point the reader may be inclined to say, "What you have written thus far about getting started with teaching may help some teachers, but it doesn't help me. You have written too much about things that don't trouble me, and too little about things that do."

To such a reader we can answer only, "You well may be the best judge of your own needs. Moreover, there is more to be said about teaching than can be put into any single chapter of a book, or even into any book. And only occasionally, in partial ways, can certain teachers or prospective teachers be helped by reading about how to teach." The parallel between learning to speak and learning to teach speech is complete at this point. One teacher, out of experience, may try to give another help in anticipating some of the problems which he will face. An experienced teacher may try to say things which will help a beginner to make better use of his experience in meeting new problems. But in the last analysis, teaching, like speaking, is learned by doing and thinking.

Our effort has been to emphasize for the speech teacher the central fact that, as a thoughtful student of speech, he already has had a variety of experiences and a background of learning, which are directly applicable to his problems as a teacher. Speech teachers ought to be superior teachers. The career which they follow is an application of the art which they teach.

SELECTED BIBLIOGRAPHY

Basic Considerations in a Functional Speech Program, Curriculum Bulletin No. 18, Madison: Wisconsin State Department of Public Instruction, 1948.

Evans, Dina R., "Report of a Speech Survey in the 9A Grade," *Quarterly Journal of Speech* (February, 1938), 24: 83–90.

Highet, Gilbert, *The Art of Teaching*. New York: Alfred A. Knopf, Inc., 1950.

Havighurst, Robert J., and Hilda Taba, *Adolescent Character and Personality*. New York: John Wiley & Sons, Inc., 1949.

Jones, Arthur J., et al., *Principles of Unit Construction*. New York: McGraw-Hill Book Co., 1939.

LaBrant, Lou, *We Teach English*. New York: Harcourt, Brace & Co., 1951, Chs. 8 and 9.

Loban, Walter, "Making Pupils Responsible for Self-Diagnosis," *English Journal* (College Edition), 24 (Nov., 1937), 729–734.

National Society for the Study of Education, *Adolescence*. Yearbook 43, Part I. Chicago: Department of Education, University of Chicago, 1944.

Rasey, M. I., *This Is Teaching*. New York: Harper & Brothers, 1950.

Robinson, Karl F. *Teaching Speech in the Secondary School*. New York: Longmans, Green & Co., Inc., 1951, Chs. 5 and 8.

Smith, Esther G., "Let the Pupils Do the Planning," *English Journal*, (May, 1943), 32: 261–264.

PART II

The Development of Basic Habits and Skills

THROUGHOUT the first part of this book we have emphasized the fact that high school students always approach the study of speech through their participation in speaking activities which are necessary to their daily living. They do not begin the study of speech by drilling on articulation, or practicing gestures, but rather by using speech in situations which are stimulating to them, and which pose real speaking problems for them.

At the same time, we have argued that students who hope to improve their speaking need to identify specifically the problems which they face as individuals, and set limited, well-defined goals for their own improvement. In analyzing acts of speaking, and in setting specific, attainable goals for growth, students will need to examine the processes which underlie all speech. They will need to learn that an act of speaking incorporates a vocal code, a visible code, and a language code. Moreover, they will need to discover that attitudes and mental processes—thoughts and emotions—which are revealed through these codes play important roles in effective speech. Having developed their capacity to view the complex act of speaking analytically, students will be in a position to define specifically their own problems, to appraise correctly their own strengths and weaknesses, and to work out plans for their own development.

The chapters in Part II analyze each of the basic elements of the speech process, indicating the typical problems students face in their use of each, and some of the workable ways in which the teacher can help students to gain both knowledge of speech and greater personal proficiency in using it.

These chapters describe classroom procedures which have been found effective in actual practice. Techniques and principles are not set forth with the thought that they represent *the* way in which all teachers of speech must organize or teach their courses, for we already have suggested the variety of methods by which speech may be taught successfully, either as a separate course, or in combination with other curricular studies. Instead, it is our hope that the speech teacher will find in these concrete descriptions of teaching procedures material which will stimulate and assist him in planning the particular ways in which he will seek to help the students with whom he works to become more intelligent and capable speakers.

CHAPTER 6

Developing Effective Action

ACTION: A PRIMARY CONSIDERATION IN THE SPEECH PROCESS

Fifteen high school freshmen were to give their first talks in a speech class. Before the final program, the class decided to evaluate each person's performance and to aim at improvement. One student went to the blackboard to list what was important in all forms of speaking. The students decided that the speaker (1) should have something worth saying, (2) should express his ideas in acceptable language, (3) should use appropriate voice, and (4) should use effective action. Effective action was listed only after prompting from the teacher.

The class was then divided into pairs, and each student was to criticize the performance of his partner. The criticisms were to be written, and the students receiving them were to evaluate the criticisms. In spite of the facts that no one had mentioned action as the first essential element of speech, and that the class had included it only after prodding by the teacher, twelve out of fifteen students commented on action in their criticisms—nine put it first, and no other speech element was referred to so frequently. Furthermore, in the three instances where critics failed to mention action, the speaker who had been evaluated noted the omission and asked specifically for comments on that phase of his performance.

The foregoing incident is typical; the importance of bodily action scarcely can be overrated, though we seldom may be conscious of it.

TEACH ACTION BEFORE VOICE

Charles Henry Woolbert, in attempting to organize a method for teaching the elements of speech, suggested that bodily action should be considered first. He said, "Body or voice, which should be studied first? First ask, Which is mastered earlier in the struggle to learn how to communicate? Clearly the body; true of the race and of the individual man; primeval man communicated by signs before he ever talked, and children get control of their sign making apparatus before they can control the apparatus of voice. If all children could get and keep a mastery of the body, arms, legs, viscera, head, and face there would be few poor speakers in the world. It seems almost safe to say that all speech difficulties get their origin in defects of bodily structure or of mastery of bodily parts. Hence in the study of how to improve speaking and reading the body properly comes in point of precedence, ahead of voice." [1]

Another good reason for beginning the improvement of speech with an improvement of visible bodily action is that students like to work on it and are therefore easily motivated.

THE INFLUENCE OF ASSOCIATION

In a "Letters from the People" section of a recent news magazine, a subscriber called attention to what he considered a little noted fact: In selecting mates people tend to choose those who look like themselves. He went on to say that he and his wife had made a hobby of identifying such couples for years and that the phenomenon was very common. He accounted for it on the grounds that likes are attracted to likes, and that in looks, as in interests and experiences, "birds of a feather flock together."

Other persons who have observed the same fact account for the resemblances between husbands and wives in a different way. They believe that couples do not necessarily look alike when they first meet, but that after living together for a long time they *get* to look alike. The proponents of the second theory think that it is not so often features or general physical builds which are alike, but that postures, gestures, facial expressions, mannerisms, and tensions be-

---

[1] Woolbert, Charles Henry, *Fundamentals of Speech*. New York: Harper & Brothers, 1920, p. 83.

come alike through constant association. Furthermore, they believe that couples look more alike when they have great influence over one another than when they are more or less indifferent to each other.

When two individuals, continually in the company of one another, have the same problems, the same aims, and many of the same experiences, they react repeatedly to the behavior which they observe in each other. Many times at breakfast the wife learns of the husband's restless night, not by asking him about it, but by reacting to slight changes in his facial expression and general tension. No doubt if some instrument could be devised to test minute muscular adjustments, it would be discovered that unconsciously the same muscles are tensed and the same muscles relaxed in both individuals. Everyone has observed numerous instances when, in a social situation, husbands and wives have similar expressions; he saddens with her as he notes her reaction to the mention of an incident which has hurt her deeply; she shows signs of insecurity with him when she senses that he feels inadequate with his new boss; her facial expression reflects his when particularly distasteful food is set before him; or he is tense and trembles with her when she anticipates taking off from a high diving board.

Years of such sympathetic mutual mirroring of muscle tensions cannot fail to bring about similarities in general bodily set, mannerisms, and, particularly, facial expressions.

EMPATHY DEFINED AND APPLIED

This tendency which all human beings have to reflect the expressions and the muscular "sets" of others, or the physical characteristics of things to which they react, is called empathy. It is a process worth studying, in observing and understanding how individuals in society get along with and control one another.

When the husband or the wife feels the need to secure from the other some help, favor, or particular response, the success of the entire process may depend on whether he or she is skillful in empathizing. There is an interchange of responses, beginning with an understanding of the situation and resulting in the control of it. From such simple requests as for the preparation of a favorite dish, the entertainment of a business associate, or attendance at a movie, to the recommendation of a college for "Junior" or the resignation from one position and the selection of another, the husband watches his wife's attitudes for the right time to broach the subject. He wants an affirmative response and he selects the moment when his wife will be rested, happy, relaxed, and optimistic. Without realizing, it, he knows her state of mind by his own as he responds to her visible action. His muscles reflect the set of hers and, therefore, he feels as she does. This process is the first step in the control of others. It is by the way he feels as he is stimulated by her muscle set that he moves to the second step and decides, in the light of the way he now knows she feels, on just the right approach to bring about the desired response. If the situation at the moment is not favorable, he plans how he can make it so. Experience has taught him certain effective techniques, such as to appear comfortable himself, or confident, or carefree, or optimistic, or relaxed, or rested, when he wants her to be so. He knows that she is likely to be happy when he is happy, sad when he is sad, discouraged when he is discouraged, and therefore, often without realizing it, he plans precisely how he will prepare her for his request.

Having decided, consciously or unconsciously, upon the right attitude for him to take in order to get the desired response, he moves to the third step, which is for him to *take* the bodily attitude which will bring out in her the right attitude. He is clearly most successful if he himself is able to look and act exactly as he wants his wife to look and act. The fourth step will come when his wife assumes the muscle set which gives her the feeling that he wants her to have.

From the very beginning of their acquaintanceship, life for this typical couple has been made up of thousands of interactions of muscular sets. Little wonder that the two get to *look* alike; they act alike and, as a result, they get to *be* alike.

FOUR STEPS IN BODILY CONTROL FOR SPEECH

This "feeling into," empathy, or *einfühlung* as the Germans call it, usually is not conscious; it is more useful in social control than if it were conscious. Normal human beings participate in it constantly without realizing it; they control others, and are controlled by them. It is a process which speakers can and do use in audience control.

The steps in empathic control are the same whether it is a husband influencing his wife; a boy, his mother; or a speaker, his audience.

In step 1, the speaker gets a general overview of the characteristics of the speech situation by empathizing in the bodily sets of the other participants. Their empathic responses will reveal to him the nature of the audience he desires to influence.

In step 2, the speaker decides upon the appropriate visible action to use with the particular audience. In the light of the circumstances, including the physical set of the audience, the speaker decides what is the best bodily action for him to use, viz., that which, if mirrored by the observers, will stir up in them the ideas and feelings he wants them to have.

In step 3, the speaker actually does with his body what he has planned to do in step 2, and what he wants the members of the audience to do with their bodies.

In step 4, the members of the audience get the speaker's meanings because of the visible action which they have followed empathically; they react to the speaker by developing the physical basis of the meanings which he intended.

CONTROL THROUGH BODILY ACTION REQUIRES KNOWLEDGE OF HUMAN BEHAVIOR

From the foregoing it is not difficult to see that to teach boys and girls in high school an understanding of bodily action through empathic response is very different from teaching specific rules—where to stand, when to gesture, and how to move. Such instruction requires an understanding of psychology—why human beings behave as they do, and how they are likely to behave under various conditions. It requires a knowledge of how individuals of different ages, backgrounds, vocations, training, and education vary among themselves. In short, it requires not a memorization of specific rules, but an understanding of the one constant factor in the successful speech process—*adaptation*. It is easy to see also that an understanding of the physical interaction of speaker and audience will prepare a student to determine how much and what kind of bodily action to use in reading, speaking, or acting in a great variety of situations and before all kinds of audiences.

INTRODUCING A CLASS TO THE PRINCIPLE OF EMPATHY

One good way to demonstrate that observers tend to do what they see done, is to have students come before the class and give some type of demonstration which will result in audience responses.

Since the empathic response is typically unconscious, the only way it can work in a class is to have part of the class uninformed as to what is to be done and another part prepared by the teacher to co-operate in the demonstration. For example, the teacher might call two students aside and ask them to work out a little game. She will tell them to cut some lemons into sixths and eat the pieces before the class. The teacher will then give each of these students a lemon and a very dull knife. Then the teacher will ask two other students to watch the audience. She will ask them not to look at what the first two students are doing before the class, but to observe every member of the audience closely, to note changes in bodily sets, facial expressions, and hand and arm movements. Since the knives are dull, the students cutting the lemons will be forced to use considerable pressure. Inevitably they will pucker up their faces when they eat the lemons. The students observing will usually note that when the performing students are pressing very hard on their knives in order to cut the lemons, some members of the audience will try to "help" them, with movements of head and mouth muscles. While the lemons are being eaten, members of the audience will have the same "sour" facial expressions as those of the students eating. After some members of the class have made the observation that the expressions of the audience are like the expressions of the performers, it will be a good time to discuss the principle of empathy, and make clear why in speaking it is a good idea to take advantage of this tendency of human beings to do what they see being done. Students will be able to recall and report other times when they have observed empathy at work. They may have seen pictures of actors and audiences taken at the same moment and have noted expressions that were similar; they will have followed football and basketball players with their own empathic action and watched others do likewise; and they will have caught others and themselves following the movements of dancers without conscious intention. A class discussion will bring out many examples of empathy and, at the end, students should be ready to use their added knowledge in demonstrations before other groups.

EXPERIMENT IN MANY MEANINGFUL SITUATIONS

There are always opportunities to experiment on audiences made up of individuals or groups of individuals such as: Friends in social situations at home and at school, other high school classes, the general school assembly, and 4-H, church, college, Y.W.C.A., Y.M.C.A., Girl Scout, Boy Scout, and P.-T.A. groups. All such organizations often want some type of program and a demonstration of empathy will be both educational and entertaining for them.

It is well to encourage boys and girls to get empathic reactions from members of their families. They will find it helpful to report on attempts to get their parents to react as they want them to react by themselves being co-operative when they want parents to be co-operative, by being relaxed when they want brothers or sisters to be relaxed, and by appearing good-natured when they want others to be good-natured. Let them recall how they have put guests at ease by themselves being at ease, and how they have frightened their friends by appearing frightened. Ask them to try to get reactions from family and friends by balancing on a narrow ledge or the edge of a platform, carrying an over-filled cup, pushing a lamp to the edge of a table, or by dozens of other acts which members of the class will think of quickly.

EXPERIENCE AFFECTS EMPATHIC RESPONSE

Instead of using the lemon demonstration which is so familiar to everyone, students may try for audience empathic reaction by coming toward the group very rapidly on a raised platform. When they get to the very edge let them stop abruptly, almost fall forward, and then regain balance. Most members of the audience will jerk with them and then regain balance with them.

After this exercise, the students may try eating something which is familiar to only part of the observers and which is either very sour, very salty, or very bitter. For example, one student may nibble on the type of salted plum or sour seed common in China and in the Hawaiian Islands. In China it is called wah-mui and in Hawaii see-moi. Very sensitive people may be able to catch subtle differences in the reactions of various members of the audience. For example, if the actors are eating see-moi for the first time, their expressions may have a questioning look as well as one revealing that the seed is salty. If the actors have eaten it many times and like it, they may have become accustomed to the salt and like it very much and their expressions will show that.

In the audiences there will likewise be a variety of responses, vary-

ing from those which are merely the empathic physical reactions to
the actors who are eating see-moi, to those who add their own experiences with the taste of see-moi. Such an experiment may
demonstrate to high school students how experiences tend to inten-
sify, subdue, or modify responses to the visible behavior of others
and how, by knowing what people's experiences have been, a
speaker can predict their behavior and get what he wants from
them. Students should try to select from the audience those who
have never tasted see-moi, those who have tasted it and like it, and
those who have tasted it and dislike it. The demonstration with
see-moi, or with something similar, will suggest many others to
resourceful teachers and students.

DEMONSTRATE EMPATHIC RESPONSE IN A
VARIETY OF WAYS

In this game of proving that a speaker can get an audience to
mirror what he is doing, it is entertaining to try opening a very
tightly covered fruit jar before an audience unaware of the game;
breaking a short and tough stick; handling gum or sticky, messy
paper; lifting a heavy package; or running fingers along the razor-
like edge of a sharp knife. The audience will jerk when the jar
cover is finally loosened and when the stick is broken; they will
show with face and fingers that gum and paper are sticky; they will
appear to try to help with the heavy package; and they will display
apprehension and discomfort at the testing of the knife edge.

When high school students have had experiences like the foregoing they will be able to add more and more examples of audience
response and resultant meanings. They then will come to understand the physical reactions of the speaker to the audience and of
the audience to the speaker. They will begin to see that empathy,
this unconscious tendency which all normal people have, is an extremely valuable tool for all speakers.

TRAINING STUDENTS TO LEARN
AUDIENCE CONTROL

Classroom training well may center around the four steps which
have been sketched on pages 150–151 and which will be explained
here at greater length.

Step I: Learning to Interpret the Actions of Others

A person who is skilled and effective in using expressive bodily action sizes up speech situations quickly and unconsciously. He may be able to point to times when he received training in doing this, or it may be that for him circumstances and surroundings were so favorable that he never knew just how or when he learned to read the visible behavior of other people. In the average high school class, at one extreme, there will be students who always read situations at once through empathy and, at the other extreme, those who misinterpret situations, through empathy.

It is essential that time be spent on this first step in improving bodily action. All students should analyze their abilities, and the successful ones should help the less successful. It may be valuable to have class discussion center around techniques of reading the bodily action of others. Students may be assigned to size up strangers to see how much meaning they can get from empathic responses. As they stand on street corners, ride on busses, attend interschool games, travel on trains or planes, and appear at social functions, they may try to analyze various situations through the bodily action which they themselves feel. Before long, most of them will realize that they do not analyze carefully and consciously but that they sense at once whether people are formal or informal, relaxed or tense, happy or unhappy, reserved or unrestrained. They will understand that such definite meanings are the result of instantaneous, unconscious empathic bodily adjustments. Students may not at first realize it, but the teacher will soon discover that, because high school students are young and very much alive, they are quicker to sense situations and interpret the feelings of others than are older people. Students will very early become intrigued with evaluating their individual skills in this first step in learning to use good bodily action.

Step II: Determining the Type of Action
Appropriate for a Given Situation

Boys and girls will soon learn that bodily action affects observers in different ways and that, if they are to persuade others, they must appeal to each type of person in his own medium, that is, by the peculiar actions which he uses to express his own ideas. This means that, if a person wants to influence a small child, he must plan to use the kind and amount of action that the small child uses; if he wants to influence a high school boy or girl, he must plan to use the kind and amount of action used by an adolescent; and if he wants to influence his grandparents or people of their age, he must use the kind and amount of action used by older people.

The high school student will observe also that the same people in the different situations react differently, and he will learn that the best way to get the response desired is to use the kind and amount of action that the observer would use to express the ideas to which the speaker wants him to react.

Out of such considerations, high school students will learn that they can use their natural bodily behavior before an audience only when that behavior is like the behavior the members of the audience would use in expressing the same ideas.[2]   This principle means that usually high school boys and girls will be most natural in the use of bodily action before people of their own age, and that they may need to use less than the natural amount of action before adults and more than the natural amount before children.   They will find that the experiences, habits, and vocations of audiences also must be taken into account, and that the individual accustomed to a sedentary life is moved by kinds of action different from those which appeal to one accustomed to an active life.   Thus, Step II is to decide exactly what kind of action will be required to get the person with whom one is communicating to empathize so that the right meanings will be stirred up.   In this particular step the teacher may be very helpful to the students because of his broader experiences.   His superior training in speech has prepared him to predict audience response to various types and amounts of bodily action.   Students may raise such specific questions as the following:

1. From a senior boy: "May I put my left hand in my pocket when I speak for the United Givers Fund at the Kiwanis Club luncheon?"

If this problem is to be solved on the basis of empathy, the question really becomes, Are members of this club accustomed to speaking with their hands in their pockets?   The answer probably is

---

[2] Of course, this principle assumes that the observer is in sufficient control of his muscles to permit him to express himself as he would like to.

"Yes." In fact, it is so with older men more often than it is with boys in the first years of high school, and for this reason the men probably will react to the hand-in-pocket position comfortably. A second consideration should be the *way* the boy puts his hand in his pocket and the ease with which he can remove it, if he finds that he needs to use it in making a gesture. If his pockets are tight and he cannot take his hand out easily, his awkwardness may draw attention to itself and away from the meaning. If that is the situation, the teacher should advise against putting the hand in the pocket.

2. From a seventh grade girl: "Since my announcement of the high school play in assembly is very short, do you think it is all right for me to stand at the side of the stage just at the head of the steps?"

The girl reasons that it is unnecessary and perhaps presumptuous for her to go across to the center of the platform. The answer is that she must think of her purpose: To let all members of her audience know when and where the play is to be given, and to urge them to attend. When a speaker stands far over to one side of a stage the empathic response is one of imbalance. Furthermore, when a speaker stands too near the edge of the platform the audience in following her bodily set, is likely to feel uncomfortable, for fear of her falling. These feelings are not the ones which the speaker wishes to stir up in her listeners, and therefore she will be wise to stand nearer the center of the stage, and far enough back from the front to leave the audience unconscious of her position and free to concentrate on the announcement.

3. From a ninth grade boy: "I am going to tell the story of *The Three Bears* before the four-to-six-year-olds down at the city library. Is it all right for me to pretend that I am really crying when the wee bear says, 'Someone has been sitting in my chair and has broken it'?"

The first issue is, How do four to six year olds themselves tell stories? and the answer is that they make their actions much more literal than adults do and even more literal than ninth graders do. This means that the ninth grader will please his audience most if he pretends that the bear *is* crying, just as members of his audience would cry if they were telling the story. He should act not like a ninth grader but a good deal like a four- or five-year-old if he wants his audience to enjoy the story.

4. From a tenth grade girl: "When I report on *How I Won the 4-H Award for the Best Landscaped Yard*, before members of the 4-H Clubs of our county, shall I use gestures and move around or shall I stand still and just talk?"

In settling this problem the girl should remember that most 4-H Club workers are active people. When they speak in conversation they are usually energetic and animated. Moreover, they use all of their muscles daily in broad general activities. It is not easy for them to keep their bodies quiet, and they will be least conscious of their bodies if they have opportunity to respond in both general and specific ways. What is more, they will react to movement easily without the fatigue which might be a part of the response of individuals two or three times as old. Therefore, the speaker will stir up more exact meanings in her listeners if she moves and gestures frequently, but, of course, always in ways appropriate to the meaning.

5. From a junior boy: "When I read *Casey at the Bat* before the Physical Education Club shall I reach down and actually pretend to rub my hands with dirt, and then wipe them on my shirt, when the lines say that? Do you think I should do it the same way when I read it at the P-.T.A. meeting?"

Casey at the Bat is a very well-known poem, particularly to adults. Some people have heard it so many times that they want it presented as a comic reading. Others, less familiar with it, may want it read as a semi-serious description of what really happened in an exciting baseball game. The Physical Education Club members will not know the poem as well as the P-.T.A. members will, and it may be that they will want to think of it as serious. The reader will have to decide how he wants the audience to react. If he elects to describe the game so that the audience will not forget it, he will try to act out each part as high school students would do it if they were telling the story. Few adolescents would reach down clear to the ground and pretend to pick up dirt, but they might stoop a little and suggest filling their hands and then start to wipe their hands on their shirts. With such suggestions in their minds the audience will understand and appreciate the meaning.

If the student is reading the poem for adults with the same purpose (seriously) as he had for his high school friends, it will be better for him to use action even less literal than what he used before the Physical Education Club; the adults themselves use less action. They have more inert cells in their bodies than the high school students have and it is more tiring for them than it is for younger persons to follow the total response of an active speaker. However, if the reader wants to burlesque the poem because adults have heard it so often that it is trite for them, he can do it by making the actions markedly literal in all details.

6. From a senior girl: "When I give my declamation from Edmond Rostand's *Cyrano de Bergerac*, should I stagger and fall down as Cyrano gives his last speech and dies? I am reading before the city Woman's Club."

Most members of a Woman's Club would employ only slight movement and suggestive gestures as they speak in most situations. If they reacted empathically to a speaker actually falling down, the feeling which resulted would usually be so foreign to their normal behavior that they would not be able to concentrate on the meanings of the lines, and the purpose of the speaker would be defeated.

7. From a tenth grade girl: "When I go to the home of the principal for a reception is it all right for me to sit on the floor? We all did when the debate club met at my house."

When the girl reaches the reception she will unconsciously feel the general atmosphere of the occasion. If it is very informal, if the guests have come in sports clothes and informal attire and many are lounging about, it may be quite appropriate to sit on the floor when conversing. However, if the reception is more formal, if the refreshment table is unusually attractive, if guests have on their best attire, if everyone is speaking quietly and with restraint, the tenth grade girl should behave so that her action will concentrate attention on what she is saying and not on her behavior.

Step III: Analyzing Action Potentialities to Determine Degree of Ability in Actual Practice.

At some time, when a high school student is working to improve his speech, he deserves to know in what ways he is effective in the use of his visible action and in what ways he is ineffective. One of the best techniques of making these individual analyses interesting and helpful is to take moving pictures of every student and have the class discuss the strengths and weaknesses of each. This procedure permits a student to see himself as others see him and to compare his own use of bodily expression with that of others in the class. This process will help him to predict what he will be able to do under various circumstances. He will see that some of his faults are the common faults of all boys and girls of his age, that he has some peculiar personal weaknesses, but that he also has some strong points that make him more effective in certain ways than any of his classmates.

If movies are not possible, similar results can be obtained by having each student go before the class and, in the light of what he does as he stands there, and what he has done before, get the opinion of his classmates as to how effective he is in posture, movement, gesture, and facial expression. It is often wise for him to record, on a card or a page in his notebook, his strong and weak points in bodily action. It is also well for the teacher to make clear that the normal boy or girl may be awkward, grow rapidly or grow slowly, and feel jittery and insecure. Such analyses may not always be comfortable, but they prove to adolescents that they are developing as they should develop.

Step IV: Improving Each Speaker's Action.

After a student knows how to size up a speech situation by means of empathy; how to determine what bodily action is appropriate for a given individual or group of individuals, and what his own strengths and weaknesses in bodily action are, he should set about to improve his use of visible action.

1. Aim at the ability to do whatever is appropriate.

It is a safe generalization that if an individual is able to do with his body anything he wishes to do, he will be able to adapt his speaking to any situation, and he can make whatever he does appear natural, even if, at times, it is not really natural until training has made it so. In accomplishing Step IV, training of all parts of the body will be in order, and will no doubt require more time and concentration than that devoted to the direct teaching of any of the other steps.

2. Train the body as a unit as well as in parts.

While total bodily action is the general aim of all training, a teacher may help her students to make marked progress by concentrating at various times on those elements which most need attention. For example, pantomimes which portray stories, including the location of the scene, the identification of characters, and the clarification of plot and climax, require skill in the use of all parts of the body. Some may be failures and difficult to interpret because of poor facial expression, inappropriate posture, stiff gestures, or awkward movements which call attention to weaknesses in elements of the performance. In such cases training of parts of the body selected according to the student's needs will be worth while. Classes will be interested in planning games to see if all members of the class can interpret changes in facial expressions, positions and movements of hands, sets of shoulders, and movements of feet, as well as in the action of the body as a unified whole. It is a good idea to work also for relaxation and tension, inhibition and expansion, and so on. Textbooks will have many interesting suggestions for training in all-over bodily response. Look at the exercises at the close of the chapters on Action and Gesture in high school speech texts. The bibliography at the close of this chapter will also be a helpful source of ideas for activities in bodily action.

3. Encourage experimentation with action.

One of the advantages to be sought in using a variety of stimulating activities in bodily action is that of encouraging students to experiment in using action during speech. Most speech teachers will observe that many of their students have far greater resources in bodily action than they ever put to use in their speaking. Students have learned, in the process of growing up, a variety of facial expressions, bodily attitudes, and movements which arouse meanings in others. Often, however, they will not make use of these actions in speaking before strangers, or in speaking in a public situation, because of their embarrassment. If, during activities in pantomime, students can be encouraged to put to use their full resources, they frequently will have the vital experience of receiving public, social approval for their use of action. This approval may help to free the student from the constraint which has handicapped him in putting his own skill to use. Free and effective use of bodily action is closely related to the development of social confidence in the speaker. Not only are students frequently helped in overcoming social fears through the study of bodily action in speaking, but also those activities in the speech class which help to reduce the social fears of speakers will usually have a good effect upon skills in using bodily action. Chapter 10 contains a more complete discussion of the whole problem of reducing social fears.

Step V: Testing for Improvement.

After training to improve bodily action it is well to help students to evaluate their progress. A second series of moving pictures will give opportunity for comparison between what they were able to do at the beginning of training and at the end. Let the students examine each set of pictures and list what they like and dislike about each. See whether for the class in general and for specific individuals there are more items of approval than disapproval. The use of improved action in all types of speaking situations will show how the new skills function. Frank class discussion will help boys and girls to understand wherein they have succeeded in substituting good action habits for poor ones. Encourage students to demonstrate, before the class, telling stories, acting in plays, giving reports, holding conversations, and so on. The criterion of success will be whether or not the action calls attention to the ideas and feelings rather than to itself. If members of an audience remember graceful action, skillful use of hands, and smooth movements rather than the meanings to be communicated, the action has been poor. The final test is: *Do members of the audience get the meaning?* Take time for students to understand the fundamental principles of evaluation.

1. *Direct students in working out evaluation scales.*

Students with the guidance of the teacher will profit by preparing evaluation sheets on which they can rate themselves and others on each of the steps through which speakers go in persuading or influencing audiences. First, they can place themselves at some point between always catching the set of an audience and never catching it; second, they can place themselves on a scale between always selecting the right kind of action and never selecting it; third, they can evaluate themselves on all of the items involved in producing the right action to get the desired result; and, fourth, they can decide how much progress they have made with bodily action as a whole, and on its various elements.

2. *Train students to determine amount and kind of action for a variety of situations.*

At the end of a project on action, it is often interesting to have students offer to answer questions concerning the amount and kind of action in terms of adaptation, and speaker-audience relationships, rather than set rules. Let them dare an audience to stump them and welcome such questions as: How should a speaker walk to the platform? Where should a speaker stand on a platform? What kind of standing or sitting position should a boy or girl use at a tea or a reception? How many, and what kinds of, gestures should one employ in a given reading? How many times should a speaker move in a public speech? and so on. All such queries should be answered in terms of empathic interchange of response and adaptation to various audiences rather than by any rigid rules.

If the teaching of visible action is based on a plan such as the foregoing, students will not resort to stiff, artificial, studied, meaningless gestures and actions to stir up meanings in their audiences; they will approach the problems of visible bodily action in terms of what is best for a given individual or group of individuals, on a specific speech occasion.

SELECTED BIBLIOGRAPHY

Baird, A. Craig, and Franklin H. Knower, *General Speech.* New York: McGraw-Hill Book Company, 1949, Chapter V.

Borchers, G. L., and C. M. Wise, *Modern Speech.* New York: Harcourt, Brace & Co., 1947, Chapter II.

Langfeld, H. S., *The Aesthetic Attitude.* New York: Harcourt, Brace & Company, 1920.

Lees, C. Lowell, *A Primer of Acting.* New York: Prentice-Hall, Inc., 1940.

Rasmussen, Carrie, *Speech Methods in the Elementary School.* New York: The Ronald Press, 1949, Ch. 3.

Robinson, Karl F., *Teaching Speech in the Secondary School.* New York: Longmans, Green & Co., Inc., 1951, Ch. 13.

Robinson, Karl F., and W. Norwood Brigance, "The Program of Basic Skills in Speaking," *Bulletin of Secondary School Principals.* (November 1945), 19–30.

Sarett, Lew, and W. T. Foster, *Basic Principles of Speech*, Rev. ed. Boston: Houghton Mifflin Co., 1946, Chapters V–VII.

Weaver, A. T., *Speech: Forms and Principle.* New York: Longmans, Green & Co., Inc., 1951.

Woolbert, C. H., and Joseph F. Smith, *Fundamentals of Speech.* New York: Harper & Brothers, 1934, Chapters V–VII.

CHAPTER 7

Developing Effective Voice

A POINT OF VIEW

Iᴍᴘʀᴏᴠᴇᴅ action for speech will indirectly improve voices, but the maximum improvement of poor voices requires direct concentration upon the problem. Frequently, voice and pronunciation irregularities will not be completely corrected during the period of high school training. Poor habits which have been learned in twelve to eighteen years of daily use may not be changed to good habits in a semester, a year, or even four years of directed, conscientious, concentrated, and intelligent practice. However, it has been proved that overdoing an activity in one direction for a short time can counteract the performance of that activity in another direction for a long time. For example, if a man's work requires that he bend over steadily a large part of an eight-hour day, he can overcome his tendency to stoop by practice in standing overly erect for a few minutes during every day. The same principle holds true of improving voice habits. Remedial over-drill on effective habits, if it is well motivated, will do much to weaken ineffective habits of long standing.

VOICE IMPROVEMENT IS AN ALL-SCHOOL SERVICE

In helping boys and girls to develop improved habits in any one of the elements of speech, the teacher must think of his work in terms of service to the entire school. Voice-training will not be successful if attention is centered on voice *per se*. The students who want to *use* good voices will make more progress than those who want to *have* good voices. This means that students must improve their voices because they want to read literature well, give effective science demonstrations, take part in social studies discussions, clarify mathematics problems, report on the lives of music composers, give physical education directions, describe pictures, act in plays, be masters of ceremonies at dinners, introduce speakers in assembly, teach Sunday school classes, use the telephone effectively, be interesting in conversation, read for club meetings, or participate in any one or more of hundreds of occasions, when a good voice will help them to be successful.

START VOICE TRAINING WITH A WELL-MOTIVATED PROJECT

The circumstances in which a teacher is endeavoring to give speech training will determine to a large extent how he will motivate his class to want to improve their voices. These circumstances will vary markedly from school to school.

Projects Organized Around General Educational Purposes

If the entire school program is organized around such large units as Health, Civic Responsibility, Vocations, or Recreation, the speech teacher, like all of the other teachers in the school, will be a consultant and will work with the students at such times as his particular contribution can help to bring a given project to a successful conclusion. Teacher and students together will select those individuals who will profit by voice training and will meet them either individually or in groups at such times as the director of the project designates.

Projects Organized Around Speech Activities

If, on the other hand, the work of one grade is organized around a core of speech activity such as a dramatic production, the discussion of a school problem, a radio or an assembly program, the speech teacher may be the director and not only decide with her students when special voice training is necessary, but also determine with them when other specially trained teachers can best make contributions to the success of the whole project.

Projects Organized Around Student Problems

In a special speech class, the motivation may be problems such as: Teen-age Driving, The Need for an Improved School Building, The Conduct of School Parties, High School Sororities and Fraternities, A Community Recreation Center for Teen Agers, Selecting a Vocation, Dating, or How to Get Along With Others. The problem may involve one or more speech activities such as talks, plays, readings, discussions, debates, and the like. For maximum success, such projects will require from students effective use of voice, and they will work to improve their voices because they want to carry out the projects.

Projects Organized in Courses Other Than Speech

The speech teacher may be engaged to teach speech in connection with social studies, English, art, mathematics, science, or any other subject matter area. In such a situation, he and his class will decide on the best time to concentrate on voice improvement, in order to further the aims of the course. Sometimes voice will be taught constantly in short concentrations almost every day, and sometimes it will be taught in larger units, weekly or monthly, or when needed.

Projects Organized by the Visiting Speech Teacher

Finally, the teacher trained in speech may make periodic visits to a school, and, with the help of other teachers, invite students to receive special voice training in order to facilitate the accomplishment of the aims of individual classes or of the school as a whole.

All Projects Related to Student Needs

In all instances students will approach voice improvement with enthusiasm only when there is some project which they wish to complete or some problem which they wish to solve, and when they can feel that their task can be accomplished more easily and more satisfactorily with improved voice habits. Only when students see the need for good voices in order to do what they want to do, will they earnestly set about the improvement of their voices.

STUDY INDIVIDUAL AND GROUP INTERESTS IN PREPARATION FOR VOICE TRAINING

It is not always a simple matter to provide effective motivation for high school students. Some are interested in every project which is brought to the attention of the class, and, unfortunately, some appear to have no genuine interest in any project. The teacher and students must discover interests. One teacher cites an example of a ninth grader who was a poor speaker and showed no co-operation in solving problems which seemed vital to most of the other students. The teacher visited him in other classes. In science, English, social studies, mathematics, and music he appeared bored. When she visited shop, she saw that the other students came and talked to him as he cut lumber for a table. The topic of conversation was horses. Later the speech teacher visited the art class and saw this boy draw horses and model horses in clay; he appeared to enjoy what he was doing. One of his models was put on display. Several times the speech teacher casually walked near the show case, until she found the boy looking at his own work. She commented on the interesting figures he had constructed and, engaging him in conversation, found him to be deeply interested in horses, a good rider, a member of a 4-H Club, and an authority among his friends on topics in any way connected with horses and riding. Discussing the boy's accomplishments before the class, the teacher found that eight students out of twenty-eight were members of 4-H Clubs, and that all students were enthusiastic about learning how to ride. The result was a project on riding which was led by the boy who previously had shown no interest in any class work, and who had indicated no desire to improve his slovenly articulation. In this discussion he wanted to be a success. He was willing and eager to get rid of his weaknesses, to meet effectively this situation which was meaningful to him.

One such victory with a problem student often changes the attitude of an entire class. Enthusiasm is contagious, and other boys and girls catch empathically the co-operative spirit of interested classmates.

COMMUNITY NEEDS INFLUENCE VOICE TRAINING

Voice problems in Texas are different from those in New York, and both are different from those in Michigan. The voice problems of boys are different from those of girls, those of freshmen from those of seniors, and those of prospective farmers from those of prospective teachers or housewives.

The teacher and the students together should discuss individual vocal habits and needs in terms of foreign influences, economic strains, health, physical inheritance, life purposes, and all of the circumstances which taken together make the voices in a given group what they are. Such considerations should determine the future aims of that group, in the field of vocal habits.

TEACHING PRODUCTION OF VOICE

A knowledge of how vocal sound is produced will help in understanding how to improve voice. It will make clear the justification for individuality in quality, force, and pitch. It will help boys and girls to understand why yelling at football games causes hoarseness, and how complete rest may cure it. The change of voice in boys at adolescence will mean more than words memorized from a book. In short, the relationship between physical structures and types of voice will be made clear, more specifically and definitely than it could be through any amount of discussion. One effective method of interesting students in this subject is to secure for class demonstration two animal larynges, one from a pig and one from a sheep, each with the lungs and diaphragm attached. These materials can be obtained from a packing plant or a butcher's shop at very small expense and are more interesting and helpful to students than expensive models, although the more fortunate students will have opportunity to examine both. Students can examine the diaphragm, lungs, trachea, esophagus, larynx, hyoid bone, and so on. The lungs can be inflated by blowing through a rubber tube inserted into the trachea or one of the bronchi, and students thus can discover how air moves into and out of the lungs. After severing the trachea from the lungs, a student can attach a rubber tube to the lower end, press the vocal folds together, blow air through the larynx, and produce the pig's grunt or the lamb's bleat. This demonstration will illustrate the fact that the physical structure of the vocal mechanism determines the character of the sound it produces. Students will enjoy dissecting out the cartilages of the larynx and will be interested to see the true and false vocal folds clearly when the voice box is cut up the back through the wide part of the cricoid cartilage, between the two arytenoids. Some teachers hesitate to direct a demonstration with fresh animal larynges lest they themselves may not be able to identify the parts. This difficulty can be turned to advantage if students understand that the teacher as well as they are examining these materials for the first time. They will then assume a larger share of responsibility for care and accuracy in the study and thus learn by helping each other to learn. The teacher will find her own knowledge increasing with each demonstration.

USE OF MODELS, CHARTS, AND PICTURES

Every available type of visual aid should be used in helping boys and girls to understand the complicated process of voice production. Models and charts of the larynx, the chest, the head, the ear, and the entire body are available. It is well to remember that if students learn the process of vocal production from ten sources they will doubtless understand it better than if they learn it from only one source.

IMPORTANCE OF CO-OPERATION OF OTHER DEPARTMENTS

The science department can be of great help in making voice production, and especially the phenomenon of resonance, clear. Science teachers not only have the equipment with which to give vivid demonstrations, but also are well informed concerning the factors that control the production of well-resonated tones.

Movies showing the details of voice production, from the time the diaphragm moves downward reducing the pressure in the lungs so that the air rushes in, to the time the word is formed by the articulatory organs, can be secured from visual aid loan libraries.

Often an expert on voice may be invited to come and talk to the class. In one city a throat specialist not only came and talked but brought a human larynx which he left in the school museum. An understanding of the production of speech sounds is important in

improving voice, and students master this subject matter most readily
if it is discussed and reviewed in a variety of ways, and with and by
interesting people.

EVALUATION OF INDIVIDUAL VOICE NEEDS

Early in the study of voice each student has the right to know how
his voice sounds to other people. It is well to keep in mind that
when he hears it from the inside of his own head he gets an impression very different from the one his classmates get. It is important
to develop a classroom spirit which makes students and teacher feel
free to speak to each other more frankly than they would speak to
people outside the class. The group is organized for specific purposes, one of which is to improve voices; anything which contributes
to the accomplishment of that end, without impeding the accomplishment of other purposes, is desirable. All good ways of getting
favorable results should be discovered and carried out in the classroom procedures.

EVALUATION METHODS VARY

One simple way of making individual evaluations of voices is to
have students rise, one after another, and each speak the same simple
sentence. If each student says, "This is my best voice," for example, students at once notice that human voices are different, and
that, as in the pig's and sheep's larynges, the sound each produces is
determined by the physical structure of the instrument. They will
not be surprised that voices are different, for as one fourth-grader
said, "They should be, because people are different shapes." After
the class has heard a number of individual voices, it is expedient to
stop and discuss the strengths and weaknesses of each. Individuals
will want to record in their notebooks what the class and the teacher
have observed.

Often it is worth while to have students read sentences designed
for the purpose of revealing specific articulatory difficulties. Teachers can make up sentences in which sounds are placed in initial,
middle, and final positions. In this way one sound at a time may be
studied. For example, for "l"—"*L*et the li*ll*y remain in the we*ll*,"
and "t"—"*T*ell the li*tt*le girl to si*t*." Many textbooks in speech contain lists of such sentences, as well as many other tests for discovering

specific weaknesses. In using such sentences, the boy or girl to be tested should not know what particular sound is in question, for if he does he is likely to give it a pronunciation different from that which is his habit. It is well to give the student who is being examined the benefit of more than one hearing, because studies show that more accurate ratings can be made by both trained and untrained judges when these ratings are the sum of analyses made at different hearings on different days.

EMPHASIZE INDIVIDUAL DIFFERENCES

There was a time in voice training when some teachers made an effort to get all students to sound alike. There is some evidence to show that low tones were recommended over high tones, that the use of specific lip muscles was recommended for the production of certain sounds, and that one kind of breathing was advocated over all others. Such practices are pretty much a thing of the past. The modern speech teacher examines every student, notes his physical and mental equipment, and sets out to help *him*, using *his* apparatus, to become the best possible speaker. No two speakers' voices should sound alike; each speaker, if he is successful, will do as well as he can do with the physical and mental mechanism which he has inherited, in the specific situation in which he finds himself. Briefly, then, the good voice teacher aims to help each individual to develop a useful voice out of the materials with which he has been endowed and to adapt himself to the community in which he is to live.

HELP STUDENTS TO DEFINE A GOOD VOICE

When student and teacher work together to define a good voice they usually emphasize the same characteristics—pleasantness, clearness, intelligibility, expressiveness, and appropriate volume. Such factors call attention to ideas and feelings rather than to the voice itself. In all speech, stirring up meanings is the end. Voice is the means to that end. Having analyzed a good voice, such student will want to test himself on each desirable characteristic and see how he measures up to the standards set by the class.

CONSIDER RELATIONSHIP OF VOICE TO
MODE OF LIVING

Voice improvement is so closely tied up with the everyday living that the teacher may hasten his students' progress by knowing them well personally. All experienced speech teachers can cite cases where information about the life of a student has opened the way to the removal of the causes of his voice difficulties. A student with a harsh, strident voice kept it unchanged in spite of comments by teacher and fellow students, until it was discovered that the cause of the tension was the strain induced by earning both room and board and, at the same time, maintaining high standards in school. When the economic pressure was reduced, the student's voice improved. A girl spoke with too little volume to be understood in class. Her fellow students helped her to recognize her difficulty but thought her inconsiderate because she did not increase her volume at once. Later it was discovered that there was serious illness in her home, which required absolute quiet; the girl had formed a habit of using low vocal volume in all situations. The discovery of this cause pointed to a thoughtful consideration for others rather than the opposite. This analysis, followed by training in adaptation to different situations, solved the girl's problem. A boy who substituted "d" for "th" in the initial position, unconsciously retained his habit, in spite of his ability to make the preferred sound, because friends in his community talked like that and told him he was a sissy when he spoke correctly. The class helped him to prepare to meet people in a larger social area than his limited community. It is safe to assume that every student has a real reason for his voice behavior. The teacher and the class must furnish him good reasons for better voice habits.

USE OF AUTOBIOGRAPHIES IN DISCOVERING
CAUSES OF POOR VOICES

Perhaps the best way to get to know students is to talk to them; observe them in and out of class; visit them in their homes; talk to fellow students, faculty, and other people in the community about them; and read the records in the school office. Clearly this is impossible when one teacher may have more than 150 students in one term and change his groups twice each year. A fairly satisfactory method for getting acquainted, one which is economical in both time and effort, is to ask for written autobiographies. Such an assignment is easily motivated, if in no better way than by drawing attention to the fact that famous people all over the world publish stories about themselves which in many cases turn out to be best sellers. In addition to making this point, the teacher should explain how every bit of information about an individual is related to his habitual voice patterns.

The assignment to write an autobiography should come after the boys and girls have been in the class long enough to have sufficient confidence in the teacher and the other students to write freely. Usually the method of presentation should be carefully worked out. One teacher said she always chose a day when she was rested, when she felt friendly toward every student in the class, and when she could devote at least forty-five minutes to talking over the assignment with the boys and girls. Her suggestions were helpful because at the end of the period each student had a list of recommended questions to be answered and knew why each was related to voice proficiency. The teacher further encouraged the students themselves to think of informing questions and to justify the inclusion of each in an autobiography written for the purpose of improving voice. She usually started with questions like: How old are you? Where were you born? How many brothers and sisters do you have? How old are they? Where were your father and mother born? Are they older or younger than the average parents? In your home, do you speak any language other than American? Have you ever had any serious illnesses? Have you ever skipped a grade? Have you ever failed a grade? What subjects do you like best in school? Which ones do you like least?

At this point she turned to the students for help. Questions raised by the students included: Where have you traveled? What are your favorite hobbies? What are you most afraid of? Have you ever had any serious accidents? What books and magazines do you like to read? What is your religion? Have you ever earned any money? Have you ever met any famous people? Do you like to speak before a class or the high school assembly? What do you intend to do for your life work? What are some of your favorite movies, radio programs, or television shows? Do you like to go to stage plays? What interesting incidents of your life occurred when you were two, or four, or ten years old?

It is wise to make clear to students that they may omit questions they prefer not to answer and also may have the autobiography kept as confidential as they wish by writing across the top, "For the teacher only," or "For the teacher and members of the class," or "For any one who may find this interesting," or "Section I for the teacher only, Section II for members of the class," and so on. Teachers will find that if they have earned the reputation for never violating the confidence placed in them, students will write freely and helpfully.

CALL FOR EXPERT HELP FOR SERIOUS VOICE DIFFICULTIES

A speech teacher should be able to decide when he himself should undertake to direct the improvement of a voice and when he should refer the case to a specialist. In every section of the United States there are expertly trained speech pathologists who can deal with marked voice defects. Many times the regular classroom teacher is prepared to do this specialized work. However, when this is not so, he should feel free to admit his inadequacy at once and be prepared to recommend some specialist to whom the boy or girl can be referred. He should make himself familiar with the professional services available in his area, rendered by special teachers, state departments, colleges, and universities. Persons who are not trained to re-educate individuals who have poor speech because of inadequate hearing, birth injury, cleft palate, and the like, should not attempt trial-and-error methods; it is far better to seek the advice of an expert and carry on remedial training under his direction.

THE RELATION OF BREATHING TO SPEECH IMPROVEMENT

Research on the relation between specific types of breathing and good voices gives very little support to the theory that all individuals should try to breathe in any one certain way. Rather, it appears to support the view that each person must find the type of breathing which is best suited to his physical structure, the way his blood circulates, the shape and character of his vocal mechanism, and so on. There is some evidence to support the belief that, in breathing for speech, movement lower rather than higher in the chest should predominate. These facts may be discouraging to the teacher who has long pointed to breathing exercises as proof that he is doing something concrete and definite to improve voice, and thus has given students confidence in his methods. All voice teachers should be alert to evaluate research in this area, with the hope that they can recommend to their students more modern, scientifically supported breathing methods than are at present available.

While our present evidence does not demonstrate that breathing exercises, designed to teach a specific type of breathing, have much influence on developing improved voices, neither does the evidence suggest that speech teachers should ignore the breathing habits of students. Individual students may find breathing exercises conducive to relaxation prior to speaking. Sometimes students may be helped to produce more effective vocal tones before the class, by being asked to experiment with lower-chest breathing, as well as other activities designed to relax the throat and face muscles, and to provide an ample supply of air for phonation. Teachers should encourage students to experiment with breathing and tone production before the group, only to the extent that the teacher has good rapport with the students, and to the extent that the students can carry out such experimentation without developing undue tensions or antagonisms. Of course, it is not clear that experimentation with breathing before a social group has any direct effect on the students' vocal quality, but some teachers have found such activity helpful to students in voice production, whatever may be the psychology involved.

Encourage Experimentation with Voice

In working with many students who have ineffective vocal habits or adjustments, the teacher may find it useful to encourage the student to experiment with his voice. Students may be asked to practice exaggerated changes in rate or pitch. They may be asked to try a variety of adjustments for tone production—maintaining open vowel sounds, developing a feeling for an open throat, with the sound directed through the mouth, combining vowels with lip consonants, as *pa, ba, wa,* and so on—and to develop a feeling for placing the tone well forward in the mouth. In asking students to experiment with vocal effects, the teacher is joining the student in the search for a voice which will win the approval of a listening group. The teacher recognizes the complexity of the muscular adjustments which accompany vocalization, but depends upon the probability that students with voice problems can find better patterns of production if they are willing to experiment with their voices. Moreover, students who win social approval with such experimentation may be stimulated to further practice in the direction of using the particular new adjustments which have proved satisfying.

It should be apparent that a speech teacher cannot ask a student to experiment with vocal production in front of a group of fellow students unless (a) rapport between the student and teacher is high, and (b) both the student in question and the class as a whole have become interested in improving voice.

TWO IMPORTANT PRINCIPLES OF VOICE IMPROVEMENT

Two important principles must be kept in mind in voice training: First, the student must know what poor habits he is trying to change and, how to change them and, second, he must be provided with meaningful situations in which to use his improved habits. Support for these tenets can be found in many studies. At the University high school in Madison, Wisconsin, and at the high school in Neenah, Wisconsin, students made maximum progress only when they recognized their special voice weaknesses and worked directly to improve them and used effective voices where they thought it mattered.[1] Henrietta Prentiss recommended that voice improvement be brought about through direct drill, but primarily in speech activities such as reading interesting literature.[2] When a teacher keeps in mind these two essentials of effective voice training, he can find dozens of ways in which he can use individual and group projects, choric verse speaking, plays, drill exercises, recordings, expert analyses, models,

[1] Gladys L. Borchers, "Direct vs Indirect Methods of Instruction in Speech," *Journal of Educational Research* (March, 1936), 512; and Ruth Dieckoff, "An Experiment in Methods of Instruction in Speech" (Master of Arts Thesis, University of Wisconsin, 1939).

[2] Henrietta Prentiss in A. M. Drummond, ed., *Speech Training and Public Speaking for Secondary Schools.* New York: The Century Co., 1925, p. 63.

and the like, to make voice improvement activities interesting and effective.

IMPROVEMENT A RESULT OF HEARING FINE DIFFERENCES

In voice training, hearing is an important consideration. If a student is unable to discriminate differences in pitch, if all vocal qualities sound much the same to him, if a voiced consonant sounds to him like a voiceless one, or if he does not hear high frequency sounds at all, there is little chance of his changing undesirable vocal habits to desirable ones. Therefore, hearing and pitch discrimination tests should be given early to avoid wasting time in asking students to measure their improvement in voice by what they hear. The sense of touch may be substituted for the sense of hearing with more satisfactory results. Let a student feel how his larynx moves up when pitch is raised, how the vocal folds vibrate in voiced sounds and fail to vibrate in voiceless sounds, and how the diaphragm and abdominal wall jerk and move, in producing quiet and loud sounds.

COMMON VOICE WEAKNESSES

In the following paragraphs, the common voice difficulties found in high school classes are classified according to *volume, quality, time, pitch,* and *pronunciation.* The teacher is urged, wherever possible, to remove causes rather than symptoms, and often when a student understands the cause of his vocal inadequacies, the symptoms disappear almost without effort. Frequently, however, direct and conscious concentration on symptoms is essential to an understanding of causes.

How to Change Ineffective Volume

When 120 high school teachers were asked to list the most common voice weakness among high school students, inappropriate volume was named more times than any other difficulty. Many high school students do not use volume enough to be heard in class discussion, in talking before high school assemblies, in contributing to club meetings, or in acting in plays. Yet they often use too much volume in conversation at the dinner table, over the telephone, and on the playground. "It's a funny thing," one high school freshman said. "You want me to talk louder, and my mother always says, 'Not so loud, I'm right here.'"

The problem basically is not one of more volume or of less volume; it is one of adaptation. It is learning to read the expressions of listeners to determine at what point they are able to hear without strain because the sound is too weak, or without irritation because the sound is too loud. After a general discussion of the problem, students will be quick to think of ways to get practice in correcting their bad habits. One class made the following suggestions:

1. Practice speaking to individuals in the front, middle, and back of the classroom, the high school assembly, and the town auditorium.

2. Go to the playground and make yourself understood by the person with whom you are walking, by a friend ten feet away, and by a friend a block away.

3. Attend a social gathering and put into practice what you have learned about appropriate voice volume.

4. Go to a large auditorium with one classmate. Practice adapting your voice to all parts of the room.

5. Divide the class into groups of two, four, or any number. Agree to call one another and get your friends to evaluate your volume over the telephone.

6. Note your volume when buying at a local store. Report to the class.

7. Note the volume of people's voices on busses. Report to the class.

8. Select material which requires variety in volume for meaningful interpretation.

9. Listen to your minister and see how he adjusts his volume to the meaning, the auditorium, and the audience.

10. Select recordings of plays, readings, and speeches and play them for the class, illustrating effective use of volume.

11. Make recordings of plays, readings, and speeches illustrating how you can use effective volume.

12. Experiment with different kinds of breathing in order to discover which method is most effective with the least effort.

13. In high school texts, find exercises for improving volume and assign them to members of the class for practice.

14. Try to make conversation, reading, public speaking, and acting more interesting by variety in volume.

15. Apply *all* you have learned about volume adaptation to *all* of the speech activities in which you participate.

One word of caution should be a part of this project, however: There are a few students who, because of weak vocal mechanisms, are unable to use adequate volume. In dealing with such cases, the teacher should seek the advice and help of the speech pathologist in discovering the exact cause of the trouble and the appropriate remedy.

How to Change Ineffective Quality

Understanding how voice is produced should help boys and girls to improve vocal quality. Common faults are too much or too little nasal resonance. Some speakers use their nasal passages to resonate sounds other than *m, n,* and *ng,* the three sounds that should have full nasal resonance in the American language, and other speakers fail to resonate these three sounds through their nasal passages.

The first step in any remedial program for nasal resonance is to discover if the nasal passages are in healthy condition and free from obstruction. If a nose and throat specialist assures the student that there is no physical reason for his improper use of nasal resonance, it is wise to let him see what happens in the back part of the mouth when a sound is resonated. (After surgery cleft palate cases may profit by the same treatment as that given the normal student.) With the use of a mirror it can be made clear that the soft palate and uvula rise and press against the back of the pharynx when vowels are produced without nasal resonance, and that in the production of the same sounds with nasal resonance the soft palate and uvula hang relaxed at the back of the mouth. A student should learn to feel the differences between these two positions, and consciously use the right one until it becomes habitual.

In order to make sure that the student can tell whether or not his sounds are nasalized or denasalized, and whether or not he is eradicating bad habits, let him try some of the following tests:

1. Produce the vowel sound (ä) and sustain it. Close the nostrils by pinching the nose. Release the pressure. If there is no difference in the sound when the nostrils are closed or open there is no improper nasality.

2. Hold a cold mirror under the nostrils and utter the following sentences: (a) My Mary's asleep by the murmuring stream. (b) She gave the book to Alice. The mirror should cloud on (a) and not on (b). Practice with other sentences containing nasal and non-nasal sounds.

3. Close the ears with the fingers and hear the difference between sounds that are nasalized and those that are not nasalized.

4. Ask other students in the class to judge whether nasality has been eradicated or developed.

5. Record the voices of students and evaluate them from the recordings.

6. Note the feeling in the back of the mouth when a tone is nasal, and when it is not nasal.

7. Alternate nasal and non-nasal sounds until the distinction is clear to you and to your listeners.

8. Make lists of words and sentences containing nasal sounds. Practice until the resonance is full and "round."

9. Make lists of words and sentences without nasal sounds. Practice until there is no trace of nasal twang.

10. Practice relaxing the throat and jaw to relieve nasality.

11. Practice yawning before speaking, to reduce nasality. Observe back of throat in mirror.

12. Strengthen the muscles in the back of the throat with such sounds as *g* and *k*, and sentences containing those sounds.

13. Strengthen the muscles in the back of the mouth by forcing them to react to the pressure of a tongue depressor.

14. With a stethoscope listen to nasal vibrations as nasal and non-nasal words are uttered. Try to eliminate nasal vibrations on non-nasal words.

15. Raise and lower the soft palate, without breathing.

16. Use the appropriate nasal resonance in meaningful speech activities.

Another problem of vocal quality is *breathiness*. Some students seem to allow air to pass over the vocal folds without setting them into vibration and this adversely affects vocal quality. The student should be helped to get a clear, sharp attack on vowels. He should learn to start tones clearly and definitely, sustain them properly, and cut them off abruptly.

Some students use hollow tones resonated far back in the throat; the effect is as if they were speaking into a barrel. They should work to "form their sounds in the front part of the mouth." The activity of lips and tongue should be emphasized, and it sometimes is helpful to imagine that the vocal tone is a ball which the speaker is trying to bounce off the wall in the back of the room.

Hoarseness may be the result of either a structural pathology, improper mental conditions, or the misuse of the mechanism. The remedial program for structural pathologies should be laid out by a good medical authority who can treat chronic laryngitis, growths in the larynx or on the vocal folds, adenoids, diseased sinuses, nasal infections, or the other abnormalities which may cause hoarseness. If none of the foregoing causes exist, the undesirable quality may be due to tension, strain, or fatigue. The remedy then appears to be rest, relaxation, relief from worry and strain, and control of voice by central, rather than upper-chest, breathing. Silence which rests the vocal folds usually helps this condition more than any other therapy.

How to Change Ineffective Pitch

Usually, the pitch which the majority of high school students employ is optimum for them, *i.e.*, the pitch at which they produce the best tone with the least effort. But this is not always true. Sometimes the pitch of a voice does not seem to suit the particular mechanism which produces it. For example, a voice which is hoarse in quality may lose this hoarseness when the pitch is lowered or raised. Whenever there is a question about a student's optimum pitch, he should be encouraged to test his voice with the help of a piano. If he will sing up the scale as high as he can go, and down the scale as low as he can go, following his voice on the keyboard, counting the semitones between the low and the high points, and adding one-fourth of the number of semitones to the lowest tone, he will have located his optimum pitch. He can discover his optimum pitch also by stopping his ears with his fingers, humming up and down the scale and listening for the maximum resonance which will come at the best pitch level. After having discovered his optimum pitch, a student should train himself to use it and get vocal variety by moving up and down from that central level.

The monopitched voice is another problem. Many students' voices are dull and uninteresting because they do not have enough variety in pitch. Drill on musical scales and on words and sentences may help, but reading and speaking interesting and meaningful material usually will bring more rapid progress. The pitch discrimination test,[3] mentioned earlier, is a "must" here. If a student cannot hear differences in pitch, he has much less chance of knowing when he is varying his pitch properly than if he both hears and feels the changes. The remedial plan will depend on his pitch hearing, and feeling discrimination. If he can hear pitch differences, he should be motivated to make distinctions in pitch as he acts, speaks, or

---

[3] Carl E. Seashore, Don Lewis, and Joseph Saetveit, "Measures of Musical Talent," Camden, N. J.: Educational Department R.C.A. Manufacturing Company, 1939.

reads. Most texts contain exercises for this purpose, and any resourceful class can supplement what is found in books.

How to Change Ineffective Rate

The rate at which a student speaks is very closely bound up with his physical construction and his habits of living. If he is constantly under pressure, strained, and tense, he may hurry in his speech. If his bodily rhythms are rapid, his speech may be rapid, too. Some people believe that climate affects rate of speaking; they believe that people in cold climates move faster and, as a result, speak more rapidly. The vital question is, however, Is the student's speech so fast or so slow that it is hard to understand? If a speaker can be understood easily there is no reason to change the rate of speech. On the other hand, if he cannot be understood easily, he may need to change his rate. Sometimes the remedy lies in trying to find a cause for the ineffective rate, which can be removed, or in trying to improve the other elements of speech until speech becomes easily intelligible in spite of the rate. Here, as in other speech characteristics, there is no right rate per se, but there is a correct rate for a particular student, with his particular needs, in his particular community, and in his specific situation.

How to Change Ineffective Pronunciation

Many of the speech weaknesses of high school students can be classified under pronunciation which calls attention away from the ideas and feelings to be expressed. Slovenly speech in which sounds are slighted is an example. In some sections of the country adolescent students ignore almost entirely final ng's, t's, d's, and s's. Another common fault is to substitute one sound for another:

(i) for (e); (d) for (th); (v) for (w); (th) for (s); (sh) for (zh);

and so on. Some of these errors are given special labels, such as foreign accent, lisp, intrusion, and the like, but all are corrected by the same procedure: *First*, help the student to identify his weakness; *second*, get him to want to remove it; *third*, teach him exactly how the desirable sound is different from the undesirable sound; *fourth*, train him to produce the desirable sound; and *fifth*, give him interesting ways to practice the preferable sound, until its use becomes habitual.

Such a program requires an understanding of what is considered standard pronunciation. In the United States three dialects are recognized: Eastern, spoken by the cultured people in the New England area east and north of New York; Southern, spoken by the cultured people south of the Ohio River and east of Central Oklahoma and Central Texas; and General American, spoken by the cultured people in the rest of the United States. Phoneticians have worked out detailed sub-standard pronunciations for each area and a knowledge of these studies will be very helpful for high school teachers. Many high school and college speech texts are useful as references for high school students. *Modern Speech*, by Borchers and Wise,[4] for example, is so indexed that a student can turn to those pages devoted to his particular needs and find out exactly how what he *is* saying differs from what he *should* say *in his locality*. The sound systems of foreign languages are described in order to help students understand just how American sounds differ from foreign sounds. This remedial program also requires an understanding of why students often are not eager to remove speech weaknesses. They must be persuaded that the pronunciations used by the majority of cultured people in their localities will be more serviceable to them than the particular idiosyncrasies which they are using.

There are numerous devices for making clear differences in pronunciations. Personal demonstrations, with and without a mirror, is the first and most obvious. Recordings, moving pictures, models, and text descriptions should supplement all methods. Some method for recording what *is* being done and what *should be* done is essential. Some teachers do this by teaching the International Phonetic Alphabet, and some prefer Diacritical Markings. Whichever is used, it must make precise and detailed distinctions clear, until the student sees and hears the differences in the vocal vibrations, in resonance, and in the positions and movements of the articulatory organs. In dealing with pronunciation, students and teacher should keep in mind the fact that every time a correct utterance is substituted for an incorrect one, the old habit loses strength and the new habit gains strength. They should remember also that, when the improved habit brings satisfactions and rewards, it will become fixated more quickly.

---

[4] Gladys L. Borchers, and Claude M. Wise, *Modern Speech*. New York: Harcourt, Brace & Company, 1947.

The Study of Voice as Training in Listening

Students who study voice as a factor in spoken communication may view their study not only as a means to using more effective vocal habits, but also as a means of becoming more intelligent listeners. As students become aware of the relationships between voices and individual differences, and between voices and modes of living, they may be helped to drop some of their prejudices about voice. For example, a student who has not studied regional speech differences in the United States may make unfavorable personality judgments about individuals whose speech represents a section of the country different from his own. A high school student from the Middle West may stereotype an Eastern accent as that of a "sissy," or a Southern accent as that of a lazy person. Such judgments reflect a form of ignorance that the study of voice ought to eradicate. High school students find it interesting to compare their readiness to judge the personalities of other persons on the basis of voice with their beliefs concerning the accuracy of such judgments. They may be helped to see the important effects their own voices have upon other persons, and also to see how desirable it is that listeners should avoid snap judgments about the personalities of speakers, based solely upon their voices.

KEEP IN MIND FUNDAMENTALS, METHODS, AND PURPOSES

Any consideration of voice must end as it began, with a reminder that vocal habits are improved maximally only if they are directly considered and meaningfully applied. The speech teacher helps students to improve their voices in order that they may improve their lives, not only after they graduate from high school but also while they still are in high school.

SELECTED BIBLIOGRAPHY

Anderson, Jeanette O., and Giles W. Gray, "Voice and Articulation Improvement," *Bulletin of Secondary School Principals* (November, 1945), 30–36.

Anderson, Virgil, *Training the Speaking Voice*. New York: Oxford Press, 1942.

Borchers, G. L., and C. M. Wise, *Modern Speech.* New York: Harcourt, Brace & Co., 1947, Chapters III, IV, V, VI, Appendix.

Brigance, W. Norwood, and Florence Henderson, *A Drill Manual for Improving Speech.* Philadelphia: J. B. Lippincott Co., 1939.

Fairbanks, Grant, *Voice and Articulation Drillbook.* New York: Harper & Brothers, 1940.

Gray, G. W., and C. M. Wise, *Bases of Speech.* New York: Harper & Brothers, 1946.

Grim, Harriett, *Practical Voice Training.* New York: Appleton-Century-Crofts, Inc., 1948.

Holmes, F. Lincoln, *A Handbook of Voice and Diction.* New York: Appleton-Century-Crofts, Inc., 1940.

Levy, Louis, Edward W. Mammen, and Robert Sonkin, *Voice and Diction Handbook.* New York: Prentice-Hall, Inc., 1950.

Monroe, Alan H., "Testing Speech Performance," *Bulletin of Secondary School Principals* (November, 1945), 156–164.

O'Neill, J. M., et al., *Foundations of Speech.* New York: Prentice-Hall, Inc., 1941.

Prentiss, Henrietta, in *Training the Voice.* (A. N. Drummond, ed.) New York: The Century Co., 1925, pp. 63–75, "Speech Training and Speaking for Secondary Schools."

Westlake, Harold, "The Classroom Teacher and the Speech Correctionist," *Bulletin of Secondary School Principals* (November, 1945), 61–66.

CHAPTER 8

Developing Effective Language

INTRODUCTION

AT THE present time both educators and laymen are showing unusual interest in language. This interest has arisen in the main because of concern over misunderstandings which are the result of the ineffective or improper use of language. In the communicative process, a particular stimulus (language symbol) will stir up different meanings for different individuals. At a given moment, words do not mean to one person what they mean to another. At different times, words have different meanings for the same person. Furthermore, time changes the meanings of words and all other symbols. Therefore, in this chapter we are dealing with shifting phenomena, no elements of which are ever fixed and finally settled.

THE MEANING OF LANGUAGE

Teachers of speech will need to consider carefully the meaning they attach to the word *language*. Are *language* and *speech* interchangeable words? Or is the study of *speech* a branch of those studies which deal with *language* skills? Or are *language* skills an aspect of the general skill of *speech*? Often two teachers of speech, or teachers of speech and English, have difficulty in talking to one another about their work in teaching *language* because they attach different meanings to this word.

The confusion over the use of the word *language* is understandable enough if one considers the variety of meanings which have been given to this word. We shall consider here some of the various ways in which educators have thought of *language*, coming finally to a definition of the word as it is generally used by teachers of speech, and as it will be used in this chapter.

Language Defined Broadly

In the discussion of the meanings of the term *language* which appears in the 1950 edition of Webster's dictionary, there is one passage which illustrates the use of this term in its broadest possible sense: ". . . language may mean (1) expression that conveys ideas, (2) expression that symbolizes ideas. Bodily expression whether gesture or articulation, and inscription, as printing, writing, etc., are its chief forms, but any systematic symbolism, in a more or less transferred sense, is called language; as the language of art."

Some educators in our day have become interested in the study of *language* as defined in this broad sense. They see *language* as embracing all the symbolic activity of man, and are interested in the relationships of the particular symbolic activities involved in speech writing, painting, sculpturing, music, and the like. With *language* defined thus, it is apparent that the study of speech would be one aspect of language study.

Language Defined More Specifically

While the use of *language* in an exceedingly inclusive sense has become common, the use of this term in a much more specific sense has been usual among teachers of speaking and writing, and scholars in the field of linguistics. In the more specific sense, the term language is applied to the body of words, and the methods of combining words, which are used and understood by a considerable community. Some linguists at the present time would restrict the use of the term *language* to the "conventional use of vocal sounds," thus defining writing as a device for recording *language*.[1] While this restriction may be useful for the scientist who studies *language*, it is likely that the teacher and students of speech will find it convenient to think of these conventional vocal sounds as the words and word groups used in speaking.

Under a specific definition, the term *language* may be used to describe one body of skills which comprise an aspect of the general-

---

[1] See Leonard Bloomfield, *Linguistic Aspects of Science*, University of Chicago Press, 1939, p. 6.

ized skill of speech. This has been the sense in which the word *language* has been generally used by teachers of speech. In this view, the act of speaking is considered as a totality in which a speaker's physical actions, his voice, and the word patterns which he articulates, combine in their effects. In 1920 Charles Henry Woolbert analyzed speech into four factors, "meaning, words, voice, and bodily action." [2] Woolbert's statement still holds true; for students and teachers of speech the traditional and generally accepted definition of *language* has limited its meaning to the conventional sounds which make up words, used singly, and in combination. Language, clearly limited by this definition, visible action, voice, and subject matter, taken together, form the general process known as speech.

The Usefulness of a Limited Definition of Language

In any practical teaching situation, that which works to the advantage of teachers and students tends to be retained. Such is the fact with the limited, clearly circumscribed definition of language as an aspect of speech. It is probable that, early in life, students should begin to perceive the relationships which exist between the language of speaking and the language of writing. It is also probable that as the student grows older, and has direct experience with music, art, and other methods of symbolic formulation of experience, he should begin to perceive the interrelationships of a variety of means of communication, and the importance of all of man's symbolic activity to his mental life. Students who are learning skills, however, need to start not in terms of great generalizations about symbolic and communicative processes, but in terms of immediate, purposeful experience in using language.

The student sees speech as a natural unity, an act useful in attaining his purposes. He can see how care in the choice of words, in forming sentences, in making his meanings clear, precise, and interesting, are resources which he will need to develop in order to speak most effectively. Thus he can set up specific and immediate goals for improvement in language skills, as they are specifically defined. Similarly, teachers of speech are able to prepare themselves specifically in ways of helping students to select and organize language for speaking. The close relationships between the lan-

---

[2] Charles Henry Woolbert, *Fundamentals of Speech*. New York: Harper & Brothers, 1920, p. 7.

guage of speaking and that of writing—and the more abstract and complicated relationships between the language of speaking and writing, and the "languages" of art and music—may be understood by students as they mature through a variety of specific experiences with many ways of "communicating," and as they may be helped to generalize from their experience.

HIGH SCHOOL TEACHING OF LANGUAGE SKILLS
A WIDELY SHARED RESPONSIBILITY

Teachers of speaking or writing too often consider themselves the exclusive "custodians" of instruction in the use of language. Actually, language skills are so important to all education that the responsibility for the development of them must be shared by all teachers. The development of an adequate vocabulary gives the student a language resource which is of great importance to him. Students are aided in the development of vocabulary by nearly all of their studies. In science classes they learn many of the words which may be used to talk clearly and accurately about the subject matter of the various branches of science; in social studies classes they develop the specialized vocabulary for talking about matters of history, government, and so on.

The Opportunity of the Speech Teacher for Developing Language Skills

Although the development of language skills is the responsibility of all high school teachers, the speech teacher has particular opportunities and responsibilities in the language field. The special opportunity of the speech teacher derives from the particular emphasis on repeated experience in a wide variety of speaking activities. In such circumstances the teacher is able to help students to determine inductively their own needs in using language. The speech teacher observes the student who fails to make use of his own experience in the development of his speaking; he observes the word which is used loosely, so that listeners get a variety of imprecise meanings as they listen; he observes the talk in which ideas are not related logically to one another—in which conclusions are drawn without reference to the evidence upon which they are based; and he observes the improprieties, or errors, of taste or usage which interfere with the speech of the student. From all of these observations, the teacher may help the individual student to set specific goals for improving his own use of language, and may help the whole class to learn the nature of effective language.

A Particular Responsibility of the Speech Teacher

High school speech teachers will discover many students who do not understand the specific ways in which the nature of the speaking situation affects the language which must be used by the student. Many high school students seem to feel that good speaking may be achieved by reading aloud material written to be read. These students need to be helped to perceive the way in which language must be adapted to the particular audience for which it is selected, and the circumstances in which it is used. By showing the effects of the speaking situation upon the language of the effective speaker, the speech teacher makes a particular contribution to the language skills of high school students. Consequently, many speech teachers feel a unique responsibility for the development of the skills of "oral" language.

Often, in the past, when a teacher attempted to assume responsibility for developing language skills in the broad sense—written and spoken communication, music, art, architecture, radio, drama, and so on—even though he could see the relationship of them all to life, he found himself overwhelmed and insecure. He was not prepared to deal adequately with each area, and he soon saw that teaching only important elementary essentials required more background than teaching quantities of material—anything and everything he could lay his hands on—in each area. Therefore, when language was defined to set off a particular area for which the teacher was able to prepare adequately, and when such a thorough understanding of language for speech was contributed to the thorough understandings of other clearly defined areas supervised by experts, students were more likely to grasp the concept of a unified whole made of parts. The result has been scholarly instead of superficial treatment of language skills in both the specific and the broad sense. Results of this kind account for the persistence in the speech field of the treatment of *language* as an element of *speech*, rather than vice versa.

WHAT IS ORAL LANGUAGE?

Oral language includes the words, phrases, clauses, sentences, and paragraphs used in speaking, and is used in conversation, informal and formal, face-to-face, and over the telephone; in public and private speaking where reports are given, sermons are delivered, and audiences are instructed or moved to respond; in problem-solving and voting, where decisions are arrived at and accepted or rejected; and in reading or acting literature in small or large groups. All material prepared for speaking should be phrased in oral language, while all material prepared for reading from the page silently should be couched in written language.

REASONS FOR DIFFERENCES BETWEEN ORAL LANGUAGE AND WRITTEN LANGUAGE

The circumstances surrounding listening to talk are always vitally different in certain respects from the circumstances surrounding the silent reading of written material. *First*, in speaking, the person who has composed or selected the language is usually seen, or heard, or both, while in reading silently, the appearance and the vocalization of the author are seldom known. *Second*, the speaker usually employs spoken language with both voice and action. The author records his language on the page and the reader gets his meanings from that record. *Third*, the reactor to oral language is often uncomfortable physically; the seats may be hard, the lights glaring, the room poorly ventilated, or the hall filled with a noisy audience. The reader usually is able to make himself comfortable; he finds a chair he likes, he adjusts the light, opens or closes windows, and removes environmental factors which are distracting. *Fourth*, the reader gets his meaning from black marks on a white page, the listener from the speaker's audible and visible actions. *Fifth*, the speaker can change his language as he observes the effect of what he says, while the writer's language remains unmodified, regardless of its effect. *Sixth*, the reader can go back and re-read until he understands; the listener must get the meanings as the words are uttered, or not at all.

SPEECH TEACHER'S RESPONSIBILITY FOR LANGUAGE

Very often at the beginning of a school term a principal will meet with his teachers for a period of planning. In such a session, aims and purposes are considered. "What are we trying to accomplish?" is the question always before the faculty. Having decided on basic objectives, the group usually tries to discover what contributions each teacher can make to the accomplishment of these purposes in the time assigned to him. The responsibilities which each assumes will depend upon the size and organization of the school. If a person has been engaged to teach in a one-room rural school, he, of course, is the only teacher with whom students will work in solving their problems. If, on the other hand, there are two teachers, they will undoubtedly decide together what responsibilities each will carry. In larger schools where the number of teachers is increased to three, ten, twenty, or one hundred, each teacher will be wise to decide early just what he personally hopes to accomplish in his classes.

The organization of the school will affect every teacher's decision. In some high schools, the teacher may be engaged to teach seventh grade, in some to solve problems centered around "making a living," in some to be a social studies and speech teacher, in some to be a speech and English teacher, in some to be a speech teacher alone, and in others to be a teacher of certain phases of speech, such as drama, public speaking, debate, or fundamentals. No matter what the special conditions, when the faculty has the planning meeting, or when they confer with the administrators, each teacher should come away knowing what specific contribution he is to make to better living for the high school students.

Every teacher learns early that his objectives usually fall into two categories—essentials and desirables. This is very true in the teaching of language. For the speech teacher, *oral* language is an essential while the languages of writing, music, art, architecture, sculpture, and so on, are desirables. The understanding of oral language should make some contribution to all of the others.

THE FOUNDATIONS OF GOOD LANGUAGE

The general foundations of good oral language are the same as the foundations of all good language: (1) Experience, (2) the recognition of its universal characteristics, and (3) the expression of experience in precise symbols. The life of every high school boy or girl usually is rich in the first element, but one of the teacher's basic responsibilities is to help students master the other two elements. Adolescents often see their own lives as humdrum compared with those they read about. They often ignore, or even attempt to hide, honest, universal experiences and incidents which might be the essence of great language. Suggestions for helping students to recognize the significance of their experiences will be given considerable emphasis in Chapter 9 in discussing how to develop effective subject matter for speech.

Discovering Universalities

After having persuaded himself that he has had significant experiences, the student should learn to select from what has happened to him those incidents which have happened to others also. This selection process is necessary in the use of every type of language. Appreciation results from the stimulation, by means of symbols, of the recall of universal experiences. In order to help students to accomplish this stimulation, numerous examples may be gathered, examined, and discussed to prove that every writer or speaker who stirs up meanings effectively does so, first, because he has experienced what he tries to describe, and, second, because he selects from his own experiences those which are also significant for others. Certain types of experiences always have universal appeal: They involve hopes and fears, successes and failures, wise and unwise behavior, and relations with a supreme being and with fellow men. Some authorities identify these fundamental experiences with "impelling motives," because they are related to survival in a broad sense. It is often pointed out that appeals to sex, self-preservation, wealth, power, prestige, reputation, health, patriotism, fairness, food, affection, and so on, are intimately related to life itself and therefore influence man profoundly. An examination of all the causes of human behavior supports the theory that man is essentially self-centered, and responds unconsciously to any stimulus which makes or keeps him stronger than those about him. Usually he does not analyze this selfish behavior, but follows it because it results in satisfaction. The mother's love and sacrifice for her child, which make him successful, reflect favorably on her; the social worker, who gives freely of his time and money, is repaid in community appreciation; and the philanthropist, who helps thousands of the handicapped, finds that according to the measure with which he metes, the rewards are measured to him again. Both speakers and writers take advantage of these human tendencies and see in them sure ways of bringing about desired responses. They do not spend time questioning whether human beings should be as they are; they accept the world as it is and turn their knowledge of it to the accomplishment of their purposes.

Working for Precise and Meaningful Phrasing

Unless language stimuli are presented in a properly meaningful way they do not get the desired responses. Teachers must help boys and girls so to select and organize their words that they will make readers and listeners see, hear, taste, smell, and feel as the speaker or writer wants them to. This process requires skill in the use of language, in both oral and written forms.

One of the most famous descriptions of the process by which meanings are stimulated or stirred up is quoted on the following pages. It is well worth reading carefully, because it makes clear by illustration the importance and the potency of economy and precision in language style. Proust demonstrates how experience resides in the individual and how, out of the record of past living, the mind creates truth. He shows how one taste symbol stirs up an ever expanding pattern of experience, beginning with the house and then extending to the garden, the street, the town, the square, the country roads, the park, the folks in the village, and finally the whole of Combray. This quotation demonstrates, in a remarkable way, the nature of great style, both oral and written. It is included here not as an example of style to be imitated by high school students (it is much too advanced for that), but for the teacher to consider and appreciate. The reader is urged especially to apply the test of repetition and note how new meanings are added with each re-reading.

I feel that there is much to be said for the Celtic belief that the souls of those whom we have lost are held captive in some inferior being, in an animal, in a plant, in some inanimate object, and so effectively lost to us until the day (which to many never comes) when we happen to pass by the tree or to obtain possession of the object which forms their prison. Then they start and tremble, they call us by our name, and as soon as we have recognized their voice the spell is broken. We have delivered them: they have overcome death and return to share our life.

And so it is with our own past. It is a labour in vain to attempt to recapture it: all the efforts of our intellect must prove futile. The past is hidden somewhere outside the realm, beyond the reach of intellect, in some material object (in the sensation which that material object will give us) which we do not suspect. And as for that object, it depends on chance whether we come upon it or not before we ourselves must die.

Many years had elapsed during which nothing of Combray, save what was comprised in the theatre and the drama of my going to bed there, had any existence for me, when one day in winter, as I came home, my mother, seeing that I was cold, offered me some tea, a thing I did not ordinarily take. I declined at first, and then, for no particular reason, changed my mind. She sent out for one of those short, plump little cakes called 'petites madeleines,' which look as though they had been moulded in the fluted scallop of a pilgrim's shell. And soon, mechanically, weary after a dull day with the prospect of a depressing morrow, I raised to my lips a spoonful of the tea in which I had soaked a morsel of the cake. No sooner had the warm liquid, and the crumbs with it, touched my palate than a shudder ran through my whole body, and I stopped, intent upon the extraordinary changes that were taking place. An exquisite pleasure had invaded my senses, but individual, detached, with no suggestion of its origin. And at once the vicissitudes of life had become indifferent to me, its disasters innocuous, its brevity illusory—this new sensation having had on me the effect which love has of filling me with a precious essence; or rather this essence was not in me, it was myself. I had ceased now to feel mediocre, accidental, mortal. Whence could it have come to me, this all-powerful joy? I was conscious that it was connected with the taste of tea and cake, but that it infinitely transcended those savours, could not, indeed, be of the same nature as theirs. Whence did it come? What did it signify? How could I seize upon and define it?

I drink a second mouthful, in which I find nothing more than in the first, a third, which gives me rather less than the second. It is time to stop; the potion is losing its magic. It is plain that the object of my quest, the truth, lies not in the cup but in myself. The tea has called up in me, but does not itself understand, and can only repeat indefinitely with a gradual loss of strength, the same testimony; which I, too, cannot interpret, though I hope at least to be able to call upon the tea for it again and to find it there presently, intact and at my disposal, for my final enlightenment. I put down my cup and examine my own mind.

It is for it to discover the truth. But how? What an abyss of uncertainty whenever the mind feels that some part of it has strayed beyond its own borders; when it, the seeker, is at once the dark region through which it must go seeking, where all its equipment will avail it nothing. Seek? More than that: create. It is face to face with something which does not so far exist, to which it alone can give reality and substance, which it alone can bring into the light of day.

And I begin again to ask myself what it could have been, this unremembered state which brought with it no logical proof of its existence, but only the sense that it was a happy, that it was a real state in whose presence other states of consciousness melted and vanished. I decide to attempt to make it reappear. I retrace my thoughts to the moment at which I drank the first spoonful of tea. I find again the same state, illumined by no fresh light. I compel my mind to make one further effort, to follow and recapture once again the fleeting sensation. And that nothing may interrupt it in its course I shut out every obstacle, every extraneous idea, I stop my ears and inhibit all attention to the sounds which come from the next room. And then, feeling that my mind is growing fatigued without having any success to report, I compel it for a change to enjoy that distraction which I have just denied it, to think of other things, to rest and refresh itself before the supreme attempt. And then for the second time I clear an empty space in front of it. I place in position before my mind's eye the still recent taste of that first mouthful, and I feel something start within me, something that leaves its resting-place and attempts to rise, something that has been embedded like an anchor at a great depth; I do not know yet what it is, but I can feel it mounting slowly; I can measure the resistance, I can hear the echo of great spaces traversed.

Undoubtedly what is thus palpitating in the depths of my being must be the image, the visual memory which, being linked to that taste, has tried to follow it into my conscious mind. But its struggles are too far off, too much confused; scarcely can I perceive the colourless reflection in which are blended the uncapturable whirling medley of radiant hues, and I cannot distinguish its form, cannot invite it, as the one possible interpreter, to translate to me the evidence of its contemporary, its inseparable paramour, the taste of cake soaked in tea; cannot ask it to inform me what special circumstance is in question, of what period in my past life.

Will it ultimately reach the clear surface of my consciousness, this memory, this old, dead moment which the magnetism of an identical moment has travelled so far to importune, to disturb, to raise up out of the very depths of my being? I cannot tell. Now that I feel nothing, it has stopped, has perhaps gone down again into its darkness, from which who can say whether it will ever rise? Ten times over I must essay the task, must lean down over the abyss. And each time the natural laziness which deters us from every difficult enterprise, every work of importance, has urged me to leave the thing alone, to drink my tea and to think merely of the worries of to-day and of my hopes for tomorrow, which let themselves be pondered over without effort or distress of mind.

And suddenly the memory returns. The taste was that of the little crumb of madeleine which on Sunday mornings at Combray (because on those mornings I did not go out before church-time), when I went to say good day to her in her bedroom, my aunt Léonie used to give me, dipping it first in her own cup of real or of lime-flower tea. The sight of the little madeleine had recalled nothing to my mind before I tasted it; perhaps because I had so often seen such things in the interval, without tasting them, on the trays in pastry-cooks' windows, that their image had dissociated itself from those Combray days to take its place among others more recent; perhaps because of those memories, so long abandoned and put out of mind, nothing now survived, everything was scattered; the forms of things, including that of the little scallop-shell of pastry, so richly sensual under its severe, religious folds, were either obliterated or had been so long dormant as to have lost the power of expansion which would have allowed them to resume their place in my consciousness. But when from a long-distant past nothing subsists, after the people are dead, after the things are broken and scattered, still, alone, more fragile, but with more vitality, more unsubstantial, more persistent, more faithful, the smell and taste of things remain poised a long time, like souls, ready to remind us, waiting and hoping for their moment, amid the ruins of all the rest; and bear unfaltering, in the tiny and almost impalpable drop of their essence, the vast structure of recollection.

And once I had recognised the taste of the crumb of madeleine soaked in her decoction of lime-flowers which my aunt used to give me (although I did not yet know and must long postpone the discovery of why this memory made me so happy) immediately the old grey house upon the street, where her room was, rose up like the scenery of a theatre to attach itself to the little pavilion, opening on to the garden, which had been built out behind it for my parents (the isolated panel which until that moment had been all that I could see); and with the house the town, from morning to night and in all weathers, the Square where I was sent before luncheon, the streets along which I used to run errands, the country roads we took when it was fine. And just as the Japanese amuse themselves by filling a porcelain bowl with water and steeping in it little crumbs of paper which until then are without character or form, but the moment they become wet, stretch themselves and bend, take on colour and distinctive shape, become flowers or houses or people, permanent and recognizable, so in that moment all the flowers in our garden and in M. Swann's park, and the water-lilies on the Vivonne and the good folk of the village and their little dwellings and the parish church and the whole of Combray and of its surroundings, taking their proper shapes and growing solid, sprang into being, town and gardens alike, from my cup of tea.[3]

---

[3] Marcel Proust, *Swann's Way*. (C. K. Scott Moncrieff, trans.) New York: Random House, Inc., The Modern Library, pp. 54-59.

HELP STUDENTS TO EVALUATE AND
CREATE LANGUAGE

The ability to evaluate and create effective language comes only with practice, and whether evaluation or creation should come first in teaching depends upon the particular problem-solving project which is the immediate motivation for studying language. Whether students are preparing to improve reports in a social studies class, composing original orations for inter-school competition, appearing in an assembly talk, appealing for funds, or simply engaging in everyday informal talk, they will gain much from an analytical comparison of selections like *Hokum About The Eskimos,* and "Freedom's Back Is Against the Wall." These examples, each good for its purpose, illustrate many points which are important in the study of language. They are included in this chapter to make clear certain basic concepts common to both oral and written language—concrete and abstract symbols, differences in meaning due to differences in experience, meanings and change, context and meaning, voice and action as related to language, and ethics in the use of language.

Miss Thompson's speech is an example of good oral language. *Hokum About The Eskimos* is not intended to be oral in style.

HOKUM ABOUT THE ESKIMOS
by
Vilhjalmur Stefansson [4]

Having invented a fictitious country and named it Eskimo-land, the textbooks find it necessary to invent a fictitious people, and the Eskimos are misrepresented even more than the territories they inhabit. They are supposed to be all alike, though some of them live farther away from others than Canada is from Mexico and have less contact. Their climate has only one description in most textbooks, although they really live in several different climates. . . . The schoolbook accounts of the Eskimo presumably arouse in the child pity and amusement. Here are some of the quotations:

"The Eskimo has an environment which forces him into constant conflict with nature. He is in continual danger of freezing and starving to death."

---

[4] From *Hokum About The Eskimos* by Vilhjalmur Stefansson; copyright Robert M. McBride Co., used by permission of Crown Publishers, Inc. (This appears in Roberts, Rand, and Tardy, *Let's Read.* New York: Henry Holt & Co., 1940, pp. 333–338.)

"The Eskimo suffers from intestinal diseases, malnutrition and scurvy, and his resistance to disease is greatly lowered."

"The ravenous eating of tallow candles and soap by Eskimo children is well attested."

"When the Eskimo boy is thirsty, he drinks oil."

Against this picture stands in my mind my own experience of living more than ten years as an Eskimo among Eskimos. To me it seems that as a race they have more leisure than city dwellers. For instance, some of the geographies mention their ivory carving and ornamental ceremonial dress, but they leave it a mystery how a people under terrific strain for a livelihood find time for such things. My observation has been that in many communities the needed work to provide food, shelter and clothing requires from the Eskimo less than half of our standard eight-hour day. Four hours of work and eight of sleep give him twelve hours of leisure. Accordingly, a man will spend a week carving an ivory handle which he could have made plain in half a day. A woman who could sew a warm coat in two days will spend two months making one not so warm (but in her opinion prettier) by cutting up whole skins and piecing them together in complicated designs. Entire communities spend weeks singing and dancing and listening to story tellers spinning out long tales of adventure with spirits and with men. The winters, so frightful in the textbooks, are their holiday season, spent in carrying out elaborate festivities.

Most of the textbooks say or imply that most or all Eskimos live in snow or ice houses in winter. This is geographical hodgepodge. No Eskimos live in ice houses, or at least I never heard of it. Some live in snow houses, but more than half the Eskimos in the world have never seen them. . . . Many Eskimos live in houses built of earth and wood, or with bone rafters and walls of stone or earth.

The case is worse about the use of oil. . . . Physiology teaches that thirst is quenched only by water, and chemistry that there is in oil no water which the human stomach is capable of extracting. The Eskimo stomach is similar to your stomach. If you think he drinks oil for any reason, I would suggest that you take about a water tumbler of whatever oil you prefer. If you have a strong will you may be able to get it down, but the chances are three in four that you will not be able to keep it down. If you are the one in four who can keep it down, you will very soon wish that you weren't.

The truth is that Eskimos use oil with their food, as we do salad oil or gravy. They eat it but they don't drink it, and, therefore, instead of being weird monstrosities, they are just like us in this respect, as they are in most fundamental human things. . . .

That Eskimo children eat soap is ridiculous on the face of it. I have never seen Eskimos eat candles, nor heard of a case. But if they did eat tallow candles it would be no stranger than the eating of tallow in any other form. Tallow is only suet, and many a well ordered meal in our country still includes suet pudding.

As for the "deficiency diseases and scurvy," the Eskimos are, as far as we know, free from them so long as they live on their own accustomed diets. Once they begin to live on white men's groceries and neglect to secure fresh meat, these diseases grow. Dr. William A. Thomas, of Chicago, found in Labrador, for instance, that the Eskimos who suffered most were those nearest the trading stations and supplied with white men's food. In sections beyond the reach of the traders, or little affected by them, the deficiency troubles vanished. . . .

To balance all these unfavorable truths about the northern half of Canada, I have been able to discover in the school texts one—and only one—favorable mistake. A geography says, "Mosquitoes are found all over the North American continent except in the extreme north." Anyone who has been there will tell you that the contrary is the fact. Until you approach the Arctic you do not know how bad mosquitoes can be.

FREEDOM'S BACK IS AGAINST THE WALL!

by

Dorothy Thompson [5]

It is more than twenty years since I sat where you are sitting this morning. The year of my own graduation was a portentous year; a fateful and fatal year. It was 1914. Hardly was I out of college when the World War broke out, and from that day to this the world has never been remotely the same place that it was before.

I suppose that I have been asked to speak to you this morning, because I have lived those twenty odd years more intensively, perhaps, than most people. It has been given to me to live in many parts of the world, to see many of the events of my times—my times, which are also yours, for there is no break in the continuity of history, no real break. One may say, as I have just said: In 1914 the World War broke out, and since then nothing has been the same. But the World War was only the crystallization of what had been done up to that time. Wise men saw its shadow darkening the world long before the first shot was fired. And out of the war, directly out of the war, opened other phases of history, quite logically, although never inevitably. It is customary now to say that the generation of 1914 was "fated." Some people have said it was "lost." But the generation of 1937 is no less fated, and whether or not it will be lost depends upon you.

. . . You are born and you come of age as Americans, citizens of a country which spans a continent, which stretches between two oceans.

. . . And yet, when all that is said, when so much is acknowledged, what does it mean to be an American, a young American?

---

[5] Dorothy Thompson, "Freedom's Back Is Against the Wall!" *Vital Speeches* (July 1, 1937), 3: 546–551.

. . . Your generation will have to ask yourselves that question more earnestly than any generation before you. Because the values, the beliefs, the myths, if you wish to use that word, upon which this country was founded are being challenged in the world today, as they have never been since this nation was founded. You are going to have to ask yourselves: Are those values, beliefs, and myths exhausted? Must we find totally different ones? Or is there, still in them, the stuff out of which to make a great culture and a great civilization?

What is the fundamental thing in the American idea? What is it that Americans, in past generations, have loved? Is it prosperity? Is it security? Is it the welfare of the masses? What is the American quality? Is it obedience? Is it subservience?

On the Plymouth Rock monument in Massachusetts these words are inscribed:

. . . "They laid the foundation of a state wherein every man through countless ages should have liberty." And when they laid down the principles to govern that state, in the Declaration of Independence, men who came many years after them said: "We hold these truths to be self-evident; that all men are created free."

. . . The love of freedom is the American quality, and independence is the American virtue.

. . . But the areas of the earth where men and women may be free in their consciences, in their work, in their religion, in their ideals, become narrower and narrower.

. . . It is into this world, a world where freedom has her back against the wall, that you graduates of 1937 go out. And it is your generation, and the generations that follow you, who will have to decide: first, whether freedom is worth the price, and second, what in terms of the modern world, freedom is.

. . . Others will tell you, perhaps, that the issue in the world today is between fascism and communism or socialism. But I shall tell you that I believe that the issue in the world is between freedom and slavery. I know that the economic system under which we live will undergo vast changes. It has undergone tremendous changes in my lifetime. Never from me will you hear that the period of our history from the Civil War to the Great War was a golden age unsullied by greed, injustice, plunder. I am profoundly dissatisfied with the world as it is. All of my adult life has been lived in revolutions. I have lived in Russia under communism; in Germany under the social republic and under Hitler; in Austria under a socialist republic and under Catholic fascism. I do not believe that the revolutions which have shaken the world in my generation happened without cause, or were merely the machinations of evil men. In Russia men sought to escape the tyranny of the Tsar. In Germany they sought, first to escape the tyranny of war, and then to escape the tyranny of chaos. In Austria peasants revolted against the tyranny of a politically powerful city proletariat. And all of these countries fastened upon themselves, in their revolt, new tyrannies, the tyrannies of all-powerful, all-controlled states.

When this country was founded the world was in revolt against the all-powerful state. Our revolution was followed by the French Revolution, whose object, like ours, was to take power away from the crown and vest it directly in the people. But today the world is in revolt against freedom, and knowing no other course, is returning the power to the crown, or to some modern symbol of it, whether he call himself president, or king, or dictator, or popular leader. And the reason why the world is in revolt against freedom is because freedom has been abused.

In the name of freedom our hills have been stripped of their forests, forests which draw the water from the air and hold the soil on the earth. In the name of freedom people have been drawn here by false promises of gold in the streets, to work and sweat in mines, treated like peons. In the name of freedom we imported black slaves to work for free men, and fought a war to set them free to starve. And today, generations after that war, the whole South is still in poverty, settled by an agricultural proletariat, black and white, which lives in many places below the material and cultural level of the Balkans. In the name of freedom part of the press has been given over to a debauch of sex and crime. In the name of freedom powerful industries have ruthlessly crushed smaller competitors, and men's labor has been treated as a mere commodity.

The revolt against freedom is a revolt against anarchy. Freedom has produced, men say, wealth, but it has not produced a good society. It has made fortunes for some, and poverty for many. It has wasted our resources in material and in men. It has turned us into a nation of speculators. Thus goes the case against freedom.

But it is freedom itself which has produced the revolt! We rebel against poverty because free enterprise, and the free enquiring mind, modern science, plus technology, both of them products of the free mind, have led us to believe that poverty might and could be eliminated. Do you think that greed alone was the motive power that subdued a continent, netted it with railroads, dragged iron from the ground, spun it into steel, and shot it sheer fifty stories into the air to support thousands of tons of stone and masonry? Did greed alone wipe out yellow fever and smallpox and diptheria? Was it the profit motive and that alone that caught fire from heaven to imprison light on a tungsten thread or harnessed the waves of the ether to propel sound, or caught a voice on a disk of rubber, or shot tons of metal in swift ships through the air, or dissolved trees into silk stockings and velvets?

No, it was not greed. It was the human mind, restless, inventive, searching, untrammeled, taught to respect truth, believing in itself, creative, searching, and free.

. . . Your problem, the problem of your generation, is to find some way of reconciling freedom with order; of keeping the creative powers of the free personality and harmonizing them with the collective life which science and technology have made inevitable. Your problem is to find some substitute for the ideal of self-interest, which is compatible with human freedom.

. . . What do we mean by freedom?   What has it meant in the past, and what does it mean today?

It is based first of all, upon a conception of people.   It affirms that men and women are creatures of will, capable of choice, and capable of reason.   Without the belief in reason, there could obviously be no justifiable democracy, no self-government, and no freedom.   The basic conception of freedom is in the dignity and inviolability of the personality, in the belief, if you want to put it in religious terms, that man is made in the image of God.

. . . For freedom has a corollary.   Its corollary is responsibility.   The free human being is the responsible human being.   A free society must be a responsible society.

. . . Either man will set himself a model, toward which to aspire, or he will be pressed, eventually into a model to which to conform.

Freedom is threatened in this nation today because too many people have forgotten that freedom has a price, the price of responsible action. Prophets are abroad amongst us, teaching that work is in some way incompatible with freedom; that leisure is synonymous with it.   But if we can find nothing better to do with freedom than to vegetate and gape at motion pictures, why preserve it at all?   We want freedom as plants want air; in order to grow in it.   And our growth as free personalities is in direct proportion to the demands that we make, not upon society, but upon ourselves.   In all great civilizations great numbers of men have lived, not with the least possible effort, but actually beyond their physical, mental, and spiritual means.   Thus they lived in the Athens of Pericles; thus they lived in the Renaissance; and thus we shall live one day, I hope, in the United States of America.   The Grecian urn described by Keats; the cathedrals of Cologne and Chartres and Exeter, the palaces of Venice, were not built by workmen whose chief concern was shorter hours and longer wages.   They were built by men, from the commonest workman to the lord above him, whose concern was perfection, and who, through his own love of perfection, knew that he was contributing to a great society.

And in this country today are thousands of people, who against all the tendencies of the times cherish that old ideal.   They are the scientists, toiling late, seeking eternally for some little shred of truth to add to the great body of truth.   They are the artists, who sacrifice what most men hold most dear, to create a single perfect sentence of poetry, or a single perfect line.   They are the workmen, deferent to materials, proud in accomplishment.   They are the mothers, devoted, self-sacrificing, wise. They are the teachers, staying after hours, struggling to pull through and pull up some recalcitrant child.   And they are leaders, in any free society.   For they do not invest themselves with power, but with responsibility, and society itself invests them with its appreciation and its love.

There is a measure by which you may judge the good or the evil of almost any social program: Does it invite you to live below the level of your own capacities? . . . You have but one gift: the gift of life; you have but one right; the right to live it through, to its fullest, and to its highest.

. . . You go out into a world where the free mind of man has mastered nature, but in the struggle has forgotten somewhat man himself. Our generation added greatly to man's mastery over the earth, the sea, and the air. Your generation may push ahead the greater and more eternal task: Man's mastery over himself, and his own conduct.

I welcome you to participation in this high adventure.

CONCRETE VERSUS ABSTRACT SYMBOLS IN UNDERSTANDING

One of the most obvious differences between the two foregoing selections is that the words in the former represent more concrete things and occurrences than do the words in the latter. For most people such nouns as *Eskimo, oil, soap, Canada, candles, meat, climate, stations, bone, disease, earth, skins, carvings, coat,* and *mosquitoes* carry more specific meanings than *freedom, world, event, war, citizen, American, generation, values, beliefs, liberty, quality, religion, issue, fascism, slavery, communism,* and *order.* Such words as *different, intestinal, ravenous, tallow, city, ivory, ornamental, warm, prettier, whole, complicated, holiday, elaborate, ice, snow, bone, fresh,* and *trading* make meanings more definite than *free, greater, more, eternal, social, perfect, mental, spiritual, human, creative, searching, inventive,* and *untrammeled.* On the one hand we are dealing mainly with the concrete symbols that stand for real, actual, material things, which can be handled and touched. On the other hand, we are concerned with abstract symbols which stand for attributes of things, qualities derived from things, and general rather than specific ideas.

Since the usual purpose of language is to stir up precise meanings, and since meanings evoked by concrete symbols are usually more precise than those suggested by abstract symbols, the question arises, Should students be taught to use concrete rather than abstract language? The answer might be in the affirmative, if no student ever wanted to present an abstract idea! Our illustrations show that the point Stefansson wanted to make was concrete, while the point Thompson wanted to make was abstract. Both were unusually successful, and teachers must expect from their students the same variety of purposes and they must prepare their students to meet needs for the use of both concrete and abstract language. But they must remember that there is greater danger of misunderstanding in the latter than there is in the former.

Vocabulary training, enriching experiences by reading, visual aids, travel, conferences, interviews, and direct concentration on understanding and verbalizing abstract concepts become necessities in successful teaching. The task of helping students to understand and use both concrete and abstract symbols rests upon every teacher. The speech teacher should assume, however, special responsibility for finding real situations in which both types of symbols will function in developing clear, vivid, and precise meanings.

COMPARISON OF THE MEANINGS FOR DIFFERENT STUDENTS

Dorothy Thompson mentions World War I early in her speech. Since meanings are found in people as a result of their experiences it will not be difficult for the speech teacher to help boys and girls to understand why language symbols stir up radically different meanings for different people. The following are thoughts which might quite reasonably have come to the minds of members of Miss Thompson's audience:

"My father is small because he was a war baby. My grandmother died of starvation just after he was born. I'm glad my dad came to America."

"My grandfather has a gun he used in the first World War. He won't let me use it but I wish he would."

"My uncle was on a boat that was torpedoed off the coast of Ireland during World War I. I like to hear him tell about how they took to a life boat in rough waters."

"Who fought in World War I? When was that war? What did they fight about?"

Class discussion may reveal startling differences in the meanings different students derive from the selection, *Hokum About The Eskimos.* The words, while definite in denotation, may call up surprising connotations. For one person, the word "Eskimo" means an Eskimo girl who talked in high school; for another, a hero in a moving picture; for still another, a picture from *The National*

Geographic Magazine. The fact that words are symbols which re-call what different people have experienced, rather than things per se, makes this process of communication exceedingly difficult. Before language codes were established, when communication was accom-plished through the use of objects rather than the names of objects, there was less chance of misunderstanding. Nevertheless, the proc-ess of comparing the variant personal meanings of language symbols, which have resulted from differences in the experiences stored up in the minds of the students in an average high school class, is a valuable exercise in understanding.

THE CHANGING MEANINGS OF WORDS

Boys and girls will enjoy considering how the meanings of sym-bols change. They read, "We hold these truths to be self-evident; that all men are created free," as recorded on Plymouth Rock in Massachusetts and referred to in "Freedom's Back is Against the Wall." One girl sees the rock in her mind's eye, because she has stood near the inscription and thrilled as she read it; for her Dorothy Thompson's speech recalls that feeling. Then she learns that one of her classmates does not consider America to be free. Her family was refused housing in a restricted neighborhood. She was snubbed at a school dance. After hearing about her experi-ences, although the word "free" sounds the same, it has a different meaning for the first student, and all through the class period the word's meaning continues to change with every comment, as it will for all symbols through her entire life. In attempting to use lan-guage effectively we must take into consideration the shifting and enlarging of meanings. Examples can be selected from the written article and speech given here or from many other sources. Students can demonstrate how meaning is never static, and how this fact complicates communication by language symbols.

CONSIDER CONTEXT IN GETTING MEANINGS

Dorothy Thompson says, "Freedom has made fortunes for some, and poverty for many." Some reader may use this statement as evidence that Miss Thompson opposes freedom. He does not quote her completely enough. He should go on to discover that she is advocating *freedom with order*, and not the abolition of freedom. Again, someone uses her speech to prove that teaching is a dull, thankless job, by quoting, ". . . teachers, staying after hours, struggling to pull through and pull up some recalcitrant child," but fails to add that the author places the teacher with the "leaders, in any free society." A student who wants to show that life in the Arctic is unpleasant and uncomfortable, implies that Stefansson found it so by quoting, "Until you approach the Arctic you do not know how bad mosquitoes can be." However, taken in its full context, the impression which Stefansson gives of the Arctic is very favorable rather than unfavorable.

UNDERSTANDING AND ETHICS

When we see how easily misunderstandings can result from the use of language, we are impressed with the importance of avoiding unnecessary misunderstandings. Some people go so far as to say that not all students should be trained in the use of language, because it is so powerful in influencing others; they contend that only good people should have such skill. They cite the unscrupulous propaganda of politicians, the fraud of smooth-tongued salesmen, and the dishonest promises of ranting dictators, and point out that the world would be better today if such individuals had never learned the techniques of moving listeners through language and speech.

The speech teacher, therefore, with all the other teachers in the school, must concern himself with the purposes, ideals, and moral standards of his students. Like Quintilian he must make every effort to train "the good man" in speaking. He must be alert to every evidence of satisfaction derived from stirring up intentional misunderstandings by means of speech symbols and, somehow, effect a change in the attitude of those who thus prostitute the high art of communication.

MASTER CHARACTERISTICS OF ORAL LANGUAGE

Earlier in this chapter we pointed out the *reasons* for differences between good language for writing and good language for speaking. After that, we dwelt in some detail on certain characteristics common to both. After such consideration, the speech teacher will do well to help students to master certain specific characteristics of good oral language.

The famous quotation from Owen Wister's *The Virginian*, "When you say that smile," illustrates the importance of taking into consideration the sound of the voice and the expression of the body, in determining the meaning of spoken language. From the standpoint of the speaker, oral language must be integrated with voice and action as it is created, and, from the standpoint of the audience, these combined elements of speech must be interpreted in getting meanings. In addition to the importance of recognizing that voice and action are represented in the full effect of oral language, the words and sentences themselves differ when differently presented to the eye and to the ear. Dorothy Thompson makes use of all of the known qualities of oral style in "Freedom's Back is Against the Wall." Perhaps some speech teachers will carry on research to add to the following list of known differences.

Good Oral Language is Adapted to the Speaker

Students will be interested in finding how this speech fits the speaker. Seven times Miss Thompson refers to herself so specifically that no other person could appropriately deliver her speech. That is good oral technique.

Good Oral Language is Adapted to the Audience

Ten times we find references to the particular audience, the 1937 graduates who are getting ready to find a place in the world. Successful speakers use such references to make each member of the audience feel that the speech is for him.

Good Oral Language is Adapted to the Occasion

At the very outset Miss Thompson refers to the occasion twice and, at the end, once more reminds her listeners that they are about to find their places in the world. A good speech is prepared for a specific occasion, and an examination of speeches composed by recognized authorities shows that they contain numerous special references to time and place.

Good Oral Language Has Variety in Sentence Length

In the first ten sentences of her speech, Miss Thompson uses 208 words, an average of 21 words per sentence. No single sentence is exactly 21 words long, however; they contain 15, 15, 3, 31, 27, 42, 23, 17, 15, and 20 words respectively. Good speakers realize that, just as change in the use of action and voice gets and keeps the attention of an audience, so change in sentence length helps to achieve the same result. Spoken sentences should not, on the average, be shorter or longer than written sentences, but *the variation in sentence length should be more marked in oral language.*

Good Oral Language Has Variety in Kinds of Sentences

Dorothy Thompson uses numerous questions in the part of her speech quoted in this chapter—nineteen questions, as well as commands and exclamations. The title is an exclamation! In written style, declarative sentences predominate, but in good oral style interrogative, exclamatory, and imperative sentences are numerous, and give life and interest to a speech. The teacher should help boys and girls to use this device which is employed by successful speakers.

Good Oral Language Uses Numerous Personal Pronouns of the First Person Singular and Plural, and of the Second Person Plural

In the excerpt of her speech quoted on pages 200–204, Dorothy Thompson uses pronouns of the first person singular (I, me, my, mine) twenty-two times; pronouns of the first person plural (we, our, us) nineteen times; and pronouns of the second person plural (you, your, yourselves) thirty-two times. One way to get the effect of talking directly to an audience is to use pronouns as they occur in direct conversation.

Repetition is Frequent in Good Oral Language

If a listener misses some essential meaning in a speech or in conversation, he has no way of retrieving it as a reader may by rereading the language. Therefore, a good speaker watches his listeners and repeats ideas which obviously may not be clear in the first presentation. Students will be interested to analyze "Freedom's

Back is Against the Wall!" for repetition in the same words, in slightly different words, by illustration, and by comparison. The speaker makes her points clear by restating them to her audience several times, in a variety of ways to avoid monotony. Lincoln was famous for the skillful way he repeated his ideas with stories. He was aware that to state the idea once was not enough, but he was also aware that to repeat it over and over in the same words was dull and ineffective. His storytelling method held attention, and fixed his ideas in people's minds in a disarming fashion.

DEVELOP LANGUAGE SKILLS BY DISCUSSING THE SPEAKER'S PROBLEMS AND RESULTS

A skillful teacher will first guide his students to *want* to improve language in order to solve some specific vital problem. He will then use the materials in this book to illustrate principles, but will find for his own classes other examples which will fit his students and his community more directly. Thus, his class will find how, with voice and action, language contributes to a total process—speech.

SELECTED BIBLIOGRAPHY

Aristotle, *Rhetorica*. Translation by W. Rhys Roberts. New York: Oxford University Press, 1924, pp. 1413a–1414a.

Baird, A. Craig, *Representative American Speeches*. New York: H. W. Wilson Company, 1937–38; 1949–51.

Baird, A. Craig, and Franklin H. Knower, *General Speech*. New York: McGraw-Hill Book Co., 1949, Ch. X.

Blumenthal, Joseph C., "Without Form and Void," *English Journal* (September, 1946), 35: 376–380.

Borchers, Gladys L., "An Approach to Oral Style," *Quarterly Journal of Speech* (February, 1936), 114–117.

Borchers, Gladys L., and Claude M. Wise, *Modern Speech*. New York: Harcourt, Brace & Co., 1947, Chs. VII and IX.

Brigance, W. Norwood, *Speech Composition*. New York: Appleton-Century-Crofts, Inc., 1937, Ch. VI.

Chase, Stuart, *The Tyranny of Words*. New York: Harcourt, Brace & Co., 1938.

Cooper, Lane, *Theories of Style*. New York: The Macmillan Co., 1907.

Crocker, Lionel, *Public Speaking for College Students*. New York: American Book Company, 1941, Ch. XVII.

Flesch, Rudolph, *The Art of Plain Talk*. New York: Harper & Brothers, 1946.

———, *The Art of Readable Writing*. New York: Harper & Brothers, 1949.

Gilmartin, John, *Building Your Vocabulary*. New York: Prentice-Hall, Inc., 1941.

Goldberg, Isaac, *The Wonder of Words*. New York: Appleton-Century-Crofts, Inc., 1938.

Hart, Archibald, *Twelve Ways to Build a Vocabulary*. New York: E. P. Dutton & Co., Inc., 1939.

Hayakawa, S. I., *Language in Action*, New York: Harcourt, Brace & Co., 1941.

Hook, J. N., *The Teaching of High School English*. New York: The Ronald Press, 1950, Ch. 9.

Johnson, Wendell, *People in Quandaries*. New York: Harper & Brothers, 1946.

La Brant, Lou, *We Teach English*. New York: Harcourt, Brace & Co., 1951. pp. 3–90, 202–224.

Lee, Irving J., *The Language of Wisdom and Folly*. New York: Harper & Brothers, 1949.

Lee, Irving J., *Habits in Human Affairs*. New York: Harper & Brothers, 1941.

Ogden, C. K., and I. A. Richards, *The Meaning of Meaning*. New York: Harcourt, Brace & Co., 1936.

Progressive Education Association, *Language in General Education*. New York: Appleton-Century-Crofts, Inc., 1940.

Sarett, Lew, and William T. Foster, *Basic Principles of Speech*. Boston: Houghton Mifflin Co., 1946.

Sarett, Lew, William T. Foster, and J. T. McBurney, *Speech: A High School Course*. Boston: Houghton Mifflin Co., 1947.

Thonssen, Lester, and Howard Gilkinson, *Basic Training in Speech*. Boston: D. C. Heath & Company, 1947, Ch. 12.

Weaver, Andrew T., *Speech: Forms and Principles*. New York: Longmans, Green & Co., Inc., 1951.

Weaver, Andrew T., and Gladys L. Borchers, *Speech*. New York: Harcourt, Brace & Co., 1946.

Winans, James A., *Speech Making*. New York: Appleton-Century-Crofts, Inc., 1938, Chapter IX.

Witty, Paul, "Some Suggestions for Vocabulary Development in the Public Schools," *Educational Administration and Supervision* (May, 1945), 31: 271–282.

Woolbert, C. H., "Speaking and Writing: A Study of Differences," *Quarterly Journal of Speech* (1922), 8: 271–285.

CHAPTER 9

Developing Meanings

INTRODUCTION

EVERY high school teacher who aims to improve the speech of boys and girls must concern himself with meanings, a vital element of every speech activity. He must recognize the fact that all types of speech are effective only when the speaker has something worth while to say. In conversation, formal or informal, an individual is happy and makes others happy only when he can contribute something interesting. In public speaking, discussion, or debate, the facts, arguments, reasoning, and authorities must be well selected, apt, and honest. In reading, storytelling, and acting the literature must be of high quality and worthy of the audience.

CHARACTERISTICS OF ACCEPTABLE SUBJECT MATTER

Subject matter should be sufficiently meaningful to challenge the audience. School administrators sometimes have raised questions about the quality of what students discuss in speech classes. We have all been concerned about what men and women discuss outside of speech classes. In both instances, the concern has arisen from two possible causes: Either (1) what is said gives the impression that the speaker does not possess sufficient integrity to present only material which he has investigated carefully to make sure it is as near the truth as it is possible for him to get, or (b) what is said is so superficial, so empty, so trite, and so lacking in substance that it reflects on the intelligence of the listeners.

The quality of what is said has always been the concern of speech teachers. Quintilian's insistence that a person must be a "good man" in order to be an effective speaker is still sound advice, because usually when a person *is* honest, he *appears* honest. If he is honest, he will seek out honest material, well supported by sound reasoning and recognized authorities. He will appreciate the ability and training of his listeners and aim to select material which will challenge their thinking and carry them a little ahead of where they are.

THE SPEECH TEACHER'S RESPONSIBILITY FOR SUBJECT MATTER

Every speech teacher must decide for himself what degree of responsibility he is to assume for the subject matter which his students present. If he is wise, he will base his decision on careful investigation and consideration. For thousands of years this question has been a controversial one. Some authorities have taken the stand that, since *what* a speaker says is fully as important as *how* he says it, the speech teacher should assume complete responsibility for all the subject matter used by his students. The advocates of this viewpoint have written, compiled, and recommended books containing materials to read and talk about in speech classes. They devote a large share of the class time to the study of such materials. Some even go so far as to suggest teaching subject matter alone and ignoring the teaching of delivery entirely. Many have contended that if a speaker really has something to say he can say it effectively.

Other authorities, who can cite numerous well-informed speakers who because of their ineffective use of body, voice, and language are unable to make their audiences feel that they *are* well informed, are not willing to leave delivery to chance. They do not believe that the speech teacher is, or can be, trained to direct students in their treatment of all kinds of subject matter. Many of them recall instances when high school students have given superior speeches on atomic energy, airplanes, interior decorating, cooking, or travel; have read from newly created literature; or have acted in excellent plays unfamiliar to the teacher, because they were encouraged to make use of all the sources of subject matter in the community. Such speech teachers insist that all speech subject matter should be worth-while, but do not undertake to direct the acquiring of subject matter. They try to guide students always to the best sources of worth while subject matter in each field. Such teachers follow Max Mason's advice to emulate Professor Michelson who said to his students, "These are *our* problems, these are *our* desks. I look to you."

SOME SUBJECT MATTER BELONGS TO THE SPEECH FIELD

If a student wishes to give a talk on how voice is produced, he should find the speech teacher well prepared to evaluate his subject matter. If he wants to talk on how a panel discussion should be conducted, or the differences between discussion and debate, he probably will do well to consider his speech teacher an authority on the material. If he wants to explain to the class how to prepare literature for oral reading, his speech teacher will be a good guide. But if he wants to talk on the history of the League of Nations or the San Francisco Conference, he usually will be wiser to look to the history or social studies teacher as an authority. If he is to report on the natural resources of a section of his country, his geography teacher may give him the most help in finding and evaluating his subject matter. The assignment of a talk on music or art should no doubt lead the prospective speaker to the music expert or the art expert. The fact that *any* and all subjects may be selected for discussion in the speech class does not mean that every idea should originate there, any more than the fact that speech is used in every class means that every teacher should go through all of the steps of improving speech habits. The well-prepared speech teacher should see his contribution in relation to the school, the home, and the community, and he should help to familiarize his students with all of the well-informed authorities available to them. He should be an authority, when experience and training make him an authority, but he should not limit the subject matter of his students to what he himself has mastered. There are no restrictions on the sources of subject matter, and the speech teacher need make no apology for the fact that he is not an authority in all areas of human knowledge. It is better for him to become an authority on the subject matter of speech and then help students discover superior authorities in other areas. It has often been said that the test of an educated person is not what information he can quote, but rather what he is able to locate.

TYPES OF SUBJECT MATTER FOR SPEECH

What speakers say can be classified roughly under two categories: (1) Materials gathered, organized, and phrased by the speaker; and (2) materials presented as phrased by someone else. The first materials are used in conversation, public speaking, discussion, debate, and in original stories, poems, and plays; the second, in oral reading, storytelling and the acting of dramatic literature.

HOW TO HELP STUDENTS RECOGNIZE
WORTH-WHILE IDEAS

The first and best place for high school students to find material for creative speaking is their own minds. It is gratifying to learn how well-informed teen-aged boys and girls often are. It is a common experience for a teacher to hear adolescents talk about a great variety of subjects with considerable understanding. Many times, however, students themselves do not realize that what they are prepared to talk about may be more interesting to others than are some more remote subjects. Explaining how to take care of a dog usually will be more entertaining in conversation than discussing how to take care of a monkey, especially if one knows precise details from first-hand experience in the one case and is forced to depend on reading and second-hand information in the other. There are numerous examples of writers who left their homes to search for materials for stories, novels, and plays and were unsuccessful as authors until they returned to familiar regions and wrote about what they understood well. It is the teacher's responsibility so to motivate his students that they will find in their immediate surroundings varied and worth-while speech content.

Boys and girls not only fail to realize that pastures are just as green in the home region as they are in a foreign country, but also at times intentionally conceal their greatest assets. Two students will let the same background be for one an asset, and for the other a liability. When Hugh Walpole, in his novel *Fortitude*, developed the thesis, "It isn't life that matters. It's the courage you bring to it," he had in mind that it is not the circumstances of one's life that make happiness or tragedy, it is the way the individual acts in those circumstances which makes all the difference.

One girl may be ashamed that her parents are of foreign birth; she will blush over their accents, urge her mother to prepare American food, and overemphasize American ways. Another girl of similar parentage will try to become familiar with two languages and understand the sound systems of each, and will encourage her mother to prepare and serve foreign foods in just the way it is done in Italy, Russia, Norway, or Germany. In the first case, both daughter and parents will become increasingly insecure, apologetic, and dull, while in the second they will broaden their horizons, gain confidence, and have interesting and original things to talk about.

Two boys have fathers who support their families by grueling work in factories, with little hope for advancement. One boy tries to forget about his father's employment and never mentions it to his classmates. The other learns about his father's problems, the attitudes of the workers toward the factory owners, the arguments for and against piece work, why unions were organized, the history of strikes to increase wages, and then uses this material effectively not only in conversation but in class reports and discussions.

Two girls drive in from farms to attend high school. Both help with chores before and after school. One thinks of farmers as ignorant and crude "hicks," does her farm work hurriedly, and talks at school about the sophisticated city where she hopes to live in the future. The other interests herself in the creative and scientific aspects of farming. She finds material for all her classes in her home environment. She discusses soil conservation, tests milk, paints a barnyard scene, reads Robert Frost, Mark Twain, and Louis Bromfield, and models an original poem after Coffin's *Winter Milking.*

Two boys are Negroes. One never mentions his race and does not encourage his associates to do so; the other, when the class is discussing housing, volunteers information on life in "restricted areas." He demonstrates the beauty of Negro spirituals, reads orations by Frederick Douglas and Booker T. Washington, and proudly introduces his mother, who accompanies him to class and tells Negro folk tales to his school mates.

In one school a resourceful teacher has assembled one of the world's finest collections of costumes for high school plays because it was her good fortune to get her first position in a foreign district. After a P.-T.A. meeting at which she was introduced to Bohemians,

Italians, Russians, Scandinavians, Germans, Japanese, Chinese, and Mexicans, she proposed to her students that their mothers might help in costuming the next play. The response was gratifying; the costumes were authentic, and the needlework was beautifully done. Over the years practically every nation has come to be represented in the costume wardrobe. The collection has gained wide fame. More important, however, than the costumes (now insured for thousands of dollars), has been the subject matter for speeches discovered by students and their families because one teacher saw the advantages to be derived from bringing together first generation Americans in a co-operative speech enterprise.

HOW TO UTILIZE MATERIAL FROM THE ENTIRE SCHOOL

In every high school there are experts in various subjects who direct students in areas other than speech. All of these may be helpful in speech activities; their judgment can be utilized in the evaluation of subject matter and in insuring desirable integration throughout the school. Thus every other class may contribute to the success of the speech class and the speech class to the success of every other class. Moreover, both the delivery and the content of speeches will be watched over by trained supervisors. Excursions to public exhibits, lectures, or social gatherings, whether under the sponsorship of the speech class or any other class in the high school, provide first-hand information which can be used in conversation, public speaking, discussion, and debate, or in creation of original literature.

HOW TO USE LIBRARIES

The thrill of discovery, so intriguing to all mankind, may motivate a thorough understanding of how to find information in a library. In most high schools the librarian is pleased to be invited to teach units on where to find books, magazine articles, newspapers, encyclopaedia references, publications of special commissions, photostats, recordings of music and speech, and moving pictures. Such units will familiarize students with the sort of materials most likely to be located in the card catalog, Poole's Index, the Reader's Guide, the Dictionary, Encyclopaedias, Almanacs, and documents.

In some cities there are public libraries which serve different groups, Agricultural, Engineering, Law, Educational, Artistic, and Scientific, and their respective literature is often housed under separate roofs. If a class is working on a problem for which students are eager to get material it will be worth while for the entire class, or for committees, to visit every place where references can be found.

HOW TO USE PERSONAL INTERVIEWS

The teacher of speech will be wise if, very early in the course, he provides training in the use of the personal interview. Such instruction contributes to speech education by giving students practice in making and keeping appointments, approaching strangers to request help, planning questions to acquire information without wasting time, showing appreciation for assistance, and taking leave. All of these activities are by-products of the search for subject matter which is the first consideration of this chapter, but they are essential elements of many speech projects, and no opportunity to offer training in them should be overlooked.

HOW TO TEST AUTHORITIES AND EVIDENCE

"I know that East is a better school than West because our neighbor knows a man who graduated from East and that man now owns a ten million dollar factory in New York State." This is not an unusual argument for a high school student to present in a class discussion before he has learned to evaluate facts, evidence, and opinions. But there is real training involved in dealing effectively with responses like, "Of course your neighbor supports East because he graduated from there," "One case doesn't prove anything," "What do you mean by *better*?" "What proof does your neighbor have that the man *owns* the factory?" "How does he know it's a ten million dollar factory?" "You have to have more facts than that about a school to prove it's a better school," "And, anyway, are you sure your neighbor is telling the truth?" "Maybe he just wants to give the school a good reputation so his house will sell for more. Isn't that a 'For Sale' sign on his house?"

Students quickly learn how to evaluate authorities and evidence. They are able to decide whether an individual is mentally and physically competent to testify, whether he is honest and unprejudiced, and whether he has had opportunity to secure worth-while information. They are challenged to distinguish between facts and opinions, to decide whether a statement is clear and specific, to evaluate documentation, to consider the quantity of proof, to learn the difference between primary and secondary sources, to discover whether facts are consistent with prior and subsequent facts, and to recognize fallacious reasoning and argument.

SELECTING LITERATURE FOR SPEECH ACTIVITIES

"Never substitute anything for your own opinion," an eminent professor said repeatedly to his class in oral interpretation. "Literature is judged by the people, all of the people; therefore you are some of the judges, and you must prepare yourselves to be good judges." One of the responsibilities of the teacher of speech is to help students learn how to select good materials to relate in story form, to read orally, and to present in dramatic productions. Students may be influenced by experts; they may examine long lists of recommended stories, poems, or plays; they may read reviews by literary critics; and they may solicit the opinions of teachers, their parents, and other students; but if they themselves do not make the final evaluations, their teacher will have failed.

Five questions should direct the teacher and the students as they attempt to select worth-while literary materials. (1) Do the characters behave like normal human beings? (2) Will the incidents have universal appeal? (3) Does the language stir up precise meanings? (4) Does repetition enrich the meanings? (5) Is the material appropriate to the speaker, the audience, the occasion?

Do the Characters Behave Like Normal Human Beings?

When Walt Whitman wrote his famous poem celebrating himself, he was writing of all mankind. "In all people I see myself—none more, and not one a barley corn less; and the good or bad I say of myself, I say of them. . . . I do not trouble my spirit to vindicate itself or be understood; I see that the elementary laws never apologize. . . . I exist as I am—that is enough." [1] He be-

---

[1] Walt Whitman, *Leaves of Grass*. New York: Universal Library. Grosset & Dunlap, p. 26.

lieved there was no need to apologize for behaving like a human being with the emotions, the appetites, the urges, the tastes, and the
reactions of normal boys and girls, and men and women. All discussions and solutions of high school problems, in and out of school,
should help with the recognition in literature of plots and characters
which are true to life. If the speech teacher is an opportunist, he
can help students to apply this first test by an understanding of individual behavior problems in and out of school such as: family conflicts, community controversies, international mistrust, wars, and all
other situations in which human beings are trying to live together
and need to understand one another in order to do so. A recognition and acceptance of normal human behavior is not the result of
one project in direct discussion; it is the result of constant application
of an understanding point of view to all the life situations in which
students in a high school participate.

Will the Incidents Have Universal Appeal?

Since all human beings are fundamentally alike, and have always
been so, there are certain emotions, relationships, and incidents which
have appealed and will appeal to everyone.   Great writers recognize
this fact and apply their knowledge in poetry, stories, and plays.
The speech teacher can give his students the opportunity to test
their critical ability by applying this second criterion in selecting
plays for school production, in evaluating movies and stage dramas,
in reviewing books in the school and community libraries, in criticizing stories from magazines and newspapers, and in making estimates
of radio programs.   The aim, of course, is to teach boys and girls
how to handle the tools of criticism.

Does the Language Stir Up Precise Meanings?

If a high school boy is on the football team and sometimes plays
and sometimes sits on the bench waiting to play, he experiences
certain specific feelings.   When an author writes a description of
those feelings and makes it so precise that the boy says, "That's just
right.   That is *exactly* the way *I* feel," language has been used effectively.   It has stirred up subtle and detailed meanings which are a
part of the reader's experiences but which have lain dormant until
words have recalled them. Students will enjoy testing literature
by the quality of its language and by what it does to them; they

soon will be able to bring examples of the appeals to tastes, smells, sounds, sights, feelings, temperatures, and combinations of all which make literature vividly meaningful. At this point it will be well to read once more the quotation from *Swann's Way* on pages 195–197.

Does Repetition Enrich the Meanings?

A teacher reports the following incident illustrating the application of the foregoing criterion. Students in a speech class selected and read aloud literary material. Each selection was evaluated according to standards set up by the group. One test was positive relationship between reading and meaningfulness. Some students urged that a selection is better when it is meaningful at once, but the class finally agreed that if it is rich in ideas at the first reading, and more rich in ideas at each subsequent reading, it is greater literature than when it measures up to either test alone. They finally decided to select two poems of approximately the same length on similar subjects, have them read aloud and discussed at the beginning of the class period each day, and in this way place each on a five-point scale:

Very Poor	Poor	Average	Good	Excellent	Superior

For the first five meetings the class got new meanings from each poem. Later they came to be more bored with one than the other. They decided that neither of the following was poor literature, but that one was better than the other because of its meaning as revealed in repetition.

LINCOLN

On seeing the George Grey Barnard head of Lincoln that was donated to France to repose in the Luxembourg Gallery, Paris.

Edwin Leibfreed

Abraham Lincoln, what's in your eyes,
Hollow and sunken, and deep as the skies?
    The figure of Sorrow, silent and lone,
    Listening for God in the heart of a moan.

Abraham Lincoln, whose was the art
That touched you with humor, though broken of heart?
    Infinite Tenderness furrowed of face,
    Saw humanity's tears to laughter give place.

Abraham Lincoln, what is your thought
Of the woes of the world that Injustice has wrought?
    Though the blood of the profits of Freedom be spilled,
    The thunders of Sinai cannot be stilled.

Abraham Lincoln, what says your soul
Whose gesture, heroic, spans history's scroll?
    That the feet of Devotion with glory be shod,
    Earth's martyrs keep step with the strides of a God.

Abraham Lincoln, why are you sad
When all of Love's world would be smiling and glad?
    The Ages are pallid with deeds of wrong,
    And Brotherhood cries, and the night is long.

Abraham Lincoln, how came your power
Of setting Fate's clock to the stroke of Time's hour?
    In the quiet of prayer, was the world set apart,
    The better to hear the tick of God's heart.

Abraham Lincoln, immortal of fame,
Will Righteousness rule in Democracy's name?
    When the nations strike hands, and in love are made one,
    The shackles will fall, and my work will be done.[2]

OH CAPTAIN! MY CAPTAIN!

Walt Whitman

(Written upon hearing of the assassination of Abraham Lincoln)

1.

Oh Captain! My Captain! our fearful trip is done;
The ship has weather'd every rack, the prize we sought is won;
The port is near, the bells I hear, the people all exulting,
While follow eyes the steady keel, the vessel grim and daring:
        But O Heart! heart! heart!
            O the bleeding drops of red,
                Where on the deck my Captain lies,
                Fallen cold and dead.

2.

Oh Captain! My Captain! rise up and hear the bells;
Rise up—for you the flag is flung—for you the bugle trills;
For you bouquets and ribbon'd wreaths—for you the shores a-crowding;
For you they call, the swaying mass, their eager faces turning:
        Here, Captain! dear father!
            This arm beneath your head;
                It is some dream that on the deck,
                You've fallen cold and dead.

---

[2] From Edwin Leibfreed, *Windows of Gold*. Philadelphia: Dorrance &
Company, 1923.

3.

My Captain does not answer, his lips are pale and still;
My father does not feel my arm, he has no pulse nor will;
The ship is anchor'd safe and sound, its voyage closed and done;
From fearful trip, the victor ship comes in with object won:

> Exult, O shores, and ring, O bells!
> But I, with mournful tread,
>   Walk the deck my Captain lies,
>   Fallen cold and dead.[3]   1865.

Is the Material Adapted to the Speaker, the Audience, and the Occasion?

If high school boys and girls are able to recognize true life situations, universal appeals, precise language, and quality that will grow with repetition, they will be able to find material which will suit any speaker, any audience, and any occasion. Unfortunately, however, only a small part of the literature of the world passes all four of the above tests. Therefore, it is wise to use some materials which seem to suit particular speakers, which will appeal to specific audiences, and which are well adapted to special occasions. One of the great weaknesses of literature used for and by high school students is that, in too many instances, it is selected by adults. They have decided what adolescents should like rather than what they do like. Furthermore, among adult judges there is great disagreement. For example, many teachers and parents believe that the literature which high school students like is overly emotional and melodramatic, while other experts believe that although it may seem so to adult critics, it does not to readers of high school age. These latter experts conclude that high school students should read and play heavy tragedy and extremely emotional material because it is not so close to most young people in real life and therefore they enjoy it more in story and drama. Selecting material appropriate to speakers, audience, and occasion may well be turned over to high school boys and girls. Their teachers should lead them to decide what fits them as speakers and listeners, on all occasions.

---

[3] *Leaves of Grass, op. cit.,* p. 413.

HOW SHALL IDEAS AND LITERATURE BE RECORDED?

Every teacher and every student will find some method of recording ideas and literature which suits him best. Three items always should be included in what is recorded: (1) The name of the topic or selection; (2) the authority or author, and (3) where the material can be located. Many people find cards useful in keeping records; 3 x 5 or 6 x 9 inch cards are easily available. If the student uses one for each topic, selection, or book, he can arrange and re-arrange them without re-writing. It is usually wise to have the topic, authority, and source near the top of the card. If this is done and the cards are filed in a box or an envelope, they can be removed for use without pulling out all of them, since the top can be read easily. However, evaluating different methods of recording makes an interesting problem for teacher and students to work out together.

Files of plays, readings, records, and pictures will be useful in teaching. If materials are alphabetized, and kept in folders or boxes of uniform size, they may be made readily available. The successful speech teacher is always collecting good literature. When he sees plays, reads magazines or novels, and listens to the radio, he has his students in mind and adds to his ever-increasing library of materials.

SUBJECT MATTER AN ELEMENT OF THE TOTAL SPEECH PROCESS

In spite of a separate consideration here of subject matter, meanings are only a part of the total speech process. The teacher with his students concentrates on them in order that they may make the richest possible contribution to every type of speech activity.

SELECTED BIBLIOGRAPHY

Borchers, G. L., and C. M. Wise, *Modern Speech*. New York: Harcourt, Brace & Co., 1947, Ch. VIII.

Gates, Arthur I, Arthur T. Jersild, T. R. McConnell, and Robert C. Challman, *Educational Psychology*. Boston: Houghton Mifflin, 1949, Ch. 13.

Gislason, Haldor, *The Art of Effective Speaking*. New York: D. C. Heath & Co., 1934, Chs. III–IX.

Sarett, Lew, and William Trufant Foster, *Basic Principles of Speech.* Boston: Houghton Mifflin, 1946, Chs. XIII, XIV.

Weaver, Andrew Thomas, *Speech: Forms and Principles.* New York: Longmans, Green & Co., Inc., 1951, Ch. 8.

Winans, James A., *Speech Making.* New York: Appleton-Century-Crofts, Inc., 1938, Chs. III–IV.

CHAPTER 10

Developing Social Adjustments

INTRODUCTION

SPEECH used to be taught almost exclusively as an art. Students practiced to attain control over the specific skills of speaking which conventionally were associated with effective platform speaking and reading. In the last fifty years we have come increasingly to view speech not only as an art, but as a form of human behavior; not only as an act by which a speaker tries to control his environment, but as his most characteristically human response to that environment. We observe a speaker perspiring and trembling before an audience. We note his wandering and evasive eye movements, his rigid body, and his strained or inaudible voice. We observe that, whatever his capacity for clear thinking and orderly verbalization, whatever his desire to elicit responses from his audience, whatever his vision of the way he wants to sound and look, these considerations are secondary to his problem of social adjustment. His speech is symptomatic not so much of what he knows about speaking or language, but of what he *is* as a person; not so much of what he consciously wants, or wants to be, as of the deep-seated patterns of adjustment which govern his behavior.

Some speech teachers regard their primary task as that of helping students to develop better social personalities, or to acquire better patterns of social adjustment. They feel that since much of speech is symptomatic of the speaker's state of adjustment, that the only efficient road to improved speaking is through improved personal adjustments. Other teachers regard the development of better patterns of social adjustment as one of many goals for their class—an important goal which they will try to help students to achieve, along with the study of all the specific skills needed for effective speaking. They feel that some students may develop better social adjustment as they acquire specific skills in speaking effectively.

THE PREVALENCE OF ADJUSTMENT PROBLEMS

Even if, in their classes, speech teachers wanted to ignore any direct attention to problems of social adjustment, it is doubtful that their students would permit them to do so. If the teacher asks his students what they desire to get from the study of speech, he is likely to find that they will indicate, as their first choice, increased poise, or freedom from nervousness, or some other improvement in social adjustment. Gilkinson reports a study of 420 men and women enrolled in a beginning college speech course, in which these students described their reactions to the experiences of addressing their classmates. The following are some of the statements which the students checked as descriptive of their reactions, and the percentage of the total group which selected each statement:

I am in a nervous state of tension before getting up to speak.	70%
It is difficult for me to search my mind calmly for the right word to express my thoughts.	57%
I feel awkward.	46%
Fear of forgetting causes me to jumble my speech at times.	40%
My legs are wobbly.	26%
I am so frightened I scarcely know what I am saying.	9%

Only 6% of these students reported that speaking in public was "a pleasurable experience unaccompanied by any doubts or fears." [1]

Social fears are extraordinarily common, so much so that some degree of tension should be considered a normal state for a speaker under the pressures of a public speaking situation. But students for whom such fears are exaggerated find them debilitating in their effects on speaking skill.

---

[1] Cited in Lester Thonssen and Howard Gilkinson, *Basic Training in Speech.* Boston: D. C. Heath & Company, 1947.

Students are conscious of their adjustment problems, when these problems lead to feelings of fear. Such feelings are unpleasant for the speaker, and are easily identified by him. The speaker usually does not have much insight into the problem of adjustment which underlies these fears, but he realizes that he does have a problem. However, speakers face problems of adjustment other than those involving fear of speaking. Students who want to talk all the time may cause their listeners considerable anguish, while producing nothing but pleasurable sensations in their own nervous systems. Students who are uncommonly dogmatic in their modes of statement, or superior in their attitudes, may arouse reactions in their listeners quite different from the evaluations they place on their own behavior. In some ways their problems of social adjustment are aggravated by the fact that they have no conscious awareness that they have such problems.

"SOCIAL ADJUSTMENT" AS A GOAL OF SPEECH TRAINING

Speech teachers who list "improved social adjustment" as one of the goals of their instruction are dealing with a concept so slippery that they ought to spend some time in worrying about its meaning.

As we see it, the speech teacher will find it useful to observe that a student's capacity for social adjustment depends upon both the specific skills the student brings to social situations and his habitual reactions to them. Thus, a student may appear awkward or ill-at-ease at a party, because he does not know how to meet strangers, or to introduce strangers to one another; or he may appear rude at times because he fails to observe the requirements of a situation more formal than those to which he is accustomed. These failures involve shortcomings in specific speaking skills. However, another student may know what should be done in a social situation, but appear awkward, or ill-at-ease because of his habitual, negative emotional reactions to such situations. He may appear rude in an effort to control or compensate for his fear of other persons. He appears to lack skill in speaking as a result of his unfortunate emotional reactions to his speaking problems.

This chapter is primarily concerned with the problem of how students may be helped to develop more effective reaction patterns to speaking situations. The skills requisite to effective social adjustment are simply those of speech generally. They are dealt with in other chapters. In talking of the reactions of students to speaking situations, we also shall consider the attitudes students take toward speech. The habitual reaction patterns of students are in constant interaction with their attitudes. Thus, a student who is nervous or tense in speaking usually dislikes speaking activities. A student's attitudes toward his fellow students influence his pattern of reaction to them. A student's attitudes toward himself also will affect his reactions to the problem of speaking to other persons.

INEFFECTIVE PATTERNS OF SOCIAL ADJUSTMENT

The Pattern of Withdrawal

Because of the extraordinary variety of speaking situations, most persons develop patterns of withdrawal or avoidance for some of them, or to some extent, for all of them. Indeed, withdrawal is an effective adjustment to some situations. Good speakers may avoid an argument, if it seems unlikely to be productive of pleasure or value.

The speech teacher observes the student primarily in his reactions to the learning activities of the school room, or to the specific speaking activities of the school. In these situations he may find a considerable number of students practicing habits of withdrawal, at times when withdrawal is inappropriate. Most of these students are not seriously maladjusted. The girl who limits her classroom verbal activity to an occasional monosyllable, reluctantly uttered, may erupt into a torrent of verbalization when with her close friends or family. Pathological seclusiveness, in which the student avoids all social contacts, is fortunately rare, although it is so serious a manifestation of social maladjustment that schools have come increasingly to recognize the necessity of giving all possible aid to such students in the development of proper social activity.

Even in its more specific and less aggravated forms, the pattern of withdrawal presents a real challenge to the speech teacher. There is every reason to believe that the student who evades participation in classroom discussions and in the relatively simple formal speaking activities of the school, is cutting himself off from an important avenue of learning, and is limiting his potential development as a person, and as a member of society.

In the speech class tendencies toward withdrawal manifest themselves in many ways. Relatively often among high school students, the teacher may observe the following types of behavior.

Non-participation in Classroom Speaking

The non-participating student seldom volunteers information or opinions in class discussions. If called upon, he frequently takes refuge in a simple, "I don't know." If given the option, he avoids practically all speech activities. If circumstances force him into speaking, his utterances are usually fragmentary, accompanied by real evidences of social fears like trembling or blushing.

Of course, non-participation may stem from sources other than a pattern of withdrawal. Teachers may make a practical check of non-participating students by consulting with other teachers to see how characteristic the students' patterns are. The teacher may also want to observe the students' out-of-class social activities when opportunity presents itself. He will be interested in evidence as to the students' mental capacities. The non-participating students often appear dull. They may actually be dull; persistent fears of social activity may effectively stifle normal intellectual growth.

Vocal Behavior Associated with Withdrawal

There is considerable evidence that vocal behavior is closely associated with the emotional states of the speaker. Students whose speech is characteristically inaudible, because of insufficient force, often seem to be practicing an effective technique of withdrawal; speech which cannot be heard is almost as inconspicuous as no speech at all! Moreover, although inaudible speech may subject a student to occasional pressures (for example, teacher and classmates may demand audibility), its long range effect will be to reduce the number of demands made upon the speaker for contributions to social situations.

For some students, speech without color or emotional tone may be an effective form of withdrawal. Of course, the student who speaks habitually in a monotone, or seems to show no emotional reaction in his voice, may be imitating a vocal pattern used in his family, or in some familiar social group. He may, however, be using such an unresponsive vocal pattern to conceal his feelings or to reduce his sense of personal involvement in any matter of which he speaks. This lack of spontaneity in speech patterns seems to be associated with general tendencies to withdraw from social participation.

Expressions of Fear, Pessimism, and Antagonism

Social fears precipitate the child's immediate rationalization of his desire to avoid speaking activity. Although he may have little insight into the causes of these fears, he may exaggerate them as a way of reducing the normal social demands for speech. He may express pessimistic views concerning his own capacities, not only as a speaker, but as a student, or a person. This pessimism may be viewed both as a source of his fear, and a rationalization of it. He may depreciate speaking activity, as another method of rationalizing his fears, and occasionally he may "strike back" at his speech teacher by placing rather low estimates on the value of speaking skills and speech training.

The speech teacher has a special contribution to make to the school program in releasing the non-participating student from his sense of inadequacy. The students with tendencies toward withdrawal from social activity generally do not provide the same challenge to teachers as do the aggressive students. If the non-participators have a modest capacity for school work, many teachers may welcome their negative pattern of social adjustment, since it carries a very low nuisance value. Studies have shown that teachers generally do not regard unsocial behavior as a very serious problem in children, although clinical psychologists rate it as a most dangerous manifestation of maladjustment. To the speech teacher, of course, unsociality is a real problem, since the techniques to be developed in the speech class are essentially social skills. For this reason, the unsocial student, of necessity, will challenge the special attention of the speech teacher.[2]

It also should be observed that the tendency to withdraw from speaking situations is a particularly difficult one for teachers to combat; it feeds upon itself. The child who avoids speaking activities closes to himself the only path by which he can overcome the fears which have caused his trouble. He becomes increasingly in-

---

[2] N. M. Campbell, "The Elementary School Teacher's Treatment of Classroom Behavior." New York: Teachers College, Columbia University, 1935.

competent in dealing with speaking situations, and consequently, as he matures, his reasons for avoiding speaking become increasingly potent. The child who avoids short public speeches in the junior high school years is not likely to "outgrow" his difficulties. If his teachers permit him to establish a pattern of "never standing to talk" during some period of his schooling, this habit is apt to be a regressive one, leading to increasingly rigid patterns of withdrawal. It is an unhappy fact that a great deal of the speech training given to senior high school students and college students must be directed at changing attitudes, relieving fears, and eradicating habits which have been built up over considerable periods of time.

The Pattern of Aggressiveness

It is not uncommon to find both withdrawal tendencies and outbursts of aggressiveness manifested by the same student. Since withdrawal may stem from a fear of social criticism, such criticism, when it appears in the speech class, may evoke intemperate statement or irrelevant aggressive activity on the part of the student criticized. Of course, aggressive patterns of adjustment may become so pronounced as to mask any tendency the student may have toward withdrawal; he develops habits of over-verbalization, and contentious and irresponsible verbalization.

Some of the aggressive patterns of speech behavior which will be encountered by the speech teacher are considered in the following paragraphs.

The Search for Favorable Attention

All speakers confront the problem of getting attention from their listeners, and the extent to which attention-getting activity is to be approved, or disapproved, depends upon its form and amount, and the situation in which it occurs. The speech teacher will usually become critical of attention-getting only when it reveals itself as the persistent and paramount goal of the student's speech, omnipresent despite the group's purpose or the requirements of the situation.

The search for praise and favorable attention seems to dominate the speech activity of one type of aggressive speaker, although he may have trouble in discriminating between favorable and unfavorable attention. He may be an overly active participant in classroom discussion, verbalizing well beyond the "call of duty," yet quite insensitive to the legitimate desire of other students to be heard. Sometimes his speech will be closely adapted to the interests of the teacher, and sometimes to those of fellow students. The speaker may develop facial or bodily mannerisms which produce "laughs," or he may seek to play the role of "clown," studiously avoiding sustained and serious concentration upon information or opinion. The inability of some students, who seem to want favorable attention, to judge the nature of the attention they attract is an interesting phenomenon. One teacher reported a conference with a student who protested at receiving a grade of "C." To the teacher, the grade seemed a generous one, since the student persistently used grotesque facial and physical mannerisms, and sprinkled his speeches with outlandishly irrelevant comments. He was laughed at by the class, and consistently criticized by them for his failures to make any headway toward the accomplishing of his supposedly communicative purposes. The student informed his teacher, quite seriously, that the class thought he was the best speaker, "because, notice how much more response I get than anyone else in the group." He seemed unable to remember any of the specific suggestions made to him for improving his speech by the teacher or by his fellow students.

The Search for Unfavorable Attention: Contentiousness, Negative Criticism

It has been observed that the attention-seeking student who has been unable to get favorable attention, sometimes will settle for unfavorable attention. He may seek opportunities to disagree with his fellows, to assert unpopular opinions, or to be adversely critical of the actions and opinions of others. He may resent directions and suggestions, and go out of his way to offend the teacher or his classmates. One high school teacher reports the case of a tenth-grade student who made speeches favoring fascism during the final year of the war with Germany. Two years later he had apparently found this theme devoid of "shock" value so he had shifted to the more unpopular support of communism and atheism. Needless to say, this boy faced serious adjustment problems; his aggressive search for "unfavorable attention" was apparent in all his school work. Students who are contentious and negative in their criticism of others often present difficult problems to the teacher in the conduct of the speech class.

Unless a student's aggressive speech behavior is extreme and represents a deep-seated feeling of fear, or insecurity, the prognosis for his developing attitudes and skills useful in social adjustment is reasonably good. Unlike the withdrawing student, the aggressive one has innumerable opportunities to learn social skills. His problems are usually attended to by many persons—parents, teachers, associates, and friends, if he has any! If his aggressiveness is accompanied by a genuine liking for praise, the speech teacher is in an exceptionally good position to point out to him patterns of social activity more effective than those he has hit upon. The very nature of speech instruction is calculated to provide an outlet for the energies of the aggressive student; even those who seem impelled to search for unfavorable attention frequently like the activity of the speech class. This liking does not guarantee that they will become better adjusted socially, but it gives the speech teacher an important source of motivation with which to work.

SOURCES OF ATTITUDES WHICH ACCOMPANY INEFFECTIVE ADJUSTMENT

Often it is easier to discover the attitudes which accompany ineffective adjustment patterns in the speech of high school students than it is to discover the sources of these attitudes. We shall consider these attitudes in three general relationships, trying in each to indicate some of the possible sources of the attitudes in question. But we must concede that the exact complex of circumstances which has caused a student to develop certain types of attitudes is difficult to identify, and that the classroom speech teacher ought to be exceedingly cautious about assuming that he "knows" the source of a particular student's trouble.

Attitudes Toward Self

The most frequently observed attitude accompanying ineffective speech adjustment is that in which the student places a low valuation on his own personal abilities. Generalized feelings of inferiority seem to accompany social fears in speakers. The speaker who has a low regard for his own worth obviously may find the speech situation terrifying, since it draws the attention of the group to him. Gilkinson's study of college students, previously cited, furnishes interesting evidence of the prevalence of feelings of inferiority among fearful speakers.

COMPARISON OF FEARFUL AND CONFIDENT SPEAKERS [3]

	Percentage of fearful speakers	Percentage of confident speakers
1. Had no previous experience in public speaking	12	4
2. Had no previous instruction in speech	38	13
3. Usually regarded as leaders in common activities	11	31
4. Regarded themselves as being "good" or "very good" speakers	10	52
5. Frequently take pride in their accomplishments	49	63
6. Have felt disgraced by an incident such as forgetting a speech	30	19
7. Are sensitive about blushing	29	16
8. Are sensitive about their personal appearance	30	13
9. Are sensitive about being snubbed	28	14
10. Worry about mistakes in etiquette	25	13
11. Worry about lack of ability	17	8
12. Frequently feel discouraged	19	8
13. Frequently feel uncertain	35	24
14. Frequently feel determined	27	47
15. Describe themselves as being thorough	9	19
16. Describe themselves as being persistent	16	40
17. Describe themselves as being observant	22	41

In addition to the items mentioned in this table, fearful speakers mentioned the following sources of worry or sensitivity: committing some sin, dimples, being small, poor complexion, physical deficiencies, personal habits, bad effects of heredity, violations of religious teaching, speech defects, acts of close relatives, language spoken in the home, clothing, nicknames, failures, and being criticized severely.

In studying this table one observes not only the prevalence of feelings of inferiority among students troubled by fears of speaking, but also some inklings of the extraordinary variety of causes for these feelings, a variety readily observed in the study of high school students who have trouble with speech. Physical defects or "insufficiencies" seem to be a frequent source of trouble for high school students. Boys during the junior high period often find themselves quite overshadowed in stature and strength by girls in the same group—a situation hardly conducive to the development of

---

[3] Thonssen and Gilkinson, *op. cit.*

feelings of confidence and security. The junior high years are particularly trying for many students. Complexion problems often accompany physical changes at puberty, boys may be conscious of voices which defy control, and most students will have a strong awareness of their own physical maturation changes, and may find it unpleasant to be "looked at."

A common, but extremely important, source of feelings of inferiority is specific or prolonged experience with failure, or embarrassment. Many students attribute their fears of speaking to actual speech situations in which they have been severely or unfairly criticized or ridiculed. It is not likely that such experiences would have produced enduring social fears unless they had fallen upon a personality already basically uncertain of its own personal worth—perhaps one which had been subjected to repressive discipline or persistent mistreatment in the home, or one in whom strong feelings of guilt had been aroused.

Exaggerated Ego

As with feelings of inferiority, exaggerated self-respect can usually be traced to the past experiences of the child. He may have come from a protected environment in which praise for his accomplishments has been phrased continuously in superlatives. Coming from such an environment into the school, the student may feel it necessary to assert his possession of the good qualities which his classmates seem unable to see in him. Low estimates of one's own worth are not the only attitudes toward self which interfere with effective social adjustment, although they may be the most important in the immediate impact upon speech. The student who over-values himself also may develop unfavorable speech patterns. Although many students who seem to place a very high estimate on their own personal worth are compensating for an underlying feeling of inferiority, there are some cases in which exaggerated pride in self seems to be real enough. Younger students, particularly, have a tendency to make unblushing public estimates of their own abilities which surprise adults. In one school, a seventh-grade student amazed both his friends and the class sponsor by nominating himself for the class presidency, making a considerable statement of his own capabilities. After he had been roundly defeated, a more perceptive classmate gave him his first lesson in speech. She suggested that the class vote again, but that this time she would nominate the ambitious student, rather than having him present his own name. In this way, said she, the class would be permitted to vote on his merits, rather than on its reactions to his display of self-esteem.

One of the speech teacher's major aims is to help students develop attitudes toward themselves which will be useful in accomplishing effective social adjustment. Such attitudes seem to require a reasonable measure of self-confidence. It is desirable, of course, that the student value himself on the basis of his real achievements, and that his estimates of his own potentialities be as objective as possible, and that they be tempered with strong regard for the feelings of others.

Attitudes Toward Others

It is very difficult to analyze those attitudes toward others which are associated with ineffective patterns of speech. However, since a student's attitudes toward himself are always inextricably linked with his evaluations of other persons, it is possible to observe a number of specific attitudes toward others which seem to hamper effective social adjustment.

Low estimates of one's own personal worth often are accompanied by exaggerated opinions of the abilities of other persons, and by hampering sensitivity to the opinion of others. The fearful student attributes to others reactions which are only a projection of his own feelings about himself. A vastly different problem is faced by the student who builds up his own self-esteem by developing and cultivating suspicions and prejudices about other persons. His capacities for social adjustment are limited by his seeming insensitivity to the opinions of others, or by the deliberate aggressiveness with which he talks to persons whom he has classified as belonging to inferior or undesirable types.

The speech teacher seeks the development of increased objectivity in the judgments made by students of one another, but objectivity tempered by a tolerant acceptance of the variety of persons who possess real value, and who need to be valued in our society. Good speaking seems to be a function of an openness of response to the various types of persons who make up any social group—a recognition of the truth in the old axiom, "It takes all kinds of people to make a world."

Attitudes Toward Specific Speaking Situations and Subjects

The speech teacher will often observe students whose most immediate problem in social adjustment seems to be their attitudes toward specific speaking situations. Students frequently become conditioned to avoid, or dislike, or misuse certain forms of speaking, and, sad to relate, this conditioning is sometimes produced in the speech class. For example, a student who seems to have a normally sociable disposition, and who participates freely and without excessive tension in conversations or informal discussions, may become exceedingly tense and uncomfortable if called upon to give a public speech. This reaction may have developed from unfortunate experiences in this form of speaking; perhaps the speaker assumes that public speaking is something vastly different from informal speaking; perhaps he has had a succession of unpleasant experiences in giving oral reports to sleeping classmates and an unsympathetic teacher.

It is also common to find students avoiding certain types of subject matter. The study of poetry in school should help students respond to it, and enjoy it, but all too often it seems to produce negative responses to the whole literary form. A student may approach the study of oral interpretation with little enthusiasm, and may do very badly in it. Other examples of avoidance may be found in the subject matter high school students choose for their speeches. Many student speakers avoid all references in the classroom to their own reactions and opinions, and this despite the fact that speeches devoid of personal references and attitudes are almost certainly inappropriate to most social situations. Students find it "safe" to talk as long as they are messengers, repeating tonelessly and impersonally facts gathered from the encyclopedia, or reciting the words and ideas of the author of some magazine article. But they feel it "unsafe" to open their own experiences to the scrutiny and comment of classmates, and more particularly to the teacher who represents the adult world.

The speech teacher seeks to help students generalize their specific capacity for adequate social adjustment to some situations, to a capacity for adjustment to a wider variety of situations. The student who has learned successfully to relate himself to other persons in some situations, may be led to see the development of his ability to do this in a variety of situations as an extension and adaptation of skills which he already has. If he can converse or discuss with other persons, he may be trained to view a public speech as involving the same skill and the same capacity for relating himself to other persons, attending to their views and needs, and to their potential interest in his own experiences. If he can talk effectively, he may come to see reading aloud as but another facet of this basic competence. He will learn to enjoy reading materials which say especially well the things he would like to say.

Certainly, few students can be expected to develop equal enthusiasm for all types of speaking, in all sorts of situations. It would be difficult to contemplate cheerfully a world in which all persons should seize enthusiastically every opportunity to make a speech, or read a poem. But it is possible for students to develop a willingness to use a variety of speech forms, and to enter into a variety of speech situations.

HELPING STUDENTS TO ACQUIRE IMPROVED ADJUSTMENT TO THE SPEAKING SITUATION

It is easier to criticize a student for reacting ineffectively to a speaking situation than it is to help him acquire a more successful pattern of adjustment. To tell a student who experiences strong social fears that the way to speak well is to stand confidently before the audience and speak in a strong, pleasant voice, may not do much more good than to tell a golfer that the way to play golf is to drive the ball 275 yards down the middle of the fairway. Helping students modify ineffective patterns of adjustment, or modify attitudes which result in these patterns, is not a task to be completed all at once by the speech teacher; it is not one which can be accomplished with all students by any set routine of experiences, or through the teaching of any specific body of knowledge. Nevertheless, the speech class offers exceptional opportunities for helping students with their problems of adjustment, and there are a number of ways in which speech teachers have set about giving specific assistance to students who lack capacity in social adjustment. We shall indicate some of the aspects of speech training which serve to make it a sort of routine therapy for students with problems in social adjustment, and also certain of the specific ways in which speech teachers may be able to help them.

Speech Training as Normal Training for Social Adjustment

The expectation of social activity is a powerful stimulus for such activity on the part of the high school student. The class in speech eliminates for the natural non-participator any possibility of effective withdrawal from the social situation. We should distinguish the force of expectation in the speech class from the pressures exerted on the student by the speech teacher, or any other teacher, who seeks to force him into social participation. The speech teacher approaches speaking as a customary, everyday activity, in which all students take part. It requires skills possessed by all students to some extent, and capable of improvement. There is no tendency to emphasize speech as an "extra" activity, indulged in by only a few students with special abilities. Thus, the student is under pressure to develop speaking skills, but it is the pressure of normal expectation from his own social group. His reaction to this expectation is far different from that to the pressure which might be focused on him, as particular student, by a particular teacher. Most teachers learn quickly the futility of attempting to "require" Jimmy to make "voluntary" contributions to a classroom discussion. The expectation of the speech teacher and the speech class, of course, must be tempered by flexibility of judgment on the part of the teacher as to the amount and sort of speaking to be elicited from any given student. One teacher describes her own practices with non-participating students as follows: "I don't call on non-participating students in an effort to get them to take part in class discussion, although I watch closely any indication on their part that they are ready to make a contribution. I do indicate, in a matter-of-fact way, that all students ought to take part in discussion, and the class considers the reason for this participation. If the class is studying in preparation for a classroom discussion, I may talk to a non-participating student to see what information or opinions he has that would be pertinent to the discussion. Then I may suggest that we will want his material for the whole group on the following day."

Probably studying about problems of social adjustment, in and of itself, does not help students very much in developing their skill. But when such study accompanies the opportunity to practice these skills in making adjustments, there is every reason to believe that it does help students to improve their patterns of adjustment.

The following list indicates the range of information and generalization about problems of social adjustment which will ordinarily be covered in a fundamentals class in speech. Some teachers may find their students much interested in discussing and learning about problems of social adjustment, and accordingly may extend considerably the range of materials to be studied by the class.

Getting "Facts" About the Nature of the Physiological Reactions People Have to Speaking Situations

The class may find it useful to study the physiological reactions people have to speaking, e.g., "social tensions," indicating a state or readiness in the organism to meet a challenging situation. Such tensions may be distinguished from "social fears" or "stage fright." For some speakers such fears may represent a false evaluation of either the nature of the situations, or the meaning of the physiological tensions. One speaker realizes that the speaking situation is not actually a threatening one, and that for the most part audiences are disposed to give friendly support to speakers. This speaker may interpret his tensions as a state of energy to be used in more effective speaking. Another speaker may regard the speaking situation as threatening, although this may not be a conscious evaluation. His physiological reactions are interpreted as fear—a marshaling of energy to be used in escaping from the situation. It is likely that the teacher should emphasize the normality of social tensions, as well as the fact that for most people, such tensions do not prevent effective speaking, or even preclude the deriving of reasonable pleasure from speaking.

Getting Facts About the Methods Various Speakers Use to Control Their Ineffective Reactions to the Speaking Situations

Students should become familiar with various ways of controlling withdrawal tendencies. Some of these are:

(1) Thorough preparation by the speaker. Some speakers feel poorly prepared because they *are* poorly prepared, and few high school students understand, without study, the amount and kind of preparation desirable for successful speech activity.

(2) Students cannot simply dismiss nervous reactions by an exercise of will power. They can, however, refuse to acknowledge defeat because of these nervous reactions. There is good reason to believe that the student who habitually completes his speaking activity, more or less as he has planned it and regardless of the nervous reactions he may experience, will achieve rapid progress in gaining control over these reactions.

Students who face problems of social adjustment may be challenged to seek out opportunities for social experience. Chapter 12 describes a method of having students report back on their speaking activities outside of speech class.

The Speech Class Can Use Discussion Activity to Study Directly Problems of Social Adjustment Faced by High School Students

Some speech classes use discussion techniques almost exclusively in connection with problems of public affairs. High school students often face their most pressing problems in areas of personal and social relationships. They may have their interest in discussion stimulated by the consideration of the problems of social adjustment and they may find the discussion technique useful in increasing their insight into, and information about, these problems.

A teacher reports: A tenth-grade speech class had observed how skills in social adjustment seemed to be related directly to skills in speaking. The members had discussed some of the difficulties of social adjustment which they had experienced in speaking, and indicated a desire to pursue further this sort of discussion. Two film showings were arranged for the class—*Social Development*, and *You and Your Friends*. A committee from the class previewed these films, and prepared a panel-forum discussion to follow the showing of them. Discussions were organized, in which the class considered interesting general problems of adjustment such as, "What are the opportunities for social activity in our school?" and "Should you cheat in examinations?"

The Speech Teacher Can See to It That Each Student Participates in Speaking at a Level Which Assures Him of Some Success

This is done by arranging for each student to speak for purposes which he understands and accepts, and in the amount and manner suitable to his past learning. The speech teacher also seeks to have each student receive such support and encouragement from the group as he may need to stimulate further speaking. Students vary greatly in the amount of encouragement and praise they need, but it is likely that a great number of the students who have problems of social adjustment have experienced too little social praise, and too much social disapproval.

The Speech Teacher Can Encourage a Maximum Degree of Openness and Objectivity Among the Members of a Speech Class

High school students are usually interested in the fact that life provides them with very limited opportunities to observe the variety of ways in which people think and feel. The speech class is an excellent place for developing in students the capacity to use, rather than reject, negative criticism; and to evaluate, rather than wallow in, praise. If group rapport is high, students may make great progress in the frankness with which they talk with persons having a variety of interests, values, and habits.

The Speech Class Enables Students and Teachers to Approach the Study of the Student's Habits of Adjustment at the Level of His Manifest Behavior, Rather Than with a Critique of His Personality

An aggressive and opinionated junior high school student can accept and understand his need to modify some of his habits of statement before he can accept and understand his need to make fundamental changes in his attitudes toward other persons, and toward social situations. Moreover, as he practices modes of statement which get a more favorable response from other persons, he may find his attitude toward other persons changing. He not only seems better adjusted; he is better adjusted.

MEETING THE NEEDS OF STUDENTS WITH
SEVERE ADJUSTMENT PROBLEMS

Most students will show improved social adjustment as the result of the normal procedures of speech training. Some students will not, and, unfortunately, students with the most severe problems of social adjustment tend to be among those least likely to make progress through the normal activities of the speech class. This situation is not hard to understand. The few students who reveal extremely severe behavior problems are usually those who are maladjusted generally. Their difficulties will be evident in *all* their school work, in their home life, and in all other social situations. Some of these students are sick emotionally to the extent that they need more help than can be given them in a speech class, and perhaps more than can be given them within the resources available to most schools. The problems of such maladjusted students are never the problems of the speech teacher alone, and his approach to them should be in terms of the provision made by the school system as a whole for helping such students.

Larger school systems often have developed special counseling services for severely maladjusted students, including in some cases the services of persons trained in clinical psychology or in psychiatry. When such personnel are available, the speech teacher will be able to get assistance in helping the students with severe problems of adjustment. In smaller schools, without specialized counseling services, provision is often made for co-operative study, by the faculty, of the needs of severely maladjusted students. Faculty members, working together, seek to develop the best possible understanding of the causes for the troubles which plague these unfortunates. They also seek to plan helpful methods of working with such students.

The Speech Teacher as Counselor

The speech teacher probably will spend some time counseling students with severe adjustment problems, since these problems are so readily observable in the speech class, and since they affect so immediately and obviously the skills sought in such a class. It is possible to list here certain practical considerations which ought to guide the speech teacher in these conferences. Needless to say, this discussion is incomplete; counseling techniques have become an area of specialized educational study, with a literature of its own.

The Speech Teacher Should Plan the Purposes He Wants to Attain from a Conference with the Handicapped Student

The speech teacher may wish to add to his knowledge of the student, as an aid to understanding better the reasons for the speech problems. He may wish to judge how seriously the student recognizes that he has problems, and his readiness to accept help in solving them. He may wish to improve his personal relations with the student, to seek a basis of mutual confidence and good will from which he may be able to operate in dealing with the student. He may feel that the student would like to talk about his own problems, and that he will profit from the chance to talk to a sympathetic listener. Too often, the teacher who has not planned the purpose of his conference will seek to accomplish too much. Lacking a clear picture of what he wants from the conference, the teacher will feel called upon to give a lot of "good advice" to the student—to solve all his problems for him in thirty minutes!

The Speech Teacher Will Usually Want a Specific Reason for Arranging the Conference

The ostensible purpose of the conference may be to discuss a specific assignment. It usually is desirable that the first conference with a severely maladjusted student should not be in terms of some failure he already has made.

The Speech Teacher Will Usually Seek to Establish a Limited, Specific Goal to be Achieved in the Student's Next Speaking Activity

One conference leads to another, if an attainable purpose comes out of each conference. Moreover, the basis has been laid for the subsequent conference to be started on the ground of some success achieved by the student, rather than with the contemplation of past failures.

Counseling with Small Groups

The teacher may find it profitable to meet with small groups of students who seem to face similar problems. One teacher reports using this technique successfully with a group of four students who conspicuously avoided all participation in informal classroom discussion. The small group set about analyzing the nature of the problem they faced. They set a modest goal for each of the individual members in terms of increased participation in discussion in all of their classes. Each student also was given the job of observing the participation of another member of the group, and a second meeting was scheduled, at which each student was to report on how well his "colleague" had succeeded in reaching the goal set for him.

SPEECH TRAINING SEEKS NO SINGLE PATTERN OF SOCIAL ADJUSTMENT

It would be unfortunate if speech teachers thought that all students ought to develop one single pattern of social adjustment. It is neither possible nor desirable to force a personality mold upon high school students. They will, and should, exhibit wide differences in their needs for speaking and in their enjoyment of it. Few students mature as healthy, happy, useful persons without some measure of social life and some capacity for enjoying the company of others. Moreover, there is no reason why the student whose habits of living carry him away from social life, should need to fear, or avoid, or be incompetent in speaking. In the speech class it should be assumed that all persons can enjoy some type of speaking situation, that some persons will get exceptional pleasure from a variety of speaking activities, and that no person need face life fearful or inept in making the simpler social adjustments of speaking.

SELECTED BIBLIOGRAPHY

Baird, A. Craig, and Franklin H. Knower, *General Speech.* New York: McGraw-Hill Book Co., Inc., 1949, Ch. XII.

Borchers, G. L., and C. M. Wise, *Modern Speech.* New York: Harcourt, Brace & Co., 1947, Ch. IX.

Bryngelson, Bryng, "Educating the Emotions and Developing Objective Attitudes Toward the Self," *Bulletin of Secondary School Principals* (November, 1945), 39–41.

Gates, A. I., Arthur T. Jersild, T. R. McConnell, and Robert C. Challman, *Educational Psychology*. New York: The Macmillan Co., 1949, Chs. 4, 5.

Gilkinson, Howard, "Speech and Personality," *Bulletin of Secondary School Principals* (November, 1945), 36–39.

Knower, Franklin H., "A Study of Speech Attitudes and Adjustments," *Speech Monographs V*, 1938, 130–203.

Lomas, Charles, "The Psychology of Stage Fright," *Quarterly Journal of Speech* (February, 1937), 23: 35–44.

——————, "Stage Fright," *Quarterly Journal of Speech* (December, 1944), 30: 479–485.

Murphy, G. L., B. Murphy, and T. M. Newcomb, *Experimental Social Psychology*. New York: Harpers, 1937.

Murray, Elwood, "Developing Self-Sufficiency and Social Responsibility," *Bulletin of Secondary School Principals* (November, 1945), 41–44, p. 29.

O'Connell, Wm. V., "Speaking and the Guidance Program," *Bulletin of Secondary School Principals* (January, 1948), 136–143.

Pratt, Shirley, "Counseling and Speech," *Bulletin of Secondary School Principals* (November, 1945), 45–47.

Prescott, D. A., *Emotion and the Educative Process*, American Council on Education, 1938.

Robinson, Karl, *Teaching Speech in Secondary School*, Longmans, Green & Co., Inc., 1950, Chapter XI.

Shaffer, L. F., *The Psychology of Adjustment*. Boston: Houghton Mifflin Co., 1936.

Thonssen, Lester, and Howard Gilkinson, *Basic Training in Speech*. New York: D. C. Heath & Company, 1937, Chs. 3 and 4.

CHAPTER 11

Developing Effective Listening

LISTENING, A NEGLECTED AREA.

THIS chapter is on a topic about which the authors have very little information. In fact, no one in the world is well informed on it, and yet it is very important. It is important because high school students participate in listening more than they do in speaking, and they speak more than they write or read. Studies show that for every minute a boy or girl spends in talking, he or she spends a minute and a half in listening. He listens to face-to-face and telephone conversations; class reports and discussions; planning sessions for all types of school activities; public speeches in assemblies, churches, and community auditoriums; radio programs of many varieties; and readings and plays on records, in the movies, and on the stage.

Common skills frequently are overlooked in education. "Everyone does that," is often the reaction when someone recommends training in a particular technique. "Everyone eats, everyone sleeps, everyone walks, everyone talks, everyone listens," are typical thoughtless statements by individuals who have never stopped to consider that not everyone does eat, sleep, walk, talk, or listen, as well as he might. Many people have never taken time to educate themselves on how much better each of these activities might be performed if special training in them were provided. The values of training in listening have been largely ignored in our schools.

It is only in the last ten years that attention has been centered on helping students to improve their listening habits. And, even now, much of the teaching consists in urging boys and girls to try hard to listen better, rather than in showing them how to do it. The reason is clear; an examination of the listening process reveals that it is much more complicated than teachers at first believed. At present no one is ready to say, "Do this and you will become a better listener." Authorities on listening have focused attention on many factors of the process, including: Perception, attention, motivation, experience, speaking, reading, concentration, recognition, thinking, control, hearing, seeing, habit formation, comfort, entertainment, and the like. Listening seems to be as broad as life itself, and, because of that fact, a study of it discourages researchers.

All Teaching of Speech Can be Teaching of Listening

Teachers of speech emphasize the fact that the speaking situation always involves two or more persons, and that there is reciprocal stimulation between the person who speaks, and the persons who listen. For this reason it is possible to look upon all speech teaching as being equally teaching in listening. The values of speech training to the listener, however, are not automatically achieved; instead they are likely to be achieved only by teachers and students who are constantly aware of the part played by the listener in every act of speaking.

In the past, some speech teachers looked upon the listener as simply so much raw material, to be manipulated by the speaker. All of the responsibility for successful communication was placed on the speaker. If a listener slept, it was because the speaker was too dull; if a listener didn't catch on, it was because the speaker did not make things clear. Today's speech class does not lessen the emphasis on the responsibilities of a speaker to his listeners, but it emphasizes also the reciprocal responsibility of the listener to the speaker. It points not only to the different degrees of success in speaking, but also to the different degrees of success in listening.

That portion of the activity of the speech class during which listeners react to speakers by discussing their ideas and methods, becomes especially important to the development of listening skills. For example, if a speaker has drawn a conclusion not warranted by his evidence, and has been criticized by some members of his audience, the criticism may affect not only the care with which the speaker will make future assertions, but also it may affect the care with which he will evaluate the assertions of other speakers. Similarly, listeners who did not catch the error in reasoning may be more alert to a similar error the next time they hear it.

In a very real sense, all discussion of techniques in the speech class gives the teacher an opportunity to direct the development of the values, or preferences, that students will bring to speaking. For example, if the speech teacher can succeed in getting high school students to give greater value status to speaking that seeks to be clear and exact in its statements of facts and conclusions, he will have influenced the listening habits of these students in a direction which would be generally approved in our society.

These observations about the effects of speech training upon listening habits do not, however, tell much about the specific types of activities which teachers may be able to develop to aid specifically the growth of definable listening skills. As speech teachers we have developed many specific activities for improving the skills of voice, action, and language; but our cultivation of listening skills has remained general in nature, a fact which should challenge the attention of speech teachers.

LISTENING AN AREA OF OPPORTUNITY

Undoubtedly, intelligent and resourceful teachers eventually will make important contributions to education by discovering effective methods of improving listening. A few have already done so, but the field is so broad that these individual contributions in the early stages of investigation, each representing careful, scholarly, time-consuming research, have not carried the problem far on the road to solution. They have proved, however, that the area is a fertile one for study, and, perhaps, in the future, some readers of this text will be able to answer questions now being asked, and to direct teaching, now based largely on trial and error with uncertain results, to specific, well-defined methods of improving listening habits.

INVESTIGATIONS OF FACTORS IN LISTENING

Although there have been fewer than twenty reported investigations of listening, certain findings have sufficient support to justify their consideration in attempting to improve the listening techniques of high school students: (1) Listening comprehension and reading comprehension help learning equally; (2) reading and listening are closely related skills; and (3) the rate of assimilation in reading and listening does not alter the efficiency of the two skills.

Professor Ralph G. Nichols found that the following factors influenced listening comprehension: Intelligence, reading comprehension, recognition of correct English usage, size of listener's vocabulary, ability to make inferences, ability to structuralize a speech, listening for main ideas as opposed to specific facts, the use of special techniques to improve concentration, real interest in the subject discussed, emotional adjustment to the speaker's thesis, ability to see significance in the subject discussed, curiosity about the subject discussed, physical fatigue of the listener, and audibility of the speaker. Nichols also found some evidence to suggest the presence of additional factors, although these were not definitely proved to be operative determinants of listening effectiveness. These less well substantiated factors are: speaker effectiveness, admiration for the speaker, respect for listening as a method of learning, susceptibility to distraction, parental occupation, sex of listener, room ventilation and temperature, use of only the English language at home, rearing in an only-child home environment, high school scholastic achievement, high school speech training, and experience in listening to difficult expository material.

Nichols also found student ratings of factors in listening, answers to questionnaires, and interviews helpful in the analysis of listening. He also noted that poor listeners overrated their own conscientiousness.[1]

Phillips found that 180 students out of 287 listing the factors of success in conversation checked good listening as a factor, and 165 out of 287 checked poor listening as a factor of poor conversation. Only five items were rated higher as factors of effective conversation.[2]

---

[1] Ralph Nichols, "Factors in Listening Comprehension," *Speech Monographs*, Vol. XV: No. 2, 1948, p. 161.
[2] David C. Phillips, "Factors of Effective and Ineffective Conversation," *Speech Monographs*, Vol. XVI: No. 2, 1949, p. 208.

APPLYING FINDINGS TO TEACHING METHODS

Out of such a mass of detailed conclusions, a teacher may select items which will point the way to improved teaching procedures. It is good experience for teachers to work with their students on some such real problem as listening, and the very fact that little has been done makes the job more challenging.

SUGGESTED PROCEDURES UTILIZING PRESENT KNOWLEDGE

Often one example of what actually has been done is more stimulating and suggestive than many detailed discussions of principles, theories, and methods. Some teachers reading a description of the procedure may follow it closely, some may vary it slightly and some more markedly, and others will discard it entirely, substituting original methods. On the one hand, knowledge of what has been done will point the way toward a more desirable plan; on the other, it will draw attention to a plan to be avoided. In either event, discriminating analysis will be promoted. It is with such ideas in mind that we set down in this chapter a fairly detailed description of what actually happened in one high school when a ninth grade class decided to improve the listening habits of the citizens of their state!

HIGH SCHOOL STUDENTS FIND AND SOLVE A REAL PROBLEM

The teacher in one of the high schools in a midwestern city was invited to speak at the annual meeting of the Better Radio Listening State Convention. She was asked to suggest methods for improving the listening habits of high school students. The teacher saw in this problem significant possibilities for the motivation of her speech class. Therefore, before giving her answer to the committee, she sought advice from her high school group. Class discussion disclosed that her students recognized listening as a real problem. Some wanted to listen to programs which did not have the approval of parents, some objected to programs recommended by the State Better Radio Listening Committee, and a few had some specific ideas on how to improve listening. In directing the discussion, the teacher kept in mind Nichols' suggestions regarding student ratings on the factors in listening, the value of student opinions, and the importance of listening as a method of learning. She was attempting to use proved facts about listening as well as accepted educational principles regarding the value of real problems in effective teaching. At the end of the first hour devoted to discussing the problem, the teacher was delegated to go to the committee with the proposal that she accept the invitation to present material on Better Radio Listening for High School Students, on condition that the exact nature of her contribution should be determined only after the class had given it further consideration. Some students were in favor of having members of the class demonstrate listening techniques, some wanted to prepare a pamphlet of suggestions for improving listening, some wanted to leave the matter in the teacher's hands, but suggested that they be allowed to attend the convention, and a few appeared completely uninterested.

High School Plan Accepted, Class Assumes Responsibility

The Better Radio Listening Program Committee accepted the ninth grade's recommendation and gave the class two weeks to decide on a specific title for their contribution to the program. When the action of the committee was reported to the students, they realized that, having accepted this responsibility, they had to do something definite about it. In beginning, they decided to spend one class period and considerable time outside of class in listening to radio. The teacher had brought in radio schedules and lists of programs recommended by various agencies and committees. The class elected a chairman and a secretary. They concluded that they could save time if the meetings were run according to parliamentary law. Each student was then assigned to study a definite radio program, at a time when it was convenient for him to listen, and a committee was appointed to arrange for obtaining a radio receiver so that all could listen to programs together.

The Question, "What Are We Looking For?"

Some students pointed out that there were things wrong with radio performers and some said there also were many things wrong with listeners. Before the first period closed, the boys and girls had decided that in this project they would concentrate on themselves as listeners. They realized that in the other class projects they had concentrated on themselves as speakers, people who were trying to stir up meanings in others. Now they were the ones in whom the meanings were being stirred up—they were at the receiving end of the speech process. Because of time limitations, each student had no more specific directions for listening than to do the best he could and come to the next class discussion ready to tell what he thought made listening effective and what he thought made listening ineffective.

One Class Hour Devoted to Preliminary Listening

During the class period, which was devoted to radio listening, the committee tuned the radio to almost every program suggested by anyone. The listening was not purposeful but most of the students were interested and attentive. A few minutes before the close of the hour, the chairman reminded everyone to listen to some program in addition to the one assigned and to be prepared to contribute to a class discussion on how to improve listening.

Students Discover Some Important Factors in Listening

On the following day the chairman led the discussion and asked for comments on what this class could do for the Better Listening Convention. At first the comments centered pretty much around putting effort into listening. Practically every student said he could be a better listener if he really tried. The chairman then asked each student to make suggestions and he directed the secretary to write them on the blackboard. The first two items listed were, "Pay attention," and "Keep quiet"; these, all agreed, were two good ways to help themselves as well as others in listening.

The chairman then called for comments on experiences in listening to specific programs. A number of students reported that they had been unable to get the meaning of some speeches. In attempting to find the reasons for this difficulty, eight factors named by Professor Nichols were listed by the ninth graders. On seven of these factors they concurred with his point of view, but on the eighth they came to the opposite conclusion. The teacher pointed out that there was much to be learned in the area of listening and showed that their findings were much like those of authorities on the subject, but expressed in different words.

The first reason for failing to get meanings was that listeners did not know exactly what the speaker had said. Some reported that they could not hear and some that they could not understand the words. "Static," "too little volume," "running words together," and "foreign accent" were cited as causes of failure to comprehend meanings. Students saw no way to get rid of static, except by using FM sets, no method to counteract too little volume except turning the radio up and listening more carefully, no way to interpret slovenly speech except by concentrating attention on it, and no way of understanding foreign accent except by training in foreign language. The students said that if German or French or any other language was spoken in a home, the members of that family could understand dialects in the language which they understood and spoke. Therefore, they believed that speaking foreign languages in the home was an advantage in listening. But they could understand how such experiences might be a disadvantage to listening in general as Nichols had found it to be. The teacher encouraged this type of discriminating analysis and played up the fact that they did not give 100 per cent support to Nichols' findings regarding the correlation of foreign language fluency and listening.

Some programs heard by several students were understood by some and not by others. It does not take long for members of any group to identify superior and inferior students. Some who failed to understand what they heard were less intelligent and did not know the meanings of many of the words. No student expressed the cause quite so bluntly as that, but one did comment to the effect that of course some of them understood because they were good in everything. The students finally concluded that two good ways to improve listening would be to try to improve all their school work and to enlarge their vocabularies. It was the teacher who explained that a relationship had been found between reading comprehension and effective listening and suggested that some might want to take advantage of a remedial reading program which was being made available to high school students that fall.

The list on the blackboard now read: (1) *Pay attention*, (2) *keep quiet*, (3) *get FM radio*, (4) *turn radio high*, (5) *know foreign languages*, (6) *improve grades in school subjects*, (7) *enlarge vocabularies*, and (8) *improve reading comprehension*. The chairman pressed for further suggestions. One boy said the program came on so late that he went to sleep, and one that he was so tired from playing football that he could not listen. Others said that the programs assigned to them were boring. The discussion then turned to the kinds of programs that kept one awake and interested. One of the boys said that ball games kept everyone awake. When he encountered disagreement among both boys and girls, he was so shocked that he wanted an explanation and only the teacher was brave enough to admit that she was bored because she did not understand football, basketball, and baseball well enough to picture in her mind what was taking place. It then developed that different members of the class were well informed on different subjects and therefore liked to listen to different programs. Two had happened to hear a discussion of *Wind in the Willows*. One who had read the book, liked it. The other turned the program off.

As a result of the discussion, the students concluded that the listener had to be informed and interested, to listen well. They also pointed out that they could listen better when they were rested. At this point they added to their list: (9) *Try to become interested in whatever you are to hear*, (10) *bring some knowledge to what you are to hear*, and (11) *try to be rested when you listen*. These are very close to factors which authorities have found to have high correlations with effectiveness in listening.

Unlike many adults, most of these adolescent students did not object to radio advertising. They remembered the songs, repeated the slogans, and knew the names of sponsors. A little questioning however revealed that they were not persuaded by the programs as readily as one might think. In fact many of them prided themselves on the fact that they were too smart to be tricked. Such comments as, "They just say that to flatter you," or, "Of course it makes you hungry to hear them tell about it, but I don't like that cereal," or, "How can you make teeth beautiful when they are already decayed?" Some students, it is true, were opposed to advertising but most of them found it interesting and thought that, as a result of it, they got better programs. They all agreed that a listener had to be alert not to be taken in. At this point they added: (12) *Don't be tricked by advertisers*.

Statement number (12) reminded the students that listeners could be tricked by speakers who were selling ideas instead of merchandise. This observation brought on a heated discussion of political speeches and the students decided to make (12) read, *Don't be tricked by propaganda*, and explained that such a statement would include all types of emotional appeals.

The feeling in the class ran very high in discussing propaganda. Each student saw himself in the light of a clever detective; one boy said, "They want you to do things, but they don't talk straight out. You have to see through them." He was doubtless feeling for the "ability to draw inferences," as a factor in listening. The class added: (13) *Discover what a speaker means, not what he says.*

News commentators received consideration next. Many students had favorites and listened to them regularly. One student, who up to this time had showed little interest, said he liked to listen to war progress reports. He explained that he had maps with different colored cords for various armies and he moved them each time he got a report of progress. His maps were on large pieces of wall board. He invited members of the group out to his home to see them. This was more interest than he had theretofore shown in any project. Other students then told of special aids to listening which they used, including diagrams of ball games, paper and pencils to get directions and recipes, music scores, and books which were being discussed. They added: (14) *Find individual devices to make points clear.* The teacher pointed out that "use of special techniques while listening to improve concentration," had been found scientifically to be effective.

In the discussion, which lasted for several class periods, students hit upon certain points which were close to what researchers had discovered. For example, some said they "couldn't stand" certain programs, or that the title of the program did not make them want to listen, or that they hated the way some people talked. They then added to their listening factors: (15) *Try to like the speaker,* and (16) *make the program seem important.*

No one mentioned any relationship between speech training and ability to listen. Even the chairman looked blank when the teacher brought up the idea; he said, "I don't see what you mean." After some discussion, the students thought that an understanding of how to plan a speech might help them to anticipate what was coming because they would then know certain characteristics of all speeches. The teacher then asked if they ever had difficulty remembering, because there were so many things to remember, and they at once saw the need for selecting that which is more important over what is less important. With a little encouragement they added: (17) *Know how to organize a speech*, and (18) *know how to pick out main points.*

Since students are usually aware that a teacher has a general plan which is modified by student needs, interests, and recommendations, these students asked how many factors that experts had written about were missed in the class discussion. The teacher presented the following for their consideration: (a) recognition of correct English usage, (b) speaker effectiveness, (c) susceptibility to distractions, (d) parental occupation, (e) sex of listener, (f) room ventilation and temperature, (g) experience in listening to difficult expository material, (h) gesture of speaker does not affect comprehension, and (i) rearing in an only-child home environment. After examining the nine items they decided that there were only four that they could do anything about, and they added: (19) *Learn to recognize correct English*, (20) *train yourself not to be distracted*, (21) *do everything possible to make yourself comfortable*, and (22) *get experience in all kinds of listening.* They pointed out that (b) and (h) were under the control of the speaker and (d), (e), and (i) under the control of fate. They could see that children with parents in some occupations might get more help in listening than those with parents in other occupations. The boys expressed no surprise that there was some evidence they were better listeners than the girls, and someone suggested that since an only child did not have to shut out as much racket as a child in a big family perhaps he paid attention better and therefore listened better. The determination to concentrate on themselves, because they had direct control over themselves, had taken root with the ninth graders and they were discriminating in selecting methods for improvement.

The Final Compilation of Listening Factors Which Can be Improved by Students

1. Pay attention.
2. Keep quiet.
3. Get FM radios.
4. Turn radio up for more volume.
5. Know foreign languages.
6. Improve grades in school subjects.
7. Enlarge vocabularies.

8. Improve reading comprehension.
9. Try to become interested in what you are to hear.
10. Bring some knowledge to what you are to hear.
11. Try to be rested when you listen.
12. Don't be tricked by propaganda.
13. Discover what a speaker means, not what he says.
14. Find individual devices to make points clear.
15. Try to like the speaker.
16. Make the program seem important.
17. Know how to organize a speech.
18. Know how to pick out the main points.
19. Learn to recognize correct English.
20. Train yourself not to be distracted.
21. Do everything possible to make yourself comfortable.
22. Get experience in all kinds of listening.

THE CONVENTION PROGRAM

The long list of ways to improve listening was at first discouraging, in the light of the immediate need to submit a title, and, in two weeks, a complete program for the Better Radio Listening Convention. The students saw that they could not consider all radio listening because they had not even mentioned some phases of it. They had been concentrating on how to listen to speech and they decided they would not go beyond that; after all, they argued, this was a speech class and the place to learn how to listen to music was in a music class! Did that mean, the game enthusiast asked, that they could not talk about what was learned in Physical Education, or in English, or in Social Studies? They all agreed that they could talk about anything they wanted to talk about if they really understood the topic! They were going to have other teachers and other classes help them to test their knowledge. They even thought it would be all right to talk about music if they got some expert help so they would not "make fools" of themselves.

For the convention program, however, they did not wish to be too ambitious. Most of them were too timid to wish to appear on the program, although all were eager to help with the preparations. They finally decided to have the teacher report on what the class had discovered, and have two students demonstrate: (a) How to improve listening to ball games, (b) how to keep from being tricked by propaganda, (c) helps in understanding war reports, and (d) how to understand book reviews. Student number one would take (a) and (b), and student number two, (c) and (d). They entitled their contribution to the program, "Suggestions for Improving the Radio Listening of High School Students," and all members of the class helped in the preparations.

How to Enjoy a Sports Broadcast

The boy who was to demonstrate how football, basketball, and baseball broadcasts could be made more interesting, brought a diagram of a football field with tiny players, which he had used many times. The class helped him to design and work out similar plans for basketball and baseball. The boy prepared a short explanation of the way in which these materials could be used by a radio listener as he followed the game.

How to Keep from Being Tricked by Propagandists

When the students started to work on propaganda they soon discovered that what they were doing had implications beyond radio listening. They saw that propaganda was used in conversation, public speaking, class reports, discussion, debates, sermons, oral readings, stage plays, and moving pictures. They asked their representative to make this clear, but they limited the demonstration to radio advertising.. The class collected examples of emotional appeals from dozens of radio programs. These appeals to survival, sex, prestige, wealth, and so on were displayed in poster form with questions like, "Did you examine the suit or were you taken in by an appeal to prestige?" or, "Were you tricked by these slogans?" or, "How do you react to these loaded words?" In addition to these posters, the boy giving the talk had dozens of cards, each of which carried a quotation from advertising based on some impelling motive designed to influence human behavior. Finally, he was to explain briefly how these appeals to fundamental emotions could be a service as well as a disservice to listeners.

Helps in Understanding War Reports

The maps mounted on wallboard were to be displayed by the second boy. He was to give credit to his classmate who had used them and to show the audience how, as the newscaster was describing the troop movements, he moved the pins which held the cord showing where the troops were stationed. All battle lines were brought up to date for the demonstration.

How to Understand Book Reviews

The second boy to speak at the convention was motivated most of all by his knowledge that *The Talmud* was to be discussed on the *Invitation to Learning* program on the next Sunday. Some members of the class, including the teacher, were not well informed on this collection of religious-legal decisions developing the laws of the Old Testament and had cited this lack of information as the reason for their inability to listen effectively. The boy selected to speak was looking forward to being a Rabbi, was receiving religious training, and therefore was well equipped to prepare the class and the members of the convention to listen intelligently to the book review program.

THE PROGRAM BROUGHT NEW INVITATIONS

Since all members of the class had provided materials for the teacher and the two student speakers who were to appear at the convention, and since all were eager to put into practice some principle of effective listening, they attended the convention. The program went off as planned. The teacher explained how the problem had been considered and the partial solutions which had been reached. She presented the list of factors in effective listening suggested by the class and supported them by calling attention to scientific findings. Then she introduced the two boys who demonstrated as they had planned. The audience showed more enthusiasm than either students or teacher had anticipated. The president of a woman's club in a neighboring city invited the first boy to come and talk on propaganda, and one of the teachers from a neighboring school asked the second boy to come and show his maps and emphasize the importance of knowledge in effective listening.

The fact that the two boys who talked were among the most effective speakers did not mean that they could not profit from further opportunities to speak, but there were twenty-eight students in the class and the teacher was eager to give all consideration. She believed that it might be possible to plan two programs in which all students would share, and she was gratified to find that every student wanted a part. Both women who had extended the original invitations were eager to co-operate and left the matter in the hands of the students and the teacher.

The Program on How to Listen to Propaganda

Twenty-eight students participated in a discussion on how to keep from being tricked when listening to propaganda. Half of them spoke from the platform and the other half contributed to an open forum with other members of the audience. Preparation for the program took four weeks, and included attention by some students to every one of the twenty-two factors in good listening and, in addition, training on how to conduct a panel-and-open-forum discussion, how to speak to be understood in a large auditorium, and how to meet members of the Woman's Club and members of the ninth grade from the host city who had been invited to be guests at the program. This time the students considered listening to propaganda not only on radio programs but also in all types of speaking. The students made more elaborate charts, collected many more revealing illustrations, and climaxed their program by distributing through the audience fifty pamphlets containing public speeches, in which the listeners were asked to find words, phrases, or sentences which seemed especially effective. Then, from the platform, these students described the impelling motives in terms of these words, phrases and sentences. While both classes of ninth graders were being treated to milk and doughnuts, a good deal of the conversation among the students was on how to listen to propaganda!

The Program on the Importance of Knowledge in Effective Listening

In a program at a neighboring school much the same arrangement was followed, save that those who were in the audience at the Woman's Club meeting spoke in a symposium from the platform and those who had been on the panel before spoke from the floor. Each person gathered some material which helped him in listening effectively to a specific radio program and then prepared a one-minute report which he presented. When the meeting was turned into an open forum, the half of the class seated in the audience gave very brief contributions on how to become informed. Questions and comments from teachers, parents, and host students in the audience followed.

The Class Invited to Work with the State Radio Committee

The State Better Listening Committee sent the class two invitations: First, to have representation on their committee, and, second, to present a program on listening over a local radio station. The class accepted both opportunities with enthusiasm and included in their training not only further work on all of the items considered for the earlier discussions but also on learning the techniques of radio speaking.

The radio program became a general overview of all that the class had learned about listening. It climaxed the work of the entire semester. Representation of high school students on the Listening Committee became a permanent policy. The students had worked, and were continuing to work, on a problem which was important not only to them but also to other high school students, as well as to adults, throughout the state.

LISTENING IS A COUNTERPART OF SPEAKING

The example of the ninth grade project just discussed shows clearly that improvement in listening and improvement in speaking are interdependent, though each skill demands individual concentration. Because the implications and applications of the listening-speaking process are so important and widespread, teachers will find work in this area as satisfying as that in the other elements of the communicative process.

SELECTED BIBLIOGRAPHY

Berry, Althea, "Experience in Listening," *Elementary English* (March, 1951), 28: 130–132.

Borchers, Gladys L., *Living Speech*. New York: Harcourt, Brace & Co., 1949, Chapter VI.

Borchers, G. L., and C. M. Wise, *Modern Speech*. New York: Harcourt, Brace & Co., 1947, Chapter XI.

Brown, Don, "Teaching Aural English," *English Journal* (March, 1950), 34: 128–137.

Brown, James, "Construction of a Diagnostic Test of Listening Comprehension," *Journal of Experimental Education* (December, 1949), 18: 139–146.

Drake, Francis L., "How Do You Teach Listening?" *The Southern Speech Journal* (May, 1951), 16: 268–271.

Freeman, Bernice, "Listening Experiences in the Language Arts," *English Journal* (December, 1949), 38: 572–577.

Herzberg, Max (ed.), *Radio and English Teaching*. New York: Appleton-Century-Crofts, Inc., 1951.

Hook, J. N., *The Teaching of High School English*. New York: The Ronald Press Company, 1950, Chapter VIII.

La Brant, Lou, *We Teach English*. New York: Harcourt, Brace & Co., 1951, Ch. 12.

Mercer, Jessie, "Listening in the Speech Class," *Bulletin of Secondary School Principals* (January, 1948), 102–108.

Nichols, Ralph G., "Factors in Listening Comprehension," *Speech Monographs XV*, 1948, No. 2: 154–63.

——————, "Listening Questions and Problems," *Quarterly Journal of Speech* (February, 1947), Vol. 33: 84.

——————, "The Teaching of Listening," *Chicago Schools Journal* (June 1949) 30.

Robinson, Karl, *Teaching Speech in the Secondary School*. New York: Longmans, Green & Co., Inc., 1950, Ch. XVII.

Turner, Alice L., *Skill in Listening*. Chicago: National Council of Teachers of English, 1941.

Wilson, C. E., and Frazier, Alexander, "Learning Through Listening to Each Other," *English Journal* (September, 1950), 39: 367–373.

PART III

Applications of Basic Skills and Understandings

A SPEAKER may study the essential processes of speech separately, but he can never use them separately. Speech is always a total act, involving all of the basic elements, voice, visible action, language, and mental processes, in an inseparable integration. For this reason, we commonly describe an act of speaking or a speech situation not in terms of its characteristic elements, but in terms of the *forms* of speech which it involves. We recognize a clearly defined group of speech situations in which we say the form is *public speaking;* another group, in which the form is *reading aloud,* or *the oral interpretation of literature;* and still another group, in which the form is *drama.* Debate, discussion, conversation, and *storytelling* are other common forms of speaking.

THE FORMS OF SPEAKING OVERLAP

To classify speech behavior according to its *forms* may seem unsatisfactory to those interested in discrete categories which do not overlap. Was there ever a discussion which did not involve debate? Are not all the participants in a debate practicing public speaking? How often does a public speaker read a poem as part of his speech? Is a speech read from manuscript a form of public speaking, or an oral reading?

Yet these classifications have value and significance in speech instruction. Despite its uncertain boundaries, each form of speaking has conventional characteristics peculiar to itself. For example, a parliamentary meeting involves public speaking, discussion, and debate, but it involves all of these within a special frame of reference—parliamentary law. A parliamentary meeting may fail because the participants use poorly a number of the forms of speaking, or it may fail because the members and the chairman are unable to handle the conventions of parliamentary law. Thus, training in basic speech processes may make one eventually a better participant in parliamentary meetings, but only persons who have studied parliamentary procedures directly are capable of handling successfully this specific speech situation.

SPEAKERS AND LISTENERS ORGANIZE THEIR BEHAVIOR IN TERMS OF FORMS

Not too much is known about how speakers organize their speaking behavior, or how listeners organize their expectations of the speech behavior of others. It seems probable that forms of speaking enter heavily into the organizing activity of speakers and listeners. Thus, a speaker may develop a bundle of skills associated with the form of public speaking. When he is called upon to give a public speech, he has available procedures for determining and limiting his subject, gathering and organizing his material, practicing, and eventually delivering his talk. He thinks of these skills in terms of the form of public speaking, and calls them into play whenever he faces this sort of job. Similarly, some listeners respond favorably or unfavorably to an act of speaking in terms of the way in which it meets their conventional expectations of the form which it involves. For example, audiences of a century ago at Fourth of July gatherings seemed to expect the "orator" of the day to make the eagle scream. The successful patriotic oration was characterized by heightened emotional statements plus a certain extravagance of vocal and physical behavior. Today audiences expect a more "conversational" manner and style in both the content and delivery of such speeches. We tend to speak of the oratory of a century ago as conventional—using that word in a derogatory sense, and to speak of our own preferences as natural. But with a little thought we can recognize that preferences for form always involve conventional behavior and expectations, and that often what we call "natural" is simply the conventional which we ourselves have come to anticipate and expect.

It seems probable therefore, that to some extent all speakers and listeners organize their speaking behavior and expectations in terms of those skills, conventions, and processes which they associate with some particular form of speaking.

SPEECH INSTRUCTION RECOGNIZES THE INTERACTION OF FORM AND PROCESS.

Do speech teachers teach their students the general skills of voice, action, language, and thought which are useful in all speaking situations? Or do they teach the specific skills needed for satisfactory and efficient handling of particular forms of speaking? The student uses speech in the service of his needs. In meeting those needs, he selects some specific speech form. Therefore, the student's consideration of ways and means in meeting his problems always involves both consideration of the processes common to all speaking, and the development of specific skills in handling identifiable particular forms of speaking.

CHAPTER 12

Informal Speech

INTRODUCTION

SPEECH teachers rightly may feel that one of their most perplexing and challenging problems is helping students to increase their skills in using the speech of everyday life. We have already observed (see Chapter II) that one of the significant changes in speech education during the 20th century has been the new emphasis upon informal speaking. It is easy to appreciate the logic of this change. Our present-day schools are trying to provide an education suitable to the needs of all students. Students use speech in informal situations far more than on formal occasions. Moreover, this informal use of speech is not unimportant per se. It is altogether probable that more decisions are reached, more information is exchanged, more questions are raised and answered, and more of the essential business of society is transacted through informal speaking than through all formal speaking activities combined.

To some teachers this has meant that most of the emphasis in speech education ought to be on informal speech, with little or no attention paid to such activities as public speaking or formal dramatics, and the like. Other teachers, while conceding the importance of everyday speaking, have regarded the totality of its skills as unsuitable for direct teaching. They would say: "Informal speech activities, at one time or another, embrace all of the purposes for which people speak, and all of the skills which make up effective speech. One cannot teach everyday speaking directly, but only particular speech skills which may go into everyday speech."

We believe that a balanced view of the place of everyday speech in the high school curriculum will neither ignore such informal activities as conversation and telephoning nor direct the attention of students solely to these activities to the neglect of the more formal speech activities. Our view is that students in high school find immediate need to use both a variety of informal speaking activities and many of the more formal ones. Therefore, experiences of both sorts should be part of their education. Moreover, as students participate in a great variety of speaking activities, they may be helped to see the interrelationships of all acts of speaking—to see, for example, the way in which public speaking, debate, and discussion grow out of conversation, and involve the same purposes and skills. Thus, the student may come to understand that observing and practicing effective speech in any situation, formal or informal, may contribute to the development of those skills which are common to all speaking.

THE SCOPE OF THIS CHAPTER

This chapter is concerned with only a part of the job of teaching everyday speech. It is devoted to those aspects of informal speech which we believe can be taught directly in class; it omits those aspects which are best taught indirectly as by-products of the study of more formal speech activities. We have listed five types of informal speech as appropriate for direct consideration by the speech class. These are discussed in the following paragraphs.

Conversation as an Enterprise in Human Relations

One of the paramount functions of language in our culture is that of easing tensions between people. Language is used not merely to exchange information, or to solve problems, or to win consent, but also to create the climate of mutual good feeling between people, without which the other functions cannot be carried on effectively. Much conversation is almost exclusively devoted to the promotion of a sense of well-being among the participants. The use of speech to promote effective human relationships may be observed more extensively and commonly in conversation than in any other form of social activity. Thus, while conversation embraces all of the purposes for which speech is used, and involves all of the speech skills, the time devoted to the study of conversation in the speech class is really directed at helping students to improve their skills in human relations.

Telephoning

Not much time need be spent in the speech class on the study of telephoning, but there are certain basic formalities of telephoning to be learned and certain understandings about the appropriate uses to which the telephone may be put which can be acquired to good purpose by all students. Ways and means of meeting these needs should be devised by the teacher and the students.

Social Forms

A significant portion of informal speech is carried on according to customary ways of introducing persons, of expressing pleasure or appreciation for the acts of others, and of extending sympathy to others. Knowledge of conventional forms is important to the security of high school students in their social life, and may be viewed as contributing to the ease with which people meet and talk with one another. Social forms govern conversation and telephoning, and they offer a convenient center of interest within which high school students can carry out a useful unit of study.

Interviewing

Interviewing fills an important need in our society; it serves many purposes with varying degrees of formality. The first practical interest students have in interviewing is in gathering information from other persons. Interviewing as an informal method of inquiry should be part of the speech activity of all students. More specialized uses of interviewing for job applications, or other persuasive purposes, may also need attention.

Parliamentary Procedure

Parliamentary meetings usually include a variety of somewhat informal public speaking, discussion, and debating. It is for this reason that we place the study of parliamentary procedure among informal speech activities. The most distinctive aspect of the study of parliamentary procedure, however, involves learning and practicing principles which are an important part of the tradition of democratic societies. Students who understand the purposes of parliamentary law understand better the nature of democracy. Those who can conduct themselves skillfully in parliamentary meetings are in a position to contribute effectively to the processes of democracy throughout their lives. For this reason, most high schools include the study of parliamentary law, and the practice of parliamentary procedure among the learning experiences which ought to be available to all students. Parliamentary procedure is not always taught in the speech class. Teachers of social studies, and class or home room advisers, often include the study of parliamentary procedures in their teaching. Thus, in any given school, the exact method of organizing the instruction in parliamentary procedure may be a matter for co-operative determination by the teaching staff.

TEACHING CONVERSATION

No more ambitious and perhaps less attainable purpose can be set by the speech teacher than that of teaching students to be good conversationalists. A person's conversation may be viewed rightly as an index of his entire character and education. No one course of study or program of training can give the student the range of information and insight which characterizes the skillful conversationalist. No short period of classroom instruction can develop the necessary awareness of and sensitivity to the feelings of other persons. The speech teacher who assumes that speech training should help students to improve conversational skill faces the important task of defining and limiting his goal. He must select specifically the particular aspects of conversational skill which are to be emphasized and the definite procedures suitable for teaching them.

The Goals of Instruction in Conversation

The following statements seem to define both significant and feasible goals for direct instruction in conversation.

To help students:

1. To understand the importance of conversational skill in effective living.

2. To develop the range of understandings, attitudes, and skills revealed by effective conversationalists.

3. To develop increased skill in observing effective and ineffective conversational procedures.

4. To appraise their own conversational abilities and needs.

5. To practice purposefully certain specific conversational skills.

Observing, Reporting, and Discussing Conversations

Since conversation takes place in a range of situations which cannot be realistically reproduced in the classroom, the study of conversation may be introduced through student observations of conversations, followed by classroom reports on these observations.

A teacher reports:

The class had read about and discussed the importance of conversational skills. They had also seen the film, *Ways to Better Conversation.* Various students then indicated the situations in which they had had need for conversational skill, and some of the more significant purposes for which they recently had used conversation. The class developed two categories for classifying conversations. The first was based on the types of persons involved in the conversation, and included:

1. Conversing with strangers.
2. Conversing with older people.
3. Conversing with younger people.
4. Conversing with friends.

The second category was based on the purposes of conversation, and included:

1. Conversation to get or share information.
2. Conversation as a part of buying or selling.
3. Conversation to ease social tensions.
4. Pseudo-conversation (in this category the students placed wasteful talking, which had no real purpose except to fill time, and conversations in which each person was attempting to control the talk, without listening to the other persons).

Each student was asked to report to the class on a conversation in which he had participated, classifying both the conversational situation and purpose. This report was to answer such questions as:

1. Who opened the conversation, and how?

2. Were you able to discover a topic of common interest? If so, how was this topic introduced?

3. What impressed you about the other persons' speech?

4. How good listeners were the other persons? How good a listener were you?

5. Could this conversation have been improved? How?

The first conversations observed were reported in class, and on a basis of the ensuing discussion, a list of topics for classroom discussion about conversation was drawn up. This list raised such questions as:

1. What are the general characteristics of a good conversationalist?

2. How may a conversation be initiated?

3. How does one decide what topics should be avoided in a conversation?

4. How may one change the subject in a conversation?

5. How do people with a wide range of interests and information acquire these tools so useful in conversation?

A number of discussions followed, while members of the class continued to observe conversations in order to gather data. Each student turned in brief written reports on observed conversations in several of the eight categories which had been set up by the class.

Reading About and Discussing Personality Development

After observing conversations, students usually will come to the conclusion that much of what is called conversational skill is really skill in human relations. Students may be interested in reading about personality development and observing films dealing with it. Such reading and observing may lead to the discussion of problems which are of particular interest to the members of the class.

A teacher reports:

This class determined to investigate the personality development which affects conversational skill. They set up as their purposes a better understanding of the causes of personality problems, and a better understanding of the ways in which personalities can be improved.

The initial procedure of the class was to organize three film-forums based on films dealing directly with personality problems. These films were, *Shy Guy* (Coronet); *Are You Popular?* (Coronet); and *You and Your Friends* (*Look* magazine). Following the discussion of these films, the class worked out a series of general problems for investigation, and divided up into committees, each of which was to make an investigation of one problem, and report back to the class on the information they had acquired. The problems selected for investigation were:

1. Should we try to be like others, or different from them?
2. Can we change our personalities?
3. What is the best way to grow up?
4. What are the opportunities for personality development in our school and community?
5. What causes feelings of inferiority and superiority?

Library materials had already been found and arranged for the first four questions, while the group used interview procedures as their basic method for gathering data on the fifth. Each committee reported to the class, and conducted a brief forum discussion on the subject matter brought in from its investigation.

Demonstration: Dramatized Conversation

In all likelihood, simulated conversations have value only to illustrate, and thus make more vivid, certain general principles. Therefore, we should regard such classroom exercises as dramatizations of conversation useful for the purpose of studying techniques, rather than as actual practice in the art of conversation. Certain types of dramatized conversations can be prepared and presented by high school students to good effect. These include:

1. Demonstrations of good and poor ways of opening a conversation.
2. Demonstrations of good and poor ways of changing the subject.
3. Demonstrations of good listening and poor listening.
4. Demonstrations of strange people we meet in conversations— the person who is interested only in himself, who always finishes the other persons' sentence, who thinks that only he and his friends know the right way of doing things, who mumbles, and who can never reach a decision.

An interesting variation on dramatized conversations may be produced by reading parts from plays or novels which illustrate certain principles of conversation, or give insight into the behavior of different types of personalities. Students may be directed by the teacher to specific conversations for dramatic presentation, or they may prefer to bring in examples from their own reading.

TEACHING TELEPHONING

Telephoning is usually regarded as a particular form of conversation. There may be some reason, however, for giving it brief, special emphasis in the speech class. Most people in this country use the telephone not only frequently, but also somewhat ineffectively. One of the sources of ineffectiveness may be the fact that many persons do not distinguish the special requirements of telephone conversation from the requirements of face-to-face conversation. Junior high school students may be introduced to the study of telephoning by a discussion contrasting telephoning with social conversations. Such conclusions as the following may be reached by students:

1. The use of the telephone for prolonged social conversation is seldom legitimate.

2. Certain formal procedures in answering the telephone would greatly increase the efficiency of conversations. Thus, there is generally one best way of starting a telephone conversation, as contrasted with the unpredictability of social conversation.

3. Telephone conversation requires more careful articulation than does face-to-face conversation.

4. Usually the person initiating a telephone conversation should plan his remarks carefully before calling.

Having established the differences between telephoning and social conversation, high school students may proceed to the consideration of telephoning with many of the same procedures previously used for studying conversation generally:

1. Reports on a variety of telephone conversations initiated by the student.

2. Viewing and discussing the films distributed by the Bell telephone system.

3. Dramatizing effective and ineffective telephone procedures.

4. Practicing customary forms of answering the telephone, asking for information, stating a complaint, and so on.

TEACHING SOCIAL FORMS

While social form must be considered an integral part of the study of conversation, we have already indicated that there may be good reason for singling out the problem of social conventions in speaking for separate consideration by the speech class. The significance of a knowledge of social forms lies in the fact that they give a degree of predictability to the generally capricious, impromptu nature of conversation. To the extent that a group of people possess a common understanding of certain formal ways of greeting one another, of introducing strangers to one another, of expressing sympathy, or congratulations—to this extent they are more comfortable and secure in all their social relations. Thus it is that the acquisition of specific knowledge of certain social forms in speaking can do much to give high school students a sense of security in their social activities.

A teacher may make a very real contribution to this feeling of security by discussing with boys and girls the development and acceptance of social forms. It will not take long for them to see that back of all rules of etiquette is the desire to make others comfortable and happy. The reason one refrains from eating soup noisily is that such behavior is unpleasant for one's associates. The reason one rises when an older woman enters the room is to make her feel comfortable and important. With the training students have had in speech they should be in a position to analyze the effects of their behavior on others. They can go beyond such rules as, "A man does not shake hands with a lady when being introduced." They can analyze the situation and decide what action would be most appropriate in the circumstances. For example, if a lady, upon being introduced, has held out her hand or has appeared insecure and hesitant, the proper thing for the man to do may be to step forward and offer to shake hands. This point of view will do much to give adolescents confidence. If they understand that they have but one rule to apply in all situations they can solve their problems themselves and they feel an increased sense of security. To be more considerate of others than of oneself is the rule which will answer nearly all questions of social form that matter.

Students enjoy forming a panel of eight or ten members and challenging the class to present to them accepted rules of etiquette which they are unable to explain as results of efforts to be considerate of others. They enjoy, too, choosing sides and conducting a "spell down" on social forms with a board of judges who determine the merit of each explanation.[1]

Classification of Social Conventions in Speaking

The conventions of speech may be taught as a part of some general study of manners or etiquette by high school students, or they may be studied in common speaking situations in which they appear. The latter approach is more common in the speech class, although, in any event, conventions will need to be related to the general function of good manners in society. The following speech situations will serve to introduce most students to important social forms in speaking:

1. Making and acknowledging introductions in informal situations.
2. Introducing a friend, or a speaker, to a group of people.
3. Congratulating someone for an achievement.
4. Acknowledging the congratulations of another person.
5. Expressing sympathy, or condolences for the misfortune of another.
6. Acknowledging expressions of another person's sympathy.
7. Extending an invitation to a party, or some other social occasion.
8. Making a date.
9. Accepting or rejecting an invitation from another person.

Classroom Procedures in Teaching Social Form

Either classroom demonstrations of social forms in speaking or films dealing with them may be used to introduce high school students to the consideration of these conventions. In general, demonstrations of social form should be brief illustrations of correct procedures, presented by students, who will then call attention to the

---

[1] Gladys L. Borchers, *Living Speech.* Rev. ed. New York: Harcourt, Brace & Co., 1951, p. 116.

essential features which have been emphasized in the illustrations. Speech teachers may wish to examine films for possible use in teaching social forms.

Reading About and Discussing Problems of Social Form

A considerable body of reading materials dealing with social form has been prepared for high school students. The bibliography at the end of this chapter lists a number of interesting books on the subject. The speech teacher will find a constant flow of periodical writing on problems of manners and etiquette, much of which is directed to the high school reader. The speech class should not, of course, launch high school students into a comprehensive program of studying good manners without regard to their immediate social needs. As suggested previously, all reading and discussion should be initiated in connection with specific problems faced by members of the class. However, the interests of individual students in reading about social forms will ordinarily extend well beyond the problems raised for the whole class. It frequently is possible, and always desirable, to introduce high school students to the study of social forms at times when they will have immediate need for skill in using them.

A teacher reports:

The students of a seventh grade class had invited their parents to a hobby show being given by the class. The class discussed the speaking problems which they would encounter during this event, including social conversation with adults and making and acknowledging introductions. Forms for introductions were illustrated and practiced in class, and the responsibilities of each student for making the parents welcome were discussed.

Other occasions developed during the course of the year for the consideration of social forms. Prior to class parties, students explored the methods of announcing games, awarding and accepting prizes, and dispensing refreshments.

TEACHING INTERVIEWING

For many reasons speech teachers find it advisable to encourage high school students to make extensive use of interviewing as a form of speaking. The student who bases all, or part, of a report to his class on information obtained by interviewing has had two speaking experiences, as compared with the single experience of the student whose talk is not based on an interview. The student who talks over his ideas with another person prior to giving a classroom report has had an additional chance to check the reactions of others to his thinking, and to make progress in developing and clarifying his ideas in relation to such reactions. The student who interviews friends, or experts, or comparative strangers, faces challenging problems of being courteous, efficient, and purposive in his conversation. These problems exist in all his speaking, but they may be more keenly felt as the high school student talks to persons other than his classmates.

Nearly all of the speaking activities of the classroom may serve as occasions for interviewing by the members of the class. Public speeches may be based on information gathered by interviews; some teachers ask students to try out their ideas with a number of persons prior to speaking in class. Discussions and debates may make wide use of the interview for gathering information. High school students studying vocational opportunities often use interviews with local representatives of various occupations as one important source of information. Consequently it is nearly always possible to introduce students to the study of interviewing in some situation where they sense an immediate need for skill in this form of speaking.

A Classification of Interviews

The student using the interview technique will find himself faced with different problems, depending upon whether he is using (1) the interview which seeks information, or (2) the interview which has a persuasive purpose, like applying for a job, selling a product or an idea, or soliciting money or support. Generally, the information interview will come closer to the needs of most high school students than will the interview seeking a persuasive end.

Many high schools include some unit in the curriculum to assist students in making vocational choices, and frequently the job-application interview is taught in connection with such a unit. Before emphasizing persuasive types of interviewing, the speech teacher should check on the extent to which this form of interviewing is receiving attention in connection with some other course.

Classroom Procedures in Teaching Interviewing

Demonstrating and discussing interviewing

If a number of members of the speech class are faced with the immediate necessity of interviewing, the speech teacher may open the problem of planning the interview with the entire class. Through reading and discussion, students are able to understand certain characteristic types of preliminary planning which ought to be done by an interviewer.

A teacher reports:

A discussion group in this eleventh grade speech class was considering the question, "What is the purpose of student government in this high school?" Members of the group had decided to interview the faculty to get their reactions, and the teacher raised with the entire class the question, "What sort of planning ought to take place prior to these interviews?" Students suggested the following:

1. The interviewer should formulate his purpose carefully. (Does he want opinion on the function of student government; does he want facts on the past operation of student government; should he try to get the prospective interviewee to give illustrations of his concepts of the function of student government? and so on.

2. The interviewer should plan certain key questions, or lines of questioning he proposes to follow with the interviewee.

3. The interviewer should decide what information the interviewee will want as to the purpose of the interview, and prepare to give this information quickly and clearly.

4. The interviewer should plan time and place arrangements for the interviewee's convenience.

As a demonstration of this sort of planning, one of the prospective interviewers was asked to demonstrate to the class his planned approach in the interview. Under questioning by the teacher, he told how he had arranged for the interview, and what considerations had prompted these arrangements. Using another student as a simulated "interviewee," he explained his purpose in seeking the interview, and proceeded to develop the line of questioning he planned to use in the actual interview. The class then discussed the adequacy of the questioning.

An interesting point to be demonstrated about interviewing is the importance of accurate reporting of the results of the interview. A student may be asked to conduct an unrehearsed demonstration interview with one of his fellow students. The interviewee may be a student who has prepared certain information and opinions on a subject of interest to the group. The interviewer may be asked to organize his data, and report to the class on the information he has received. Then the class can discuss the accuracy of the interviewer's reporting, asking, "Were important facts accurately reported?" "Were the attitudes and opinions of the interviewee fairly reported?" This discussion may lead to consideration of the propriety of asking an interviewee to check the accuracy of statements which are to be attributed to him, and of various ways of keeping notes on an interview. The students may be interested in examining interviewing from the standpoint of the job of a newspaper reporter.

Checking the Reactions of Interviewees

The speech teacher may develop an interesting activity by getting the co-operation of certain faculty colleagues who agree to be interviewed by a number of students, and to report their reactions. These interviewees can call attention to actions on the part of the interviewers which inconvenienced them, or made them uncomfortable, or otherwise reduced the effectiveness of the interview, as well as to exceptionally good techniques. The speech teacher may wish to get the reactions of the interviewees, and select for consideration by the class those reactions which seem to have the greatest general significance.

Developing the Habit of Questioning; Seeking Information

Almost any high school class will be the scene of a number of arguments over matters of fact or interpretation, carried on by students who have neither looked for the facts, nor sought the opinions of experts. The speech teacher should be alert to the possibility of suggesting the use of an interview to settle arguments which are futile because of lack of information. Of course, the interview is only one method of inquiry, and its suitability is to be determined by the nature of the problem at issue, and the availability of persons who may be expert in relation to it. Nevertheless, the interview is an avenue of inquiry often neglected by high school students, even by those who may have established somewhat effective habits of seeking information through library research.

Reporting Reactions to Interviewees

Most of the practice of high school students in interviewing will necessarily come with the student serving as interviewer, and seeking information from adults with special knowledge or experience. The behavior of the interviewee is, of course, as essential to the success of the venture as is the behavior of the interviewer. After a number of the members of the speech class have had experience in interviewing, they may wish to discuss the characteristics they most liked in the behavior of the persons they interviewed. Such a discussion must be handled carefully, of course, and should not be allowed to involve direct criticism of specific persons. Indeed, the impropriety of such personal criticisms may need discussing by the class. However, if the discussion emphasizes the positive characteristics of interviewees, and calls attention to negative characteristics without reference to particular persons, it can prove a helpful learning activity for the members of the speech class.

TEACHING PARLIAMENTARY PROCEDURE

Much public speaking, discussion, and debate takes place in meetings operating under parliamentary law. These assemblages may be as significant to the life of the nation as the United States Congress, or as obscure as a seventh grade class meeting, but the laws which govern their conduct of business have much in common. They are laws of procedure designed to protect the rights of each individual member, promote fair play and harmony among the members, and guarantee the efficient, orderly conduct of business by groups of any size. While individual organizations may have certain procedural rules of their own, they are likely to act under that common system of regulations, derived from experience and set down formally as parliamentary law.

Why High School Students Study Parliamentary Law

In a sense, parliamentary law simply provides one set of rules within which debate, discussion, or public speaking may take place.

Yet these parliamentary rules have received specific attention in the
high school curriculum to an extent not accorded any other rules
for speaking. The reason for this emphasis is twofold: Skill in
using the forms of parliamentary procedures, and an understanding
and appreciation of their significance, seem to be learnings appropriate to the needs of all high school students. Most students will
be participating in class and club organizations in which business
will be expedited if the members have a knowledge of parliamentary
law. After high school, most adults will be similarly involved in
meetings, clubs, or societies requiring some measure of adherence
to parliamentary procedure for the efficient conduct of their business. Groups in which knowledge of parliamentary law is widely
shared are not automatically efficient; laws do not guarantee good
speaking and listening, good discussion, or good debating. Groups
in which the knowledge and appreciation of parliamentary law are
lacking, however, are almost inevitably inefficient. High school
students, therefore, study the principles of parliamentary law because they have both immediate and future need for them, and
because widespread sharing of knowledge in this field will serve to
promote effective social and political action in our society.

The Study of Parliamentary Law Should Derive from Immediate Needs

Much of the teaching of parliamentary law illustrates the desirability of tying classroom instruction closely to the immediate needs
and interests of students. The following report from a speech
teacher describes a situation in which students were studying
parliamentary law, but were not practicing it on appropriate occasions.

A teacher reports:

In this high school, short units in parliamentary law were taught
in the eighth and the eleventh grades. Students studied the principles and practiced them within the classroom by developing a club
and holding meetings. At the same time, nearly all students in the
school were members of one or more organizations which were
supposedly using parliamentary procedure in conducting their
meetings. Each class in school elected officers and conducted business; there was a student council; and most students belonged to at

least one club. Observation by the speech teacher, however, disclosed the fact that the principles of parliamentary law were being ignored by nearly all of these student groups:

1. Few organizations kept accurate minutes.

2. Discussion of two or more proposals or problems at the same time was often permitted.

3. In some groups student leadership broke down and the faculty adviser took over.

4. Groups handling money seldom had clear financial records.

5. Class organizations made limited and ineffective use of committees.

6. Voting on motions was often delayed by confusion over the nature of the motion up for consideration.

The speech teacher at this school concluded that the classroom instruction in parliamentary law was getting limited results, even though it seemed well motivated and organized. Students seemed to be obtaining more practice in using ineffective procedures out of class than in using effective procedures in class.

The unfortunate situation pictured in this report is not an uncommon one. The obvious conclusion is that instruction in parliamentary law, as far as possible, should grow out of the immediate needs faced by students in their own organizations. Use of effective procedures should be sought, as a whole school objective, in all student organizations. The following is another report showing how instruction in parliamentary procedures may be developed from the needs of a student group.

A teacher reports:

In this small high school, the seventh grade class held its first organizational meeting during one of its regularly scheduled class hours. The speech teacher was invited to this meeting to discuss with the class the problem of insuring efficiency in its activities. Students were asked to list some of the procedures they would need for conducting class business. They listed:

1. A fair method of selecting officers.

2. A written statement of the purposes of their group, the duties of the officers, and the duties of the members.

3. A secretary who would keep accurate minutes.

4. A treasurer who would keep accurate records.

5. A president who knew how to keep only one item of business before the group at a time.

6. Members who knew how to state and amend motions.

7. Co-operation by all members of the class.

The speech teacher offered to take time in speech class to discuss the foregoing problems. He also offered to attend the class meetings, when possible, and observe the procedures being used. Thus the classroom study of parliamentary principles, in the seventh grade, was initiated in terms of immediate needs, and was expanded as the class met new problems. Some of the verbal forms which were being poorly used were drilled on in class. These were:

1. The form for stating a motion.

2. The form for amending a motion.

3. The forms for getting a vote.

4. The form for ruling a member out of order.

At the end of the year, the seventh grade students discussed the increased need they would have for parliamentary law as (1) their class groups faced more problems, and (2) as they entered more school clubs. They were of the opinion that a knowledge of parliamentary law helped to make meetings efficient, and fair to everyone.

Developmental Possibilities in Teaching Parliamentary Law

We have emphasized the fact that the study of parliamentary law ought to start from the immediate needs of students in conducting the business of their organizations. Until students accept the practicality of parliamentary law, extensive study of its intricacies may cause them to view it as a system of rules designed to harass ordinary people who "want to get something done."

However, beyond the immediate practical basis for studying parliamentary law, lie the possibilities of developing further significant learnings in the speech classroom.

1. *Extending leadership training*

Conducting a parliamentary meeting is an activity with obvious merit for developing the leadership potentialities of students. Ordinarily, a very small group of students will exercise such leadership roles in all student class and club organizations. Classroom parliamentary groups can be organized, therefore, to provide an extension of this leadership training to a wider group of students. The following report illustrates such an effort by a speech teacher.

A teacher reports:

The tenth grade speech class decided to practice parliamentary procedure in connection with a follow-up to its study of radio listening. The class organized a radio listening club. This club was to meet one period each week for nine weeks. The group set a standard agenda for each meeting, part of the purpose of which was to extend the sharing of leadership experience by the members of the class. Their agenda was planned as follows:

1. The meeting is called to order.
2. The secretary's report.
3. The report of a program committee, assigning (a) a radio program for listening during the following week, and (b) a speaker to make a report of evaluation on the assigned program at the subsequent meeting.
4. Hearing and discussing a talk evaluating the program which had been assigned by the program committee at the previous meeting.
5. Entertaining a motion of praise or censure for the program discussed. (The resolution was to be offered by the speaker, with opportunity for discussion, amendment, debate, and so on, by members of the club.)
6. Nomination and election of a new president and secretary for the following meeting.
7. Adjournment.

Adjournment was required by rule 10 minutes prior to the end of the hour to allow time for a critique of each meeting.

2. *Developing parliamentarians*

While the skills and understandings of parliamentary law need to be widely shared in our society, extensive and detailed knowledge of such principles is also especially needed by certain persons. Students with exceptional interest in the study of parliamentary law may well be encouraged to acquire expertness in this area. All students may be helped to see the value of the expert parliamentarian. The following report illustrates the way in which an intensive knowledge of parliamentary law was achieved in one speech class.

A teacher reports:

The tenth grade speech class decided that if each student group would appoint a parliamentarian, the effect would be to improve parliamentary practices in the school, and to give valuable additional training to the students who were appointed. Members of the class carried their proposal to all student groups, and got the co-operation of most of them. The class prepared a short mimeographed "Guide to Parliamentary Law," to be given to all parliamentarians. The guide was based on an analysis of a parliamentary law text, to which the parliamentarians were referred for further information. The main headings of the guide were:

1. The purpose of parliamentary law.
2. Fundamental principles of parliamentary law.
3. How to present a motion.
4. How to amend a motion.
5. A list of frequently used motions in their order of precedence.
6. Types of committees.
7. Uses of committees.
8. How to speed up business in small, informal groups.
9. References to be used to decide points of controversy on parliamentary procedure.

In the process of preparing this guide, students in the speech class developed considerable detailed knowledge of the forms and purposes of parliamentary law.

Increasing the Opportunities for Informal Speech in the Classroom

This chapter has considered certain specific categories of activities in informal speaking which may be given direct attention in the speech classroom. There is another consideration with regard to everyday speech which deserves the attention of the speech teacher. This is the question of how best to increase the opportunities for purposeful informal speech in the classroom.

The speech teacher who examines carefully the activities of his classroom may discover many opportunities of this sort which are being neglected. Frequently the teacher is carrying out activities involving speech which could be carried out by members of the class to their profit. At other times the teacher simply is overlooking the learning possibilities of situations in which informal student speaking might accomplish a real purpose. Listed below are some of the common plans used by speech teachers to increase the amount of informal student speaking.

1. The class is frequently given five to ten minutes for the discussion of local or national news events which have immediate interest. A student leader conducts the conversation, which occasionally is evaluated in terms of such questions as, "Was every speaker easy to hear?" "Were the comments sufficiently brief?" "Pertinent?" "How many students took part?" "Were references to people courteous?" "Did the students seem interested in the opinions of others, as well as their own?"

2. The class reviews a reading assignment, by having members of the class ask questions, and evaluate the answers to these questions given by their fellow students.

3. All student speakers in the class are introduced by a student chairman. Introductions are brief, informal, and designed to secure favorable attention to the speaker's subject.

4. Students bringing materials for the class bulletin board are usually asked to call the attention of the class to their contributions.

5. The teacher asks a question about speech which seems to call for an answer based upon thought, rather than recall. Members of the class divide into groups of five or six students, each with a student chairman. The chairman asks each member of his group to give his answer to the question. The group then selects the student whose answer they believe to be the best offered in their group. Finally, each group has the selected student present his answer to the class as a whole.

Developmental Levels for Everyday Speech

Everyday speaking activities appear at every level of the curriculum. Accordingly, the speech teacher properly may view the development of skills in everyday speaking as related constantly to the skills, needs, and potentialities of each student at each stage in his growth. In other words, the speech teacher does not introduce the study of everyday speaking at some one grade level, the seventh grade for example, and then assume that all, or any of the students have learned all they need to know about everyday speech.

Nevertheless, certain decisions should be reached by the speech teacher regarding the purposes of the school curriculum as a whole and the placement of certain specific items of instruction. These decisions are in a sense arbitrary, and are reached only to avoid wasteful duplication of instruction in a variety of classes in any one school. The following is the report of one teacher on the placement of certain types of study of everyday speaking in the curriculum of one school, together with some of the circumstances which led to the decisions on placement. This report is not offered as an ideal solution to the problem of placement of instruction in everyday speaking, for we have already asserted that there may be no such ideal placement. It is offered to illustrate the process by which the speech teacher, or the faculty of a given school, may reach a decision on placement.

A teacher reports:

The faculty of High School A decided to place classroom instruction in conversation and social forms in the seventh grade, in connection with a broad social program developed for this grade in this school. The program included at least one social gathering to which all seventh grade parents were invited. The study of the class started in terms of the immediate problems raised by seventh grade social events, but was broadened to include the uses of conversation and social form in situations encountered by the student outside of school affairs. Observation, classroom discussion, reading, and films were used to develop the unit of study. This same school planned a unit on personality development in the ninth grade, in which additional reading materials and films were used. This unit reviewed with students their earlier experiences, and organized their generalizations relating to the study of conversation and social form.

The decision was reached that interviewing as information seeking should be taught in the eighth grade in connection with a unit on discussion procedures. Included in this unit were problems which involved the use of the interview as a research method, and it was planned that time would be taken by the eighth grade students for the careful development of interview procedures. All teachers were to call attention to the requirements of effective interviewing on all occasions for which this technique of research was to be used. Interviewing for job applications was to receive emphasis in the twelfth year in connection with a unit on vocations.

Everyday Speech as a Goal

The study of informal, everyday speech is not limited to the direct study of such activities as conversation, telephoning, social forms, or interviewing. All speech activities in the school may contribute to the development of skills in everyday speaking. They do this by helping the student to develop speech skills and attitudes with general utility, and understandings about speech applicable to all speaking situations. They do this also by emphasizing constantly the interrelationships of the skills the student uses in public speaking, discussion, debating, reading aloud, storytelling, dramatic activity, and the skills he uses in the less formal speech of everyday life. In the chapters which follow, we shall emphasize the thought that all speech activities may contribute to the developing of speaking skills useful in all the situations of everyday life. Public speaking and discussion will be viewed as extensions of good conversation. Debate will be considered as both an extension of discussion, and an integral element of both discussion and conversation. Reading aloud, storytelling, and dramatics will all be treated as means of developing skills useful in all other forms of speaking.

SELECTED BIBLIOGRAPHY

Allen, Betty, *If You Please!* Philadelphia: J. B. Lippincott & Co., 1942.

Allen, Betty, and Mitchell Pirie Briggs, *Behave Yourself!* Philadelphia: F. A. Davis Co., 1948.

Barbour, Ralph Henry, *Good Manners for Boys.* New York: Appleton-Century-Crofts, Inc., 1947.

Betz, Betty, *Your Manners Are Showing.* New York: Grossett & Dunlap, 1946.

Black, Kathleen, *Manners for Moderns.* New York: Dodd, Mead & Co., 1938.

Borchers, G. L., *Living Speech.* Harcourt, Brace & Co., 1949. Chs. 4 and 6.

Borchers, G. L., and Claude M. Wise, *Modern Speech.* New York: Harcourt, Brace & Co., 1947, Chs. 12, 15.

Bro, Margueritte, *Let's Talk about You.* New York: Doubleday & Co., Inc., 1945.

Brockman, Mary, *What Is She Like?* New York: Charles Scribner's Sons, 1936.

Burnham, Helen, *Boys Will be Men.* Philadelphia: J. B. Lippincott Co., 1942.

Chapman, Paul, *Your Personality and Your Job.* Boston: Little, Brown & Co., 1941.

Crawford, Claud, *Living Your Life.* Boston: D. C. Heath & Company, 1940.

Crawford, John Edmund, and Luther E. Woodward, *Better Ways of Growing Up.* Philadelphia: Muhlenberg Press, 1948.

Daly, Maureen, *Smarter and Smoother.* New York: Dodd, Mead & Co., 1944.

Daly, Sheila, *Personality Plus.* New York: H. W. Wilson Co., 1946.

Eldridge, Elizabeth, *Poise and Popularity for Every Girl.* New York: E. P. Dutton & Co., Inc., 1936.

Fedder, Ruth, *A Girl Grows Up.* New York: H. W. Wilson Co., 1948.

Gilman, Wilbur, Bower Aly, and Loren D. Reid, *The Fundamentals of Speaking.* New York: The Macmillan Co., 1951, Ch. 27, "Parliamentary Procedure."

Harris, Jessie, *Everyday Living.* Boston: Houghton Mifflin Co., 1946.

Hile, Frederic W., and Joseph A. Wigley, "The Telephone Conversation Project," *Western Speech* (January, 1951), 15: 31–37.

Hogue, Helen, *Bringing Up Ourselves.* New York: Charles Scribner's Sons, 1943.

Howes, R. F., "Training in Conversation," *Quarterly Journal of Speech* (April, 1928), 14: 253–260.

Human Relations in the Classroom. Book I and II. Bulletin of the Delaware State Society for Mental Hygiene, 1950.

Hunter, Lucretta, *A Girl Today: The Woman Tomorrow.* Boston: Allyn and Bacon, 1932.

Jonathan, Norton, *Gentlemen Aren't Sissies.* Philadelphia: John C. Winston Co., 1938.

Mawhinney, Clara Krefting, "Speech in Informal Social Activities," *Bulletin of Secondary School Principals* (November, 1945), 29: 133, pp. 47–50.

Miller, Francis, *Personal Problems of a High School Girl.* New York: H. W. Wilson Co., 1946.

Murphy, George, "Conversation—A Lost Art?" *Childhood Education* (February, 1951), 27: 256–259.

Oliver, Robert T., "A Working Bibliography on Conversation," *Quar-*

terly Journal of Speech (November, 1934), 20: 534–535. (253 essays and books on conversation).

O'Neill, J. M. (ed.), *Foundations of Speech.* New York: Prentice-Hall, Inc., 1941, Ch. 10.

Pierce, Beatrice, *It's More Fun When You Know the Rules.* New York: Farrar, Straus & Young, Inc., 1936.

Pierce, Wellington, *Youth Comes of Age.* New York: McGraw-Hill Book Co., 1948.

Priestley, J. B., *Talking.* New York: Harper & Brothers, 1937.

Ryan, Mildred, *Your Clothes and Personality.* New York: Appleton-Century-Crofts, Inc., 1947.

Schacter, Helen, *Understanding Ourselves.* Bloomington, Illinois: McKnight & McKnight Publishing Co., 1945.

Sondel, Bess, *Are You Telling Them?* New York: Prentice-Hall, Inc., 1947, Chs. 1, 6.

Sorenson, Robert, and Marguerite Malm, *Psychology for Living.* New York: McGraw-Hill Book Co., 1948.

Weaver, A. T., *Speech: Forms and Principles.* New York: Longmans, Green & Co., 1951, Ch. 11, "Conversation and Interviews."

Weaver, A. T., and G. L. Borchers, *Speech.* Harcourt, Brace & Co., 1946, Chs. 8, 16, 18, 19.

Wilson, Margery, *Charm.* Philadelphia: Stokes, 1948.

Winans, James A., *Speech Making.* New York: Appleton-Century-Crofts, Inc., 1936, Ch. 1.

Youngblood, Dorothy, "Informal and Business Speech," *Bulletin of Secondary School Principals* (January, 1948), 32: 151, pp. 98–101.

CHAPTER 13

Public Speaking

INTRODUCTION

No SHARP line divides public speaking from the conversation, telephoning, buying and selling, and so on which make up the speech of daily living. All speech, public and private, normally involves a speaker and a listener, a social situation, purposes and attitudes, language, voice, and visible action. Yet, in certain circumstances, speech begins to take on aspects of form and deliberateness which mark the appearance of public speaking. From the standpoint of this book, public speaking appears whenever a single speaker addresses a group of listeners, using relatively continuous discourse, for a specifically defined and delimited purpose. Characteristically, public speaking is planned. It concentrates attention on the *one* as speaker, as opposed to the *many* as audience. It involves substantially continuous discourse by the speaker, whether the time allotted is one minute or several hours.

SOME HISTORICAL NOTES

The teaching tradition in the field of public speaking is older and more continuous than that for any other form of speech. As we already have observed, the schools of ancient Greece and Rome were concerned with teaching speech, and particularly with the teaching of public speaking. For many centuries, indeed as recently as the nineteenth, the educational discipline of *rhetoric* was directed primarily toward the development of public speakers.

294

This history, extending in our own western European culture from the schools of ancient Greece and Rome to the immense educational structure of twentieth century America, has already been considered in some detail in Part I, Chapter 2. From the standpoint of the teacher, it is significant to note that this long tradition in teaching public speaking has given us an unusual opportunity to define by experience the skills needed for effective public address, and the areas in which students may study to acquire these skills.

It is of great importance to note that the instruction in public speaking which has been most successful historically has been that which stresses public speaking as whole activity—the systematic study of a great complex of skills which come into focus in the act of speech making. Thus, classical rhetoric came to define the field of public speaking as embracing the divisions of *invention*, or the discovery of ideas (subject matter); *disposition*, or the arrangement of materials for speaking; *style*, or the selection of language most suitable to the total speaking situation; *memory;* and *delivery*. Modern texts in public speaking usually cover, in some form at least, four of these divisions, without giving as much attention to *memory* as was common in the ancient books. The success of instruction which treats public speaking as a whole art has been as clear as the failure of that instruction which attempts to concentrate on only one or two aspects of public speaking. Thus, in medieval times instruction in rhetoric was frequently narrowed to instruction in style—the casting of ideas into suitable language. Well intentioned though it may have been, this instruction seems to have had notably bad results. It led to an excessive concentration on the art of ornamenting thought, and resulted in speech making which was notable for flowery, effusive language. It neglected both the problem of getting sound subject matter and the problem of delivering speeches effectively.

One of the reactions against the neglect of speech delivery was the growth of instruction in elocution, which attempted to focus on instruction in actual speaking to audiences, exclusive of other considerations. The elocutionary movement had great influence in England, and in the United States in the eighteenth and nineteenth centuries, but again, despite good intentions and the contributions of some skilled and thoughtful teachers, it ultimately narrowed down to developing speakers who were so extravagant in their use of posture, vocal expression, and gesture that the art they practiced fell into disrepute.

Teachers would do well to ponder these historical changes of emphasis in the teaching of public speaking, for they contain a clear message: Public speaking should be taught as a whole art, in which the student views his speaking as the combination of a number of interrelated skills and activities.

THE SIGNIFICANCE OF PUBLIC SPEAKING IN SCHOOL AND PUBLIC LIFE

The emphasis on everyday speaking in our own century has caused some teachers to conclude that public speaking is an activity seldom indulged in by the majority of students, and of significance in the adult life of only a few persons. It is true that public speaking does not have quite the same significance to the American citizen in 1952 that it had to the citizen of ancient Athens, who had to plead his own cases in the courts and defend himself publicly if accused of wrongdoing. But it does require a kind of magnificent disinclination to face facts to conclude that public speaking is no longer an important form of speaking in our own century.

Public speaking is one of the common forms of student activity in the modern American high school. Usually, in classroom work, it appears under some pallid title like "oral report" or "topic," but no one can tour the classrooms of a contemporary high school without being impressed with the functional character of public speaking in the lives of students. On a single day, a student in Biology 9 will be giving a report on the "Causes and Control of the Common Cold," another student in Social Studies 7 will be recounting the story of "The Indian Tribes of Our State," in English 11 a student who has read *All The King's Men* will be recommending it to others in the class; and the president of the student council will have some words to address to the student body on the care of the school lunch room. In many schools, of course, too few students will be giving too many of these talks, but one of the reasons for this unfortunate state of affairs is the inadequacy felt by many students in handling even simple informational speeches.

Moreover, public speaking always will remain an important functional activity in the lives of most students. As adults, many of them will continue to feel the need to speak in public, as salesmen, lawyers, doctors, teachers, businessmen, and members of churches, clubs, civic organizations, labor unions, or co-operatives. In all of these ways, adults become effective, participating citizens in proportion as they are able to engage effectively in public speaking. Furthermore, public speaking will bulk large in their lives even when they are not doing the speaking. They will live in an age when the spoken word, in radio and television, has vast influence in all the significant decisions of society. As students and as adults they will need to listen with critical judgment to an immense amount of public speaking. Listening skills cannot be exclusively the product of instruction in public speaking, but may be aided greatly by it.

TEACHING PROBLEMS AND PROCEDURES

The Problem Students Face in Finding Subject Matter

A common complaint heard by speech teachers from students is, "I have nothing to talk about." Perhaps a student may make such a statement because he is nourishing a desire to withdraw from situations in which he will be the center of attention, or because he has been asked to make a speech under circumstances in which too little attention has been paid to creating the conditions of need. The problems of student attitude have already been covered in Chapter 10; the problems arising from the speech situation will be considered now.

In general terms, the problem of subject matter does not arise in speeches which are connected with meeting the needs of a social situation. Thus, the subject matter of most speeches, in classes other than speech, is set, or should be, by the general purposes and needs of the class in which the speeches are made. There is a special problem, however, in teaching the class in which students are *practicing* public speaking skills—skills which will be put to functional use in other classes. Here the attention of the class is on the practice of speech making, and the subject matter may seem incidental to the immediate purposes of the group. It is exactly because subject matter is thought of as incidental, that many speech students encounter difficulties in finding something to talk about. An obvious answer then is to attack the problem at its source by making certain that there is more than incidental need for subject matter in the speech class.

Speech teachers use at least three kinds of approaches to this problem in their classes:

1. The first approach demands that the class raise a problem, the solution of which involves the need for speech making. Note the unit described earlier in this text, in which the teacher suggested an intellectual problem relative to speech, "Do animals speak?" Because of the nature of the problem, it was possible for the teacher to schedule a considerable number of speeches arising out of the investigation.

a. One teacher reports starting his tenth grade class in speech fundamentals by identifying with the group a large number of problems of personal behavior, public policy, and information which the group desires to investigate. The public speaking of the class follows upon group investigation of these problems.

b. Another teacher reports starting the speech class with the investigation of problems in which other classes or adult groups will be interested. The class ultimately carries the results of its deliberations to interested groups outside the speech class, using various forms of speaking, but including carefully prepared public speeches.

2. The second approach to the problem of subject matter involves stimulating class interest in some general topic which is likely to be of interest to students of the age and background of the particular group, or which may be stimulating in terms of a local or national event which has brought it to the attention of the students.

a. A teacher reports that a discussion of "Our state as a Vacationland" provided most students with subject matter for talks. These talks ranged from reports on vacation experiences to investigations of facts about the vacation industry, and to the expression of hopes concerning vacations.

b. The community chest drive in this town wanted a group of student speakers to explain the need for funds, and methods of contributing. The teacher reports using this occasion for study and preparation of speeches to be used in the drive.

3. The third approach makes use of the speech class as an opportunity for all students to talk in terms of their own interests, skills, and experiences.

    a. Most students have skills or interests which they are anxious to talk about with other persons. These skills and interests may have been the product of work in other classes of the school, or they may have been the product of hobbies, and other out-of-school concerns. The speech class offers an excellent opportunity for students to try out their thinking and knowledge on others, and to observe the range of interests and information of their classmates.

    b. A teacher reports that a discussion of "What do you know that might interest others, and what would you like to learn from others?" led to a series of informational talks which were either requested or approved by the class as a whole. Another discussion of "What can you do, and what would you like to know how to do?" led to a similar series of talks, demonstrating, and instructing in certain skills.

Extending student experience

The speech teacher must be aware of his responsibility not only to draw upon the subject matter latent in his students' interests and activities, but also to direct students to the sort of activity which will enrich their range of interests, information, and communicable experiences. This responsibility is shared by the speech teacher with all other teachers. There are, however, special contributions possible in the discovery of subject matter for public speeches in the speech class. These include the effort to widen the students' range of reading, listening, and discussion. The speech teacher can emphasize the significant interrelationship of the students' own thinking to the subject matter which has come to him through reading and observing. It should be emphasized that good speeches are never the product of a simple effort to reconstruct facts or ideas set forth by another person. Rather, they result from the thoughtful selection and appraisal of these facts and from the confirmations or questions provided by a student's own experience and reflection upon the thoughts of other persons.

A teacher reports asking each of his students to talk to six people about the material he had gathered for a speech, prior to actually preparing the speech. This was to stimulate the speakers' own thoughtful examination of their subject matter, as well as to give them insight into the way in which others viewed their subjects. It should be emphasized that many junior high school students cannot be stimulated effectively to thoughtful contemplation of subject matter, and that their speeches will not represent the product of real interaction of self, personal experience, reading, and talking to other persons. Yet this is the process of invention which underlies all speaking of real significance to speaker and listener. It should be hailed when it appears, and urged upon the consideration of all students.

The Problems Students Face in Limiting Subject Matter to a "Statement"

Nearly all texts dealing with public speaking recommend certain procedures designed to help speakers make more specific the ends they hope to accomplish with their speeches. These procedures unquestionably arise out of the experience of teachers with speeches which seem to fail because the speaker does not have his own purpose clearly in mind, or because he attempts more than is possible in the available time. This problem is apparent in the public speaking of junior high school students, whose primary purpose in speaking often seems to be the joy of hearing themselves talk, and who frequently seem to identify the boundaries of a speech as "all that which I know that is remotely related to my subject." Certain routine procedures and pressures may be used by teachers to help students in achieving purposiveness and unity in their speeches.

1. Teachers should insist that the student identify his statement—what it is that he wants to say—prior to planning and delivering his speech. Some teachers refer to this statement as the central proposition, or topic sentence, or thesis sentence. Regardless of the term used, the process involved for the speaker is that of stating in a single, complete sentence the unifying idea of this speech. The statement

may appear as a statement of fact, of belief, of desire, or of proposal, but it always identifies the focus of the speech in question. Some typical student statements follow:

> "I believe that the U.N. deserves the full support of the American Public."
> "Motion pictures are getting worse."
> "This is the way to build a model airplane."
> "You should support the Red Cross."

2. It is of the utmost importance that students come to differentiate titles, or topics, and statements. Thus, a student may have George Washington as the topic for a report, but it is necessary that he make a statement telling the essence of what it is that he intends to say about George Washington, prior to planning the content of his speech. The concepts of unity and relevance, so important to good composition and good thinking, have no significance save as a speaker identifies that which gives unity to his talk—his statement.

3. Students should be helped to see their statement as related to and arising from a purpose centered in the audience. Thus students who have some proficiency in setting forth in a single sentence the essence of their talk, may be asked to convert this statement to a single sentence describing what it is that the speaker wishes to accomplish with his audience. Thus a person whose statement is, "I believe that the U.N. deserves the full support of the American people," may create an audience-centered statement in terms of his purpose with his audience, as:

> "I want my audience to believe that the U.N. should get the full support of the American people,"
> or "I want my audience to understand my reasons for believing that the U.N. should get the full support of the American people."

Note that two rather different wordings of audience-centered purpose are possible from the same statement. The first audience-centered purpose sets a persuasive task for the speaker, while the second sets an informative task for the speaker.

A teacher reports asking some of his students on occasion to check the effectiveness of their speaking in terms of its audience-centered purpose. Thus the student who has been making a speech to inform his audience may follow this speech with a short test to check the extent to which his purpose has been achieved.   Another, who has wanted his audience to believe some proposition, may check their belief, both before and after his speech.   The exercise emphasizes for students a number of important concepts about public speaking—its purposive nature, the fact that the purpose involves the responses of an audience, and that responses of an audience are difficult to control, and vary widely from person to person.

4. Senior high school students gradually may be led to understand that speeches hold different general purposes, and that the general purpose of the speaker determines to some extent the sort of materials and procedures he selects for his speech, and the standards of criticism which will be applied to the speech.   Although different classifications of the general ends of speech are common, distinctions are usually made among speeches which aim: (a) to entertain, (b) to inform, (c) to persuade, and (d) to actuate, or move to overt action.

The concept of the relationships of the general end of a speech, its specific audience-centered purpose, and the form of the speech, is not easily developed with high school students.   It involves the highly abstract notion of the relationships of purpose and form in language—relationships which are sufficiently complicated to trouble linguists at any level.   Yet, to some extent, many high school students who have had sufficient experience with speech making will be ready to observe the differences in the general ends for which we use speech, and to make distinctions important to the practice and criticism of speeches based on these observed differences.

The Problem of Gathering Material

Good speeches are built out of a plentiful supply of materials. When the speaker has to tell all he knows in order to fill an allotted period of time with his speech, the probability is slight that his speech will be good.   Characteristically, many high school students seem unable to solve this problem.   Unlike some of their more fluent classmates, their difficulty seems to be not that of limiting their talk to the most pertinent available materials, but of discovering enough material.

Using library facilities

The problem of gathering material is a hard one for students who are deficient in reading or library skills. Accordingly, the development of such skills is a direct concern of the speech teacher, although it is one he shares with all other teachers. In most schools, responsibility for teaching the efficient use of the library will be specifically assigned to some teacher. Perhaps this instruction will be given as a unit in seventh grade language arts, and repeated in the same sequence in the ninth grade. The speech teacher should be familiar with the sort of skills students are supposed to have acquired, or to which they have been "exposed." In this way he can encourage students to use these specific skills in the preparation of speeches, and can help students who have not learned these skills to acquire them.

It is extremely important that students be given ample time for research and investigation from the moment they have arrived at their audience-centered statement to the moment they present their speeches; that specific plans be laid for the use of this period; and that, when these plans include reading and library research, the speech teacher assume responsibility both for the existence of materials available to the students, and for their ability to use library and reading skills.

There are, of course, other sources of speech material. And, while a student's deficiencies in reading and library skills are often observed, his deficiencies in other methods of investigation are frequently neglected. Three sources other than reading that need special mention are discussed in the following paragraphs.

Using radio and television

Speech teachers are aware of the significance of student listening and viewing habits in their personal development. Frequently the speech class will study these communication media, and the use being made of them by students, as a part of the work of the class. It may be observed here that directing students to radio or television programs which will give them useful materials for speech making is an effective way of improving their listening and viewing habits.

Using interviews and conversations

Materials gathered through interviews are particularly significant in speech preparation. The student not only collects materials, but also hears others verbalize these materials, and he may begin to see what aspects of his statements interest other people, and what the attitudes of others toward his purpose actually are. Interviewing as a form of inquiry has already been considered in this book (pages 271–283), and should be freely employed in the investigation process preceding public speaking.

Using student's own experiences

The finest speaking often represents genuine reflection on the part of the speaker. His materials reveal the thoughtful interaction of his own emotional and intellectual experiences with ideas and information gathered from others. Speeches thus reflectively prepared are in sharp contrast with those in which the student attempts to re-say the things said in a book or magazine article. The teacher often tells the student who parrots the speech of others, "Say it in your own words," or, "But what did *you* think of this writer's ideas?" Such gentle prodding usually does not do much good. Students frequently avoid using their own real experiences, and their own reflective reactions to facts, ideas, and events, either because of the poverty of their experience, or because they like the security of parroting the ideas of others, because audience criticism in that case is aimed at the original, not the present, speaker.

Probably during their high school years only a few students will prepare speeches representing the reflective interaction of their own real experiences with events, facts, and ideas, but the importance of such creative speaking, to the speaker and to his audience, warrants every encouragement by the teacher to those students who try to achieve it.

A teacher reports:

The class had discussed the difference between relating an event and describing one's own reactions to the event. Students were asked if they could remember some simple happening in their lives which had stirred deep reactions of emotion or of thinking. Several could. These students were given the challenge of trying to re-create their experiences for others. Speeches of unusual interest followed, and the class discussed the importance of relating oneself to events and audiences as a part of speech making.

The Problem of Organization

The activity of public speaking may afford the speech teacher his best opportunity for teaching skills of organization. The construction of a speech involves both the problems of organizing the materials in the speech, as they relate logically to one another; and the problems of creating a structure or form for the speech which will please the audience.

1. The simplest concept of structure considers the speech as having three parts—*introduction, body,* and *conclusion;* or four parts—*introduction, statement, supports for statement,* and *conclusion.* Ordinarily it is desirable that students, as a matter of routine, prepare plans for their speeches, indicating these simple structural divisions, prior to the delivery of the speeches. Most speech texts consider in some detail the functions of these parts of a speech, and present exercises for studying types of introductions and conclusions.

2. It is important that the student see that the statement and its supports will be prepared first, and that the introduction and conclusion ordinarily will be worked out afterwards. Speeches need not and should not be planned in the order of their structural parts.

3. More elaborate concepts of structure, in which students will observe the variety of plans which may be used for preparing speeches of different sorts, ordinarily are not needed for fundamental instruction in speech. Special courses in public speaking may deal with structure more intensively. An exception to this may be the use of speeches in which the entire speech consists of the statement and a supporting anecdote—a structure illustrated in the following report.

A teacher reports:

Students were asked to present talks in which a general statement was supported by an anecdote, or to give an anecdote from which they could draw a general statement. Anecdotes were to be found by reading, or in personal experiences; or imaginatively created to fit the statement. The class discussed the simplicity and effectiveness of such a speech plan.

The Problem of Language (Style)

As with organization, the activity of public speaking affords the speech teacher many opportunities for teaching skills in the use of spoken language. The nature of these skills, and the procedures in-developing them have already been considered in Chapter 8.

The Problem of Delivery

Students face serious problems in developing skill in the delivery of public speeches. Skills of delivery embrace the generalized skills of action and voice discussed in Chapters 6 and 7, and also raise special problems associated with the activity of public speaking. Three of these problems will be considered here.

Developing desirable characteristics

Although students are able to agree upon the desirable characteristics of delivery in public speeches, they often complain that they do not know how to go about developing these characteristics. The student may be criticized for the lack of physical animation, and then, when he essays animation in his next speech, he is criticized because his gestures are not co-ordinated or natural. He has been told that his actions ought to arise out of sincere feeling, and yet he reports, "I feel like standing like a post," or, "I feel that I want to look out of the window." The student needs to study delivery very carefully so that he may come to an intelligent understanding of his problems, and learn not only the goal he is seeking to achieve, but also the sensible path he must follow to reach it. Certain types of understandings may be developed by discussion and will help the student.

1. Students may be led to see that physical and vocal animation have already been learned by most people, and that they naturally use a great variety of facial expressions, movements, vocal qualities, and inflections which are useful for supporting specific types of meaning. Observation of other students and adults, and classroom exercises in pantomime and in symbolizing emotions by vocal quality or facial expressions will help to establish this point. Thus the student may observe that his problem is not so much learning postures, expressions, and inflections, as it is using the tools he has already acquired. His problem may be one of poise, or freedom,

and therefore his delivery should improve with practice and experience in speaking.

2. Students may be encouraged to eliminate certain distracting movements from their speech, by being made aware of these movements. The teacher must exercise judgment in advising such eliminations. Speakers who have serious problems of social fears may be better off when they employ certain random movements to relieve their tensions, than when they add one more problem to the business of speech making.

3. Students may see that extensive practice is necessary to acquire good delivery, and that such practice should involve talking out loud, with movement and gesture. It is important that teachers help fix the habit of preparation for delivery as a part of the routine of speech making. If space is available it is frequently desirable to provide time for actual rehearsal of delivery during class time.

A teacher reports:

Students in a class preparing public speeches were paired off, and the pairs of students were given corners of the classroom, or other available rooms, for practicing their speeches with one another. Each speaker was asked to present his talk aloud at least three times prior to reassembling the class for the final presentation of the talks. The speeches were considerably improved in delivery over previous speeches given in the class, and the class discussed certain obvious implications of this result for the preparation of public speeches.

Developing extemporaneous techniques

Many high school students will be reluctant to speak extemporaneously, without notes, even for short periods of time. Fundamental instruction in speech should emphasize extemporaneous speaking. Extemporaneous speaking is widely useful in our society; it is close to the informal speech of conversation. The student who develops skill in extemporaneous speaking, therefore, is likely to see more clearly than will the student who relies upon a manuscript the close relationship between public speaking and informal speaking. This statement does not mean, of course, that speaking from manuscript is always prohibited for the high school student.

In encouraging the use of extemporaneous speaking, the speech teacher will often encounter difficulties with students who seem to assume that an extemporaneous speech is, by definition, a poorly prepared one. The teacher can dramatize the possibilities of careful preparation for extemporaneous speaking by pointing out that speakers who are well prepared for short, extemporaneous speeches are often able to give their speeches without the use of notes; they have developed such a clear mental picture of the structure of the speech, and have practiced its delivery so thoroughly, that they no longer need the support of a written outline to assure an orderly speech.

GRADE LEVEL CONSIDERATIONS IN INTRODUCING PUBLIC SPEAKING SKILLS

Teachers are generally agreed that the learning experiences of high school students ought to be appropriate to their level of maturation. This would indicate that there ought to be some differentiation made in the study of public speaking by a seventh grade student, and the study of the same form of speaking by a student in the twelfth grade. Speech teachers need to exercise extreme care, however, to avoid jumping from this general acknowledgment of the need for differentiation to arbitrary decisions about specific concepts or skills in speaking which may or may not be introduced at certain grade levels. Characteristic errors in making such arbitrary decisions are described below.

1. Some teachers assume that younger students use language primarily for such simple functions as relaying information, asking questions, giving directions, and so on, and that it is not until they are more mature that they begin to use language consciously and purposively to control the behavior of others, to persuade, or move to action. Thus they would delay reference to language functions such as persuasion until the student is older. Actually there is no evidence to support this assumption. Children, even at pre-school age, seem to use speech for all the purposes for which they will use it as adults. Maturation is revealed in terms of the skill with which they use speech, and the level of insight they reveal into speaking behavior, but it is not represented by any hierarchy of functions.

2. Some teachers assume that younger students have enough trouble in using speech for expressing and describing—for telling what it is that they feel or believe, or for describing or stating facts

as observed or read about. They would have such students concentrate on these language activities, without raising the question of the relation of all these activities to an audience. They would not trouble the speaker with the necessity of describing his purposes in terms of what he wants from his listeners, or with the problem of selection of language and ideas to meet a particular audience situation. The teacher would delay introducing the relatively sophisticated concept of speech as related to audience, subject matter, and speaking situation until the student is relatively mature. We need to observe here, however, that children have a rudimentary awareness of the relationships between speech and the listener even before they start to school; that many children differentiate quite sharply the ways in which they speak to different auditors, on a basis of their experience with the auditors' expectations. There seems little point to deliberately delaying secondary school children in making observations about the relationships of audiences to speaking, and in drawing conclusions based on these observations. The depth of their awareness will vary with their level of maturation, but there is no age or grade level at which a child suddenly becomes capable of understanding certain concepts about the nature of speech.

If it is necessary to avoid arbitrary decisions on the significance of age or grade level in the selection of materials for public speaking instruction, what sort of approaches can the teacher make to the differentiation of instruction? Two possible answers may be noted.

1. The teacher may accept the thesis that the pattern of speech instruction—activity, criticism, and goal setting—permits each student to learn speech in terms of his own needs and potentialities. Thus the speech class considers only the sort of problems that the members of the class, individually and collectively, are able to see as relevant to their needs as speakers.

A teacher reports:

The members of a seventh grade speech class were not generally interested in persuasive speaking; other problems challenged their attention more immediately. One student in the class, however, was seriously disturbed by the monotonous regularity with which his proposals were voted down by the class. The teacher observed both his distress and the fact that his problem seemed to have something to do with the manner of his speaking. He was extremely aggressive and willing to proclaim his own superiority. In conference, the teacher found him extremely interested in learning how to speak persuasively. Decisions were reached as to ways in which the student ought to try to modify his speaking in class meetings. The student was observed to make considerable progress in the direction of the suggested modifications, and, fortunately, some of his ideas began to receive more favorable responses from the audience. The teacher pointed out that probably there were other matters besides his changed method of speaking that had influenced his success in class meetings, but that the changes in speaking might have helped.

2. The speech teacher, working with other teachers, may reach certain decisions as to grade levels at which certain specific public speaking skills may be introduced. Such decisions should be based on careful estimates of the most immediate needs of students. Thus it is common to emphasize informational public speaking for junior high school students, because such skill will be immediately functional in the oral reporting in all classes, and because skills in exposition will be generally useful in whatever type of speaking the student may employ.

PUBLIC SPEAKING IN CO-CURRICULAR ACTIVITIES

Ordinarily speech teachers will have many opportunities for developing extra-curricular work in public speaking. At the present time three types of inter-school contests in public speaking are common—contests in extemporaneous speaking, original oratory, and oratorical declamation. A number of contests in original oratory are sponsored by various civic and national organizations each year.

Extemporaneous Speaking

The nature of the contest

In extemporaneous speaking contests, ordinarily the participating students are asked to prepare short speeches in a limited period of time and on specific subjects drawn by lot. Rules for the conduct of the contests vary from locality to locality, but the following arrangements are common:

1. The contest director prepares a large number of topics, limited to areas of information previously made known to the participating students, and usually announced at the beginning of the school year. It is common to limit the range of subjects to those which have been discussed in a group of specifically named magazines or newspapers, or to subjects related to some large general area of information, such as "The United Nations."

2. Each contestant draws a specified number of subjects, usually from three to five, and selects one. This drawing occurs for a specified period prior to the time of the contest. One hour for preparation is common.

3. The speech must be given within specified time limits. The maximum time limit of six minutes has become general. Some rules specify a four-minute minimum, while others leave the matter of minimum to the discretion of the contestant. Some contests provide for a short period after each speech during which the speaker may be questioned on his subject, sometimes by the judge, sometimes by other contestants. This "cross examination" is designed to test the student's range of information and analysis.

4. Judging will ordinarily be based upon such factors as the skill with which the speech was constructed; the clarity, interest, and informativeness of the speech; the closeness with which the speaker adheres to his subject; and the skill used in presentation.

Preparing the extemporaneous speaker

Speech teachers ordinarily look with favor upon extemporaneous speaking contests, since the skills emphasized in them are so closely related to the skills sought in the public speaking classroom. The student who is effective in extemporaneous speaking contests is usually one who has an excellent background of information, and the capacity to interpret that information; who understands the need for unity and relevance in a short speech, and how to go about constructing such a speech; who has skill in organization; who has a capacity for clear, concrete, colorful statement; and who is skilled in informal, direct, conversational delivery. These skills have generalized significance, and students participating in extemporaneous speaking contests are usually quick to observe the practicality of the sort of training and experience they are receiving.

The training of the extemporaneous speaker involves essentially the same techniques as does all-round instruction in other forms of public speaking. Certain specific procedures may suggest themselves to the speech teacher in training the contestant:

1. The student should be encouraged to analyze the extent of the subject matter area within which subjects will be chosen. Within the area thus selected, he should follow an orderly, continuous program of reading, and he should be encouraged to discuss what he reads with other persons. Many teachers will hold regular informal discussion groups for the students interested in extemporaneous speaking. These discussions help the student to gain insight into the significance of the information he has gathered and skill in evaluating the opinions he has read. The student may be encouraged to discuss his reading with his parents or other interested adults.

2. The student should be encouraged to make notes on articles which seem to him to be particularly meritorious—apt illustrations, anecdotes, quotations, or statistics which seem likely to be useful in the development of ideas.

3. The student should be given as much practice as possible in preparing and presenting speeches under the conditions prescribed by the contest. Such speeches should be made the basis for giving the student specific help in speech structure and organization, methods of getting and holding audience attention, and the other considerations pertinent to effective public speaking.

Original Oratory

For the contest in original oratory students write, memorize, and deliver speeches, usually of a persuasive nature arising out of their strong personal feelings. This contest requires the same general skills in speech making as those needed in extemporaneous speaking, although it provides intensive experience in research, organization, and delivery, as opposed to extensive practice in these areas, and it manifestly emphasizes precision in the use of language, rather than the readiness and adaptability so important to the extemporaneous speaker.

Certain values in speech preparation are undoubtedly emphasized by practice in speech composition. The preparation of a manuscript is a common activity in advanced classes in public speaking. Such extensive work on a written speech often gives a student a new appreciation of the possibilities of effective rhetoric, the skillful selection of the right words in the right order. It also serves to clarify the differences between writing to be heard and writing to be read silently. Many students associate oral style with extemporaneous speaking only, and, with their first experience in written speeches, turn to the language style more appropriate to the printed page than to platform speaking.

The fact that this contest is designated as one in "oratory" seems to mislead some people as to the actual nature of the speaking involved. Despite its long and honorable history, the word oratory is associated in the minds of some persons with a form of speaking which seeks exaggerated effects in language and delivery. Speech teachers frequently refer to a manner of speaking or phrasing as "oratorical," using the adjective to imply that it lacks directness, simplicity, and naturalness. Some speech teachers feel that these contemporary connotations of oratory cause contestants and their teachers to turn away from the best practices in modern speech making, and, therefore, they would prefer to call the contest one in memorized public speaking. Other teachers would like to retain the word oratory, with its long and significant tradition, and eliminate the unfortunate practices in speech making which have been committed in its name. Only one believing in word magic would expect a change of title to change materially the type of speaking commonly found in the contests.

Arrangements for the contest in original oratory

The following arrangements for contests in original oratory are common:

1. It is specified that the oration shall be original with the student. Sometimes limitations are placed on the amount of quoted material in the speech. In certain contests copies of the manuscript are submitted prior to the event; in others coaches certify the originality of the speeches; and in still others it is assumed that the conditions of the contest will be observed.

2. Limitations on the length of the oration are specified. There may be a rule setting a time limit of perhaps 8 or 10 minutes on the speech, or setting a word limit to the manuscript.

3. Judges will ordinarily judge the oration as a speech; the content, organization, and delivery are judged simultaneously as the speech is presented.

Preparing the original oration

1. Students interested in writing original orations should be started on their preparation a considerable period prior to the date set for the contest, in order to permit careful study by the student of the problem of selecting a subject, and doing extensive research on the subject before preparing the speech outline. Student orators should not be expected always to select topics of world-shaking importance, which they propose to solve in 10 minutes; rather it is desirable that they select problems which are within the range of their own interests and capabilities as high school students. At the same time, since students will spend considerable time in the preparation of a single speech, it is well that they choose problems of sufficient significance to challenge their capacity for investigation and reflective thinking.

2. Once he has selected his subject, the student should undertake the preparation of his speech, following the routines customary in the preparation of all public speeches. The teacher has a fine opportunity to work with students who are preparing original orations on: the procedures of library research, interviewing, reflection, procedures in selecting the statement, outlining the speech, planning the introduction and conclusion, and preparing the manuscript.

3. It is often desirable that students present their proposed orations as extemporaneous speeches prior to preparing final manuscripts. Defects in the speech outline often will become apparent in following such a practice.

4. The speech manuscript should be read aloud repeatedly during the process of revising and reworking. The speaker should seek the reactions of others, to aid him in the work of rewriting.

5. With the manuscript in final form, the speech should be spoken aloud frequently, and, whenever possible, to real audiences, so that the speaker may get a feeling for the audience reactions which his speech may arouse. Memorization should be carried out by studying the speech as a whole, and, if the preparation of the speech has been thorough, should give the speaker little trouble.

Oratorical Declamation

In the oratorical declamation contest the student memorizes and delivers an oration originally written and presented by another speaker. It usually is a contest in speech delivery, with the emphasis on effective visible action and vocalization. The value of this contest is a point of controversy among speech teachers. Declamation has an ancient tradition; the practice of giving oratorical declamations was well thought of in Roman education, where it was assumed that the study of great speeches had felicitous effects on the language habits of the students. It was held that declamation developed a taste for elevated language and elevated thought. Nevertheless, the practice seems to have fallen into disrepute in Rome, although it was revived by the Latin Grammar school, with its reverence for all things Ciceronian, including Cicero's orations, and was a popular activity in American schools and colleges during the eighteenth and nineteenth centuries.

The critics of oratorical declamation usually point out the fact that while great speeches embody many of the qualities of literature, speeches are, nevertheless, essentially creatures of the moment, shaped by the requirements of the immediate situation, the audience, the occasion, and the nature of the speaker's own person and reputation. Critics question the appropriateness of a student taking a speech which is not his own, and delivering it to an audience for which it was not originally intended, on an occasion remote from that which engendered it. They also observe that the emphasis of the contest upon delivery often results in painful practices by the speaker, who seems to be attempting to display his own vocal and visible versatility, with little regard to the meaning of the speech, which becomes more or less incidental in this whole business. It is true that the delivery of extemporaneous speakers is often more effective than the studied mannerisms of those taking part in a contest in memorized speaking.

Arrangements for contests in declamation

The arrangements for contests in oratorical declamation are usually simple:

1. The selection to be memorized is designated as an oration or a prose selection in oratorical style. The intent seems clearly to

direct students to prose literature which was prepared as a public speech, although the extended definition may be valid for orations which appear as parts of plays or novels. (Original orations are usually permitted in this contest.)

2. A maximum time limit, usually 10 minutes, is prescribed for the declamation.

Preparing the student for oratorical declamation.

Although the contest in oratorical declamation is by definition one in delivery, the selection of the oration is a crucial step in the effective preparation of the declaimer. Good delivery presupposes real understanding of the material to be communicated. It follows that no student can declaim effectively a speech for which he lacks real feeling and understanding. It is often desirable to ask the student to read a large number of speeches until he finds one which interests him in theme and treatment, and which seems to fit him and the situation in which he will be speaking.

The student should be helped to a complete understanding of the speech he has selected. This may necessitate exploration of the historical circumstances under which the speech was presented originally, and it will always involve considerable discussion of the original speaker's purpose, attitude, and meaning.

The student should be encouraged to memorize the oration as a whole, reading it always in its entirety, and reading it aloud.

Frequent practice sessions should be scheduled for the declaimer, with provision for a real audience, whenever this is possible. The emphasis of those training the speaker should be upon stimulating his feeling for and response to the meaning of his material, until he achieves reasonable visible and vocal animation. Then the speaker may be given help in modifying some of his vocalization and action to more effective patterns. However, it is all but impossible to superimpose upon an unanimated or inhibited speaker specific gestures and vocalization, without producing delivery which is manifestly unnatural and affected.

SELECTED BIBLIOGRAPHY

Borchers, Gladys L., *Living Speech*. Rev. ed. New York: Harcourt, Brace & Co., 1949, Ch. V.

Brigance, William Norwood, *Speech Composition.* New York: F. S. Crofts, 1937.

Brink, Lauren, "Extemporaneous Speaking in the English Class," *English Journal* (November, 1947), 36: 474–477.

Gilman, Wilbur, Bower Aly, and Loren D. Reid, *The Fundamentals of Speaking.* New York: The Macmillan Co., 1951, Chapters 2–7; 13–16.

Loughlin, Richard L., "A Philosophy of Public Speaking," *Educational Forum* (November, 1946), 11: 55–65.

McWeiney, Ann, "Bugaboo of Oral Themes," *English Journal* (May, 1948), 37: 254–256.

O'Neill, J. M. (ed.), *Foundations of Speech.* New York: Prentice-Hall, Inc., 1941, Ch. 14.

Robinson, Karl F., *Teaching Speech in the Secondary School.* New York: Longmans, Green & Co., Inc., 1951, Ch. 20.

Weaver, A. T., and G. L. Borchers, *Speech.* New York: Harcourt, Brace & Co., 1946, Chs. 7, 13, 22.

Winans, James A., *Speech Making.* New York: Appleton-Century-Crofts, Inc., 1938.

CHAPTER 14

Discussion

INTRODUCTION

Discussion now has become a sort of magic word in American educational circles but its use to describe a specific form of speaking dates back no more than thirty years. Only within the last twenty years have we witnessed the appearance of a large number of books seeking to define discussion, describe its types, and provide instruction in its use. The popular radio discussions which have made this speech form familiar to the American public, originated no further back than 1931, when three University of Chicago professors got together for an experimental radio broadcast—a program which has become the now-venerable "University of Chicago Round Table." [1] The first "America's Town Meeting of the Air" was broadcast in 1935.

Although discussion as a speech form may be new, the process of discussion is very old. Men have discussed problems, doubtless, ever since speech became available to them. But for centuries no effort was made by scholars or educators to define, or describe discussion [2] as a form of speaking.

---

[1] H. L. Ewbank, and J. J. Auer, *Discussion and Debate*, New York: Appleton-Century-Crofts, Inc., 1951, p. 34.

[2] Greek scholars and their medieval followers were interested in a form of speaking called "dialectic" which has been considered by some as a predecessor of "discussion." Dialectic emphasized face-to-face discussion by two or more persons who attempted to use syllogistic reasoning to get at some probable truth. See Sattler, W. M., "Socratic Dialectic and Modern Group Discussion," *Q.J.S. XXIX* (April, 1943).

In our own generation, we are witnessing the effort of American scholars to give a form and a literature to discussion, exactly as Greek scholars more than two thousand years ago sought to give a form and a literature to individual public speaking. The effort has been prompted, in our age, by somewhat the same motives which started the Greeks on their study of public speaking. Just as public speaking was very vital in their society, so discussion is very significant in ours. It has come to be regarded as a form of speaking which deserves deliberate study and cultivation; it has tremendous potential use in our democratic culture.

In a very real sense, the impetus behind the discussion movement in America has been provided by teachers. It is true that today many persons desire to become more skillful in discussion. Businessmen and labor leaders have observed that effectively conducted discussions help to solve their mutual problems. Politicians now take formal note of the fact that discussion, as well as debate and public speaking, has a significant role to play in the business of government. But it was the interest of teachers in discussion as a tool for learning and teaching that started speculation about its possibilities. This speculation has resulted in giving discussion some powerful sanctions in our society. If anyone wishes to know why discussion is a type of speaking which meets with such universal approval by educators, let him examine the skills and goals which have come to be associated with it.

Desirable Skills and Goals Associated with Discussion

1. *A method of learning which emphasizes overt activity by the learner*

Few high school teachers today spend much time in lecturing to their students. They wish to make sure that the student is learning, and they believe that participating in discussion promotes significant and extensive learning.

2. *Valuable tool of democracy*

Just as an informed electorate has always been considered the basis of successful democracy, so talk among the electorate has been regarded as a major means of disseminating information. The American ideal of the individual's participation in government gives special sanction to discussion activity, which serves as both a form of and springboard for such participation.

3. *Best method for solving certain types of problems*

Problem solving is a particularly powerful sanction for discussion. We have learned that certain types of problems are solved better by groups of people thinking and talking together, than by any single individual. This realization extends beyond the limits of the old saw, "two heads are better than one," and includes the understanding that many types of problems have no one, true solution; they have to be dealt with by a social group, in a framework of the particular insights, needs, and wishes of all members of that group.

4. *Application of scientific methods and critical thinking to the problems of social groups*

Ewbank and Auer compare discussion as a non-laboratory method of solving social problems, to scientific laboratory research as a method of solving scientific problems. Many of the writers who have tried to describe the form of good discussion have emphasized for discussion groups the same methods as those which have been applied so successfully in scientific study. Thus the discussion group states problems, examines evidence, suggests tentative solutions, and explores these solutions in the light of the available evidence before it moves toward a final decision. The members of a discussion group are trying to follow the scientific method—to suspend judgment until all available evidence is in, and then to reach decisions in accordance with the evidence. Discussion is inquiry directed toward discovering possible solutions to problems, not advocacy of any one solution.

5. *A co-operative activity*

To the extent that people actually co-operate in a discussion group, they are practicing a form of social behavior which has a high ethical status in our society. Most of us desire a higher level of co-operation, a greater effort by people to understand and work with one another, rather than to exploit one another. To the extent that the practice of discussion promotes co-operation, it rises in value and stature among us.

Undesirable By-products of Discussion

Now all of these sanctions have given discussion higher prestige in the world of education, and to some extent among people generally, than is enjoyed by any other speech activity. To the extent that such esteem has promoted the study of discussion, and has called attention to the values of co-operative, problem-solving deliberation by groups of people, its effects have been good. But let us consider some strange and less satisfactory by-products of the increased use of discussion.

1. *Substitution of discussion for other speech forms*

One of these unfortunate by-products has been the tendency of some educators to decide that if discussion is good, other forms of speaking—debate in particular—must be bad. We will have more to say about this error in the following chapter on debate. For the moment it is enough to observe that discussion and debate should be thought of as complementary and not antagonistic forms of speaking. Both are vitally useful in our society.

2. *Not all attempts at discussion are profitable*

The second unhappy by-product arising from the evaluation of discussion as a good form of speaking has been the temptation to think that if students are discussing, they necessarily are engaging in a good process—automatically learning something of value, and practicing such desirable types of behavior as critical thinking and social co-operation. Nothing could be further from the truth. Not all discussion gives people skill in thinking or co-operation. We all have observed many discussions in which no skills of critical thinking were being practiced; rather, the discussants were displaying themselves, voicing their ignorant prejudices, drawing conclusions without adequate evidence, and generally behaving on a most unintelligent level. Like all forms of speaking, discussion has no inherent or magical virtue; it is good only to the extent that it offers an effective form of speaking for groups of persons who understand its uses, who have developed skill in it, and who have prepared themselves carefully for it.

Some teachers describe the activities of their students as discussions, without making any real effort to teach them the necessary skills, and then delude themselves into believing that their students are learning something worth while simply because they are discussing. The approach of the wise teacher should be to train students to discuss; help them learn the mature social, verbal, and intellectual skills needed for effective discussion; and use discussion as a laboratory for the practice of these valuable skills. Only in these circumstances does discussion deserve the great prestige it enjoys as a form of speaking. Only under such conditions does it become serviceable as a means of reaching significant educational goals.

DEFINING DISCUSSION AS A SPEECH ACTIVITY

The speech teacher needs to consider carefully the limitations to be placed on discussion as a speech form. Since it is taught as a speech form, and since it has gained recognition as a speech form by society generally, certain boundaries must be placed on the form. For the purposes of teaching and learning, we should not apply the term discussion to all of the informal, group-speaking activities which are sometimes so designated, e.g., bull-sessions, exploratory conversations moving in no definite direction, and impromptu conversations by a class on some topic or question thrown out by the teacher.

Conditions Essential to the Emergence of Discussion as a True Form of Speaking

1. A group of persons confront a problem, which they have been able to identify and state.

2. The group has planned a method of attack on the problem; an order of procedure, or an agenda.

3. The purpose of the group is inquiry, to search for a solution.

4. The members of the group have assumed certain responsibilities. At the simplest level, this means that one member of the group will carry the responsibilities of leadership, and the others, the responsibilities for participation.

5. There is interaction among the members of the group. They talk, and listen to one another, and make use of the thinking of each other, in their inquiry.

Note that we have said nothing here about dynamic skills of critical or co-operative thinking. These skills help to determine the effectiveness of a discussion, and are present in greater or lesser degree in every real discussion, but their presence or absence does not by itself determine the existence or non-existence of discussion.

Some Forms of Pseudo-discussion

A consideration of the preceding five conditions necessary to real discussion will help the teacher and the students to distinguish this speech form from closely related speaking activities which may be called pseudo-discussions and which have the following character- istics, or features:

1. *No common problem*

The most usual form of pseudo-discussion occurs in the conversa- tion of a group whose members do not envisage a common problem. Classroom groups who discuss a topic without any sense of urgency, or need, or curiosity are engaging in pseudo-discussion. This activity often occurs when student groups are assigned a problem for discussion which lies outside their range of interest or intellectual competence. A group of students may try to discuss a topic like, "What Are the Causes of War?" which seems, to an adult to be an important and urgent question. A casual examination of the activity of the discussion group will reveal that the students sense no real problem in the stated question; their range of informa- tion, analytical abilities, and interests do not extend, even in dim outline, to the proportions of the problem of which they are speak- ing.

2. *Agreement already reached*

A second form of pseudo-discussion is that which purports to deal with a problem when the attitudes and opinions of the discussants are pretty well known in advance. In one school the problem of cliques was assigned for a discussion before the student body. Only students who were known to be exceptionally democratic in outlook, and opposed to cliques, were placed in the discussion group, and they quickly found themselves in agreement that cliques ought not to exist! Their discussion was a form of persuasion, and was a legitimate enough speaking activity, but it was not a real discussion, because it had been set up in such a way that students with undemocratic attitudes did not participate. Therefore, actual discussion of the cliques that existed at this particular school was avoided.

ORGANIZING TO TEACH AND USE DISCUSSION

As with other speech activities, discussion is functional not only in the adult world, but also in a great many areas of school life. Teachers of social studies, science, and English often organize discussion groups to consider problems which have arisen in the work of their classes. Student clubs and other groups usually discuss their problems, either as entire groups, or through reference to committees, for whom discussion is then a "must." In any school, therefore, many teachers share the responsibility for teaching students how to discuss, as these students feel the need for discussion techniques to help them solve their problems. Good sense dictates, however, that every school assign to some class and some teacher special responsibility for teaching students the minimum competencies needed in organizing and preparing discussions. The teacher to whom this responsibility falls has a primary task of showing students how to use discussion efficiently, and teaching the procedures which will be generally useful in all situations where discussion is needed. This function of the teacher is to be distinguished from that of helping students to an effective solution of a particular problem, although students should perceive the relationship of means and ends as they practice discussion techniques.

Initial Procedures in Teaching Discussion Skills

The first objective of the teacher of discussion method should be to get students into the actual practice of discussion techniques, with a minimum consideration of theory. With discussion, as with other speech forms, instruction should be largely inductive in character; the students learn by observing their own failures and successes and by evolving their theories from guided observation of their own practices. At the same time, it should be emphasized that the minimum consideration of theory which precedes the first actual practice of discussion is very important, and that it must be effective if students are to avoid disaster in their initial efforts. When undertaking the study of discussion, a class generally will need to take up at least the following eight specific matters prior to the first attempt to put theory into practice:

1. *The problem for discussion should be clearly stated*

Teachers may follow a number of serviceable procedures in identifying problems for discussion, but all of them are aimed at securing a wording which will genuinely interest the class, which will fall within their range of intellectual competence, and for which study materials and methods of getting information are available.

A teacher reports:

The ninth grade class was asked to read a chapter on discussion in their speech text, and to examine the list of discussion topics suggested therein. The following day an informal discussion was held to see which of the topics interested the members of the class. They were asked if they had other problems which had developed in any of their classes, clubs, or out-of-school experiences which they thought were more interesting than the problems listed in the text. Each student was asked to bring to class one or more problems, stated as questions, which he thought would make for interesting and profitable discussion. The following day all students put their topics on the board, and each explained informally, in two minutes or less, why he thought his topic would be interesting. The group then selected, by ballot, the five topics they rated most interesting. The students were then divided into five groups. The teacher was able to follow student preferences for the most part in arranging the groups. (Whenever feasible the teacher should balance these preferences against the need for seeing that each group has the personnel likely to produce a satisfactory discussion of the problem in question.) A tentative time schedule was set for the discussions, with an intervening period of three days for further preparation. (The teacher should emphasize the importance of stating the discussion problem so that it poses the real problem at issue and so that it is readily understood by all discussants.)

If the students in the speech class are approaching the study of discussion for the first time, and seem to be slow to suggest problems of real interest, certain types of questions may be introduced by the teacher for general consideration by the class. Often questions involving problems of behavior which are faced by most high school students will be productive of immediate, animated conversation by the members of the class. From the interest in problem-solving discussion thus generated, the class can proceed to the important task of selecting problems for thorough consideration in planned discussion groups.

Questions such as the following usually elicit good response. Students are asked what they would do if:

(a) A friend asked them for help during an examination? (b) They heard a rumor that one of their neighbors was a communist? (c) Their school had no school newspaper?

2. Provision should be made for gathering evidence relating to the problem

Depending on the nature of the problem, this may imply library reading, interviewing or consulting others on the problem, or reflection—digging up ones own relevant thoughts and experiences, or all three. The class should explore possible ways of gathering material, and should set a schedule for completing preliminary research. Class members should see discussion as something which emerges from serious study and from attitudes of suspended judgment, and not as uninformed and prejudiced bickering.

3. The discussion group should plan an agenda for its discussion

High school students will want to understand the agenda first in its simplest dimensions, as a plan, agreed upon by the members of a discussion group, for organizing and limiting the sort of materials to be considered. For a symposium the agenda may represent the partition of the problem into the series of speeches to be made by the different members of the group. For a panel discussion it may be a series of sub-questions or issues, each of which will be taken up in turn by the group.

The teacher should not complicate the matter of agenda making unduly for a class having its first experience in discussion. Actually, of course, the skills involved in planning a discussion agenda are exceedingly complex, involving competence in the fine arts of analysis and structuring. Senior high school students who have had some experience with discussion may profit from a consideration of the general steps in problem solving, which can be used as a beginning structure for analyzing a problem.[3] However, the best procedure for beginners is probably for the teacher to work with the entire class on setting up an agenda for their first discussion, thus creating a model procedure which students can follow in arriving at the agenda for subsequent discussions. If the class has had earlier work in organizing speeches, the teacher may wish to compare the structure of speeches with the structure of discussions.

4. *The class should consider the duties*
of a chairman or leader

If recorded examples of discussion are available, this is a good point at which to introduce them to the class. By observing a good chairman in action, they will learn the duties of a chairman, and also develop criteria for evaluating their own subsequent discussions. If recordings are not available, students can be asked to draw on previous experiences with discussion, to read their text, or listen to radio discussions, observing particularly the leader's role.

5. *The class should consider the characteristics*
of effective discussion participants

This step can be developed through class discussion, again based on the same sort of stimuli used to motivate the study of the chairman's duties.

6. *The class should select the form of discussion*
to be used and should become familiar with the
general arrangements for the form

The forms most frequently used with high school groups are considered briefly in the next section of this chapter (see pp. 329–330).

---

[3] Most discussion texts base the analysis of a discussion group on the steps of reflective thinking first suggested by John Dewey. Thus, the group considers such steps as: (a) Defining the problem, (b) exploring the problem (as history—causes, views about it), (c) suggesting solutions, (d) examining pros and cons of each solution, and (e) deciding, "Where do we agree or disagree and what action is next?"

**7. The class should consider briefly the ways
of starting and closing a discussion**

These techniques relate directly to the duties of the chairman, since they involve forms for introductions, and for concluding or summarizing remarks.

**8. The class should plan some criteria for
the criticism of discussions**

These criteria will usually be rather general in the beginning, and will be derived specifically from the theory developed by the class prior to the first discussion. The experience in the discussion will suggest additional criteria and serve to start the process of inductive learning about the nature of effective discussion. In general, a teacher should avoid handing the class a list of criteria for good discussion; rather, he should let the students evolve their own standards and phrase them in their terms, with his help. Of course, teachers should formulate carefully their own concepts of the characteristics of good discussion before working on such matters with the class.

Co-operative Discussion Techniques

Following is a listing of fifteen "Co-operative Discussion Techniques," developed by Professor William S. Howell of the University of Minnesota, for use by high school students. This list states criteria as questions which can be answered specifically by observing students as they discuss.

Information

Is the participant willing to say "I don't know," when he doesn't?

Is his evidence pertinent and plentiful?

Do other panel members turn to him for information?

Is he able to supply information to supplement or test information contributed by other members of the group?

Does the participant stay on the subject and make every reasonable effort to bring out all points of view and all facts relevant to it?

Thinking

Does the participant answer questions directly, specifically, briefly?

Does the participant encourage critical examination of information he himself advances?

Does the participant contribute one point at a time?

Is participant temperate rather than absolute?

Can he put his finger on the essence of a disagreement and clarify it to others?

Co-operation

Is the participant willing to relinquish the center of the stage to others and hear them out fairly but critically?

Is there an honest attempt on his part to move toward a meeting of minds?

Does the participant seem anxious to help other panel members?

Is he willing to change his opinion when change is justified?

Does he follow, willingly, the guidance of the leader?

USABLE FORMS OF DISCUSSION

There are a great many forms of discussion described in textbooks. This variety of form reflects the multiplicity of circumstances in which discussion may take place. For example, there is the distinction to be made between group discussions and public discussions. In the former, the whole membership of a small group or committee considers some problem, while in the latter a relatively small group presents a discussion before an audience, which later may join in. There is the distinction to be made between conference, or committee-type discussion, in which decisions of some sort have to be reached, and discussions which are conducted under no necessity for reaching a decision, but may serve the function of stimulating thinking, or making progress toward the solution of a problem.

For the most part, the complex considerations which affect discussion form and strategy are not pertinent to the instruction of high school students. Initially, at least, the teacher will want to develop only the simplest and most basic discussion forms, four in all. Individual teachers may prefer variations of the terminology suggested here, or may find good use for additional descriptions.

The *Forum.* If used by itself, this form is sometimes called a single-leader discussion. It is applicable to the situation in which the entire membership of a group, a high school class for example, sets a problem, chooses a leader, and plans and carries out a discussion under the direction of the leader. It may be well to introduce the study of discussion with this form, since it permits joint planning of the entire discussion under the direction of the teacher, and provides a good chance to consider all of the preparatory steps. It has obvious limitations, especially for large classes, for participation of all members of the class in such a discussion seldom can be secured.

The *Symposium*. This title is applied to discussions in which a small group of speakers (usually from two to four) give prepared talks on various aspects of a problem. In such a discussion the leader carries the minimum responsibilities of introducing the speakers, and showing how their talks fit together to give a comprehensive view of the problem. The symposium is usually presented to an audience and followed by an open forum, with comments or questions from the audience. Since the structure of the symposium-forum is exceedingly simple, beginning students often find it easier than other forms.

The *Panel*. The panel discussion involves a small group, usually four or five, under the direction of a leader, who engages in informal conversation about a problem. The fact that the conversation is informal does not mean that it is unplanned. On the contrary a successful panel usually involves extensive planning, especially in gathering data and in determining the agenda. The panel discussion will usually be given before an audience, thus making possible a panel-forum, involving members of the audience.

The *Round table*. Round table seems an apt title for the small, informal, discussion group operating without an audience, or with a radio audience. The radio round table is referred to in chapter 19.

Co-operative investigation seems a good title for describing a discussion in which a larger group sets a committee to the task of bringing specific information back for its deliberation. Some teachers prepare "Town-Hall" discussions, to make use of the familiar format of the well-known radio program and also the materials available through the "Junior Town Meeting" organization.

DEVELOPMENTAL POSSIBILITIES IN DISCUSSION

Discussion is adapted to persons of any age level. Its formal characteristics are sufficiently close to the natural speech patterns of conversation so that elementary school children are readily capable of carrying out satisfying discussions of problems close to their interests and on the level of their information. Its dynamic characteristics involve all of the intellectual processes of critical thinking, and many of the social processes of human relations. Accordingly, the only practical limitation to the capacity of any person to improve in discussion skill is the limitation of his capacity for developing skills in critical thinking and human relationships. Few persons ever approach their highest potentialities in these areas.

The task of the speech teacher, of course, is to help students develop the degree of skill possible for them at any given level of maturity. The pages that follow examine these developmental possibilities in five different discussion skills, together with some suggestions as to methods of assuring development in each of these. In discussion, as in all other speech activities, the teacher is less concerned with estimates of the skills that a seventh grade student ought to have, than with observations of the skills he actually possesses, and with ways of helping him to improve in his capacity to meet his own needs.

Developing a Sense of Form in Discussion

There is always a temptation to believe that the form of discussion is incidental to its essence, and that once persons have acquired some skill in critical thinking, and in working co-operatively with others, they will automatically use efficient forms in carrying on a discussion. To some extent this is true, since the forms of discussion derive from the requirements of efficient group thinking. But it is also true that persons who hold a common feeling for the forms of discussion are more efficient in exercising their capacities for effective thinking and effective co-operation than are persons for whom this sense of form is vague and ill-defined. One of the first objectives of the teacher in introducing the study of discussion is to give students a feeling for discussion activity. At its simplest level, this involves understanding the physical arrangements for discussion, the reasons for such arrangements, and practice in making decisions about such arrangements.

At a progressively more complex level, it involves such matters as: (1) An understanding of the chairman's activity in making introductions, and stating the problems for discussion, including the adaptations that the chairman makes between discussion in small, self-contained groups, and discussion before audiences; (2) an understanding of the reasons for frequent summary, "where have we

been," and such questions as, "whither are we going," as characteristic of the verbal pattern of discussion; (3) an understanding of
the significance of some of the verbal gestures common to small
group problem-solving discussions, in which the discussant limits
the truth-claim of his ideas, or expresses consideration for the ideas
of his fellow discussants. This last class of verbal forms plays an
important part in discussion training, and will be considered in
greater detail on pages 337–338.

It is interesting to observe how many discussions carried out by
adults either fail dismally or lose effectiveness because of an inadequate sense of form on the part of the discussants or the leader.
We have observed public discussions arranged in such a way that
some of the discussants had difficulty in seeing the audience or in
being seen by the audience; discussions in which the talk began without any clear statement of the problem; and discussions in which no
provision had been made for identifying either the discussants or
their leader. Yet most seventh grade students, with a little directed
experience in discussion, are able to attain considerable independence
of judgment in providing intelligent arrangements for discussion!

While the sense of form in discussion may be taught as a part of
each discussion, the speech teacher may find it wise to single out and
make impressive certain specific characteristics of form.

A teacher reports:

Students in this seventh grade class dramatized good and poor
physical arrangements for discussions, and explained the reasons for
so classifying the demonstrated arrangements. They also dramatized
effective and ineffective ways of starting and ending a discussion;
introducing an opinion into a discussion; and disagreeing with the
opinion of another discussant. After these dramatizations in class
they listened to discussions which had been given over the radio,
and rated the leader and the speakers on how well they had observed
good form.

The teacher may find it helpful to use some of the films dealing
with discussion as a means of emphasizing both the functions of
discussion in a democracy, and the forms which it may take. Films
like *Public Opinion* and *Discussion in a Democracy* are helpful for
this purpose.

Developing Critical Thinking in Discussion

Although the speech teacher will want to emphasize the development of critical thinking ability in conversation, in public speaking, in criticism of the speeches of others, and in debating, discussion offers unusual opportunity for stressing the development of attitudes and skills associated with generalized ability in critical thinking. Two principal considerations make this true:

1. *The activity of discussion serves problem solving as its primary goal*

We have come to accept the idea that problems are solved most effectively by persons who are in possession of the greatest amount of pertinent information, who suspend judgment until all possible evidence is available, who seek actively to allay the effects of their prejudices on their judgments, who are able to state accurately the extent of the conclusions which can be supported by the evidence, and who can judge the relative worth of various types of evidence— in short, persons who know and respect scientific method of investigation, and who know and respect logical forms in handling evidence and drawing conclusions.

2. *Discussion provides a thinking laboratory*

The activity of discussion thus provides a laboratory in which students may express their thinking about specific problems, examine and appraise the thinking of their fellow students, have their thinking appraised both immediately and for a continuing period of time by other students, and evaluate the quality of the final group thinking.

Discussion at its best, therefore, gives the student simultaneous practice in his own thinking, and in the criticism of the thinking of others. It is likely that such co-ordinate development of skills in speaking thoughtfully oneself, and in appraising thoughtfully the speech of others—the practice of speech in a continuing atmosphere of inspection and criticism—is one of the straightest paths to the development of generalized skill in critical thinking.

Relating Critical Thinking to Discussion.

The teacher of speech will want to relate critical thinking to discussion in two ways, (1) by encouraging students to accept and value the relationship of good discussion to good thinking, and thus to incorporate the criticism of thinking into their practice of discussion, and their evaluation of discussion; and (2) by developing with students specific standards for controlling their own thinking and for criticizing the opinions of others.

Encouraging students to accept and value good thinking as a part of good discussion is accomplished with relative ease. Students are often interested in activities like comparing the care which good scientists exercise in drawing conclusions in their laboratories with the carelessness often revealed by people (including these same scientists) in making decisions in their everyday living.

Students may be asked to bring in examples of non-logical reasons for which people buy various advertised goods, select certain political leaders, or decide that a book or movie is good or bad. Students should be encouraged to search out non-logical behavior in their own beliefs, statements, and choices, and to see that such behavior is characteristic of all people to some extent. They should be encouraged to observe the difficulty of thinking critically, and the need for specific practice in exercising thinking skills. They should observe the usefulness of non-logical behavior at times, its appropriateness to some types of problems, and its inappropriateness to other types.

In recent years, many teachers of speech, English, and social studies have taught units in propaganda analysis, in which students analyze advertisements, editorials, and speeches to identify and study the propaganda devices used by persuaders to get desired decisions from other persons. Such units have value in making students sensitive to the non-logical bases for much human behavior, and may be useful in stimulating the ambition of students to exercise higher standards in controlling their own decisions. Such units may, in short, help students to give higher value status to suspended judgments, and to well-supported conclusions. Teachers should not regard such units as effective in giving students great skill in the exercise of critical thinking ability generally. There is evidence that students who have acquired considerable skill in identifying propaganda devices are just as susceptible to non-logical persuasion as they were before the acquisition of such skill.[4] The teacher should look upon such units as motivations for the study of critical thinking, and not as a form of study adequate in itself to developing thinking skills. There are no short cuts to critical thinking, and the search for them is apt to be unprofitable for both teacher and pupils.

The following is a list of concepts about critical thinking which have proved interesting and useful to high school students. Both the selection of these items and their grade placement have been derived empirically. There is no good experimental evidence to support the grade-level placement of critical thinking concepts in the secondary schools. This listing, however, gives some indication of the types of ideas useful in association with the teaching of critical thinking through discussion.

SEVENTH, EIGHTH, AND NINTH GRADES

Discussion at this level is often characterized by the large percentage of comments irrelevant to the actual problem at issue. Many junior high school students, however, are able to grasp the concept of relevance, and to make use of it in controlling their own discourse, and in criticizing the discourse of others.

Students can discuss the importance of qualifying the source for certain types of facts, and can develop some capacity for checking sources of surprising or incredible evidence.

Students can develop lists of ways of judging facts, as a basis for crediting the probable truth of evidence offered in discussion.

Students can develop simple tests of the probable value of certain authorities, especially tests which qualify the expertness and disinterestedness of the authority.

Students can develop an awareness of the need to qualify conclusions based on personal observation, or limited observation.

Students can understand and apply in their discourse the concept of hasty generalization. They show increasing skill in qualifying their conclusions from limited data.

---

[4] A good summary of the evidence on the effects of teaching propaganda analysis appears in Arthur I. Gates, Arthur T. Jersild, T. R. McConnell, and Robert C. Challman, *Educational Psychology*. New York: The Macmillan Co., 1942, pp. 490–493.

Students can observe the effects of prejudice on opinion in certain areas of problem solving, especially in areas involving questions of politics, religion, race, social status, and the like.

TENTH, ELEVENTH, AND TWELFTH GRADES

Students can observe differences in statements which assert that (1) something is true, (2) the speaker likes or dislikes something, and (3) some course of action ought to be followed. They are able to criticize statements which confuse assertions of preference with assertions of truth.

Students can test causal arguments, and exercise some care in asserting causal relationships in complex social phenomena.

Students can use and test argument by analogy.

Students can identify the type of intellectual disagreement that rests behind some arguments; and know some of the methods of reducing arguments which occur over verbal issues or matters of definition, over facts, over values or preferences, and over opinions about policy.[5]

Developing Skills in Human Relations

It has long been recognized that the failure of people to agree on the solution of a problem under discussion often has its source in personality conflicts, rather than in logical or intellectual conflicts. As a matter of fact, a large number of the problems faced by people in their everyday living, including the problems of high school students, originate in the difficulty people have in getting along with one another. Discussion groups offer an excellent laboratory for teachers and students to observe some of these processes in operation, and to learn how some of these difficulties arise out of personal animosities, awkwardness of statement, and failures of mutual respect.

In recent years, some teachers of discussion have become so interested in the problems of inter-personal relationships that may be studied in discussion activity that they have reduced the study of discussion almost completely to a study of these relationships. They have made discussion a training ground for developing skills in per-

---

[5] Some teachers may want to introduce students to the tests for detecting certain common fallacies. Superior high school students enjoy using the technical names of fallacies in criticizing the reasoning of others.

sonal and human relationships, rather than for developing the more formal skills of intellectual analysis and critical thinking. In this chapter, we have emphasized the more traditional approach to discussion as a form of speaking associated with rational inquiry into problems and their solutions, but we recognize the opportunities in discussion training for developing skills in human relationships, and the values of a form of discussion training which stresses such skills.

One specific way of approaching the study of skills in human relations, as an aspect of discussion training, is through the observation by students and teacher of specific verbal gestures used by discussants. Such observation may be started with seventh grade students, but it offers an extremely fertile field for cultivation at all high school levels.

A teacher reports:

While organizing a series of discussions, the seventh grade students had observed the need for co-operation among members of the class. During the first discussion, one of the students seemed especially effective in his relations with the other members of the group. After the discussion the teacher asked, "Did you notice any of the things that Mike said which might have helped the group to co-operate better?" Members of the class cited several of his statements—how he often said, "That's a good idea," to another member of the group; how he said, "It seems to me," rather than "I know"; how he asked, "What do *you* think about it, Jim?" and so on. These verbalizations were compared with other ways of contributing to a discussion, and the students expressed their feeling that Mike's method of talking with others was a good one for developing co-operation. Students listened to a recorded discussion, and tried to pick out wordings which would be likely to promote co-operation, and those which might arouse antagonistic feelings. The concepts of co-operation, mutual respect, and diplomacy came up for consideration and clarification.

Teachers will observe that some of the verbal gestures contributing to effective human relationships are also habitual forms of speech for skillful critical thinking. Students who consistently qualify and limit their conclusions, or temper the claims they make for their evidence and reasoning, have habitualized a set of verbal patterns which reflect such moderation of statement. Such habits are all too rare among high school students. Many of the useful verbal gestures combine some degree of intention on the part of the speaker to be accurate in his thinking with his intention to solicit the cooperation of other members of the discussion group. Thus, a discussant may ask fellow speaker, Jim, for his opinion, for the purpose of strengthening his own thinking, or for the diplomatic purpose of securing support from Jim. High school students will not ordinarily want to worry too much about the mixtures of motives which may lie behind the statements typically used by good discussants. However, they will be able to observe the modes of statement characteristic of effective discussion, and in some measure acquire skill in the utilization of such statements.[6]

The Development of Skills of Leadership

One of the obvious merits of discussion as a speech activity is the simultaneous opportunity it offers for training in leadership, for students who have capacities for it, and for training in participation for all students, each according to his own potentialities. To some extent, the consideration of leadership techniques will be a subject for consideration and evaluation by the entire speech class, since the functions of the discussion leader must be understood by all who would participate in the discussion. However, since in any class the leaders will always be a minority group, one of the best ways of assisting them is through individual conferences. Frequently these conferences can be arranged at periods devoted to research or the gathering of material by the class. One method of approaching the general consideration of leadership techniques with high school students is through comparing and contrasting the attributes of the discussion leader with the attributes of leaders in other activities.

A teacher reports:

After a round of panel discussions, the class was asked if discussion leadership was similar to, or different from leadership in other

---

[6] The teacher of discussion may wish to study carefully the treatment in James H. McBurney and Kenneth G. Hance, *Discussion in Human Affairs*, New York: Harper & Brothers, 1950, of the "Empirical Method" of contributing to discussion, pp. 204–208, which gives an excellent account of the general mode of statement useful in the practice of discussion.

situations—the leadership of the captain of the football team, the leadership of a business executive, of the President of the United States, or of a person like Hitler. The class hit upon some of the attributes common to leadership in all situations, and then listed some of the differences between (1) autocratic leaders and democratic leaders; (2) leaders who show others how to do things, and leaders who try to help others do things for themselves; and (3) leaders who take the spotlight, and leaders who try to give everyone else an equal chance. In this way, the type of leadership needed in discussion was defined, and its usefulness appraised.

The speech teacher will need to study carefully the possibilities for opening the opportunities for leadership in discussion as widely as possible in his class. Not all students can have such opportunities, and not all are able to profit from them. Indeed, the chance for leadership in adult society is not so general that we should expect or desire to train a large proportion of high school students as leaders. Nevertheless, it is likely that most high school classes have more students with potentialities as leaders than ever get the opportunity to develop their latent talents. The teacher must be alert to the tendency of a few students, who have become established as leaders, to get repeated opportunities for exercising their skills to the exclusion of such chances for others who may have equal potential.

Development of Skills of Voice and Attitudes

Although training in discussion usually emphasizes the verbal-thinking skills which have been considered thus far, many speech teachers have found it an excellent activity for the practice of basic speech skills. Speech teachers sometimes use discussion as the beginning activity in a speech class, setting up single leader discussions, and panel discussions with a minimum of attention to the theory of discussion, and a maximum of attention to the selection of stimulating problems. The merit of such activity is apparent: It serves to introduce students to the study of speaking as a group activity, rather than as an individual activity, an approach calculated to relieve social tensions. It also starts the study of speech under conditions in which the individual has an immediate and obvious responsibility to his fellow students, thus making it difficult for him to view speaking as a burden imposed upon him by a teacher.

The recording of student discussion offers an excellent method of studying the speech characteristics of individual participants. High school students listening to wire, tape, or disk recordings of programs in which they have participated are able to observe the contribution of good voice to the general effectiveness of the discussion, as well as the contributions of skills in critical thinking, human relationships, and leadership.

A teacher reports:

All discussions in this tenth grade speech class were recorded on tape. The records were made available for play-back by the students. Sometimes discussions were played back during the regular class hour and evaluated; sometimes the group met after school, at noon, or during a study period for a play-back session and for mutual criticism and evaluation. The recording was made available so that individual students could play it when they wished. Prior to any recording, specific consideration was given to the criteria of criticism. These criteria were held in mind and applied at the play-back sessions.

DISCUSSION AS A CO-CURRICULAR ACTIVITY

The extraordinary range of educational goals which can be reached through discussion, and the flexibility of the discussion form have made the activity adaptable to a great variety of co-curricular activities. Indeed, the only limitations on the development of discussion activities in the high school seem to be lack of time and ingenuity. No attempt will be made here to describe all of the uses to which discussion has been put as a co-curricular activity, but some of the major ones will be listed and defined briefly.

The Development of School Forums

With sympathetic and competent leadership from the faculty and from a nucleus of interested students, certain schools have been able to organize forums for the discussion of school and community problems. Such forums employ types of discussion suitable to their size and their objectives. If an effective effort is made by the student forum to interest sizable audiences of students, the program may follow the plan for such meetings set up by the "Junior Town

Meeting League," which has been promoting school discussion along the lines of the "Town Meeting of the Air," and of adult forums operating in a number of cities throughout the country.[7]

The Town Meeting pattern for public forums has obvious utility for school assembly programs, since it permits the use of a wide variety of methods of bringing material on public problems before the student body. Lecturers can be used in connection with student forums. Mixed symposiums, with speakers from more than one high school, furnish stimulation for a high school forum, and bring students from different schools together on a basis other than that of narrow and selfish partisanship. Symposiums with both student and adult speakers are also popular.

School-Community Forums

High school discussion speakers, teams, and panels are usually welcomed by various civic groups such as luncheon clubs, parent-teacher associations, and the like. Members of these adult organizations are interested in the discussion of public problems by high school students.

Inter-school Contests, Conferences, Congresses

The last few years have witnessed the development of an amazing variety of inter-school discussion contests, conferences, and congresses. Such competitions follow as many patterns as the imagination of their sponsors have been able to devise; there is little indication as yet of any tendency to standardize the inter-school contests in discussion. Probably discussion activity will not, and should not, be frozen into any relatively uniform contest-type activity, as inter-school contests in debate, public speaking, and reading have been. It is probable that, in the years to come, certain particularly successful patterns for organizing interscholastic discussions will come to be extensively imitated. We will consider here three of the major methods of conducting interscholastic discussion meetings. It should be observed that the beginning teacher ought to seek the

---

[7] Teachers may get a large number of suggestions for the organization of "Junior Town Meeting" groups from the Junior Town Meeting League, 400 South Front Street, Columbus 15, Ohio. The literature of this group includes a listing each year of topics suitable for "Junior Town Meeting Discussions."

advice and assistance of someone more experienced than himself in organizing inter-scholastic discussion meets.

The discussion-progression: Groups with fixed membership

Discussion-progression contests require considerable advance organization. A discussion problem must be agreed upon by a group of schools wishing to send students to the meeting. This problem may be one selected by a state high school league, or by the director of the meet, or by a conference of representatives of the participating schools.

An outline for the discussion of the problem in question is distributed to the various schools well before the date of the meeting. This outline is usually divided into sections which direct the student speakers in an orderly investigation of the selected problem, and conform generally to the plan to be followed in each of the separate rounds of discussion. For example, a meet might be planned to include three one-hour rounds of discussion by all participating students. The outline might then be divided into three parts: (1) Definition of the problem, and historical background; (2) causes for the problem, and solutions proposed in the light of these causes; and (3) comparison of the merits or weaknesses of various proposed solutions. The pattern of the outline will be set, of course, by the particular requirements of the selected problem. Participating students usually are divided into discussion groups with from six to eight members. Some plan is specified for choosing the leader for each of the rounds of discussion. In some meets, the leaders are furnished by the host school; in others, the leaders are appointed from the participants, in advance; and, in still others, the leader for the first round is appointed, and the group is allowed to select its own leaders thereafter. In some meets the critic serves as a leader for each discussion group he is observing. Groups maintain constant membership throughout the three rounds of discussion, with provision for a different "critic" in each round.

The discussion-progression: Groups with changing membership

This plan for organizing a discussion meet varies from the foregoing only in that the membership of each discussion group is changed for each succeeding round. This procedure has the defect of preventing the orderly progress by a single group of students through a succession of meetings, but it has the merit of giving each individual participant experience in speaking with a variety of students from other schools.

Discussion-progression culminating in debate

This plan for organization is similar to that for the other discussion-progressions, except that it provides for some form of debate after the participating students have examined various proposed solutions to the problem. The debate may take the form of a meeting of the discussion group during which speeches of advocacy for particular solutions will be made, or it may take the form of a general assembly, or congress, of all students, at which resolutions will be introduced. Parliamentary debate will accompany the efforts of the various groups to secure the adoption of their respective resolutions. The so-called student congress usually terminates in some form of parliamentary debate which culminates in the adoption of specific bills.

Discussion as a forensic contest

Some high school leagues have set up contests in discussion to accompany other contests in public speaking and reading. Such contests usually are based on a stated problem and an outline distributed by the league.

Judging inter-school discussion meets

The practices in judging inter-scholastic discussion meets are as varied as the plans for their organization. Judging presents some serious problems. Certain speech teachers insist that no individual ratings ought to be given at discussion meets, since it is inconsistent to have students competing with one another in an activity which has co-operation as its essence. These teachers would favor having the critic give comments on the work of each individual, and appraisals of the work of the group as a whole. Other teachers would combine ratings of groups and suggestions by critics to individuals, with comparative ratings of the individuals in each group. In general, the function of the expert critic for a discussion group is primarily the making of specific observations about the work of the group and its individual members, with the comparative ratings of individuals either omitted, or treated as a secondary function. As with all interscholastic speech work, teachers will find that students generally desire, and are stimulated by, comparative ratings of some sort, although, with adequate training, they can come to understand the importance of ratings of a discussion group as a team, rather than of its individual members.

Preparing students for interscholastic discussion

The procedure in preparing students for effective interscholastic discussion will not vary from that followed in getting students ready for any effective discussion. It involves careful preparation by the individual student in the analysis of the problem at hand, and in gathering material. Usually the speech teacher will want the students under his direction to participate in a number of discussions among themselves, following the outline prepared for the interscholastic meet. He will also want to develop with them the bases upon which the work at the interscholastic meet is to be evaluated, and train them to make maximum use of the critical comments offered by the expert observers and judges at the meet.

SELECTED BIBLIOGRAPHY

Baird, A. Craig, *Argumentation, Discussion and Debate.* New York: McGraw-Hill Book Co., 1950.

Educator's Washington Dispatch, *Portfolio of Teaching Techniques.* 501 Dupont Circle Building, Washington 6, D. C., 1950, 31 pp.

Ewbank, H. L., and J. J. Auer, "Decision Making: Discussion and Debate," *Bulletin of Secondary School Principals* (January, 1948), 32: 151, pp. 34–39.

————, *Discussion and Debate.* New York: Appleton-Century-Crofts, Inc., 1951.

Flesch, Rudolph, *The Art of Clear Thinking.* New York: Harper & Brothers, 1951.

Hunt, Maurice P., "Leading Group Discussions," *Social Education* (February, 1951), 15: 71–74.

Jones, R. Stewart, "A Procedure for the Appraisal of the Mechanics of Group Discussion," *Progressive Education* (January, 1951), 28: 96–99.

Junior Town Meeting League, *Make Youth Discussion Conscious.* The League, 400 South Front St., Columbus 15, Ohio. (The Junior Town Meeting League has a variety of publications to aid teachers of discussion.)

Keohane, Robert E., "The Toleration of Ambiguity," *The School Review* (March, 1950), 58: 129–130.

McBurney, James H., and Kenneth G. Hance, *Discussion in Human Affairs*. New York: Harper & Brothers, 1950.

Northwestern University Reviewing Stand pamphlets. Published weekly at 10¢ per copy. Northwestern University, Evanston, Illinois.

Roberts, Holland D., and Helen Fox, "Streamlining the Forum and Debate," *English Journal* (April, 1937), 26: 275–282.

Robinson, Karl F., *Teaching Speech in the Secondary School*. New York: Longmans, Green & Co., Inc., 1951. Ch. 21.

Salt, George E., *Thinking Together*. Chicago: National Council of Teachers of English, 1942.

Sherman, Mendel, "Films and Discussion 66," *Educational Screen* (November, 1950), 29: 384–386.

Town Meeting of the Air bulletins. Published weekly at 10¢ per copy. Town Hall, Inc., New York 18, New York.

University of Chicago Round Table pamphlets. Published weekly at 10¢ per copy. University of Chicago Round Table, Chicago 37, Illinois.

Utterback, William E., *Group Thinking and Conference Leadership*. New York: Rinehart & Company, Inc., 1950.

CHAPTER 15

Debate

INTRODUCTION

Just as the teaching of discussion has sometimes suffered from an exuberant faith in its virtues, so the teaching of debate has suffered from widespread charges regarding its alleged evils. Curiously enough, this depreciation of debate as a form of speaking has been accompanied by the notion that discussion is a speech form especially designed to replace debate. Some educators have even gone so far as to convince themselves that the replacement has already taken place; one recent book on the high school curriculum says simply, "Students don't debate any more." We are inclined to regard this burial of debating as premature. Perhaps the best way of ascertaining the proper place of debating in the high school is to examine carefully the relationships between debate and discussion, observing their complementary nature and their separate, yet related uses, by students and adults. When we understand the essential nature of debate, we will be better able to see its possibilities as a speech form.

DISCUSSION AND DEBATE: RELATED METHODS OF PROBLEM SOLVING

One of the best ways of understanding both the nature of debate and its relationship to discussion is to analyze the purposes which these two forms of speaking serve in our society. One of these purposes is *inquiry*—the search after facts, opinions, hypotheses, and, ultimately, solutions to problems.[1]   The other purpose is *advocacy*, the proposal and support of specific propositions.

The function of inquiry in our use of speech may be pretty well understood if we observe that this function appears before we actually have made up our minds as to the truth or desirability of a specific proposition.   So long as we are asking questions, soliciting opinions, searching for facts or possible hypotheses, and comparing and evaluating theories, we are engaged in the process of inquiry. Discussion has been defined largely in terms of the process of inquiry. Not all inquiry is discussion, and not all discussion is inquiry, but discussion at its best involves people in a co-operative search after solutions to problems.   One of the basic assumptions in discussion is that the discussants are genuinely seeking light and will not close their minds prior to the conclusion of the discussion.

It would be a mistake, however, to assume that processes of inquiry can actually provide satisfactory solutions to all of the problems of our society.   Even after small groups of people have discussed a complex problem honestly and intelligently, they still may differ widely as to the best solution.   Although this is true of the problems confronting all social groups, the point is best illustrated by the practices of democratic governments.   Governments must make choices among various proposed solutions, and act upon those choices.   Governing bodies, in a democracy at least, customarily use the procedures of parliamentary debate in deciding upon courses of action.   Specific proposals for action are subjected to free and open debate and are accepted or rejected by the procedure of voting. During this debate, advocates who have made choices propose and support by argument the specific actions in which they have come to believe.   Debate, thus, is an essential part of the process by which social groups come to decisions.   The individual becomes an advocate as soon as he reaches a decision; he then seeks to persuade

---

[1] The function of *inquiry* in our problem-solving activity is pretty well illustrated by Dewey's description of a "complete act of thought." Dewey's analysis divides the process of reflective problem solving into six steps: (1) Becoming aware of the problem; (2) defining the problem; (3) locating, evaluating and organizing information; (4) discovering relationships and formulating hypotheses; (5) evaluating hypotheses; and (6) applying, or testing the solution. This pattern is often applied to the verbal pattern of discussion. See John Dewey, *How We Think*. Boston: D. C. Heath & Company, 1933.

others to accept his decision. The practice of advocacy in our society takes many forms—public speeches, editorials, radio commentaries, and the like. Debate happens to be one of the fairest forms, since it subjects advocacy to certain rules of procedure which give equal opportunity for conflicting points of view to be heard from the same platform.

It should be apparent that both inquiry and advocacy are natural speech functions in our society. Both arise naturally, as men seek to solve their problems, and both are a part of the daily life of most people, including high school students. Both inquiry and advocacy are intrinsically worthy of the best powers of free men.

It would be difficult to imagine a democratic society in which people tried to solve their problems before making any effort at orderly inquiry; and it would be equally difficult to imagine a democratic society in which people were either so lacking in courage, or in the desire to win support for their decisions, that they never found it necessary to advocate specific solutions of their problems in public gatherings.

As forms of speaking, discussion and debate are inseparably related in their common concern with problems and solutions. We may view this relationship, in somewhat simplified form, as follows:

1. Individuals, confronting a problem, seek solutions.

Discussion is a form of speaking adapted to assist this process of *inquiry*.

2. Individuals who have reached decisions, try to get others to understand and accept those decisions.

Debate is a form of speaking designed to provide fair opportunity for *advocacy*, by persons who wish to win support for some particular decision.

Ideally, people always ought to discuss before they debate—they should seek maximum understanding of any problem before they advocate specific solutions. However, every discussion is likely to involve considerable debating. The members of discussion groups individually reach decisions on specific issues at different times, and in different ways. Every group discussion will usually include a series of part-debates, as conflict arises over particular issues within the discussion. This is one illustration of the way in which discussion and debate are complementary. Not only does discussion almost inevitably lead to debate, but also almost always includes debate. Not only does debate follow discussion, but also is incidental to discussion, since listening to a debate between contending advocates may promote inquiry. If one examines realistically the relationship between discussion and debate, it is difficult to see how educators can ever have looked upon them as antithetical, rather than complementary, processes.

THE ESSENTIAL NATURE OF DEBATE

We are now ready to state more specifically the conditions prerequisite to the emergence of debate as a form of speaking. These conditions are three in number:

1. *Speakers are prepared to advocate the acceptance of some proposition.* This proposition is a conclusion which they have reached and stated as a motion or resolution, which will give the listener a clearcut choice between either accepting the proposition, or rejecting it.[2]

2. *A speaker, or speakers, is prepared to advocate the rejection of this proposition.*

3. *There are rules of procedure giving both sides an equal chance to present their arguments.*

Debate may be conducted under varying conditions of formality or informality. Its only requirements are the existence of a proposition, speakers with opposing points of view on the proposition, and rules of fair procedure. In a parliamentary gathering these rules may be numerous, and may produce a high degree of formality in the conduct of the debate. Interscholastic debate also has developed rules which govern its conduct according to a somewhat fixed pattern. Debating as it appears in the classroom is often much more informal, and may be conducted without stated rules, but always within the atmosphere of fair play.

---

[2] Some critics of debate argue that it gives the listener only the choice of accepting or rejecting a particular proposition, whereas he ought to have the chance to accept it in part, or modify the proposition presented. Actually, the debate places no limitation on the ultimate choices to be made by a listener. Its form is dictated by the obvious necessity, faced by every parliamentary group and every social group, of coming eventually to the acceptance or rejection of some specific proposal.

HIGH SCHOOL STUDENTS SHOULD ANSWER THE
QUESTION: WHEN IS DEBATE APPROPRIATE?

The foregoing considerations should make it apparent that debate, far from being non-existent as a classroom activity, actually may be altogether too common. High school students are not notably reluctant to reach decisions about problems. One of the time-honored observations about the nature of young people is that they are quick to make decisions, irrespective of their readiness to gather evidence and to think carefully. Too often they are prepared to argue hotly the rightness of their decisions with whatever make-shift verbal weapons they can command. Most teachers deplore the prevalence of the " 'tis so—'tain't-either" type of debating among their students; the debaters battle about the truth of an assertion when no one has made any real effort to find the facts concerning it. Then, too, there are the futile debates over matters of personal taste: For example, one student asserts that a particular book is bad, "because I didn't enjoy it," and another asserts that it is good, "because *I* did enjoy it." The futility of debates over propositions which represent only matters of personal taste has been clear for centuries, but the popularity of such debates remains distressingly high among untrained partisans, both in and out of high school.

The mere fact that a high school curriculum may not include instruction in debate does not cause debate to disappear; it is likely to permit it to continue on unintelligent and ineffective levels. One of the realistic problems faced by the speech teacher is that of helping students to understand the particular conditions under which debate may be both useful and satisfying, and also to realize that there are numerous occasions on which debate is an exercise in applied futility!

A teacher reports:

After a speech which had raised the issue, the students in this class were carrying on an impromptu debate on the relative merits of the two major presidential candidates. The national election was close at hand and the debate was both heated and uninformed. The instructor allowed the debate to go on for a time, and then suggested that the class measure the amount of relevant information possessed by the more outspoken debaters. Cross-examination, led by the teacher, revealed the fact that none of the speakers had any considerable amount of information about either of the two men under discussion, or about the policies of the parties they represented. The teacher then asked, "When is it useful to debate?" Students began to cite a number of debates they had heard which had seemed to them futile, and to list some of the conditions which ought to prevail before a person should become involved in a debate. They decided that:

1. The person ought to debate only if his proposal is based on careful thought, and an examination of the available evidence.

2. The person ought to debate only if he and his opponent understand clearly what it is they disagree about.

3. The person ought to debate only on occasions when serious argument is appropriate. For example, usually it is inappropriate to start a full-fledged debate over some casual statement by a guest at a dinner party.

4. The person ought to debate only if he can keep his temper and be courteous to those who disagree with him.

The students decided that these rules, if followed, would reduce the amount of so-called debate in class, and would help make that which did take place more helpful in solving their problems.

SHOULD ALL HIGH SCHOOL STUDENTS ENGAGE IN DEBATING?

Two divergent points of view have been expressed about the propriety and value of debate training for all high school students. Some teachers of speech regard such training as highly specialized, demanding, and appropriate only for a minority of students with superior verbal and intellectual skills. These teachers look upon debate as training for students who may be expected to assume leadership in adult society, and who will need debating skill, if they are to be effective in such a capacity. Other teachers of speech would not so limit instruction in debate. They contend that the need to support decisions against verbal assault, and the ability to state effectively ones reasons for opposing the decision of another are skills useful to all school children and adults.

This difference of opinion is capable of sensible resolution if we look upon debate in terms of that which is essential to it as a speech form, rather than in terms of the rigorous, prolonged, and formal preparation required for interscholastic debate. At the less formal level, all students should be given the opportunity to acquire such skill in debate as they may be capable of exercising. They need practice in stating propositions and supporting them with evidence and reasoning; practice in defending propositions against the opposition of other speakers; and practice in stating clearly a proposition with which they disagree, their reasons for disagreement, and their own position on the issues. Practice in these fundamental debating skills may be given advantageously to all students.

Public speaking offers students the opportunity for propositional speaking, and it is possible to organize informal debate in the period of discussion which may follow a speech on a controversial issue. Such informal debate may be accompanied by instruction in efficient ways of expressing opposition, and clarifying reasons for opposition —in short, by instruction in the techniques of rebuttal. We have already observed that good group discussion often involves informal debate on issues subordinate to the major objective sought by the discussants. Here again is an opportunity to offer all students classroom instruction in stating and supporting propositions, and in refuting them.

At a slightly more formal level, we may regard classroom debating as an activity to be organized when good opportunities present themselves rather than developed under a rigid plan for all students. This means that the speech teacher should use debate as a separate activity if, and when, a controversy has arisen in class over an issue which gives promise of becoming a debatable proposition. If the class is a lively one, with speeches and discussions productive of a number of sensible, controversial issues, this procedure may result in a good many excellent debates during the course of a school term. Thus, experience in debating will reach a maximum number of students. But in general, the practice of debate at the more formal level will be aimed at the needs of better-than-average students, who have capacity for independent research and aptitude for elaborate argument.

Of course, these procedures should not be applied to elective courses in debate which provide prolonged, intensive training in debating for all of the members of the class, or for any speech elective which brings together a highly selected group of students.

However, the general principles for training in debate as a classroom activity, which will be discussed in the next section of this chapter, refer specifically to the problem of using debate as an activity in a speech fundamentals class.

PROCEDURES IN TEACHING SKILLS IN DEBATE

As with discussion, students should be introduced to debating with a minimum of attention to theoretical considerations, and with inductive development of principles from experience. Again, however, the nature of these minimum learning preparations is extremely important, in order that the practice of debating may be efficient from the first. Seven steps can be listed as describing the prerequisites for the conduct of classroom debating. Each of these steps offers opportunities for elaboration, as students engage in subsequent practice.

Finding Opportunities for Debate

Debate is best begun by a high school class when an argument has arisen over a student's assertion which, in the judgment of the instructor, has the potentiality of being phrased as a suitable proposition. The nature of the opportunity selected by the instructor will determine to some extent the immediate concept of debate which the class will develop. For example, some teachers prefer to organize debates after a series of discussions have revealed sharp differences of opinion among members of the class. Thus, the teacher is able to demonstrate to the class how inquiry and investigation may lead to debate.

A teacher reports:

A discussion of "Universal Military Training" by the twelfth grade class revealed sharp differences of opinion on the question of the deferment from selective service of students who have demonstrated willingness and capacity to go on to college. The class as a whole seemed interested in the problem, and the teacher suggested a debate between some of the contending discussants. The proposition, worded informally by the class, was, "Resolved: that the government should defer from military service all college students as long as these students make successful progress toward graduation." A proponent and opponent of this proposition were selected, and a chairman was appointed to preside over a two-man debate. The class considered the reasons why some discussion leads, not to consensus, but to informed conflict. They talked over the relationship between discussion and debate in a democratic society. Then they proceeded to plan the preparation and conduct of the debate, and a forum discussion to follow it.

An equally valuable opportunity is presented by the debate which arises in class over an assertion concerning which both the proponents and opponents are generally uninformed. The teacher may capitalize on this situation to organize a debate, thus stressing the futility of uninformed argument, and the concept of debate as a rational attack on muddle-headedness and ignorant prejudices.

A teacher reports:

A public speech in the tenth grade class had resulted in an especially unprofitable argument over the merits of the student council. One speaker had proposed the abolition of the council, and had presented some evidence to support his view. Some members of the class opposed his position, but both the amount of the available evidence and the manner of its use were such as to produce confusion. The teacher commented on the uselessness of the contention, and remarked that the class had been having a debate, but a pretty bad debate because of the lack of evidence, and the careless reasoning. The students were able to cite a number of examples of debates in which they had participated, or which they had observed, where the level of evidence and reasoning had been very low. They agreed that it would be desirable to prepare a debate carefully, to see if planning would produce a good debate. The proposition was phrased, and careful preparations were made.

Stating the Proposition

Considerable thought should be given by the teacher to the statement of any proposition which is to be debated in class. The major characteristics of a satisfactory debate proposition are covered by the following statements:

1. *It should be phrased as a declarative sentence*

While a discussion may take as its topic a question—"Should interscholastic athletics be abolished?"—the debate proceeds toward a declarative conclusion—"Resolved: that this high school should abolish interscholastic athletics."

2. *It should be clear*

Debates should avoid purely verbal issues based on different definitions of what is proposed, or upon differing interpretation of ambiguous statements. For classroom debates, after the proposition has been stated as clearly as possible, it is desirable that the participants agree, prior to the debate, on specific interpretations of terms. The class discussion which seeks to clarify the meaning of a proposition is a good opportunity for the teacher to teach methods of resolving verbal issues, as a preliminary to unambiguous debate.

3. *It should propose only one action or judgment*

In general, the more specific and definite the proposed action or judgment, the better the debate. Just as parliamentary meetings are more effective if motions are restricted to one proposal, so debates are more effective if the proposition is single.

4. *It should represent the affirmative position*

The burden of proof in any debate should rest upon the affirmative; it is the affirmative who propose a change in the status quo. Thus a debate proposition should not read, "Resolved: That this school should continue to publish a newspaper." If the continuation of such publication is under debate, it is because some one has proposed, "Resolved: That this school should discontinue its newspaper."

5. *It should be so phrased that reasonable people may either favor or oppose it*

The teacher needs to be careful that propositions for debate offer reasonable positions for both affirmative and negative speakers. Sometimes in discussion students adopt hasty positions, supported by no reasonable evidence or logic, but which have been taken simply for the sake of the argument. Students might be willing to debate a proposition such as, "Resolved: That the faculty has no right to censor school publications." The proposition is ambiguous because of the word, "right," but it is also possibly a poor proposition, since the faculty in any school, as a point of fact, has both the legal right and the responsibility to supervise all school activities. A more debatable proposition might be, "Resolved: That the faculty should not exercise any direct censorship over the material printed in the school newspaper." Teachers, of course, may err in their judgment as to the debatability of some propositions, but in general they will find it advisable to help students select propositions on which it appears likely that both the affirmative and the negative have the possibility of developing good cases.

Students in junior high school usually will not be interested in prolonged discussion of the phrasing of a proposition, and it may be advisable for the teacher to give them considerable help and direction. Upper senior high school students can learn how important careful statement is to good argument, and well-motivated practice in stating propositions may be a useful activity for them.

Choosing Opposing Advocates

Once a class has selected a proposition for debate, the choice of the debaters becomes the next order of business. Frequently their selection is determined by the circumstances which have caused the debate to be planned. If the initial difference of opinion which gave rise to the debate occurred between John and Jim, it is natural enough that they should be selected as the opposing debaters. Just as the proposition should give both sides opportunity for reasonable argument, so is it advisable that students of approximately equal speech skills should oppose each other in a debate. The teacher will need to be alert to secure such a balance of ability.

Arrangements Of Debates

A great variety of arrangements are possible for classroom debating, and the teacher or class will want to select the participants who will fit best into the plans which are contemplated. The following suggested arrangements will serve to illustrate some of the possibilities.

The two-man debate. This may be set up with two speakers and a chairman. A convenient time arrangement is to give each student fifteen minutes, distributed so that the affirmative speaker has 10 minutes to present his case; the negative speaker has 15 minutes to refute the affirmative, present his own case, and summarize; and the affirmative speaker then has his last 5 minutes for rebuttal—to rebuild his case, and to summarize. This pattern allows time within a class-hour for a forum discussion after the debate. The schedule may be modified in many ways.

Many of the so-called discussion programs on the radio are actually two-man debates, followed by a forum period with questions and comments from the audience. Usually only 15 minutes is allotted to the debate and the speakers talk 7½ minutes apiece. Such a pattern often leads to the inconclusive introduction of a large number of arguments, but it may stimulate a good forum discussion. Sometimes each speaker is given 5 minutes to present his case, and then there follows a 10- or 15-minute period of cross-examination, in which each speaker seeks to refute the arguments of his opponent by questioning him on the position which he has taken.

A number of patterns for debate using four or more speakers have been used in interscholastic contests. These are described later in this chapter on pages 364–367.

Provision for Research and Case Construction

The teacher who has organized a debate on the basis of the spontaneous eruption of a debatable proposition faces one very critical problem of determining the amount of time to be set aside for the gathering of evidence and the preparation of cases. On the one hand, it is desirable that every care be taken to avoid uninformed, thoughtless argument. The very purpose of organizing the debate may be to demonstrate the need for careful preparation. On the other hand, there is a limit to the length of time students will maintain their enthusiasm for a debate which has been motivated by a controversy developed in class. If each classroom debate involves endless hours of drudgery for the students who are involved, the teacher will very soon have a class thoroughly conditioned against the activity.

Judgment dictates that the teacher should secure from the debaters the maximum amount of effort in research and case construction that their interest will support, and that the debate be scheduled only if this interest is sufficient to produce a debate obviously better than the casual classroom arguments.

The class as a whole may spend some time profitably in the research and case-construction activities expected of the debaters, particularly if the debate is their first one. For the most part, however, the teacher will need to confer separately with the debaters or the teams, and give them out-of-class assistance in securing materials and organizing their cases. It may be possible to arrange such conferences in class at the time the rest of the students are engaged in some other type of individual or small-group activity. It is often possible to excuse the debaters for library research during the regular meetings of the class.

Preparation for Effective Refutation

The greatest problem encountered by high school debaters is that of meeting directly the arguments presented by opponents. Since direct-clash is the very essence of debate, the teacher must be certain that the debaters understand both the need for such clash, and the methods of statement which make for effective refutation.

One of the best approaches to the study of refutation, for students to whom the concept and techniques are unfamiliar, is through the study of a good recorded debate. Students may listen to a first affirmative speech, and attempt to outline it as they listen. Then they may listen to the refutation of this speech, noting how the negative speaker does or does not restate fairly the affirmative arguments; how well he refutes major arguments, rather than minor points; how well he shows the effects of refutation upon the affirmative case; and how skillfully he utilizes the various methods of attacking the affirmative's evidence and reasoning. It also is possible to illustrate refutation in class; one student may state a single argument, supporting it with evidence and reasoning, and then another student may refute this argument according to some general plan, as: (1) Restatement of the argument to be refuted; (2) statement of what this argument was supposed to prove; (3) refutation of the argument by an attack on the evidence or the reasoning; and (4) summary, showing how the refutation has rendered the attempted argument invalid or ineffective.

Although the study of refutation may involve all of the ramifications of argumentation, the teacher using debate as a classroom activity will find it advisable to carry on just enough practice in refutation to guarantee a direct clash. Further insight on the part of the class into the techniques of refutation should come inductively, from the study of that which is effective or ineffective in the rebuttal arguments which appear in the debate.

Attention to Formal Arrangements

The classroom debate offers an excellent speech opportunity for the chairman. The duties of the presiding officer may be discussed briefly in class, or may be developed in conference with the student who is to serve in that capacity. He may be asked to provide and instruct a student timekeeper, and to introduce the proposition and the speakers. If there is to be a forum period following the debate, the student chairman should state the procedural rules and take charge of the meeting.

Preparation for Audience Participation and Evaluation

The participation of the audience in the classroom debate may take the form of a forum discussion stimulated by the debate, or the form of evaluations of the debating. Ordinarily some combination of these two forms of audience participation will be most useful.

Since, in our society, formal debating is used in making many important decisions, students will often find it interesting to conduct some form of balloting following a debate. Although the judge's ballot on a contest debate is cast on "the merits of the debating," rather than on the attitude of the judge toward the proposition, this is a form of expert criticism which probably is better avoided by a class of high school students. One of the most interesting forms of voting by the high school class is through the use of a "shift-of-opinion" ballot. This procedure involves two ballots by the audience. Prior to the debate, the members of the audience indicate, on the first ballot, one of three opinions:

> I believe in the proposition
> I am undecided
> I oppose the proposition

After the debate, they are given a second ballot, on which they choose the one of the following statements which best indicates their position:

I believe more strongly in the proposition
I believe in the proposition
I am undecided
I oppose the proposition
I oppose the proposition more strongly

From the before-and-after ballots, a student committee can calculate the extent to which members of the audience have shifted their opinions. These changes may be weighted as one point or two points depending upon whether they represent one or two steps from the original position. The results are thus both more interesting and more significant than expressions of opinion recorded only after the debate.[3]

In addition to the balloting, the critical activities following a debate offer an excellent chance for establishing criteria of argument, including evaluations of evidence and reasoning, as well as criticism of the presentation.

DEVELOPMENTAL GOALS IN CLASSROOM DEBATING

As with discussion, the activity of debate offers developmental possibilities for students of all ages, grades, and degrees of intellectual competence. Children start debating of one sort or another long before they enter grade school, and they will continue to engage in arguments throughout their lives. Few of these children will receive sufficient training in debating to enable them to approach their maximum potentialities, but the introduction of experiences in debating into the education of all children ought unquestionably to equip a greater number of them with a basic skill which will be useful to them as individuals, as members of professions, and as citizens.

---

[3] The shift-of-opinion ballot may be used with good results in connection with discussions or public speeches on controversial issues. See H. S. Woodward, "Measurement and Analysis of Audience Opinion," *Quarterly Journal of Speech* (February, 1928), 14: 94–111, and William A. D. Millson, "Measuring Audience Reactions," *Quarterly Journal of Speech* (November, 1932), 18: 621–637.

The activity of debate offers primary opportunity for developing the skills of students in at least three significant areas.

Skills in Research

Speech teachers have long known that no activity in the school curriculum is so apt to motivate prolonged, intensive, and thorough research as the activity of interscholastic debating. Although classroom debating involves less prolonged and intensive gathering of evidence than that which develops during the year-long activity of interscholastic debating, it is nevertheless an appropriate medium for training many students in research of a more intensive, highly motivated sort than that provided by most other speech activities. While research techniques also may be taught in connection with public speaking or discussion, it is true that debate places a heavier pressure on the speaker for thorough examination of available evidence. While the discussant may depend upon his fellow speakers to fill in gaps in his own information, and the public speaker may limit the extent of his evidence to that needed for the specific talk which he is planning; the debater faces not only the possibility, but also the certainty, that his evidence will be tested by an opposing speaker, and the only way he can attain any security in carrying on the argument is by research which familiarizes him with the evidence and lines of argument used by many proponents and opponents of the proposition.

Skills in Building Arguments: The Use of Evidence and Reasoning; Critical Thinking

Just as debate motivates thorough research, so, too, it motivates the exercise of optimum skill in the construction of sound arguments. Again, the fact that the debater is confronted with the knowledge that everything he says is subject to immediate scrutiny and criticism by a speaker who is supposedly equally well prepared on the proposition at issue, presents him with a situation demanding care in the construction of arguments, and precision in the statement of them.

Skills in Extemporaneous Speaking

No other form of speaking places as much emphasis as debating upon the speaker's capacity to think on his feet. Not only must the debater exercise his critical faculties constantly during the course of a debate, but also he must adapt his statements and his organization of evidence to the immediate conditions of the argument *as it develops.* Most high school students have considerable difficulty in extemporizing argument, but the student who has once acquired this skill, has also acquired increased self-reliance and speech readiness. This is one of the skills most sought after by adults.

DEBATE IN THE CO-CURRICULUM

The high school teacher who begins to use debate successfully as a classroom activity will find that he is working in a field which has an extensive literature. Particularly, since the beginnings of intercollegiate debating, an activity which has grown up in this country since about 1890, a large number of texts have been devoted exclusively to the subject matter and disciplinary routines of argumentation and debate. Most colleges and universities offer courses in this area.

Because the practice of debating is based upon such a voluminous body of theory, high school students in the speech fundamentals course can hope to do little more than scratch the surface of understanding about debating. Good teaching, however, can make this beginning extremely useful. Only in an elective course in debating, or in the sustained activity of a squad pursuing debating as an interscholastic activity, will the high school student be able to explore deeply the variety of learnings possible in this field. Since high school electives in debate are usually offered in connection with an interscholastic program in debate, we will not differentiate the intensive curricular and the co-curricular study of debating, but will consider here only interscholastic debate, and the routines to be followed in preparing students for it.

As we see it, the co-curricular activity of debating should be reserved for a limited segment of the high school population. It provides these students with an intensive period of training in research, in the analysis of propositions, in the building of arguments, in the use of evidence and reasoning, in the exercise of critical thinking, and in the skills of extemporaneous speaking. This is not an accurate description of the debating actually done by all high school students; it is only a statement of the potential development which may accrue through intensive training under wise and capable guidance by a teacher who knows what he is doing. Some schools have included a considerable number of students in this limited segment. In one high school of nine hundred students, some sixty participate each year in the interscholastic debate program. This is exceptional, however, and the training and management of a squad of this size occupies a very large portion of the time of the speech teacher who directs the activity. It is more usual to limit the number in the debate squad rather severely. Some small high schools carry on debating with only four or six students actually taking part; others operate with squads of from eight to sixteen, which can be managed almost as efficiently as the smaller number. In any event, the debate coach should restrict his squad to a group small enough so that he can give them intensive direction in the available time. He should regard this concentrated attention to a few good students as a fulfillment of his responsibility to those with superior potentialities for intellectual development and leadership.

Preferably, debate coaching ought to be in the hands of persons who have had considerable training and experience in actual debating. This condition does not always obtain. The following capsule discussion of the interscholastic debate program is not designed to give a person untrained in debate a sufficient understanding of the activity to qualify as a coach. Such knowledge should be sought in the thorough treatments of debate which are given in a number of excellent textbooks.

INTERSCHOLASTIC DEBATE

Most interscholastic debating in this country is on propositions selected each year by a national committee, and used by state and national forensic leagues. These propositions ordinarily are announced during the summer, and by the time schools open in the fall, a quantity of materials have been prepared for the assistance of the students who will be engaged in debating.[4]

---

[4] The National University Extension Association publishes each year two volumes on the high school debate question, designed to help high school debaters to analyze the proposition and to provide them with a ready col-

The availability of reference materials on the "national proposition" makes it possible to give high school students a valuable experience in research, even in schools with very limited library facilities. Some state leagues select propositions of their own, if the "national proposition" does not seem to them to be appropriate, and some high schools debate more than one proposition during the year, but the bulk of the interscholastic debating done in the United States is on the one "national proposition."

Traditional Debating

The most popular format for interscholastic debate at the present time places two speakers on each side, with the following speaking schedule. (The short description of the function of each speech characterizes a typical debate.)

1st Affirmative—10 minutes for constructive case. Defines terms; gives cause for proposal; opens affirmative case.

1st Negative—10 minutes to attack 1st affirmative, and to open negative case.

2nd Affirmative—10 minutes for meeting the first negative attack, and completing the affirmative case.

2nd Negative—10 minutes for continuing negative attack, and completing the negative case.

Speaking order is reversed for four rebuttal speeches.

1st Negative—5 minutes

1st Affirmative—5 minutes

2nd Negative—5 minutes

2nd Affirmative—5 minutes

---

lection of articles written by both proponents and opponents of the proposition. Many private publishing ventures are also carried out each year in preparing materials for the "national" debate proposition. The *Reference Shelf Series* and the *Handbook Series,* published each year by H. W. Wilson Co., 950–972 University Avenue, New York, and the *Debaters Help Book Series,* published by Noble and Noble, 67 Irving Place, N. Y., are familiar special reference works for debaters. The debate coach should be careful of materials which furnish debaters with ready-made briefs, speech outlines, speeches, and rebuttal notes. If debate training is to be of any use to the student, this is the sort of work that the student ought to do for himself, under the direction of a coach.

Modification of the Traditional Form

A number of modifications of the traditional four-man debate have been used successfully, and some of these have genuine merit in teaching particular debating techniques. We shall describe three of these modifications which have received rather wide attention:

1. The cross-question debate

The cross-question form introduces the technique of cross-examination into the debate pattern, thus providing participants with experience in both asking and answering questions pertinent to a developing issue. This form of debating emphasizes the specific clash between the negative and the affirmative speakers, making it impossible for them to ignore one another, as they sometimes manage to do in the traditional form of debate. Furthermore, it emphasizes skills in extemporaneous speaking.

The following schedule of speeches for the cross-question debate was developed in experiments with this plan in Oregon.[5] Such a debate requires four speakers and 80 minutes, but the plan can be modified by shortening the speeches sufficiently to fit the debate into a one-hour class period.

First affirmative presents entire case	20	minutes
First negative questions first affirmative	10	"
Second negative presents entire case	20	"
Second affirmative questions second negative	10	"
First negative presents rebuttal	10	"
Second affirmative presents rebuttal	10	"

The National Forensic League, in its tournaments, has introduced a short cross-examination period into the time schedule of the traditional four-man debate. The plan followed by this organization substitutes two five-minute cross questioning periods for the first two five-minute rebuttals.

2. The direct-clash debate

This pattern for debate also emphasizes the development of specific, well-defined points of controversy between the negative

---

[5] J. S. Cray, "The Oregon Plan of Debating," *Quarterly Journal of Speech* (April, 1926), 175–179.

and affirmative, and the skills in extemporaneous speaking which are necessary to debaters who thus meet one another's arguments head on. Paget [6] reported a set of rules under which this form of debating may be used in interscholastic meetings. The following suggested procedure is a modification of his original plan, which furnishes a useful and interesting training exercise for the members of a debate squad.

From four to ten members of the debate squad are divided into negative and affirmative teams. A preliminary discussion is held, usually with the coach as moderator, during which the two teams agree on the definition of terms in the proposition, and on a set of issues.

An affirmative speaker then takes one of the issues and presents, in three or four minutes, a single argument in support of the affirmative stand on it.

A negative speaker is then given two minutes to make a direct reply to the affirmative argument. An affirmative speaker replies to the negative, and thus the argument continues until halted by the chairman. The chairman then may analyze the argument developed by both sides. The teacher usually will serve as chairman.

The second argument, which is on the second issue, is opened by a negative speaker, and is continued until terminated in the same manner as the first. The debate may continue for the allotted time or, if it is being carried on for practice purposes, as long as the coach considers the procedure profitable.

3. *The problem-solving debate*

This plan radically changes the conditions under which debate is conducted. In many ways it is designed to stress the flexible, varied, problem-solving activity of discussion, rather than the conflicting advocacies of traditional debate.[7] The major steps are as follows:

The topic is worded as a *question* rather than as a *proposition*.

There are two teams, each made up of two or three speakers. Each team prepares to make a series of three speeches. In the first

---

[6] Edwin H. Paget, "Rules for the Direct Clash Debate Plan," *Quarterly Journal of Speech* (October, 1937), 431.

[7] F. W. Orr and A. L. Franzke, "The University of Washington Plan of Problem-Solving Debate," *Bulletin of the University of Washington* (Extension Series). No. 8, January, 1938.

of these, speakers from each team attempt to analyze the problem, setting forth an unbiased explanation of what they think are its nature and its causes, and the criteria by which a proposed solution should be judged.

In the second set of speeches, a speaker from each team sets forth the solution that his team has decided is the best.

In the third set of speeches, a speaker from each team evaluates the two solutions proposed. He interprets and compares these solutions. He is under no compulsion to defend *in toto* the solution proposed by his team, but can support or criticize any portion of any of the suggested solutions, or attempt a synthesis of these solutions.

Many variations are possible within the pattern of analysis, solution, and evaluation. Some plans, for example, have only a single speech of analysis, two to four speeches on proposed solutions, and two speeches of evaluation. Other plans provide for periods of cross-questioning.

Teachers interested in developing variety in the structure of debate may be interested in other debate plans.[8]

MANAGING CO-CURRICULAR DEBATING

Managing debate as a co-curricular activity involves the same sort of educational goals, and developmental possibilities, as those that control the use of debating as a classroom activity. Since the co-curricular activity starts with a proposition, however, and aims at prolonged and intensive preparation, it involves the teacher in a number of additional considerations.

Determining the Scope of the Activity

The popularity of interscholastic debate varies greatly from school to school. The determination of the role such an activity is to play in any particular school is a matter for joint consideration by the debate coach and the school administration. It raises issues in which the school faculty as a whole have an interest, and in which

---

[8] See Warren A. Guthrie, "The Reserve Plan for Intercollegiate Discussion," *Quarterly Journal of Speech* (October, 1939), XXV: 392–396, which gives a plan for a "mock trial" as a debate pattern; and also Charles H. McReynolds, "A New System of Debate," *Quarterly Journal of Speech* (February, 1940), 6–11.

the community, too, properly may be concerned. The debate program requires support from the school and the parents; this support may be obtained through developing an understanding of its educational purposes and the requirements for working out these purposes.

Once a school has decided that it wants a debate program, and has some concept of how extensive it ought to be—how many students it ought to reach, how much of their time and the time of the coach it ought to take, how many trips are to be made, and how debate is to be financed—it becomes possible to make intelligent decisions about over-all plans for the activity. The coach should not rely on himself alone in selecting a squad, in publicizing the program, or in building up debating in competition with other school activities. Instead he must found his program on whatever community of interest, purpose, and support may exist in the school. If the activity has the backing of the school and of the community, the teacher will experience little trouble in interesting a reasonable number of superior students in it. If it does not have such support, the coach ought to take whatever opportunities are available for clarifying the purposes of debate training and making known what sort of students it is designed to reach, to all of the persons responsible for the planning of the school curriculum. Because interscholastic debating has come in for a lot of criticism, some of it from responsible sources, the debate coach may encounter considerable opposition to the debate program, even in schools in which the activity is supported, or at least tolerated. It should be remembered that debate is not the only school activity which is subjected to criticism; there are educators who view with alarm almost all of the co-curricular programs now carried on in high schools. However, the argument over debating has been particularly violent and has given rise to some pointed charges against it which have received wide publicity and acceptance. At the end of this chapter, there is a short discussion of the more important of these allegations, and an attempt is made to appraise their significance.

Directing the Squad

Decisions as to the extensiveness of the debating program will determine the amount of detail necessary in planning for it. Many coaches build the activity of the debate squad around regularly scheduled meetings held at least once a week throughout the season, with additional meetings for practice debates and conferences with small groups or particular teams, as the need arises. The responsibilities of the coach involve a large number of planning activities, such as the following:

1. *Arranging for the availability of research materials*

The coach will usually work with the school librarian, if there is one, in ordering and handling special reading materials. A debate corner in the school library or in some classroom is an excellent aid to student research. Of course, the coach must aid debaters in gathering and recording evidence. The trade mark of a debater—his evidence file—has real significance if the student has been given help in the selection, recording, and effective indexing of pertinent evidence.

2. *Scheduling the activity for each squad meeting*

The teacher will find a number of suggested plans in print for developing analysis, research, case construction, and speaking practice. Typically, the work of a debate squad starts with the general analysis of the proposition, perhaps through group discussion. Its purpose is to develop in all students maximum insight into the nature of the subject, the sources which gave rise to the proposition, and the issues which seem to be vital in the conflicting opinions of proponents and opponents. While this group analysis is going on, individuals should be carrying their research forward and sharing with others the product of their study. Only after students have a thorough background of knowledge on the proposition should they set about constructing cases and practicing debating techniques. Some coaches whose squads include both experienced and inexperienced personnel should arrange for some demonstration debates by the experienced students as early as possible to facilitate the newcomers' orientation to the general form and structure of debating.

3. *Selecting teams*

Students are interested in making the team. They are interested also in having a friend, as a colleague, traveling to tournaments, and so on. The teacher may find that some of his educational objectives need careful presentation to his debaters, if they are to accept the procedure he wishes to follow in organizing his teams. For many reasons the coach may wish to delay the establishing of fixed teams within the squad. The development of the individual debater probably proceeds upon a sounder footing if he has experience in debating with a number of different colleagues, in debating both sides of the proposition, and in presenting more than one portion of the case. Such experience aims at developing in the individual a thorough grounding in subject matter, and an adaptability in discussing it. These are skills which hardly can grow in the debater who early becomes a first affirmative speaker, with a given colleague, and a stereotyped performance.

Debate Is an Activity for Students, Not Coaches

A group of prospective speech teachers recently were questioning a high school debater about the values he thought he had received from debating. The debater had mentioned all of his own activities—analysis, research, case construction, and practice in speaking. One of the questioners, perhaps familiar with the procedures of some high school debate coaches, asked him what his coach had done for him: "Does your coach do a lot of work in developing your case?" The debater thought for a time, and then replied, "No. Mr. ———— doesn't do anything at all. He listens to us, and makes suggestions, but we do all the work." The coach in question was an exceptionally successful and hard-working teacher. While the reply of his student to the question revealed the myopia of most high school students in seeing the amount of work involved in coaching, it was also a great tribute to the success of this man's teaching. For his students, debating was the sort of activity it should have been—an activity for *them;* they were carrying the maximum responsibility of which they were capable.

It is unfortunate if the coach ever views his task in the preparation of debaters as different in any essential way from his job as a classroom teacher. His function is to help his students to acquire the skills they need to perform for themselves the exacting intellectual tasks of debating, not to perform these tasks for them. The best debaters have had coaching of this sort; self-sufficiency is a first requisite for the debater.

Debate Training and the Debater's Personality

Most of the adverse critics of debate have acknowledged the utility of debating skill, and to some extent the possibilities in debate training for the intellectual development of the participants. They have been disturbed, however, by what they believe to be the harmful effects of debate training upon the attitudes and behavior of debaters—in short, by the thought that debate develops smooth and skillful advocates at the expense of desirable personality traits. Most of these critics have not been debaters or coaches of debating. Many of them have made hasty analyses, which reflect little understanding of the functions of debate in a democratic society. None of the charges ever has been supported by actual evidence showing that debate training has the alleged harmful effects. On the other hand, there is substantial evidence pointing to the beneficial educational effects of debate training.

Some of the adverse criticism of debating has tended to clarify the responsibilities of the coach in seeing to it that the activity does make a substantial contribution to the development of the student as a person, as well as to the development of certain specific skills.

Does Debating Develop Attitudes of Insincerity?

Some educators look askance at having debaters argue first one side of a proposition and then the other, even though such practice be confined to the preparatory phase of the training. They feel that debaters thus may be encouraged to become efficient in supporting what they do not believe sincerely and that such a practice leads to sophistry and undermines intellectual honesty.

Of course the attitudes taken by the debater toward practice in presenting the evidence on either side of an issue is a matter of concern for his teacher, and may require some discussion. Some students may get the idea that the essence of debate technique is skill in outwitting ones fellow men, or that debate training is useful because there are so many occasions in life when one needs to be a successful advocate, regardless of his real convictions. We doubt that students derive these attitudes from sound debate training; like most wrong views of morals and ethics, they originate in broader and earlier aspects of the student's home and school experience. However, since the debate coach occasionally does meet these warped attitudes, he has an excellent opportunity to help students who display them in acquiring more socially constructive patterns and standards of conduct.

The student should understand that he presents both sides of a controversial issue for specific reasons: (1) Such practice gives him a more accurate, truthful understanding of the issues, and (2) such practice makes him a better advocate of the side in which he really believes. Many centuries ago Cicero discussed his practice of arguing aloud the views of all the parties to a legal dispute before taking his case to court. He viewed this procedure as the best way of developing sound arguments for his own position. The student should understand that, when he debates, he is performing the intellectually honest task of stating clearly and completely the best possible case for one side of a proposition, using all the available tools of evidence and reasoning. He is developing skills to be used later for the defense or support of his own convictions. He should be taught that sincerity based upon evidence and reasoning is more ethical than uninformed and illogical prejudice and partisanship.

Does Debating Develop Contentiousness?

Some debaters exhibit bad manners in interscholastic contests, and some debaters carry bad manners with them into their other classes and social situations, and out into life when they leave school. At times contentious personalities are attracted to debate, perhaps, but it is doubtful that the training accentuates such non-persuasive factors. Young people with superior verbal skills sometimes are less than polite and tactful in their exercise of these skills, and some unpersuasive speakers of this sort doubtless find their way into debate. When they do, their debating experience should modify their habits for the better.

A college football coach recently observed that his players were not a great deal different from other people. But one difference, he said, is that they seem to enjoy knocking one another down for two hours every day. "I don't know why they enjoy that," said the coach, "but they do. And that's one reason they come out for football." This coach had no illusions about the importance of enjoying knocking people down, to the future of civilization. But he did see the activity of football as an educational opportunity with possibilities which transcend any peculiarities of the participants. Most people seem to take satisfaction in some avocation with less than world-shaking significance, whether it be mountain climbing, channel swimming, or stamp collecting. Most students who enjoy debating do like to win an argument, a pleasure which is inconsequential in comparison with the social significance of debating but which may attract them to the serious aspects of the activity.

Actually, debating offers the teacher an opportunity for helping students who exhibit habits of contentiousness or arrogance to discipline these habits, and change the social attitudes out of which they arise. Most experienced debate coaches have watched with satisfaction the development of a student from a brash, noisy, and assertive arguer, *and a poor debater,* into a student who exercises good judgment as to the situations in which debate is appropriate, who speaks with unfailing courtesy and good humor, and who is a *good debater.*

Our point is a simple one; *the debate coach is first and foremost a teacher.* Coaching is a form of teaching which usually has the support of unusually strong motivation. As a teacher, the coach's concern is with developing the personality of his debaters in any and all ways which will make them better and more useful individuals, as well as better debaters. If he approaches his task in this light, he will find many opportunities for helping students to modify the undesirable attitudes and habits which they may bring with them to debating.

SELECTED BIBLIOGRAPHY

Baird, A. Craig, *Argumentation, Discussion and Debate.* McGraw-Hill Book Co., 1950.

Ewbank, H. L., "What's Right With Debate?" *Quarterly Journal of Speech* (April, 1951), 37: 197–202.

Ewbank, H. L., and J. J. Auer, "Decision Making: Discussion and Debate," *Bulletin Secondary School Principals* (January, 1948), 32: 151, pp. 34–39.

——————, *Discussion and Debate.* New York: Appleton-Century-Crofts, Inc., 1951.

Gray, J. S., "The Oregon Plan of Debating," *Quarterly Journal of Speech* (April, 1926), 12: 175–179.

Hance, Kenneth G., "Adapting the Teaching Cycle to Debate," *Quarterly Journal of Speech* (December, 1944), 30: 444–450.

Lahman, Carroll, *Debate Coaching.* New York: H. W. Wilson Company, 1936.

McBurney, James H., J. M. O'Neill, and G. E. Mills, *Argumentation and Debate.* New York: The Macmillan Co., 1951.

McClellan, Samuel D., "The Function of Debating," *English Journal* (February, 1947), 36: 91–93.

McReynolds, Charles H., "A New System of Debate," *Quarterly Journal of Speech* (February, 1940), 26: 6–11.

Paget, Edwin H., "Rules for the Direct Clash Debate Plan," *Quarterly Journal of Speech* (October, 1937), 23: 431–433.

CHAPTER 16

Reading

SCOPE OF TERM READING

THE TERM, Reading, covers a broad area and has a variety of meanings. Although the development of reading skills has always been considered one of the most important goals of education, the history of education records many controversies: Silent versus oral reading; training the handicapped versus training the gifted; private versus public reading; curricular versus co-curricular emphasis; individual versus group performance; reading from the printed page versus reading from memory; practicing for speed versus practicing for comprehension; and reading in view of an audience versus reading over the radio.

Many authorities have written books on silent reading, remedial reading, reading from memory, methods of increasing speed, improving comprehension, reading needs at various school levels, and other relatively small sections of the whole reading problem. By so doing these experts have helped to establish the present generally accepted point of view, that both sides of each controversy have well supported arguments, and that instead of thinking in terms of silent *versus* oral, or training the handicapped *versus* training the gifted, and so on, we should consider silent *and* oral, handicapped *and* gifted. For example, scientific studies have shown that at certain school levels training in silent reading improves oral reading, while at other stages training in oral reading improves silent reading. There appear to be points in the learning process, however, at which attention should be concentrated on one rather than the other to secure maximum development. Findings seem to indicate that the greatest progress may result from combining the training in oral and silent reading, since there is more overlapping than was at first recognized. Thus a thorough understanding of each type of reading may make a distinct contribution to the teaching of both. All present-day teacher-training institutions concern themselves with the education of the handicapped, the gifted, and those in between them. They no longer try to justify giving training to one rather than the other but spend their effort on ways and means of lifting every child or adult from the kind of reader he is to the kind he can become. In the same way teaching is directed at private *and* public reading, curricular *and* co-curricular needs, individual *and* group performance, reading from the page *and* from memory, speed *and* comprehension, training for the audience in sight *and* over the radio, and so on.

A PREDICTION REGARDING THE TEACHING OF READING

If further research continues to point up the advantages of having students study in many reading areas in order to make their training maximally effective, it is likely that reading clinics, interpretation courses, silent reading programs, choric speaking activities, and the like, instead of being scattered through many departments, will be centered under one head where reading, with all its many facets, will be taught. Students of this text may influence such a reorganization and prepare themselves to contribute to it by going beyond what is at present termed oral reading or interpretation, the areas most often assigned to speech teachers, and undertaking to work in the broader field of reading.

PRESENT LIMITS OF SPEECH TEACHER'S RESPONSIBILITIES

At the present time the average speech teacher's responsibilities in the field of reading are not nearly so extensive as they may become in the future. Unless, because of special interests and training, he elects to do so, the speech teacher is usually not responsible for directing students in silent reading. In large school systems, reading experts test comprehension and speed and set up remedial programs. Oral reading, on the other hand, is often practiced without being improved, unless some teacher accepts this problem as a reasonable part of his contribution to student growth. Most speech majors and minors in college are trained to help high school boys and girls in the sort of oral reading which will function in the home, the school, and the community.

During the six years of junior and senior high school, students use both individual and group oral reading; proficiency brings big returns in better grades, increased knowledge, the enjoyment and appreciation of literature, and improved speech techniques generally. The average student needs to read aloud, to give information; at home, in classes, in clubs, and in dozens of other situations where it is desirable to share material on the printed page with others. He is invited to interpret poetry and prose in his classes, especially in English. The ability to introduce worth-while literature to his family, fellow church members, and other friends will enrich his own life as well as the lives of others.

Group reading of two kinds can improve a high school student's speech abilities and add to his pleasures. Reading appropriate poetry in chorus is almost always undertaken with enthusiasm by boys and girls from twelve to eighteen years of age. Most of them also enjoy reading plays, seated in a semicircle with books in their hands.

SELECTING MATERIAL FOR ORAL READING

Much of the literature which a high school student wants to learn to read aloud will be brought to his attention by his own attempts to solve his day-to-day problems. In science he may read to the class the directions for carrying out an experiment; in social studies he may read information helpful in preparing for a discussion on conservation in his community; in mathematics he may read rules for writing and endorsing checks; in music he may read the instructor's plans for seating the orchestra; in assembly he may read an announcement of specific procedures to be observed by students who are attending a football game in a neighboring town; or in his living room at home he may read to the family an item from the evening paper. At home and at school there are numerous occasions when a high school student can serve himself and others by clear, expressive, reading for the purpose of giving information.

Usually the student in English courses faces no serious problem in selecting literary materials to read. The student chooses what he likes best from good literature which experts have chosen and recommended in textbooks. The reading of such approved literature certainly should help to develop standards and build independent critical habits which will give students confidence in evaluating materials from other sources. At this point the teacher will do well to make use of the guiding principles formulated in Chapter 9 on subject matter, where methods for appraising literature were clarified.

TEACH STUDENTS HOW TO GET FULL MEANINGS

The first step in oral reading, whether the material be the recipe for a cake or the climactic speech of a great drama, is to get the full meaning. It is safe to assume that listeners seldom will find what is read more meaningful than the reader has found it to be. High school students need to be taught how to go about the search for background information in developing the meanings of literature. They must be guided to distinguish between the denotative meanings which can be found in the dictionary and the connotative meanings which arise out of the reader's own experience. Every teacher is wise to keep in mind the sequence of steps to be taken in getting meaning from written language. These can be canvassed quickly, and the appropriate ones applied in each reading preparation. We shall now consider this process in detail.

STEPS TO INSURE COMPLETE MEANING

High school students will welcome the suggestion of some systematic procedure by which they can get the meaning of the material to be read aloud. The following steps may be followed by the beginner. They may serve as guides for developing an original approach which always should come out of the learner's own experience.

1. Find the significance of the title. Every author chooses his titles with care, and usually they suggest the central idea of the story, essay, poem, or play.

2. Use the dictionary. Students always should use the dictionary to get the meanings and pronunciations of unfamilair words.

3. See how punctuation marks help to make the meaning clear.

4. Relate the part to be read aloud to the entire selection.

5. Study how the author's life is related to his writings.

6. Find out when the material was written.

7. Use maps to clarify geographical references.

8. Look up historical references.

9. Check all allusions and literary references.

10. Note how rhythm reveals meaning.

11. Discover whether the purpose of the selection is to depict a character or characters or to present ideas and philosophies.

12. Picture the imaginary listener if other than the audience before whom the reader is speaking.

13. Discuss personal experiences of individual members of the group to demonstrate differences between denotative and connotative meanings, and to clarify the statement, "We read in terms of our experiences."

14. Summarize the central idea specifically and briefly in clear language.

AVOID MEANINGLESS READING

There are two common mistakes in teaching oral reading which tend to habitualize unfortunate meaningless expression: Reading aloud by the teacher, and reading aloud by students, before complete meanings have been discovered by the students.

Speech teachers usually like to read aloud to their classes, and it is fortunate that they do. High school boys and girls gain a great deal from hearing good reading. Many a student can trace his motivation for becoming a good reader to the moving interpretation of some poem or play by an inspiring teacher. The warning here is against having a teacher read the particular selection on which students are still working. Different individuals express meanings in different ways, and the aim of the teacher should be to let students see that, after having discovered the meanings, each individual should be free to stir up these meanings in his audience in the ways in which *he* can do it best. If the student hears his teacher read a selection well, he is likely to hesitate to read it differently, even though the teacher's way may not be the best way for him.

If a teacher asks the average high school class, "What is the first step in preparing material for reading aloud?" many students will respond at once, "Read it over aloud many times." This is poor advice, because the vocal patterns used in reading material not completely understood, are quite different from the ones used when full meanings have been found. The student, having set the first inflections, often has difficulty in changing them when he finally gets the meanings and recognizes that these earlier vocal patterns lead his listeners away from the author's intention rather than to it. Thus the first step in oral reading must be to get rich, complete meanings.

THE QUESTION: HOW LITERAL SHOULD THE READER'S ACTION AND VOICE BE?

In reading aloud the meanings and the language usually are provided by an author other than the reader, and for this reason the action and the voice to be used are the reader's major problems.

The question of whether the teacher should give the impression of being himself or some other character who is speaking in the selection is one of the most persistent issues faced by the teacher and the student of oral reading. High school readers sometimes are criticized for "acting too much" and, again, for "acting too little," and frequently the reasons for the unfavorable comments are not explained fully. Let us see what considerations may help in deciding how much impersonation or characterization should be used in reading.

STYLE OF DELIVERY DETERMINED BY MATERIAL, SPEAKER, AUDIENCE

There are three factors which determine how material should be read aloud: What is read; who is reading it; and where, when, and before whom it is read. It is often impossible to determine which of these three should be given greatest consideration. In answer to an inquiry from his students as to which factor is most important, the teacher will be forced to answer always, "That depends!" No single element is universally paramount, but each is absolutely essential. Furthermore, each is dependent on and affected by the others. For example, every reader tries to select material which is appropriate and interesting to his listeners, and he also attempts to choose a selection that he will be able to make meaningful to them. At this point some authorities would say, "Choose the material carefully with the reader and the audience in mind, then look to the material alone for guidance in determining how much or how little characterization to use." This text, however, supports the thesis that the same material may be read in a variety of ways by different readers, by the same reader on different occasions, and before different audiences. Therefore, throughout the entire preparation, from the choice of what is to be read until it is presented, the material, the reader, and the audience should determine the manner of presentation.

Material Affects Manner of Delivery

An examination of the material which high school students read aloud would place it on a long scale reaching from one extreme where the reader should appear to be himself and read with no suggestion of characterization, to the other extreme where the reader should give the impression that he is someone other than himself and read with complete characterization. On this scale there are no clear, definite breaks, but the meanings of the material suggest when to change voice and action and assume the semblance of some other person. Sometimes characters are portrayed partially and suggestively and sometimes completely and literally, depending on which method best expresses the author's intent and accomplishes his purposes.

Four questions may help the reader to determine the extent of characterization by studying the subject matter.

1. What is the central idea of the selection?
2. Are persons other than the reader speaking?
3. If, when the reading is finished, a central thought is remembered above everything else, will the purpose of the author be accomplished?
4. If, when the reading is finished, characters are remembered above everything else, will the intent of the author be fulfilled?

Speaker Affects Manner of Delivery

Ability, sex, age, and appearance should all be taken into account in deciding just how far to go in using action and voice for characterization in oral reading. While it is true that every teacher hopes to help his students to become so skillful in the use of visible action and voice that they can interpret any selection in any desired way, that objective cannot always be attained. Some students are more skillful in the management of voice and action than others, some have excellent control of their facial muscles, others have skill in using their hands and arms, and still others have unusual ability to employ posture and movement. The same holds true of voice. Because of natural endowment, experience, and training some readers can manage one dialect better than another, some have a wider range of pitch than others, and some have a delicacy of volume control which others can never develop. Each will need to examine himself under the guidance of the teacher and his fellow students to discover his special abilities and the most effective use of them.

Boys may often read material in ways which would seem out of place for girls. A girl reader may often be much more literal in her action and voice if the characters in the material are women, than she can if the characters are men. The reverse is true when the reader is a boy. It is usually better for the reader to suggest the opposite sex than to try to portray it literally.

The age factor must be dealt with in much the same way. Delivery which might appear exaggerated and overdone by a woman of fifty might suit a boy or girl of 15 or 16; likewise, the dignified action and subtle voice change of an older man might appear too restrained for a high school boy. As in all forms of speech, the manner of reading should call attention to the meanings rather than to the techniques of voice and action. The listener should remember *what* is read, not *how* it is read, and the reader must analyze his abilities and utilize them discriminatingly if he is to meet this test.

If a student is over- or underweight, very tall or very short, very round shouldered or very erect, unusually awkward or unusually graceful, he will need to adapt his delivery to turn the attention of the audience away from his appearance to what he is reading. Because of these physical factors the reader may decide to use visible action and voice quite differently from the way in which another of his classmates uses them, and still be equally effective in stirring up intended meanings in the minds of his audience.

Audience Affects Manner of Delivery

High school students enjoy class discussions on the problem of adapting delivery to various audiences. They are able to cite times when adults were displeased by programs which were acceptable to them; they recall how younger brothers and sisters reacted favorably to literal and extreme action; and they describe programs which were criticized favorably by some members of the audience and unfavorably by others. An understanding of appropriate action, considered in Chapter 6, and appropriate voice, considered in Chapter 7, will be useful in this discussion of how the audience factor helps in determining the type of delivery to be employed in reading.

EXAMPLES ANALYZED IN TERMS OF MATERIAL, READER, AND AUDIENCE

Following are sixteen selections which may be read aloud. Clearly they will not suit all individuals, be appropriate for all occasions, and interest all audiences. They are arranged to move from zero characterization to 100 per cent characterization. Each is analyzed briefly to show how a teacher can help high school boys and girls to come to reasonable decisions on how much and what kind of visible action and vocal characterization should be used in a given situation.

Example I

Below is an excerpt from the preface of *The First Book of Botany*, by Eliza A. Youmans, published in 1873.[1] An application of the four questions on page 381 are: (1) The central purpose is to introduce a method of teaching by means of specimens and observations; (2) no character other than the reader is referred to; (3) quite obviously the central thought is more important than the reader; and (4) the presentation will be successful if the personalities are subordinated and the ideas are made to stand out.

It is clear that this excerpt can be read by a prospective teacher, a senior in high school, or anyone interested in teaching methods, as an example of a point of view more than seventy-five years old. It is clear, also, that in order to get that same idea over to an audience a younger student would need to assume a different attitude. Likewise, an audience of students brought up in a modern progres-

---

[1] Eliza A. Youmans, *The First Book of Botany*. New York: D. Appleton & Company, 1873, p. III.

sive high school would bring to the presentation experiences different from those of students from more traditional schools, and different stimuli will be required to stir up such experiences. But no reader, before any audience, if he is to be effective, will try to appear to look and sound like anyone other than himself.

This little book has a twofold claim upon those concerned in the work of education.

In the first place, it introduces the beginner to the study of Botany in the only way it can be properly done—by the direct observation of vegetable forms. The pupil is told very little, and from the beginning, throughout, he is sent to the plant to get his knowledge of the plant. The book is designed to help him in this work, never to supersede it. Instead of memorizing the statements of others, he brings reports of the living reality as he sees it; it is the things themselves that are to be examined, questioned, and understood. The true basis of a knowledge of Botany is that familiarity with the actual characters of plants, which can only be obtained by direct and habitual inspection of them. The beginner should therefore commence with the actual specimens, and learn to distinguish those external characters which are open to observation; the knowledge of which leads naturally to that arrangement by related attributes which constitutes classification.

But the present book has a still stronger claim to attention; it develops a new method of study which is designed to correct that which is confessedly the deepest defect of our current education. This defect is the almost total lack of any systematic cultivation of the observing powers. Although all real knowledge begins in attention to things, and consists in the discrimination and comparison of the likenesses and differences among objects; yet, strange to say, in our vaunted system of instruction there is no provision for the regular training of the perceptive faculties. That which should be first and fundamental is hardly attended to at all. We train in mathematics, and cram the contents of books, but do little to exercise the mind upon the realities of Nature, or to make it alert, sensitive, and intelligent, in respect to the order of the surrounding world.

Example II

The selection below contains directions for study of bodily action, from *Speech*, by Weaver and Borchers.[2] As in the preceding selection the central idea is specific information with no reference to any character. The reader will therefore be himself, and test his

---

[2] Andrew T. Weaver, and Gladys L. Borchers, *Speech*. New York: Harcourt, Brace & Co., 1946, p. 51.

success or failure as a reader by whether or not his listeners understand what they are being asked to do.

Tell a story to the class without words. Plan to show where the action takes place in the first part, lead up to a climax in the second part, and show the climax in the third part. Do not tell your friends specifically what you plan to do. Your performance will deserve a superior rating if the audience is not confused on a single detail. Practice at home before members of your family, in order to be sure that your body does what you want it to do.

Example III

The following item from a daily newspaper [3] is the kind of material which any high school student might elect to read to members of his family in the living room. Like Examples I and II, there is no suggestion of any character other than the reader, and the success of the reading depends on making the news item clear in all details.

Dyanne Reinke has a pet that you normally wouldn't pet.

Her pet is a skunk, of mild but inquisitive manner, name of Petunia.

The baby skunk—she's about 3 months old—has been put through a rigid disarmament program, involving a session with surgery, and is harmless as a house-cat, which she resembles to some degree.

The baby skunk was an orphan, and Dyanne, who's 11 and goes to Middleton grade school, has a penchant for orphans.

Dyanne has made a harness for the baby skunk out of a wrist band, and the skunk takes her out for a walk every now and then. Skunks don't lead very well, but they do like to set out and pull their owners along behind.

The Reinke's started out feeding Petunia on cat food, but soon found out "that she eats like a goat."

She likes meat in any form, and grubs, and some roots. And she goes for American fried potatoes, too.

The Reinke's are worrying a little about the amount of food and fat that Petunia is taking on, but figure that she may be storing away energy for the coming winter, when she may go into hibernation.

Example IV

Like the three foregoing readings no specific speaker is described here in *Hound on the Church Porch*, by Robert P. Tristram Coffin, and the presentation will be successful if the listeners each recall

---

[3] As reported in *The Capital Times*, Madison, Wisconsin.

some dog who recognizes good friends and greets them in some particular way.

The selection is more personal than the preceding examples, and the connotative meanings will be richer for both speaker and audience, thus giving opportunity for individuality in pauses, inflections, gestures, and facial expressions which show what parts mean most to the reader.

HOUND ON THE CHURCH PORCH [4]

Robert P. Tristram Coffin

The farmer knew each time a friend went past
Though he was deep in Sunday and his eyes
Were on the preacher or the azure squares
The high church sashes cut out of the skies
And on the dark blue serge upon his thighs.

Every time a man the farmer knew
Went by upon the road, the farmer's hound
On the church's wooden porch outside
Would thump his tail and make a pleasant sound,
His tail struck every time that it went round.

The farmer knew how well he knew each friend
Going by, he counted up the score;
If the passer-by were a plain friend,
There would be three thumps, or maybe four,
But if it was a good friend, it was more.

That would be Sam Rogers passing now,
And that would be Dave Merryman, all right,
For the hound-dog's joy flowed down his tail
And made it pound the planks with all its might,
He could not stop it going for delight.

The man in church sat back and glowed all through,
He heard the sermon, but it did not hide
The rhythm of the comforting old hymn
Of friendship that was going on outside,
And every inch of him filled out with pride.

Example V

There Was Once a Puffin, by Florence Page Jaques, was brought to class in one high school by a ninth grader who volunteered to

---

[4] Robert P. Tristram Coffin, *Collected Poems.* New York: The Macmillan Company, 1948, p. 315. Used by permission of the publishers.

read it aloud just because she liked it so much. Here, as in all preceding examples, the speaker is any person who wishes to read the poem, but, unlike the others, in this there is a quotation from the fishes who said, "If you wishes, You can have us for playmates, Instead of for tea." The girl who read the poem successfully inflected her voice and showed by her facial expression when someone else was speaking, but the changes were slight, subtle, and suggestive, and she was always thought of as the storyteller who quoted what the fishes had said.

THERE WAS ONCE A PUFFIN [5]

Florence Page Jaques

Oh, there once was a Puffin
Just the shape of a muffin,
And he lived on an island
In the
> bright
> > blue sea!

He ate little fishes,
That were most delicious,
And he had them for supper
And he
> had
> > them
> > > for tea.

But this poor little Puffin,
He couldn't play nothin',
For he hadn't anybody
To
> play
> > with
> > > at all.

So he sat on his island,
And he cried for a while, and
He felt very lonely,
And he
> felt
> > very small.

Then along came the fishes
And they said, "If you wishes,
You can have us for playmates,

---

[5] Florence Page Jaques, "There Was Once a Puffin," reprinted from Marjorie Barrows (ed.), *One Hundred Best Poems for Boys and Girls*. Racine, Wis.: Whitman Publishing Company, 1930, p. 75. Used by permission.

Instead
of
for
tea!"
So they now play together,
In all sorts of weather,
And the Puffin eats pancakes,
Like you
and
like
me.

Example VI

The Admiral's Ghost, by Alfred Noyes, is a story which can be related by any person who can move listeners to understand the central idea—how much the English people love their country. The poem contains much dialogue, and the reader must study the material carefully and make clear that he is the storyteller, relating a *second* story which a seaman told to him.   He must never make the character of the seaman stand out over the central idea of *The Admiral's Ghost*, but he must suggest the character of the seaman enough to have his report re-emphasize English patriotism.   In addition, the reader must suggest a second speaker, make him different from the storyteller, and make him powerful enough to rise from the dead to save England, but not powerful enough to overshadow the central purpose of the poem.   Though this selection, according to the scale laid out on page 381, moves nearer to characterization the reader is still a *reader*, and he is only suggesting Drake, and the seaman telling the story.

THE ADMIRAL'S GHOST [6]

Alfred Noyes

I tell you a tale tonight
Which a seaman told to me,
With eyes that gleamed in the lanthorn light
And a voice as low as the sea.
You could almost hear the stars
Twinkling up in the sky,

---

[6] Reprinted by permission of the publishers, J. B. Lippincott Company, Philadelphia, from *Collected Poems in One Volume* by Alfred Noyes. Copyright 1906, 1922, 1947, by Alfred Noyes.

And the old wind woke and moaned in the spars,
And the same old waves went by,
Singing the same old song
As ages and ages ago
While he froze my blood in that deep-sea night
With the things that he seemed to know.

A bare foot pattered on deck;
Ropes creaked; then—all grew still,
And he pointed his finger straight in my face
And growled, as a sea dog will.

"Do'ee know who Nelson was?
That pore little shriveled form
With the patch on his eye and the pinned-up sleeve
And a soul like a North Sea storm?

"Ask of the Devonshire men!
They know, and they'll tell you true;
He wasn't the pore little chawed-up chap
That Hardy thought he knew.

"He wasn't the man you think!
His patch was a dern disguise!
For he knew that they'd find him out, d'you see,
If they looked him in both his eyes.

"He was twice as big as he seemed;
But his clothes were cunningly made.
He'd both of his hairy arms all right!
The sleeve was a trick of the trade.

"You've heard of sperrits, no doubt;
Well, there's more in the matter than that!
But he wasn't the patch and he wasn't the sleeve,
And he wasn't the laced cocked hat.

"*Nelson was just—a ghost!*
You may laugh! But the Devonshire men
They knew that he'd come when England called,
And they know that he'll come again.

"I'll tell you the way it was
(For none of the landmen know),
And to tell it you right, you must go a-starn
Two hundred years or so.
. . . .

"The waves were lapping and slapping
The same as they are today;
And Drake lay dying aboard his ship
In Nombre Dios Bay.

"The scent of the foreign flowers
Came floating all around;

'But I'd give my soul for the smell o' the pitch,'
Says he, 'in Plymouth Sound.

" 'What shall I do,' he says,
'When the guns begin to roar,
An' England wants me, and me not there
To shatter'er foes once more?'

"(You've heard what he said, maybe,
But I'll make you the p'ints again;
For I want you to box your compass right
And get my story plain.)

" 'You must take my drum,' he says,
'To the old sea wall at home;
And if ever you strike that drum,' he says,
'Why, strike me blind, I'll come!

" 'If England needs me, dead
Or living, I'll rise that day!
I'll rise from the darkness under the sea
Ten thousand miles away.'

"That's what he said; and he died;
An' his pirates, listenin' roun',
With their crimson doublets and jeweled swords
That flashed as the sun went down,

"They sewed him up in his shroud
With a round shot top and toe,
To sink him under the salt sharp sea
Where all good seamen go.

"They lowered him down in the deep,
And there in the sunset light
They boomed a broadside over his grave,
As meanin' to say 'Good night.'

"They sailed away in the dark
To the dear little isle they knew;
And they hung his drum by the old sea wall
The same as he told them to.
                        .   .   .   .   .   .

"Two hundred years went by,
And the guns began to roar,
And England was fighting hard for her life,
As ever she fought of yore.

" 'It's only my dead that count,'
She said, as she says today;
'It isn't the ships and it isn't the guns
'Ull sweep Trafalgar's Bay.'

"D'you guess who Nelson was?
You may laugh, but it's true as true!

There was more in that pore little chawed-up chap
Than ever his best friend knew.

"The foe was creepin' close,
In the dark, to our white-cliffed isle;
They were ready to leap at England's throat,
When— Oh, you may smile, you may smile;
"But—ask of the Devonshire men;
For they heard in the dead of night
The roll of a drum, and they saw him pass
On a ship all shining white.
"He stretched out his dead cold face
And he sailed in the grand old way!
The fishes had taken an eye and his arm,
But he swept Trafalgar's Bay.
"Nelson—was Francis Drake!
Oh, what matters the uniform,
Or the patch on your eye or your pinned-up sleeve,
If your soul's like a North Sea Storm?"

Example VII

A study of *The True History of the Hare and the Tortoise*, by Lord Dunsany, shows that the central idea of the story is a satire on our moral and political life. There are numerous direct quotations given by the hare, the tortoise, and the backers of each, but at all times what they say is cited only to emphasize the central idea. Keeping in mind that no character should stand out over that idea, the speaker must decide how he can deliver the dialogue to reveal something of the character of each speaker but avoid having the listeners remember those speakers instead of the weaknesses which Dunsany wishes to point up in our way of living.

A younger person in reading a story like the following, will tend to use more impersonation than will an older reader. This is quite acceptable, since the entire life of the younger person is more active, vivid, and colorful.

THE TRUE HISTORY OF THE HARE AND THE TORTOISE [7]
Lord Dunsany

For a long time there was doubt with acrimony among the beasts as to whether the hare or the tortoise could run the swifter. Some said

---

[7] Lord Dunsany, *Fifty-one Tales*. Boston: Little, Brown & Company, 1915.

the hare was the swifter of the two because he had such long ears, and others said that the tortoise was the swifter because any one whose shell was so hard as that should be able to run hard too. And lo, the forces of estrangement and disorder perpetually postponed a decisive contest.

But when there was nearly war among the beasts, at last an arrangement was come to and it was decided that the hare and the tortoise should run a race of five hundred yards so that all should see who was right.

"Ridiculous nonsense!" said the hare, and it was all his backers could do to get him to run.

"The contest is most welcome to me," said the tortoise. "I shall not shirk it."

Oh, how his backers cheered.

Feeling ran high on the day of the race; the goose rushed at the fox and nearly pecked him. Both sides spoke loudly of the approaching victory up to the very moment of the race.

"I am absolutely confident of success," said the tortoise. But the hare said nothing; he looked bored and cross. Some of his supporters deserted him then and went to the other side, who were loudly cheering the tortoise's inspiriting words. But many remained with the hare. "We shall not be disappointed in him," they said. "A beast with such long ears is bound to win."

"Run hard," said the supporters of the tortoise.

And "run hard" became a kind of catch-phrase which everybody repeated to one another. "Hard shell and hard living. That's what the country wants. Run hard," they said and these words were never uttered but multitudes cheered from their hearts.

Then they were off, and suddenly there was a hush.

The hare dashed off for about a hundred yards, then he looked round to see where his rival was.

"It is rather absurd," he said, "to race with a tortoise." And he sat down and scratched himself. "Run hard! Run hard!" shouted some.

"Let him rest," shouted others. And "let him rest" became a catch-phrase too.

And after a while his rival drew near to him.

"There comes that damned tortoise," said the hare, and he got up and ran as hard as he could so that he should not let the tortoise beat him.

"Those ears will win," said his friends. "Those ears will win; and establish upon an incontestable footing the truth of what we have said." And some of them turned to the backers of the tortoise and said: "What about your beast now?"

"Run hard," they replied. "Run hard."

The hare ran on for nearly three hundred yards, nearly in fact as far as the winning-post, when it suddenly struck him what a fool he looked running races with a tortoise who was nowhere in sight, and he sat down again and scratched.

"Run hard. Run hard," said the crowd, and, "Let him rest." "Whatever is the use of it?" said the hare, and this time he stopped for good. Some say he slept.

There was desperate excitement for an hour or two, and then the tortoise won.

"Run hard. Run hard," shouted his backers. "Hard shell and hard living; that's what has done it." And then they asked the tortoise what his achievement signified, and he went and asked the turtle. And the turtle said: "It is a glorious victory for the forces of swiftness." And then the tortoise repeated it to his friends. And all the beasts said nothing else for years. And even to this day "a glorious victory for the forces of swiftness" is a catch-phrase in the house of the snail.

And the reason that this version of the race is not widely known is that very few of those that witnessed it survived the great forest-fire that happened shortly after. It came up over the weald by night with a great wind. The hare and the tortoise and a very few of the beasts saw it far off from a high bare hill that was at the edge of the trees, and they hurriedly called a meeting to decide what messenger they should send to warn the beasts in the forest.

They sent the tortoise.

Example VIII

In *To Hide the Tears*, by Helen Caldwell Day, one person speaks throughout, which prompts the question: Shall the reader try to characterize the person speaking or shall he continue to be himself? Again we go back to the discovery of the central idea and the question of relative importance of that idea compared with the person speaking. In this case the central idea is an appeal against discrimination, and if, at the end of the reading, the listener remembers a Negro woman instead of the idea of discrimination, the purpose of the author will be defeated.

TO HIDE THE TEARS [8]

Helen Caldwell Day

"Sometimes we spoke with bitterness, sometimes we spoke matter-of-factly, so much has suffering become commonplace and sorrow part of our heritage. Sometimes we even spoke with laughter. Laughter drowns out the sound of grief, and one must laugh at times to keep from crying. . . .

"You know, they tell me that down near the Delta there's a town

---

[8] From *Color Ebony* by Helen Caldwell Day. Copyright Sheed & Ward, Inc., 1951, New York.

that's got written over the city gates, 'Nigger, read and run, and if you can't read, run anyhow.' "

"That's like that sign in Memphis, 'No Negroes, peddlers or dogs allowed.' "

"I guess peddlers must be awfully mad, if they are white, when they see themselves classed with us and dogs."

"Yeah, maybe more for us than for the dogs! Ha!"

"I heard a guy at the bus station the other day talking about a place down in Alabama where a Negro can't go out on the streets after dark except in his own neighborhood."

"I reckon they think we'll bite. Watch out, Mr. Tucker, old boy. Here I come, and I'm hungry! Grrr."

"And we laughed again. But inside, pain kindled the fires of spirits into resolutions to change things and bring freedom and justice to dark men who had long since lost all hope of either, who had slept with despair until nature forced a marriage. Then we felt most keenly the stigma of being black and destitute."

Examples IX and X are excerpts from plays. They present a new problem, and in them the reader is moving nearer to complete characterization; how far he goes depends on his attitude toward the material, his ability, and his audience. Example IX is a short part of *The Valiant,* by Holworthy Hall and Robert Middlemass, and is more familiar to high school students than are most modern plays. Example X is a part of *Midsummer Night's Dream*—the familiar wood scene with Quince, Snug, Bottom, Flute, Snout, and Starveling, the characters. In Example IX there are two characters and in Example X six. These facts alone will make the prospective reader pause to consider whether or not he is versatile enough to use the literal actions and voices of so many different speakers without calling attention to his ability to change rather than to the characters portrayed. Often through minor modifications of voice and visible action an audience is able to get definite hints which help them to imagine characters completely and clearly. The reader's estimates of his physical and vocal abilities will play a large part in the decisions he makes, because, unlike the "Once upon a time . . ." of narrative literature, there are no lines in the material which demand that the reader remain a storyteller. In plays the central ideas are closely identified with the characters themselves.

The following changes usually are made when a reader moves from partial to complete characterization: (1) Action and voice take on more literal qualities—the reader appears to *be* the characters rather than to *suggest* them; (2) the scene is laid *before* the audience in the realm of the stage; and (3) the material is usually memorized so that the reader may not have even a manuscript to suggest himself rather than the characters. A reader may aim to present the two characters in *The Valiant* in such a manner that the audience can see and hear first the girl and then Dyke, as the reader speaks their respective lines. Very few adults would care to attempt the literal presentation of the Shakespearean scene, while a high school boy or girl, with animation and skill in bodily expression, might be very successful in complete characterization. What is even more important, the audience might be offended at the strained efforts of the older reader and consider the performance of the adolescent quite acceptable and "right."

In *The Valiant*,[9] Dyke, in prison, about to be executed for murder, receives his sister, who is not sure of his identity.

Example IX

THE GIRL. What's the matter?

DYKE [frowning]. I was thinking of something—now, what on earth was that boy's name! Wait a minute, don't tell me—wait a minute—I've got it!   [He punctuates his triumph with one fist in the palm of the other hand.] Joseph Anthony Paris!

THE GIRL [amazed]. Why, that's his name! That's Joe! How did you ever—

DYKE [his manner is very forcible and convincing]. Wait! Now listen carefully to what I say, and don't interrupt me, because we've only got a minute, and I want you to get this all straight, so you can tell your mother. When the war came along I enlisted and I was overseas for four years—with the Canadians. Early one morning we'd staged a big trench raid, and there was an officer who'd been wounded coming back, and was lying out there in a shell-hole under fire. The Jerries were getting ready for a raid of their own, so they were putting down a box barrage with light guns and howitzers and a few heavies. This officer was lying right in the middle of it. Well, all of a sudden a young fellow dashed out of a trench not far from where I was, and went for that officer. He had to go through a curtain of shells and, more than that, they opened on him with rifles and machine guns. The chances were just about a million to one against him, and he must have known it, but he went out just the same. He got the officer in his arms and started back, but he'd only gone a few yards when a five point nine landed right on top of the two of them. Afterward, we got what was left—the identification tag was still there—and that was the name—Joseph Anthony Paris!

THE GIRL [carries both hands to her breast]. Oh!

DYKE. If that was your brother's name, then you can tell your mother that he died like a brave man and a soldier, three years ago, in France.

THE GIRL. Joe—my brother—is dead?

DYKE. On the field of battle. It was one of the wonderful, heroic things that went almost unnoticed, as so many of them did. If an officer had seen it, there'd have been a decoration for your mother to keep and remember him by.

THE GIRL. And you were there—and saw it?

DYKE. I was there and saw it. It was three years ago. That's why you and your mother haven't heard from him. And if you don't believe what I've said, why, you just write up to Ottawa and get the official record. Of course [he shrugs his shoulders contemptuously] those records are in terribly poor shape, but at least they can tell you what battalion he fought with, when he went overseas. Only you mustn't be surprised no matter whether they say he was killed in action, or died of wounds, or is missing, or even went through the whole war with his outfit, and was honorably discharged. They really don't know what happened to half the men. But I've told you the truth. And it certainly ought to make your mother happy when she knows that her boy died as a solder, and not as a criminal.

THE GIRL [is transfigured]. Yes, yes, it will!

DYKE. And does it make you happy, too?

THE GIRL [nods repeatedly]. Yes. So happy—after what we were both afraid of—I can't even cry—yet. [She brushes her eyes with her handkerchief.] I can hardly wait to take it to her.

DYKE [struck by a sudden inspiration]. I want to give you something else to take to her. [He picks up from the desk the envelope containing the Liberty Bonds and seals it.] I want you to give this to your mother from me. Tell her it's from a man who was at Vimy Ridge and saw your brother die, so it's a sort of memorial for him. [He touches her arm as she absently begins to tear open the envelope.] No, don't you open it—let her do it.

THE GIRL. What is it? Can't I know?

DYKE. Never mind now, but give it to her. It's all I've got in the world and it's too late now for me to do anything else with it. And have your mother buy a little gold star to wear for her son—and you get one, too, and wear it—here— [He touches his heart.] Will you?

THE GIRL. Yes—I will. And yet somehow I'll almost feel that I'm wearing it for you, too.

DYKE [shakes his head soberly]. Oh, no! You mustn't ever do that.

I'm not fit to be mentioned in the same breath with a boy like your brother, and now I'm afraid it *is* time for you to go. I'm sorry, but— you'd better. I'm glad you came before it was too late, though.

THE GIRL [gives him her hand]. Good-bye, and thank you. You've done more for me—and mother—that I could possibly tell you.

Example X

PYRAMUS AND THISBE [10]

Scene 2: A Wood

[Enter QUINCE, SNUG, BOTTOM, FLUTE, SNOUT, and STARVELING.]

BOTTOM. Are we all met?

QUINCE. Pat, pat; [11] and here's a marvelous convenient place for our rehearsal. This green plot shall be our stage, this hawthorn-brake [12] our tiring-house; [13] and we will do it in action as we will do it before the duke.

BOTTOM. Peter Quince—

QUINCE. What sayest thou, bully [14] bottom?

BOTTOM. There are things in this comedy of Pyramus and Thisby that will never please. First, Pyramus must draw a sword to kill himself; which the ladies cannot abide. How answer you that?

SNOUT. By'r lakin,[15] a parlous [16] fear.

STARVELING. I believe we must leave the killing out, when all is done.

BOTTOM. Not a whit. I have a device to make all well. Write me a prologue; and let the prologue seem to say, we will do no harm with our swords, and that Pyramus is not killed indeed; and, for the more better assurance, tell them that I, Pyramus, am not Pyramus, but Bottom the weaver. This will put them out of fear.

QUINCE. Well, we will have such a prologue; and it shall be written in eight and six.[17]

BOTTOM. No, make it two more; let it be written in eight and eight.

SNOUT. Will not the ladies be afeared of the lion?

STARVELING. I fear it, I promise you.

BOTTOM. Masters,[18] you ought to consider with yourselves. To bring

---

10 William Shakespeare, *Pyramus and Thisbe*, as arranged by Edwin Van B. Knickerbocker (ed.) in *Short Plays*. New York: Henry Holt & Co., 1948.

11 Pat, pat, just in the nick. They have all arrived at one and the same time.

12 Hawthorn-brake, a spot overgrown with hawthorn shrubs.

13 Tiring-house, the room or place where the players dressed (attired) themselves.

14 Bully. The word is used here in an old sense—that of a dashing, spirited fellow.

15 Lakin, ladykin, little lady. The term was applied by Elizabethan writers to the Virgin Mary.

16 Parlous, an obsolete form of "perilous."

17 Eight and six, eight and six syllable lines, alternating.

18 Masters: The present-day term would be "gentlemen." But in Shakespere's time a gentleman was a man of distinguished family.

—God shield us!—a lion among ladies is a most dreadful thing; for there is not a more fearful wild-fowl than your lion, living; and we ought to look to 't.

SNOUT. Therefore another prologue must tell he is not a lion.

BOTTOM. Nay, you must name his name, and half his face must be seen through the lion's neck; and he himself must speak through, saying thus, or to the same defect,—"Ladies,"—or, "Fair ladies, I would wish you,"—or, "I would request you,"—or, "I would entreat you, not to fear, not to tremble; my life for yours.[19] If you think I come hither as a lion, it were pity of my life.[20] No, I am no such thing; I am a man as other men are"; and there indeed let him name his name, and tell them plainly, he is Snug the joiner.

QUINCE. Well, it shall be so. But there is two hard things; that is, to bring the moonlight into a chamber; for, you know, Pyramus and Thisby meet by moonlight.

SNOUT. Doth the moon shine that night we play our play?

BOTTOM. A calendar, a calendar! Look in the almanac. Find out moonshine, find out moonshine.

QUINCE. Yes, it doth shine that night.

BOTTOM. Why, then may you leave a casement of the great chamber window, where we play, open, and the moon may shine in at the casement.

QUINCE. Aye; or else one must come in with a bush of thorns and a lantern,[21] and say he comes to disfigure, or to present, the person of Moonshine. Then, there is another thing: we must have a wall in the great chamber; for Pyramus and Thisby, says the story, did talk through the chink of a wall.

SNOUT. You can never bring in a wall. What say you, Bottom?

BOTTOM. Some man or other must present Wall; and let him have some plaster, or some loam, or some rough-cast [22] about him, to signify wall; and let him hold his fingers thus, and through that cranny shall Pyramus and Thisby whisper.

QUINCE. If that may be, then all is well. Come, sit down, every mother's son, and rehearse your parts. [They sit.]

The following are six examples of literature in which the aim of the author is to reveal characters. Under proper circumstances each may be given with complete characterization, that is, by coming before the audience as the person speaking, by walking exactly

---

[19] My life for yours. Bottom advises Snug to stake his life on the safety of the audience.

[20] It were pity of my life, it would go hard with me.

[21] The Man in the Moon was popularly represented as carrying a bundle of thorns and a lantern.

[22] Rough-cast, plastering for an external wall; it was composed of gravel and lime.

as he would walk, by gesturing as he would gesture, by sounding as he would sound, and by reacting as he would react. But here again the reader has a choice. Often, for example, high school and younger audiences like more literal action and vocalization than do older audiences. This is as it should be, since these boys and girls are more alive and more able to respond empathically to the performer. Furthermore, the age of a reader may make a difference. A girl or boy of sixteen may read Example XVII, *Mah Mifdis' Foot*, from memory and actually break into a jig at the end without offense to any member of the audience, while a stoutish woman of fifty would do better to suggest the jig, lest the audience become more intrigued with the idea that she is still able to do it, than with the character of the Negro, which is the point of the poem.

Sex is an important factor in determining whether to use complete characterization. Chic Sale used complete characterization in reading Example XII, *He Knew Lincoln*. He went so far as to costume the narrator and he was extremely successful wherever he appeared. A woman would be more successful merely to suggest the character of Billy Brown. In the same way Example XIV, *Tommy's Bedtime Story*, is more easily acted literally by a girl than by a boy, although the fact that both boys and girls do act as baby sitters may make the selection appropriate for both sexes.

The teacher will find that a discussion of the materials of this chapter with a high school class will reveal sensitivity in taste and judgment sufficient to support the thesis that high school students should be encouraged to develop their own standards of oral reading. They will be able to determine at what point on the scale from no characterization to complete characterization a given selection, by a given reader, before a given audience, should be placed.

Example XI

DA HORSA RACE

Thomas A. Daly [23]

Joe Cavalieri, he's w'at-you-call "jay"!
So dumb, he do evratheeng joost da wrong way.

---

[23] From T. A. Daly, *Selected Poems of T. A. Daly*. New York: Harcourt, Brace and Company, Inc., pp. 82–83. Copyright 1936 by Harcourt, Brace and Company, Inc.

You nevva can turn 'eem
    Da right way, or learn 'eem—
He just maka face to w'atevra you say.

For eenstance, een weenter he walks on da street
Weeth socks on da outside da shoes on hees feet!
An' always on toppa hees head you weell see
Da back of hees cap where da front oughta be.
He's gotta wan beeg, bony horse he call "Jack"—
You see, deesa Joe eesa diggin'-contrac'—
An' dough he don't quite put da horse een da back
An' da cart een da front, eet ees true, for a fac',
He's learna dees horse eet's a sign he shall go
More fast an' more fast w'en he call to heem: "Whoa!"
Ha! w'at you theenk dat for dees cocket-eye Joe?
But Joe he don't care; eet no bother heem none
W'en othra contrac's ees start pokin' da fun,
But wan o'dose guys makin' cracks dat'sa wise
Eees Tony Baratta—an' he gats su'prise!
Joe looks at heem cold, an' he says to heem: "Tony,
You theenka my horse ees so slow an' so bony,
Eef mebbe you got hundred dollars—good money—
You bat on your horse an' I bat on my Jack
An' we drive dem right now on da horsa-race track!"
So Tony an' Joe, weeth da cart an' da horse,
Dey race for da—how-you-call?—"Two Hundred Purse,"
An' all of our people ees out eena force.
A guy weetha peestol goes "Bang!" an' dey start!
"Hooray!" shout da people; bump! bump! goes da cart.
Eet looks as eef Joe eesa poosh on da reins,
But steell for all dat eet ees Tony dat gains,
Hees horse ees so strong an' ees jompin' so fine
He looks to be sure da first over da line—
But, joost w'en day com' een da stretch, deesa Joe
He steeck out hees cheen an' he holler: "Whoa! Whoa!"
Oh, my, you should see dat old bony horse go!
Of course, dat was joost da right word for hees Jack,
But Tony's horse heard an' stopped dead een hees track!
An' long bayfore Tony can mak' heem go on
Dees Joe an' hees Jack dey have winna da mon'—
Ha! W'at you theenk dat for a sunovagun?

Joe Cavalieri, he's w'at-you-call "jay";
So dumb, he do evratheen joost da wrong way.
    You nevva can turn 'eem
    Da right way, or learn 'eem
He jus' maka face to w'atevra you say!

Example XII

HE KNEW LINCOLN [24]

Ida M. Tarbell

Some one visiting in Springfield, Illinois, steps into a drugstore and asks the proprietor, an old man by the name of Billy Brown, "Did you know Abraham Lincoln?" Billy Brown answers:

"Did I know Lincoln? Well, I should say. See that chair there? Take it, set down. That's right. Comfortable, ain't it? Well, sir, Abraham Lincoln has set in that chair hours, him and Little 'Doug,' and Logan and Judge Davis, all of 'em, all the big men in this state, set in that chair. See them marks? Whittlin'. Judge Logan did it, all-firedest man to whittle. Always cuttin' away at something. I just got that chair new, paid six dollars for it, and I be blamed if I didn't come in this store and find him slashin' right into that arm. I picked up a stick and said: 'Here, Judge, s'posin' you cut this?' He just looked at me and flounced out, mad as a wet hen. Mr. Lincoln was here, and you ought to heard him tee-hee. He was always here. Come and set by the stove by the hour and tell stories and talk and argue. There wan't never no United States Senate that could beat just what I've heard right here in this room with Lincoln settin' in that very chair where you are this minute.

"Tell stories? Nobody ever could beat him at that, and how he'd enjoy 'em, just slap his hands on his knees and jump up and turn around and then set down, laughin' to kill. Greatest man to git new yarns that ever lived, always askin', 'Heard any new stories, Billy?' And if I had I'd trot 'em out, and how he'd laugh. Often and often when I've told him something new and he'd kin'a forgit how it went, he'd come in and say, 'Billy, how was that story you'se tellin' me?' and then I'd tell it all over.

"You know I felt kind of sorry for Lincoln when they began to talk about him for President. It seemed almost as if somebody was makin' fun of him. He didn't look like a president. I never had seen one, but we had pictures of 'em, all of 'em from George Washington down, and they looked somehow as if they were different kind of timber from us. I couldn't imagine George Washington or Thomas Jefferson settin' here in that chair you're in tee-heein' over some blamed yarn of mine. None of us around town took much stock in his bein' elected at first—that is, none of the men, the women was different. They always believed in him, and used to say, 'You mark my word, Mr. Lincoln will be president. He's just made for it, he's good, he's the best man ever lived and

---

[24] Reprinted by permission from Ida M. Tarbell, *He Knew Lincoln*. New York: The Macmillan Company, 1917. Arranged by Gertrude E. Johnson.

he ought to be president.' I didn't see no logic in that then, but I dunno but there was some after all.

" 'Was there much talk about his bein' killed?' Well, there's an awful lot of fools in this world and when they don't git what they want they're always for killin' somebody. Mr. Lincoln never let on, but I reckon his mail was pretty lively readin' sometimes.

"Of course he seemed pretty cheerful always. He wan't no man to show out all he felt. Lots of them little stuck-up chaps that came out here to talk to him said, solemn as owls, 'He don't realize the gravity of the situation.' Think of that, Mr. Lincoln not realizing. They ought to heard him talk to us the night he went away. I'll never fergit that speech—nor any man who heard it. I can see him now just how he looked, standin' there on the end of his car. He'd been shakin' hands with the crowd in the depot, laughin' and talkin', just like himself, but when he got onto that car he seemed suddint to be all changed. You never seen a face so sad in all the world. I tell you he had woe in his heart that minute, woe. He knew he was leavin' us for good, nuthin' else could explain the way he looked and what he said. He knew he never was comin' back to us alive.

" 'Ever see him again?' Yes, once down in Washington, summer of '64. Things was lookin' purty blue that summer. Didn't seem to be anybody who thought he'd git reelected. I kept hearin' about the trouble he was havin' with everybody, and I just made up my mind I'd go down and see him and swap yarns and tell him how we was all countin' on his gettin' home. So I jest picked up and went right off.

"Well, I footed it up to the Soldiers' Home where Mr. Lincoln was livin' then right among the sick soldiers in their tents. There was lots of people settin' around in a little room, waitin' fer him, but there wan't anybody there I knowed, and I was feelin' a little funny when a door popped open and out came Mr. Lincoln. He saw me first thing, and his face lit up, and he laid holt of me and jest shook my hands fit to kill. 'Billy,' he says, 'now I am glad to see you. Come right in. You're goin' to stay to supper with Mary and me.'

"Didn't I know it? Think bein' president would change him—not a mite. Well, he had a right smart lot of people to see, but soon as he was through we went out on the back stoop and set down and talked and talked. He asked me about pretty nigh everybody in Springfield. I just let loose and told him about the weddin's and births and the funerals and the buildin', and I guess there wan't a yarn I'd heard in the three years and a half he'd been away that I didn't spin for him. Laugh—you ought to a heard him laugh—just did my heart good, for I could see what they'd been doin' to him. Always was a thin man, but, Lordy, he was thinner'n ever now, and his face was kind a drawn and gray—enough to make you cry.

"Well, we had supper and then talked some more, and about ten o'clock I started downtown. Wanted me to stay all night, but I says to myself, 'Billy, don't you overdo it. You've cheered him up, and you better light out and let him remember it when he's tired.' So I said, 'Nope, Mr. Lincoln, can't, goin' back to Springfield tomorrow.'

"Well, sir, I never was so astonished in my life. Mr. Lincoln just grabbed my hand and shook it nearly off, and the tears just poured down his face, and he says, 'Billy, you never'll know what good you've done me. I'm homesick, Billy, just plumb homesick, and it seems as if this war never would be over. Many a night I can see the boys a-dyin' on the fields and can hear their mothers cryin' for 'em at home, and I can't help 'em, Billy. I have to send them down there. We've got to save the Union, Billy, we've got to.'

" 'Course we have, Mr. Lincoln,' I says, cheerful as I could, 'course we have. Don't worry. It's most over. You're goin' to be reëlected, and you and old Grant's goin' to finish the war mighty quick then. Just keep a stiff upper lip, Mr. Lincoln, and don't forget them yarns I told you.' And I started out. But seems as if he couldn't let me go. 'Wait a minute, Billy,' he says, 'till I get my hat and I'll walk a piece with you.' It was one of them still sweet-smellin' summer nights with no end of stars and you ain't no idee how pretty 'twas walkin' down the road. There was white tents showin' through the trees and every little way a tall soldier standin' stock-still, a gun at his side. Made me feel mighty curious and solemn. By-and-by we come out of the trees to a sightly place where you could look all over Washington—see the Potomac and clean into Virginia. There was a bench there and we set down and after a while Mr. Lincoln he begun to talk. Well, sir, you or nobody ever heard anything like it. Tell you what he said? Nope, I can't. Can't talk about it somehow. He just opened up his heart if I do say it. Seemed as if he'd come to a p'int where he must let out. I dunno how long we set there—must have been nigh morning, fer the stars begun to go out before he got up to go. 'Good-by, Billy,' he says. 'You're the first person I ever unloaded onto, and I hope you won't think I'm a baby,' and then we shook hands again, and I walked down to town and next day I come home.

"Yes, that's the last time I seen him—last time alive.

"Wan't long after that things began to look better. War began to move right smart, and, soon as it did, there wan't no use talkin' about anybody else for President. I see that plain enough, and just as I told him, he was reëlected, and him and Grant finished up the war in a hurry. I tell you it was a great day out here when we heard Lee had surrendered. Somehow the only thing I could think of was how glad Mr. Lincoln would be.

"We began right off to make plans about the reception we'd give him —brass band—parade—speeches—fireworks—everything. Seems as if I couldn't think about anything else. I was comin' down to open the store one mornin' thinkin' how I'd decorate the windows and how I'd tie a flag on that old chair, when I see Hiram Jones comin' toward me. He looked so old and all bent over, I didn't know what had happened. 'Hiram,' I says, 'what's the matter? Be you sick?'

" 'Billy,' he says, and he couldn't hardly say it, 'Billy, they've killed Mr. Lincoln.'

"Well, I just turned cold all over, and then I flared up. 'Hiram Jones,' I says, 'you're lyin', you're crazy. How dare you tell me that? It ain't so.'

" 'Don't, Billy,' he says, 'don't go on so. I ain't lyin'. It's so. He'll never come back, Billy. He's dead!' And he fell to sobbin' out loud right there in the street, and somehow I knew it was true.

"For days and days 'twas awful here. Waitin' and waitin'. Seemed as if that funeral never would end. I couldn't bear to think of him being dragged around the country and havin' all that fuss made over him. He always hated fussin' so. Still, I s'pose I'd been mad if they hadn't done it.

"Of course they got here at last, and I must say it was pretty grand. All sorts of big bugs, Senators and Congressmen, and officers in grand uniforms and music and flags and crape. They certainly didn't spare no pains givin' him a funeral. Only we didn't want 'em. We wanted to bury him ourselves, but they wouldn't let us.

"Ma and me didn't go to the cemetery with 'em. I couldn't stan' it. Didn't seem right to have sich goin's on here at home where he belonged for a man like him. But we go up often now, ma and me does, and talk about him.

"Yes, I knowed Abraham Lincoln; knowed him well; and I tell you there wan't never a better man made. Leastwise, I don't want to know a better one. He just suited *me*—Abraham Lincoln did."

Example XIII

INJUN SUMMER [25]

John T. McCutcheon

Yep, sonny, this is sure enough Injun Summer. Don't know what that is, I reckon, do you?

Well, that's when all the homesick Injuns come back to play. You know, a long time ago, long afore yer granddaddy was born even, there used to be heaps of Injuns around here—thousands—millions, I reckon, far as that's concerned. Reg'lar sure 'nough Injuns—none o' yer cigar store Injuns, not much. They wuz all around here—right here where you're standin'. Don't be skeered—hain't none around here now, least ways, no live ones. They been done this many a year. They all went away and died, so they ain't no more left.

But every year, long about now, they all come back, leastways their sperrits do. They're here now. You can see 'em off across the fields. Look real hard. See that kind o' hazy, misty look out yonder? Well, them's Injuns—Injun sperrits marchin' along an' dancin' in the sun-

---

[25] *Chicago Tribune.* Copyright 1912 by John T. McCutcheon.

light. That's what makes that kind o' haze that's everywhere—it's jest the sperrits of the Injuns all come back. They're all around us now. See off yonder, see them tepees? They kind o' look like corn shocks from here, but them's Injun tents, sure as you're a foot high. See 'em now? Sure, I knowed you could. Smell that smoky sort o' smell in the air? That's the campfires a-burnin' and their pipes a-goin'. Lots o' people say its jest leaves burnin', but it ain't. It's the campfires, an' the Injuns are hopping around 'em t' beat the old Harry.

You jest come out here tonight, when the moon is hangin' over the hill off yonder an' the harvest fields is all swimmin' in the moonlight, an' you can see the Injuns and the tepees jest as plain as kin be. You can, eh? I knowed you could after a little while.

J'ever notice how the leaves turn red 'bout this time o' year? That's jest another sign o' redskins. That's when an old Injun sperrit gits tired dancin' an' goes up an' squats on a leaf t' rest. Why, I kin hear em rustlin' an' whisperin' an creepin' round among the leaves all the time; an' ever' once 'n a while a leaf gives way under some fat old Injun ghost and comes floatin' down to the ground. See—here's one now. See how red it is? That's the war paint rubbed off'n an Injun ghost, sure's your born.

Purty soon all the Injuns ull go marchin' away again, back to the happy huntin' ground, but next year you'll see 'em troopin' back—the sky jest hazy with 'em and their campfires smolderin' away jest like they are now.

Example XIV

TOMMY'S BEDTIME STORY [26]

Katie Lorenz

Time: 8:00 p.m. Place: The home of the average school girl.
Characters Invisible: The Mother, brother Tommy, and friend on telephone.
Enter KATIE.

KATIE. (In surprised tone.) What do you mean, be quiet, I'm being quiet.

KATIE. (Looks at watch.) Tommy's in bed! Gee Whiz! This is the first time he's been in bed at 8:00 p.m. since he was three years old.

KATIE. O. K. Mom, I will; have a nice time. (Mother exits and Katie starts up stairs.)

KATIE. Whew! Climbing these stairs gets more like climbing stairs at school everyday!

KATIE. (Enters Tommy's room and sits by the bed.) Hi! Tommy. I heard that you wanted a bedtime story. Well let's see here. There's Little Red Riding Hood, say there's a nice story. Don't want it, huh,

---

26 Katie Lorenz. Used by permission.

well here's one, the Three Bears. No? Here is another, Jack and the Bean Stalk, now I don't know what! You want it, O. K. Let's see now. (Starts thumbing through book.) Ah! here we are!

KATIE. Once upon a time there—yes it is a very nice picture, what? Silly, that isn't the mother, it's a tree! Well, anyway, once upon a time in the land of Make Believe a—what? Well no I—I don't know where the Land of Make Believe is—but maybe it will tell in the story. Well, anyway, in the Land of Make Believe there lived a boy named Jack and —say I think that's the phone. (Runs eagerly out of the room.)

KATIE. Hello—Saturday night?—With whom?—Oh! Well, I'd have to ask my mother—she might have something planned for me. You know how it is! Well I'll call you back. Thanks Doris goodbye. (Walks back to Tommy's room.)

KATIE. (Leans over him) Ah! he's sleeping! I'll leave now. (Starts for door then is frozen to spot as Tommy speaks.) Sure Tommy, I'm going to finish the story only I—well—(Goes back to chair.)

KATIE. Well, anyway, Jack and his mother lived in the country; they were very poor and all they owned was their house and their cow. So, one day Jack's mother (yawn) asked him to—take—the—cow (is almost asleep but shakes self to wake self up) to town and trade it— (yawn) for—some food—(falls asleep—but soon regains consciousness when poked by Tommy.)

KATIE. (Startled) Oh! Where was I—well, Gee, Tommy, I'd much rather tell the story to you besides I know some new parts. Well, Jack met a man on the way to town who had a sack of colored beans, now Jack traded the cow for those beans for what reason I'll never understand and when Jack's mother found out she threw the beans out the window. And then, do you know what happened? (Leans over Tommy, then a delighted expression steals over her face as she puts covers over him, then tip-toes out of the room, turns to audience, puts finger to lips.) Shhh!

Example XV

THE RACE QUESTION [27]

Paul Laurence Dunbar

In *The Heart of Happy Hollow*. Scene—Race track. Enter old colored man, seating himself.

"Oomph, oomph. De work of de devil sho' do p'ospah. How 'do suh? Des tol'able, thankee, suh. How you come on? Oh, I was des a-sayin' how de wo'k of de ol' boy do p'ospah. Doesn't I frequent the

[27] Reprinted by permission of Dodd, Mead & Company, New York, from *The Heart of Happy Hollow* by Paul Laurence Dunbar. Copyright 1904, 1932 by Mathilde Dunbar. (Chapter VI, "The Race Question.")

race-track? No, suh; no, suh. I's Baptis' myse'f, an' I 'low hit's all
devil's doin's. Wouldn't 'a 'be'n hyeah today, but I got a boy named Jim
dats long gone in sin an' he goine ride one dem hosses. Oomph, 'dat
boy! I sut'ny has talked to him and labohed wid him night an' day, but
it was allers in vain, an' I's feahed dat de day of his reckonin' is at han'.
"Ain't I nevah been intrusted in racin'? Humph, you don't s'pose
I been dead all my life, does you? What you laffin' at? Oh, scuse me,
scuse me, you unnerstan' what I means. You don' give a ol' man time
to splain hisse'f. What I means is dat day has been days when I
walked in de counsels of de ongawdly and set in de seats of sinnahs; and
long erbout dem times I did tek most ovahly strong to racin.
"How long dat been? Oh, dat's way long back, 'fo' I got religion,
mo'n thirty years ago, dough I got to own I has fell from grace several
times sense.
"Yes, suh, I ust to ride. Ki-ye! I nevah furgit de day dat my ol'
mas' Jack put me on June Boy; his black geldin', and say to me, 'Si'
says he, 'if you don' ride de tail offen Cunnel Scott's mare, I's guine to
larrup you twell you cain't set in de saddle no mo'!' Hyah, hyah.
My o' mas' was amighty han' fu' a joke. I knowed he wan't gwine to
do nuffin' to me.
"Did I win? Why, whut you spec' I's doin' hyeah if I hadn' winned?
W'y, ef I'd 'a' let dat Scott maih beat my 'June Boy' I'd 'a' drowned
myse'f in Bull Skin Crick.
"Yes, suh, I winned; w'y, at de finish I come down dat track lak hit
was de Jedgment Day an' I was de las' one up! Ef I didn't race dat
maih's tail clean off, I'low I made hit do a lot a' switchin! An' aftah dat
my wife Mandy she ma'ed me. Hyah, hyah, I ain't bin much on hol'in'
de reins since.
"Sh! dey comin' in to wa'm up. Dat Jim dat Jim, dat my boy; you
nasty putrid little rascal. Des a hundred an' eight, suh, des a hundred
an' eight. Yas, suh, dat's my Jim; I don' know whaih he gits his dev'-
ment at.
"What's de mattah wid dat boy? Whyn't he hunch hisse'f up on dat
saddle right? Jim, Jim, whyn't you limber up, boy; hunch yo' se'f up on
dat hoss lak you belonged to him and knowed you was dah. What I
done showed you! De black raskil goin' out dah tryin' to disgrace his
own daddy. Hyeah he come back. Dat's bettah, you scoun'ril.
"Does I bet? Well I don' des call hit bettin; but I risks a little w'en
I t'inks I kin he'p de cause. 'Tain't gamblin', dough my ol' Mastah did
ust to say dat a honest gamblah was ez good ez a hones' preachah an'
mos' nigh ez skace.
"Look out dah, man, days off, dat nasty bay maih wid de white feet
leadin' right fu'm de pos'. I knowed it! I knowed it! I had my eye on
huh all de time. Oh, Jim, Jim, why didn't you git in bettah, way back
dah fouf? Dah go de gong! I knowed dat wasn't no staht. Troop
back dah, you raskils, hyah, hyah.

"I wish dat boy wouldn't do so much jummying erroun' wid dat hose.
First t'ing he know he ain't gwine to know whaih he's at.

"Dah, dah dey go ag'in. Hit's a sho' t'ing dis time. Bettah, Jim
bettah. Dey didn't leave you dis time. Hug dat bay maih, hug her
close, boy. Don't press dat hoss yit. He's holdin' back a lot o'tings.

"He's gainin'! Doggone my cats, he's gainin'! an' dat hoss o' his'n
gwine dess ez stiddy ez a rockin' chair. Jim allus was a good boy.

"Confound these spec's, I cain't see 'em skacely; huh, you say dey's
neck an' neck; now I see 'em! now I see 'em! and Jimmy's a-ridin' like
—Hugh, huh, I laik to said sumpin!

"De bay maih's done huh bes', she's done huh bes'! Dey's turned into
the stretch an' still see-sawin'. Let him out, Jimmy, let him out! Dat
boy done th'owed de reins away. Come on, Jimmy, come on! He's
leadin' by a nose. Come on, I tell you, you black rapscallion, come on!
Give 'em hell, Jimmy! give 'em hell! Under de wire an' a len'th ahead.
Doggone my cats! wake me up w'en dat othah hoss comes in.

"No, sur, I ain't gwine stay no longah, I don't app'ove o' racin; I's
gwine 'round' an' see dis hyeah bookmakah an' den I's gwine dreckly
home, suh, dreckly home. I's Baptis' myse'f, an' I don' app'ove o' no
sich doin's!"

Example XVI

MAH MIF'DIS' FOOT [28]

Wilbur Nesbit

●

I done got 'ligion las' Sunday night,
En I's livin' true en I's livin' right;
En I doan' no mo' give a passin' glance
Ter a deck o' cyahds or a ragtime dance;
En I go no mo' ter de wicked shows
'Ca'se day temp' de weak, ez a pusson knows!

●

Would yo' lissen ter dat?
Who's a-playin'? My lan'!
Dat am Eph'm's foot-pat
Ez he switches his han'—
"Tek yo' foot out de mud
En roll it in de san'!"

I done knell down at de mo'neh's bench
En mah sins come a-loose wid a monst'ous wrench;

---

[28] Wilbur Nesbit, "Mah Mif'dis' Foot," *The Saturday Evening Post*, October
10, 1908. Copyright 1908 by The Curtis Publishing Company.

En I ain't gwine fool wid no shootin' craps;
Lest I be lef' out w'en de last bah draps;
En I ain't gwine dance, dough de fiddle coax,
'Ca'se I's took my place wid de Mif'dis folks.

Would yo' lissen dis now!
Eph'm scrapin' de strings
Ez dey balance en bow
In de pigeon wings!
"Tek yo' foot out de mud
En roll it"—it sings!

Mah Mif'dis' foot it am sho'ly good—
But de t'ur foot shake lak I knowed it would!
En it trimble so w'en de fiddle squeal
Dat it beatin' de time fum toe to heel!
Stan' still; Stan' fas'!   Oh, yo' blame fool feet!
Er ol' Satin'll sco'ch yo' wid chimbly heat!

Would yo' lissen dat chune?
It am suttenly gran'!
It am mo' dan a coon
Dat's a sinneh could stan'.
"Tek yo' foot out de mud
En roll it in de san'!"

I done got 'ligion las' Sunday night—
Oh, it's shuffle en swing en bow ter de right,
En it's allaman lef' en do-se-doe
Wid a sif'-sif'-sif'! on de dusty flo'!
En a jump Jim Crow—En blame mah hide
Ef mah Mif'dis' foot ain' done backslide!

En I's out on de flo'
W'ilst dey pattin' de han'!
Ol' Eph'm, yo' bow
Is suttenly gran'.
"Tek yo' foot out de mud
En roll it in de san'!"

KINDS OF GROUP READING

There are two types of group reading which interest high school students: reading poems in chorus, and reading plays.

Choric Speaking

Choric speaking is a method of interpreting poetry by speaking together as a group in much the same way that a chorus interprets songs. Some parts of the poem are read simultaneously by everyone in the chorus, some parts are read by two or three persons together, and still other parts are read by individuals alone.

The first step to get meaning

Just as in all other reading the first step is to understand what is being said, so in choric speaking the teacher must work with students to get the full meaning. The suggestions on page 378 should be followed to make sure that the meaning is clear and complete before the choric presentation is worked out.

Analyze the abilities of the class

Study the talent in the class to see how much originality can be given to the choric reading. It is often well to divide the class into high, low, and medium voices, because a poem becomes more meaningful when some parts are read with one pitch and some, with another. It is well to make use of facial expression and gestures, if such visible symbols seem appropriate.

Choose a leader

If a group is to read in unison, if solo parts are to come in at the right moment, if high, low or medium voices are to blend to give appropriate meanings, it is helpful to have a leader, just as a chorus and a symphony have conductors. The teacher will often make the best leader but frequently more is learned when students themselves take turns at directing. Choric reading helps boys and girls to become sensitive to melody and rhythm and to the various possible interpretations of a poem.

Steps in preparation exemplified

Thunderdrums, by Lew Sarett, is a poem which high school students like to do in chorus and the steps in preparation are sketched briefly here as a guide to the preparation of other poems.

Selection for study

THUNDERDRUMS [29]

An Indian War-Medicine Dance

Lew Sarett

I

The Drummers Sing:

Beat on the buckskin, beat on the drums,
Hi! Hi! Hi! for the Thunderbird comes;
His eyes burn red with the blood of battle;
His wild wings roar in the medicine rattle.
Thunderbird-god, while our spirits dance,
Tip with your lightning the warrior's lance;
On shafts of wind, with heads of flame,
Build for us arrows that torture and maim;
Ho! may our ironwood war-clubs crash
With a thunderbolt head and a lightning flash.
Hi! Hi! Hi! hear the Cut-throat's doom,
As our wild bells ring and our thunderdrums boom.

[Then follow Part II, Double Bear Dances; Part III, Jumping River Dances; Part IV, Ghost Wolf Dances; and Part V, Iron-Wind Dances.]

VI

The Drummers Sing:

Beat on the buckskin, beat on the drums,
Hi! Hi! Hi! for the Thunderbird comes;
His eyes glow red with the lust for battle,
And his wild wings roar in the medicine-rattle.
Thunderbird-god, while our spirits dance,
Tip with your lightning the warrior's lance;
On shafts of wind, with heads of flame,
Build for us arrows that torture and maim;
Ho! may our ironwood war-clubs crash
With a thunderbolt head and a lightning flash.
Hi! Hi! Hi! hear the Cut-throat's doom,
As our wild bells ring and our thunderdrums boom.

The lines must be meaningful

The author gives the following information regarding the meaning of *Thunderdrums*.[30] Students may be given the author's statement as a point of departure and then be encouraged to bring in material on Indians and their dances which can be applied to this poem. The teacher will get an enthusiastic response if the assignment is well motivated.

The ceremony upon which the "Thunderdrums" is based illustrates the futility of translation. The poem is a broad interpretation of a war-medicine dance that was performed often in the old Indian fighting days by the Chippewas as a part of their preparation for war with the Sioux, their bitter enemies. This ancient war-dance has been preserved by some of the Chippewas and is performed occasionally by the Red Lake Chippewas and other equally remote Indians, even in these modern peaceful days.

While the Chippewa chiefs and braves danced in the ring, during the war-dance, the medicine-men made war-medicine; by means of their chants and strong medicines they render the warriors immune from injury and death; they would invoke the aid of the powerful spirits and gods, especially of the Thunderbird; and thus they would strengthen the fighting hearts of the braves for fearless struggles and for heroic deeds.

A war-dance may continue for hours; yet in the entire period no specific words may be uttered, with the exception of a defiant war-whoop, or an exultant "Ah-hah-háy!" "Háh-yah-ah-háy!,", or a blood-curdling shout. Yet consider all that transpires: hours of dancing, posturing, and pantomime; meaningful singing and drumming, varying in spirit and purpose from time to time; medicine-making and invocations to the gods,—all of which is so significant and real to the warriors in the dancing-ring that they become transported and frenzied in their will for battle.

Occasionally in the course of a dance, especially in the war-dance, an individual in the group may do a sort of solo dance. By means of gesture and posture, impersonation, and pantomime, he may enact a dramatic scene; he may tell the story of a former battle in which he killed an enemy in a hand-to-hand struggle; he may portray his method of scouting, or his power as a warrior; he may show how he will track, attack, and destroy his enemies; he may impersonate animals and wounded men, and enact a score of dramatic incidents relevant to the ceremony. The dance pantomime is the root of Indian drama, the only form of drama known to the early American Indians, with the exception of certain seasonal dances and religious ceremonies—and these are simply elaborations of the more common dance pantomimes. In "Thunder-

---

[30] *Ibid.*, p. 79.

drums"—Sections II–V, "Double-Bear Dances," "Jumping-River Dances," "Ghost-Wolf Dances," and "Iron-Wind Dances"—I have sought to capture the spirit of four solo dances or pantomimes typical of many others in the old war-medicine ceremonies.

The Thunderbird, to which many references are made in the poem, is one of the most powerful of the spirits, a force in the lives of most Chippewas and in the conjurings of the medicine men. The Thunderbird comes to the world in electrical storms; he shows himself when the black clouds gather on the horizon, when the sky rumbles with thunder, and when the fiery bolts and the jagged lightnings flash overhead.

The words "Cut-throat" and "Pucker-skin" are terms used occasionally to characterize respectively the Sioux and the Chippewa. The meaning of the other Chippewa words and phrases in this poem and in the remaining poems in the group may be gathered from their context; whenever an Indian word is used, its equivalent in English may be found generally in the same line. The spelling, syllabification, and the marks of emphasis convey the accurate pronunciation of all the Indian words.

The expressions, Ho! Ho! Ah-hah-háy!, Háh-yah-ah-háy, and Wuh! are typical Chippewa explosives and ejaculations of approval by the audience.

Note parts appropriate for group and individual reading

This poem is written for groups and individuals. Stanzas I and VI are clearly for more than one person, and stanzas II, III, IV, and V, can appropriately be read by Double-Bear, Big-Sky, Ghost-Wolf, and Iron-Wind respectively. The refrains at the end of each stanza may be taken by the group, by low, high, or medium voices, or by the individual dancer, depending on the wish of the class.

Decide on action and arrangement of speakers

Some classes may have the entire class read the lines of the drummers and let them form a background for the four individual dancers, some may plan to have the drummers arranged on steps, some may have them seated, beating with dull thuds on the floor or the wall, encouraging the dancers who step forth to show their daring. There are dozens of ways in which resourceful high school boys and girls can show the fire and enthusiasm of these Indians.

Make voices meaningful

A careful study of the lines will make clear where interest and response can be aroused by varying the vocal volume, pitch, and rate. If the students plan the presentation with the teacher, and it is made clear that no preconceived form is desired, boys and girls will gain freedom and confidence in this group activity.

Practice in groups and alone

When working out meaning and practicing delivery it is well to ask students to read single lines, stanzas, and, finally, the whole selection, alone and with others. The entire performance should proceed with life and enthusiasm. The teacher himself should show the interest which he expects from his students.

Group Play Reading

Group play reading is a type of activity which gives many students an opportunity to participate; it develops familiarity with relatively large numbers of plays; it involves no expense and work for setting, lighting, costume; and, best of all, high school boys and girls enjoy this method of play presentation.

The play should have special characteristics

Plays to be read from the book instead of being acted on the stage should depend for effect on dialogue rather than on action and setting; they should have relatively short speeches, not over ten characters, and be of good literary quality.

The play should be appropriate in length

If the play is to be given in a class period it should be adapted to fit that length of time. The teacher will need to cut long plays or help students to find short plays. Seldom does an audience listen attentively to a high school play reading which exceeds forty-five minutes. Sometimes it is possible to read one act of a longer play in a class period.

Selecting the characters

Because the persons playing the parts of the various characters remain seated and present the play mainly through voice rather than visible action, it is not so important to consider age, sex, and physical characteristics in assigning parts as it is in a stage play. However, if possible, boys should have the male parts, girls the female parts, and attention should be given to vocal skill and facial expression if an effective performance is expected.

Responsibilities of stage manager

The stage manager should arrange rehearsals, and direct the final performance. He should learn about the history and background of the play, prepare introductions for each character, rehearse with his cast until all can pick up cues effectively and read expressively, and read descriptions of the action necessary to an understanding of the play.

Seating the characters

The readers should sit in a semicircle, the leading characters near the center, and the stage manager, or director, at the end either on the right or left. If two characters have a good deal of dialogue, it is better to have someone sitting between them in order that volume enough to make the lines easily heard by the audience will not seem inappropriate to the situation. It is usually effective to arrange readers in the right order, let them walk in, stand until all have reached their places, and then sit simultaneously.

The final performance

When the characters have come before the audience and are seated, the director rises and announces the play. He gives background information of interest to the listeners, and then introduces the characters. As he announces the first character, the person reading it stands and remains standing during the time the character is being described, and then resumes his seat. Then the next character rises and remains standing until he is described. In this way the audience has time to see the characters vividly in their own minds, even though there are no costumes or stage action.

The director announces and describes the scenes. Each actor reads his part as expressively as possible in order to make the play meaningful.

If there are several scenes and the cast of characters changes, seating may be rearranged at the end of each scene. The class should decide whether or not this is advisable.

An example of a good play for reading

Friend Mary is a good play for reading by high school students. It is given here in its entirety because it can be read in the average class period. Preceding the play is information which will help readers to understand it. Part I and the introduction of Part II may be used advantageously by the director in the introduction. The rest of Part II is the play.

Part I

To be read by stage manager

HUMOROUS ACCOUNT OF HIS EXPERIENCES WITH A LADY HE WAS REQUESTED TO MARRY [31]

A letter to Mrs. O. H. Browning, Springfield, Illinois
April 1, 1838

Dear Madam, Without apologising for being egotistical, I shall make the history of so much of my life as has elapsed since I saw you the subject of this letter. And, by the way, I now discover that in order to give a full and intelligible account of the things I have done and suffered since I saw you, I shall necessarily have to relate some that happened before.

It was, then, in the autumn of 1836 that a married lady of my acquaintance, and who was a great friend of mine, being about to pay a visit to her father and other relatives residing in Kentucky, proposed to me that on her return she would bring a sister of hers with her on condition that I would engage to become her brother-in-law with all convenient dispatch. I, of course, accepted the proposal, for you know I could not have done otherwise had I really been averse to it; but privately, between you and me, I was most confoundedly well pleased with the project. I had seen the said sister some three years before, thought her intelligent and agreeable, and saw no good objection to plodding life through hand-in-hand with her. Time passed on, the lady took her journey, and in due time returned, sister in company, sure enough. This astonished me a little, for it appeared to me that her coming so readily showed that she was a trifle too willing, but on reflection it occurred to me that she might have been prevailed on by her married sister to come, without anything concerning me having been mentioned to her, and so I concluded that if no other objection presented itself, I would consent to waive this. All this occurred to me on hearing of her arrival in the neighbourhood—for, be it remembered, I had not yet seen her, except about three years previous, as above mentioned. In a few days we had an interview, and, although I had seen her before, she

[31] William H. Herndon and Jesse W. Weik, *Abraham Lincoln: The True Story of a Great Life*. New York: Appleton-Century-Crofts, Inc., 1892, pp. 148–152.

did not look as my imagination had pictured her. I knew she was over-size, but she now appeared a fair match for Falstaff. I knew she was called an "old maid," and I felt no doubt of the truth of at least half of the appellation, but now, when I beheld her, I could not for my life avoid thinking of my mother; and this, not from withered features,—for her skin was too full of fat to permit of its contracting into wrinkles—but from her want of teeth, weather-beaten appearance in general, and from a kind of notion that ran in my head that nothing could have commenced at the size of infancy and reached her present bulk in less than thirty-five or forty years; and, in short, I was not at all pleased with her. But what could I do? I had told her sister that I would take her for better or for worse, and I made a point of honour and conscience in all things to stick to my word, especially if others had been induced to act on it, which in this case I had no doubt they had, for I was now fairly convinced that no other man on earth would have her, and hence the conclusion that they were bent on holding me to my bargain. "Well," thought I, "I have said it, and, be the consequences what they may, it shall not be my fault if I fail to do it." At once I determined to consider her my wife, and this done, all my powers of discovery were put to work in search of perfections in her which might be fairly set off against her defects. I tried to imagine her handsome, which, but for her unfortunate corpulency, was actually true. Exclusive of this, no woman that I have ever seen had a finer face. I also tried to convince myself that the mind was much more to be valued than the person, and in this she was not inferior, to any with whom I had been acquainted.

Shortly after this, without attempting to come to any positive under-standing with her, I set out for Vandalia, when and where you first saw me. During my stay there I had letters from her which did not change my opinion of either her intellect or intention, but, on the con-trary, confirmed it in both.

All this while, although I was fixed "firm as the surge-repelling rock" in my resolution, I found that I was continually repenting the rashness which had led me to make it. Through life I have been in no bondage, either real or imaginary, from the thraldom of which I so much desired to be free. After my return home I saw nothing to change my opinion of her in any particular. She was the same, and so was I. I now spent my time in planning how I might get along in life after my con-templated change of circumstances should have taken place, and how I might procrastinate the evil day for a time, which I really dreaded as much, perhaps more, than an Irishman does the halter.

After all my sufferings upon this deeply interesting subject, here I am, wholly, unexpectedly, completely out of the "scrape" and I now want to know if you can guess how I got out of it—out, clear, in every sense of the term—no violation of word, honour, or conscience. I don't believe you can guess, and so I might as well tell you at once. As the lawyer says, it was done in the manner following, to wit: After I had delayed the matter as long as I thought I could in honour do (which, by the way, had brought me round into the last fall), I concluded I might as well bring it to a consummation without further delay, and so I mustered my resolution and made the proposal to her direct; but, shocking to relate, she answered, No. At first I supposed she did it through an affectation of modesty, which I thought but ill became her under the peculiar circumstances of the case, but on my renewal of the charge I found she repelled it with greater firmness than before. I tried it again and again, but with the same success, or rather with the same want of success.

I finally was forced to give it up, at which I very unexpectedly found myself mortified almost beyond endurance. I was mortified, it seemed to me, in a hundred different ways. My vanity was deeply wounded by the reflection that I had so long been too stupid to discover her intentions, and at the same time never doubting that I understood them perfectly; and also that she, whom I had taught myself to believe nobody else would have, had actually rejected me with all my fancied greatness. And, to cap the whole, I then for the first time began to suspect that I was really a little in love with her. But let it all go! I'll try and outlive it. Others have been made fools of by the girls, but this can never in truth be said of me. I most emphatically, in this instance, made a fool of myself. I have now come to the conclusion never again to think of marrying, and for this reason—I can never be satisfied with any one who would be blockhead enough to have me.

When you receive this, write me a long yarn about something to amuse me. Give my respects to Mr. Browning.

Part II

FRIEND MARY [32]

Thomas Wood Stevens

A Play for the Twelfth of February

The basis of "Friend Mary" is the familiar "Browning letter" and Herndon's account of the Mary Owens affair, together with his later interview with her, as Mrs. Vinyard. Sometimes—usually on the twelfth of February—a Lincoln play is wanted when there is no actor of exactly the Lincoln type available, and it may be possible to evoke the idea of Lincoln better without a Lincoln at all than with an imperfect type.

Characters:

> MRS. MARY VINYARD, nee Mary Owens
> JESSIE, her daughter
> JUDGE PARSONS
> MR. FLINT, of the *New York Herald*.

[32] From: *The Nursery Maid of Heaven and Other Plays* by Thomas Wood Stevens. Copyright, 1926, D. Appleton & Company. Reprinted by permission of the publishers, Appleton-Century-Crofts, Inc. Pp. 145–166.

Scene: The living room in the home of Mrs. Vinyard, at Weston, Mo.

Time: The morning of April 15, 1865

MRS. VINYARD has put aside her knitting, and is playing solitaire, and waiting. The door opens, and JESSIE enters from outdoors, taking off her
wrap and coming gaily to her mother.

JESSIE: Look, mother—the first violets.

MRS. VINYARD: Middle of April. Down in Kentucky, now, the hollows
were blue with them a week ago. . . . Jack of spades? . . . Did you
get the mail?

JESSIE: No train from the East. There's been a washout.

MRS. VINYARD: No—no other mail, from the South? From your brothers?

JESSIE: (Coming closer) I saw Virgie. She said . . . nothing.

MRS. VINYARD: Thought there might be—now.

JESSIE: (overlooking the game of solitaire) Why don't you play the ten
on the nine?

MRS. VINYARD: Who's playing this game?

JESSIE: The boys from the last squad are back.

MRS. VINYARD: Back from where?

JESSIE: Camp, at Saint Joe.

MRS. VINYARD: I need a jack of spades. I thought you said there was
no train.

JESSIE: There wasn't. The wires are down, too. They walked. They
were mud to their knees. You'd think they were the very ones that
settled the war, to hear them talk.

MRS. VINYARD: (rather bitterly) Yes, they'd talk. Never beyond their
first camp at Saint Joe.

JESSIE: Well, they're mighty gay. Lee's licked, and all that sort of
thing. All but little Bill Warren—he was about crying.

MRS. VINYARD: 'Cause they wouldn't let him capture Jeff Davis with his
own two hands, I s'pose.

JESSIE: No. 'Cause while he was gone his old black hound dog had
died. That's the calamity of the war to little Bill.

MRS. VINYARD: (with a faint, broken laugh) Babies—poor babies. . . .

JESSIE: Oh—and I saw Judge Parsons.

MRS. VINYARD: Judge Parsons? . . . What's that got to do with the jack
of spades?

JESSIE: And he said he was coming right up to see you—wanted to bring
a friend.

MRS. VINYARD: (acidly) Judge Parsons, eh? Well, he needn't trouble.

JESSIE: It was something mighty special, he said. Why don't you want
to see him? You used to like him.

MRS. VINYARD: That was different, up in Illinois, when we were children.
He was a friend of your father's. But down here in Missouri, and
now—

JESSIE: (wistfully) Yes, it's all different. I wonder when Walsh and
Dudley—

MRS. VINYARD: (rising) There's somebody at the gate now.

JESSIE: That's Judge Parsons and his friend.

MRS. VINYARD: Who is his friend?

JESSIE: I never saw him before.

(A knock is heard.)

MRS. VINYARD: Well—let them in.

(Mrs. Vinyard goes into the other room, and Jessie opens the door to Judge Parsons and Mr. Flint. The judge is about sixty, a positive, hearty, humorous man. Mr. Flint is under forty, a reporter from Boston, now employed on the *New York Herald*.)

JUDGE PARSONS: How d'ye do, Jessie . . . Bless my soul, how you've grown up! Let me introduce Mr. Flint—Miss Vinyard, this is Mr. Flint—correspondent of the *New York Herald*.

JESSIE: Mr. Flint. Won't you sit down, judge? And Mr. Flint.

JUDGE: We came to see your mother, on particular business.

JESSIE: I'll tell her you're here. I mentioned that you were coming. (Jessie goes out.)

JUDGE: I suppose the mother looked about like that girl—at the time.

FLINT: If she did—nobody'd believe the story.

(Mrs. Vinyard re-enters.)

MRS. VINYARD: (without cordiality) How d'ye do, Judge Parsons.

JUDGE: How d'ye do, Mrs. Vinyard. May I introduce Mr. Flint, of the *New York Herald*—Mrs. Vinyard.

FLINT: I'm sure I'm very glad to know Mrs. Vinyard.

MRS. VINYARD: *New York Herald*. . . . You're a long ways from home, Mr. Flint.

FLINT: Yes, Mrs. Vinyard. I'm—I'm detained in Missouri by the wash-out on the railroad. I encountered Judge Parsons, and—

MRS. VINYARD: Oh—you just happened to be caught here by the wash-out. I understood from my daughter that Judge Parsons had some particular business with me.

JUDGE: There now, Mrs. Vinyard—the war's over, you know.

MRS. VINYARD: So they tell me, down here.

JUDGE: Come now, we haven't any quarrel.

MRS. VINYARD: Have you given over being an abolitionist?

JUDGE: Yes—if you like. There's nothing left to abolish.

MRS. VINYARD: What was your particular business?

JUDGE: You won't run up the rebel flag again if I tell you? I want you to tell Mr. Flint all about your acquaintance—or shall I say your engagement—to Abe Lincoln.

MRS. VINYARD: Why should I?

FLINT: It's a matter of public interest, Mrs. Vinyard. An episode that's never been published, in the life of the President, you know—

MRS. VINYARD: I've nothing to say.

FLINT: I hope you won't be so obdurate, Mrs. Vinyard.

MRS. VINYARD: Why should I give you anything of interest—even if I had it, about a Yankee president?

JUDGE: Come, Mrs. Vinyard—I'm talking about old times in Illinois

now. His being a president has nothing to do with his having jilted
you.

MRS. VINYARD: Don't use that word, Judge Parsons.

JUDGE: Choose your own word, Mrs. Vinyard. I didn't come to quarrel
with an old neighbor, but I want you to know this story, Mr. Flint.
If I tell it to you, outside this room, you'll discount it—so will everybody. Come, Mrs. Vinyard, you might's well help me get it straight.

MRS. VINYARD: Well, of all the impudence.

JUDGE: Get out your notebook, Mr. Flint.

MRS. VINYARD: (in answer to a questioning look from Flint) Of course,
Mr. Flint, get out your notebook. I'm lending my house to the judge
—for old times' sake. (She speaks with dangerous coldness and sits
in her chair, very straight.)

JUDGE: Mrs. Vinyard was Miss Mary Owens, of Kentucky. She had a
sister, Mrs. Abel, who lived in Petersburg, Illinois. Once when Mrs.
Abel was making a visit to Kentucky, Lincoln told her that if she'd
bring her pretty sister back with her, he'd be her brother-in-law.
That's how it was, isn't it, Mrs. Vinyard?

MRS. VINYARD: It's as near it as I'd expect to get from you, Judge Parsons.

JUDGE: Of course, on this part of the story, Mrs. Vinyard speaks only
from hearsay—she wasn't there.

MRS. VINYARD: No more than Judge Parsons was.

JUDGE: This was in '38—

MRS. VINYARD: It was in '37. You would have been in short breeches
then, Mr. Flint, but Alex Parsons was a flourishing lawyer, and mighty
unreliable already.

JUDGE: Lincoln had seen the witness—I mean Miss Mary Owens, now
Mrs. Vinyard—three or four years before, and he remembered her as
a slim, willowy slip of a girl. Well, when she arrived in Petersburg
in '37, she was different from what he remembered. She's taken on
weight, as I might say. She was—

MRS. VINYARD: Take a good look at me, Mr. Flint, and tell me, does it
look likely to you that the judge is telling the truth?

FLINT: Well, Mrs. Vinyard, it's hard to say—

JUDGE: Lincoln wanted mightily to get out of his bargain—

MRS. VINYARD: (rising) Gentlemen, you have gone too far. I will not
allow Judge Parsons to say another word.

FLINT: You'll tell me yourself then, Mrs. Vinyard.

MRS. VINYARD: I think, considering his high position now, Mr. Lincoln
should be heard first.

JUDGE: But how the devil—I beg your pardon—

FLINT: Oh! You have letters—

(She moves over to the door.)

MRS. VINYARD: After all—it's nothing to be ashamed of. Just one moment
—and I'll get them.

(She goes out.)

FLINT: Letters from him? Still I don't expect much from them. He was a lawyer then, wasn't he?

JUDGE: You mean you don't expect anything damaging? No. But if it's not ridiculous it's the next thing to it, just now.

FLINT: Of course the *Herald* doesn't want anything scandalous.

JUDGE: No. I judge not. That wouldn't be popular. He's in the height of victory now. You want to take him down a peg. It's natural. Take him down a peg before he squanders the victory in his soft-hearted pity for the rebels . . . little irritations.

FLINT: That's it. You've put your finger right on the spot. And this story might be mighty welcome—especially if there are letters.

(Mrs. Vinyard re-enters.)

MRS. VINYARD: Gentlemen, do you recognize the figures in this picture? (She hands them an ambrotype.)

JUDGE: Of course. Abe Lincoln looks like no other man on God's footstool, and the lady looks just like you today, Mrs. Vinyard.

FLINT: (not so easily convinced) There's no doubt about him, but— would you mind facing this way ma'am. Thank you. There's no doubt, I should say.

MRS. VINYARD: Doubt, I reckon not. (She chuckles to herself.) I remember when it was taken. Now, why do you want this, Mr. Flint?

JUDGE: Why are you so suspicious, Mrs. Vinyard? We both know you're a Kentuckian.

MRS. VINYARD: My kin came from Carolina, in the first place.

JUDGE: We know where your sympathies have been. And you know I've always been a strong Union man—

MRS. VINYARD: Rabid, I'd say.

JUDGE: Well, then, you know I wouldn't do anything to damage Abraham Lincoln, don't you?

MRS. VINYARD: I was asking you, Mr. Flint.

FLINT: Well, it's just as I told you before. The public is always interested in anything about the President. And especially just now, when he's in the flush of victory, and when his new policies—whatever they may be—

MRS. VINYARD: I didn't know he had any policies—except to free the niggers—

FLINT: Of course the question of the treatment of the conquered South will be in his hands. . . .

MRS. VINYARD: (rising) The conquered South! . . . You and Judge Parsons say—She goes over to the door and calls. Jessie! Jessie, come here. You want my story. Well, you shall have it. It's nothing to be ashamed of. (Jessie comes in.) Jessie, take the judge out and show him the new chickens.

JUDGE: Now look here, Mrs. Vinyard—

JESSIE: Better come with me, Judge. When mother sets her lips that way, it's no use.

JUDGE: I reckon you're right, Miss Jessie. May I smoke on the way?

JESSIE: Of course. (Jessie and the Judge go out. Mrs. Vinyard comes to the table and takes up the ambrotype and the little packet of letters.)

MRS. VINYARD: I hardly know how to tell you. Not that it isn't clear in my remembrance. I can see him now, the long, lanky—and that shy. . . . Well, I wonder where I'd better begin.

FLINT: Perhaps if we began with these letters—

MRS. VINYARD: No, they come after. It all began with Ellen Jane, my sister. She was going home on a visit. She told Lincoln she'd bring me back with her for him, and he said if she would, he'd be eternally grateful and her brother-in-law to boot.

FLINT: That's a very odd sort of arrangement. Did he mean it?

MRS. VINYARD: It wasn't so odd in the Illinois country, back in '37. She said she'd hold him to it. Half joking, you know. But he never was smart about women. . . . Well, Ellen Jane brought me, never saying a word about Lincoln until we got to Petersburg. He was just setting up in law then—and in politics, too, I reckon. . . . He remembered me, he said, from three years back. I remembered him, too, but lawsy, I wouldn't have admitted it.

FLINT: Then there was an understanding about the matter between Mr. Lincoln and your sister Mrs.—Mrs. Abel?

MRS. VINYARD: A misunderstanding—more like it. I told you, when it came to girls, he was a mere child. Smart about other things, but not about girls. . . . He'd come and sit . . . and we'd go to a quiltin' maybe. Never any style, though. Just plain . . . I'd been brought up in Kentucky, and I'd been to boarding school, and I looked for something. . . . Well, I was a young lady, bless your heart. My notion wasn't a man a foot taller than me, that had worked on a flatboat, and looked it. He might be a smart lawyer, but I was looking for somebody with a dash, and a way with the ladies, and . . . Do you understand that, young man?

FLINT: I think so. You expected a suitor to be—er—romantic, and to show it in his—in his deportment.

MRS. VINYARD: That's it. Most girls are fools that way . . . I remember once we were all going out to Uncle Billy Green's to a huskin'. Mr. Lincoln was riding with me. We had a branch to cross—

FLINT: A branch? That's a—

MRS. VINYARD: A crick, I s'pose you'd call it down East. Pretty deep it was at the ford, too. The other gentlemen all made a great fuss about getting their ladies safe across. We were behind. He rode in and never looked back to see how I got along. I splashed through the branch and rode up beside him. Land, but I was mad! "You're a nice fellow," I says. "I s'pose you didn't care whether I was mired down or not." He looked kind of dashed and said he knew I was plenty smart to take care of myself. He thought it was a compliment.

I didn't. . . . That very night he asked me to marry him. He'd seen Sister Ellen Jane's eye on him at the huskin', I reckon.

FLINT: Now we're coming to it.

MRS. VINYARD: If I could make you see it—just as it was—

FLINT: So your sister, Mrs. Abel, announced your engagement?

MRS. VINYARD: (laughing) Lawsy, no. Nobody ever thought of announcing, and that sort of thing, in the Illinois country. And besides, I was that splashed, crossing the branch. My pride was soaked clean through, if my habit was only spattered. I said "No, sir," to him.

(Somewhere in the village a church bell begins to toll slowly.)

FLINT: But I understood the judge to say quite definitely—

MRS. VINYARD: He said we were engaged. I wonder. Abe was engaged —there's no doubt about that.

FLINT: But you didn't consider yourself—

MRS. VINYARD: You'd never see it. He asked me—more than half because he thought Jane thought he should. Why should a man like that be afraid of women? . . . A man like that. 'Cause he couldn't tell what they were thinking about him, I reckon. . . . He asked me again, once. We were sitting on a front stoop. Broad daylight it was. He whittled a stick, and stopped whittling to ask me. Then he whittled some more, and stopped whittling for me to answer him. I was right sorry for him that day. He was lonely . . . His sleeves weren't long enough, and his wrists were chapped with the wind. He said—can you see it, Mr. Flint?

(A second bell begins tolling.)

FLINT: Go on, Mrs. Vinyard.

MRS. VINYARD: He didn't want to offer me any false hopes. He was honest. I don't suppose any man's downright honest when he's trying to persuade a woman—but he was. I—I couldn't be sure. That night he wrote me this. Just read there, under "Friend Mary." . . . Wonder what those bells are ringing about.

FLINT: This is very curious. (He reads.) "Friend Mary—I want more than anything else to do right with you, and if I knew it would be doing right to let you alone, I would do it. If it suits you best not to answer—" And what did you say?

MRS. VINYARD: You see, I'd been to boarding school. If it hadn't been for that I might be in the White House, now. . . . My idea of a man was genteel—and he wasn't genteel. I answered that I feared he was deficient in the little links that make up the chain of a woman's happiness. . . . Can you see me—and him—as we were?

FLINT: And this is all?

MRS. VINYARD: Yes . . . No—one thing more. While he sat there whittling I remember looking at him, and thinking—Your heart was buried in the grave with Ann Rutledge.

FLINT: Oh, there was another?

MRS. VINYARD: Ellen Jane wouldn't have let that stop me.

FLINT: Then I am to understand from you, and from these letters, that he was so—uncouth—so unsophisticated, that he imagined he ought to marry you just because your sister expected him to.

MRS. VINYARD: Young man, I see it's no use trying to make you understand him. May be he was a little . . . in love with me. You might see that without my having to tell you.

(The Judge comes knocking at the door.)

JUDGE: (heartily) Come now, Mrs. Vinyard, let me in again.

MRS. VINYARD: Certainly, Judge. I'm all over my spell of temper. I was thinking of that time we rode out to Uncle Billy Green's when I got splashed in the branch and Abe asked me—you were there. La, la . . . Where's Jessie?

JUDGE: She went to see what the bells are tolling about. Well, did you get the facts in the case, Mr. Flint?

FLINT: If Mrs. Vinyard will lend me the letters and the picture—

MRS. VINYARD: Well, if you think anybody'll be interested, and if you won't use any names, and if the judge'll go bond for them. I 'lowed to leave them to my children, Abe Lincoln being President, and all.

JUDGE: Confidence restored. You trust me, and I'll trust Mr. Flint.

(Jessie comes in, pale and tearful, with a newspaper in her hand.)

JESSIE: Mother—look.

JUDGE: What is it?

JESSIE: He's been shot. The President. He's dead.

FLINT: What's that? Mr. Lincoln?

JESSIE: You hear the bells. The mail just came through.

JUDGE: Let me look . . . Ford's Theater . . . Secretary Seward wounded. The assassins—ah, God in Heaven!

JESSIE: Down street the men—they're all just like us—they're all crying. . . . Everybody—

FLINT: (With the paper) It's true—not a doubt of it. Do you see what this means?

JUDGE: (sternly) Yes, I see.

(A pause.)

FLINT: Mrs. Vinyard, you'll let me take those letters?

JUDGE: No—what can be done with them now—he's beyond all that.

FLINT: Judge, these letters are not what you thought. Now, the least word of him—don't you see? This martyr's death lifts him into immortality. Nothing can reach him now.

MRS. VINYARD: Jessie, my child, come here. Take these. Keep them always. I was about to be a foolish old woman.

FLINT: But Mrs. Vinyard—what harm? And you—you are a Southerner. Your sympathies—

MRS. VINYARD: My sympathies. My two sons, if they are alive, surrendered with Lee last week. But I have just learned from you, today, that the South's best friend in this hour is—was the President . . . I knew him when I was a girl. He was born in Kentucky, too . . . We'll—we'll keep the letters, Jessie.

Curtain.

SELECTED BIBLIOGRAPHY

Allen, Willadell, "The Oral Reading Program," *Bulletin of Secondary School Principals* (November, 1945), 29: 133, pp. 79–82.

Ballet, Arthur, "Oral Interpretation in the English Classroom," *English Journal* (December, 1950), 39: 560–566.

Bassett, Lee Emerson, *Handbook of Oral Reading*. Boston: Houghton Mifflin Co., 1917.

Borchers, Gladys L., *Living Speech*. New York: Harcourt, Brace & Co., 1951.

Borchers, Gladys L., and Claude M. Wise, *Modern Speech*. New York: Harcourt, Brace & Co., 1947.

Clark, S. H., and Maud May Babcock, *Interpretation of the Printed Page*. New York: Prentice-Hall, Inc., 1940.

Crocker, L., and L. Eich, *Oral Reading*. New York: Prentice-Hall, Inc., 1947.

Curry, Samuel Silas, *Browning and the Dramatic Monologue*. Boston: Expression Company, 1907.

————, *Foundations of Expression*, Boston: Expression Company, 1896.

Farma, William J., *Prose, Poetry and Drama for Oral Interpretation*. New York: Harper & Brothers, 1930.

Johnson, Gertrude E., *Modern Literature for Oral Interpretation*. New York: Appleton-Century-Crofts, Inc., 1930.

Keppie, Elizabeth E., *The Teaching of Choric Speech*. Boston: Expression Company, 1931.

Kerfoot, John B., *How to Read*. Boston: Houghton Mifflin Co., 1916.

Laughton, Charles, "Storytelling," *Atlantic Monthly* (June, 1950), 185: 71–72.

Lloyd, M. Pearl, and John Tryon Marshman, *Modern Short Stories for Oral Interpretation*. Boston: Expression Company, 1933.

Lovett, Robert Morse, and Howard Mumford Jones, *The College Reader*. Boston: Houghton Mifflin Co., 1936.

O'Neill, J. M. (Ed.), *Foundations of Speech*. New York: Prentice-Hall, Inc., 1941.

Rasmussen, Carrie, *Speech Methods in the Elementary School*. New York: The Ronald Press Company, 1949.

Sarett, Lew, and William Trufant Foster, *Basic Principles of Speech*. Boston: Houghton Mifflin Co., 1947.

Smith, W. Palmer, *Prose and Verse for Speaking and Reading*. New York: Harcourt, Brace & Co., 1930.

Tassin, A., *Oral Study of Literature*. New York: F. S. Crofts Co., 1932.

Tressidder, Argus, *Reading to Others*, Chicago: Scott, Foresman & Company, 1940.

Weaver, Andrew Thomas, *Speech: Forms and Principles.* New York: Longmans, Green & Co., Inc., 1951.

Weaver, Andrew Thomas, and Gladys L. Borchers, *Speech.* New York: Harcourt, Brace & Co., 1946.

Woolbert, Charles, and Severina Nelson, *The Art of Interpretative Speech.* New York: Appleton-Century-Crofts, Inc., 1934.

(Note: reference to sources of recordings in the appendix.)

CHAPTER 17

Storytelling and Dramatization

WHY TEACH STORYTELLING?

Storytelling is older than reading: It began long before printing was invented, and long before incidents were recorded with symbols in mud and stone—but it is modern, too. It touches every person's life every day. The neighbor who steps into the yard and reports an auto accident; the child who explains how his dog behaves; the minister who by narrative illustration clarifies the text of his sermon; the auctioneer who tells the history of a piece of farm machinery; the mother who entertains her child with a bedtime story; the husband who relates to his wife his experiences at work; the dinner guest who slips a humorous anecdote into his table conversation; the traveler who narrates to his friends incidents of his trip to Spain—all of these people, with thousands of others, are storytellers, and are welcomed or avoided because of their ability or lack of it in this art. If the high school speech teacher can prevent his students from falling into the "Don't-let-her-get-started-on-her-family" group, and get them in the "Try-to-get-her-to-tell-a-story" group, he will have added much to the pleasure of living for great numbers of people. Stories will continue to be told, with or without skill.

High School Students Gain Social Poise in Telling Stories

Whether it is a story told before the English, history, mathematics, science, or speech class; an incident related in the bus en route to a debate tournament; or a joke shared with a neighbor while walking to school; a high school student gains confidence and poise when the responses to what he says are favorable. Most people like to be the center of attention. The high school student is now too old to step before his friends and relatives and say "Look at me," as he did when he was three, although he often has the same urge to do so. Now he must get attention in more indirect and subtle ways. To obtain the attention which he covets, he must offer society something desirable.

High School Students Give Pleasure in Telling Stories

A recent issue of an eastern newspaper announced the observance of "Book Week," which was highlighted by story hours. In a city of several hundred thousand inhabitants, every library, every school, and every radio station offered a "Saturday Story Hour." Each of the library meetings was the beginning of a weekly series and most of the storytellers were high school students, who had probably received training and practice in school.

The occupation of baby sitting has motivated storytelling for many high school students. A good speech class project might be one in which each student is given an opportunity to prepare a story for telling to his particular charge. Almost every student has immediate need for such an assignment, either in entertaining younger brothers or sisters or in going out to earn spending money.

Storytelling has a place in community and church programs, and no one gives greater pleasure in these places than the high school narrator. But the story which ranks above all others in usefulness is the story well told in conversation. The person who is always ready with an apt story is fun, and others like to associate with him.

High School Students Give Better Class Recitations by Using Stories

Stories can be helpful in all high school classes. A demonstration in science is often made interesting and clear with a good story. Well-told stories in history may change a class hour from a boring to a stimulating experience. One of the most vivid ways to give information is by means of examples, and examples are usually stories.

High School Students Enlarge Vocabularies and Improve Language with Stories

When an individual is attempting to learn a foreign language, he is assigned the reading of story after story. The purpose is mainly to enlarge the reader's vocabulary and gain knowledge of idioms and language structure. When in addition to understanding the story, he repeats it for others, he gets double practice in the language. A good storyteller retains many of the author's most expressive words and phrases and thus improves his vocabulary and his language forms.

High School Students Develop Imagination Through Storytelling

It is not necessary to watch large numbers of storytellers to be sure that what the speaker sees, feels, and appreciates often goes far beyond the words he utters. The mere mention of an evergreen may be all that is needed for an imaginary trip to Norway, Switzerland, or Glacier Park. The "most important wish in the world" by "the princess" in the story may stimulate a far more important one for the storyteller. One of the most urgent reasons behind the telling of many stories is satisfaction of the craving to travel into the land of make-believe.

TEACHING THE SELECTION OF STORIES

Consider Appeals to the Senses

While most stories appeal to the senses or we would not understand them at all, in some stories tastes, smells, sights, sounds, and feelings are more vivid than in others. These are good stories to tell. The smell of the turkey and the pudding in Dickens' *Christmas Carol*, the father's touching and feeling of his little boy's hand in Ewald's *My Little Boy*, the sight of the liquid eyes of Flag in Rawling's *The Yearling*, the ringing sound of "Pieces of Eight!" in Stevenson's *Treasure Island*, the taste of the chocolate jacket and the fine fat currant eyes in Bryant's *Gingerbread Man*, are appeals so fundamental that they seldom fail to bring responses long remembered by listeners. The presence of such vivid evocative terms as the foregoing serves as a safe guide in selecting good stories.

Look for Action

Help students to find stories in which something is happening all the time. One may enjoy reading silently long descriptions of scenes and people, but in storytelling such literature may become tiresome. People listen attentively to stories in which change and action are prominent features.

Look for an Interesting Opening

Stories beginning with long preliminaries that prepare listeners for what is to happen later are seldom as interesting as those which start right out with what is happening. Notice the action in the following first sentences:

"Every afternoon as they were coming from school, the children used to go and play in the Giant's garden."

"Old Man Rabbit sat at the door of his little house eating a nice, ripe, juicy turnip."

"The fox was digging behind a stump and he found a bumble-bee."

" 'The whole show is dreadful,' she cried, coming out of the menagerie of M. Martin."

"It was the birthday of the Infanta."

"They used to go there every evening at about eleven o'clock just as they went to the cafe."

"When his father ran away to Buitenzorg, Saidjah was about fifteen years old."

When a storyteller uses such openings, he does not need to stop and ask his audience to listen; they are already listening.

Look for Suspense

If a story keeps people waiting to find out what is going to happen next, it holds attention. All listeners are curious, and their minds will not wander if each part of the story tells just enough about the next part to hold the attention in anticipation of what is going to happen, but not enough to make clear exactly what is to take place. The element of suspense is essential in a good story.

Choose a Story to Fit the Audience

Whether the story is an anecdote in conversation, a tall tale at a boys' camp, a Bible story for Sunday School, or a folk tale for high school assembly, it must be selected with the audience in mind. Everything that has been learned about adapting subject matter to audiences can be applied in making sure that the listeners will appreciate the story. The storyteller should analyze the past experiences of his audience, because it is through old experiences that the new experiences in the story must be made effective.

Choose a Story to Fit the Teller

Not all stories are for all storytellers. The teacher should help each student to discover just what types of stories are best for him to tell. Just as the experiences of the audience should be considered in selecting stories, so the experiences of the narrator should be considered in finding out which ones are best for him to tell. Sometimes a discussion of these matters can be combined with a consideration of hearer's attitudes. Boys and girls will learn not to select stories for which certain individual listeners may have emotional distaste, lest they find themselves unable to stir up in the listeners the meanings the authors intended. Students will be able to relate size, age, and sex to the selection of stories, and cite examples of fortunate and unfortunate choices, as a result of their understanding of these factors.

Good Stories Usually Are Good Literature

The principles for selecting good readings and good plays can be applied in selecting stories to tell to others. The suggestions in Chapter 9 should be helpful in guarding against the embarrassment arising because some student presents shallow, cheap, and poorly-written stories.

TEACHING THE PREPARATION OF STORIES

Encourage Careful Reading

A careful reading of the story is the first step in preparing it for telling. High school students may need help in understanding what is meant by careful reading. It takes experience and training to learn how to get all of the meaning from a story. The steps for analyzing literary material, beginning on page 378 of Chapter 16, will be of assistance and should be considered carefully.

After the story has been read once and analyzed, it should be read over and over a number of times, to find its subtler meanings and to familiarize the teller with its style. Students should be advised to space these readings over a period of several days or even weeks, if possible.

Help Students to Divide the Story into Units

Stories are divided like plays into important scenes and incidents. These units should be clear to the teller and he should see that each is vital to the story and is naturally related to what precedes it, and what follows. It is helpful to remember that if the story were dramatized, these units, in many instances, would be the scenes of the play, each one with a sort of minor climax leading to the major climax which is the high point of the entire story.

Help Students to Adapt the Language of the Story to the Audience

The language of a story must be meaningful to the listeners. In planning the telling of any narrative, the reader should examine its text carefully for words that may be strange to the audience. Usually familiar words should be substituted for them, unless their meaning is obvious from the context, or the language is part of a refrain which creates interest or mood. In such cases the exact wording should be used, because, as the story proceeds, the meaning will become clear.

The language of a good story is carefully selected by the author. The phrasing seems to be inevitable. Therefore, in large part, the original wording should be retained by the storyteller. Listeners, both young and old, will recognize and appreciate great style. However, few storytellers are effective when they have memorized every word of a narrative; in those circumstances, even a very experienced speaker has difficulty in making his delivery sound spontaneous. But almost everyone profits by pre-planning so carefully that some parts are practically memorized and, as the story is told and retold, the wording in these parts remains the same. Such careful preparation will prevent spoiling the climax of an anecdote by reaching it too soon.

When the rhythm of the language is an important part of the

meaning of a story, it is necessary to retain the rhythm in the telling by employing the author's exact words and phrases.

Make the Story Interesting Through Skillful Use of Voice and Action

Many principles of effective vocalization and visible action can be applied to the problem of holding the attention of the audience from the beginning to the end of a story. Chapters 6 and 7 have much to contribute to storytelling from the point of view of these two elements of speech.

TEACHING THE EVALUATION OF STORIES

Students should learn to judge the success of speaking activities by interpreting audience reactions as well as by getting the opinion of the teacher or other expert. An experienced storyteller knows whether his story has gone over or fallen flat by the way his listeners behave, by their facial expressions, and by their bodily sets. An inexperienced storyteller may not notice audience inattention, but a skilled storyteller is immediately aware of it and does something to regain attention. Furthermore, he knows what to do because he understands the interests and habits of the people he is trying to entertain. Boys and girls will profit from repeated opportunities to test their own performances in telling stories by analyzing their listeners' reactions.

TEACHING STUDENTS TO DRAMATIZE STORIES

First Tell or Read the Story

When a teacher wishes to have students dramatize a story he usually begins by telling it to them as effectively as he can. He may tell it several times. Dramatization also may start with the reading of a play or story. In either event the story must be carefully prepared and repeated until the boys and girls are thoroughly familiar with its details.

Have Students Play Leading Characters

Let us assume that the class wishes to dramatize *The Taming of the Shrew*. The teacher tells or reads certain well-selected, important scenes which make up a unified story. After that he can ask, "Who would like to play Petruchio?" and the class will discuss the character. They will describe his looks, voice, action, personality, dress, and general behavior. They will decide which one of the many scenes in which he appears they would like to try first. They will imagine the environment, and give Petruchio something appropriate to do if he is on stage alone. If Katharina is on stage with him, someone will volunteer to take her part and all will learn exactly what kind of a person she is. If the story has been well told or read, and has been repeated often, the students will be able to show in the speaking of the dialogue exactly what is happening, and will quote some of the lines precisely as Shakespeare wrote them.

The wise teacher will call on several pairs to present the same scene. He will encourage variations. He will play a part himself if invited to do so by the students. He will help students to imagine properties (the meat platter and the cap for Katharina for example), and to play with enthusiasm and abandon, expressing the meanings in many different ways.

After one scene has been dramatized by a number of students and it is clear that they have sufficient mastery and appreciation of the material, a new scene may be treated in much the same way as the first one has been. It will not be necessary to begin with the first scene and follow the play through all the way. The last scene may be tried first, and then the very first one. Students should be encouraged to play first the most vivid and most interesting scenes, and the ones they like best. Particular pains should be taken to develop an understanding of each character, until all the dramatis personae seem like friends and intimate acquaintances to the members of the class.

To such questions as, "What do you think Petruchio would have done if Katharina had surprised him by being kind and considerate at once?" or "What would Baptista have said if Petruchio had misspoken and asked for Bianca's hand instead of Katharina's?" students should be encouraged to give answers in keeping with the characters and the situations. Such experiences help to develop the informal freedom which is at the heart of dramatization.

Teach Students to Select Important Scenes

After picking certain favorite scenes at random and playing them, the class should decide what others should be added and how many should be used in the final presentation. It is easy to see that the choices of the class may be influenced greatly by the teacher's telling or reading of the story, before the dramatization begins. Any class will enjoy playing a series of scenes from a good drama like *The Taming of the Shrew*. Under the direction of a skilled teacher, they will retain enough of the original story to make their play effective.

Rehearse One Unit at a Time

Boys and girls are vastly satisfied and pleased when they begin to feel adequate in the parts they are playing. For this reason the class should work on short scenes until almost every student can play any part freely and with originality.

Plan the Staging

In informal dramatics, the acting is the first consideration, but sometimes setting, lighting, costuming, and make-up are worthy of considerable attention. If the play is to be given during a regular class period, and no outsiders are to be invited, it may not be wise to spend much time on staging or costuming. The decision will rest with the teacher and the class, but if they wish a public or semi-public production, the bibliography on drama in Chapter 18 will be found helpful.

Work with Other Departments

For an elaborate dramatization, the departments of manual training, music, art, dance, English, history, science, and so on, can be called in to make the enterprise a school, rather than a class, project. There is value in the co-operative spirit so developed. Such an undertaking requires publicity, programs, staging, lighting, costuming, and music, but the teacher must make sure that the main purpose of dramatization, the development in children of the creative spirit, is not lost. The teacher should remind himself repeatedly of that aim, and never let the desire for public acclaim of a finished performance turn him from it.

SELECTED BIBLIOGRAPHY

Bailey, Carolyn Sherwin, *For the Story Teller.* Springfield, Mass.: Milton Bradley Company, 1926.

Bones, Woutrina A., *Children's Stories and How to Tell Them.* New York: Harcourt, Brace & Co., 1949.

Borchers, Gladys Louise, *Living Speech.* Rev. ed., New York: Harcourt, Brace & Co., 1949.

Brown, Corinne, *Creative Drama in the Lower School.* New York: Appleton-Century-Crofts, Inc., 1930.

Brown, Rollo Walter, *The Creative Spirit.* New York: Harper & Brothers, 1925.

Bryant, Sara Cone, *How to Tell Stories to Children.* Boston: Houghton Mifflin Co., 1924.

Cowles, Julia Darrow, *The Art of Story Telling.* Chicago: A. C. McClurg & Co., 1916.

Kready, Laura F., *A Study of Fairy Tales.* Boston: Houghton Mifflin Co., 1916.

Sawyer, Ruth, *The Way of the Story Teller.* New York: The Viking Press, 1945.

Ward, Winifred, *Creative Dramatics.* New York: Appleton-Century-Crofts, Inc., 1931.

————, *Playmaking With Children.* New York: Appleton-Century-Crofts, Inc., 1947.

CHAPTER 18

Drama

DRAMA, A MOTIVATING ACTIVITY

THE DESIRE to act in a play is highly motivating for high school students, and the wise teacher will make use of this interest in order to promote practice in using the elements of action, voice, language, thought, and attitude in situations which are meaningful and important for boys and girls. They will see at once that a dramatic production can be successful only when the actors have bodily control, expressive voices, appropriate language, detailed meanings, and desirable attitudes, and almost without exception they will work industriously on individual improvement programs in order to insure a final performance which reflects favorably on everyone concerned. In fact, the contribution which high school drama makes to the everyday speech habits of students is the primary justification for including this activity in a secondary school speech training program. Improved habits when used with enthusiasm in an important, interesting dramatic production can be fixed more quickly than when repeated in meaningless, dull, and monotonous exercises.

THE PURPOSE OF DRAMA IN HIGH SCHOOL

As we have just observed, the purpose of drama in high school is primarily to improve the everyday talk of students. Therefore, the program should be so planned that it will aid *all* students. This means that the teacher should be resourceful enough to provide dramatic experiences for the handicapped, the average, and the superior, before appreciative observers. It is an established fact that, in acting, audience response is a powerful factor in progress and improvement. The following paragraphs set forth a suggested program which may be adjusted to secondary schools of various sizes, types and locations.

Drama for Handicapped Students

Many speech correctionists use drama in a remedial program for persons with marked speech difficulties. They choose plays very carefully and assign responsibilities and parts, keeping in mind the needs of each individual participant. Some students, therefore, are not given acting or speaking roles, but collect and arrange properties, manage lights, help with costumes or make-up, or build and change sets. These students improve their speech by working with others, and using speech informally in completing their assignments. Some individuals have acting parts but no spoken lines. They receive indirect speech improvement through the development of action for communication, through the acceptance of responsibility, and through the exchange of comments during rehearsal and after the final performance. Some students have very minor speaking parts, for which they are carefully coached, in order to make sure that the utterance of the lines will bring favorable responses from the audience and, as a result, satisfaction to the actors. Finally, some students may be cast in heavier roles for which the teacher should make sure they are adequately prepared, since in each case it is important that the experience bring pleasure and confidence to the performer.

The audiences for such productions should be carefully selected, and should be made up of parents, faculty members, interested friends, and other individuals who understand the purpose of the play and its use in speech therapy. Comparison with other performances by groups of superior students or professionals should be avoided.

Drama for Average Students

At some high schools it is announced repeatedly in assemblies, in the school paper, in conversation, and in classes, that any person wishing to act in a play may have that opportunity. Numerous plays, usually one-act plays, are then produced, and many of them are coached by high school students. They are given in and out of school, for clubs, for classes, for students at the lunch hour, for high school assemblies, for church groups, for the aged and handicapped, for the sick in hospitals, and for parent-teacher meetings. While an effort should be made to give the plays as much finish as possible, the main purpose is to provide experience and training for the actors; a perfected performance is secondary. However, if large numbers are motivated to participate in this broad dramatic program, the more capable will raise the quality of the final performance and they will serve as examples to the less skilled.

Drama for Superior Students

Every high school should have some plays produced by students with superior ability. In such performances the teacher will be wise to aim at greater finish, because the actors are more able and will derive more training and a deeper sense of satisfaction from working to capacity. The numerous short plays not brought to such high quality can serve as try-outs for the actors in these longer and more professional ones. Such a procedure will encourage more students to participate in the average offerings, and at the same time give preparatory training for acting and producing the plays which will be the dramatic high lights of the year.

SELECTING THE PLAY

The principles to be applied in recognizing good literature, considered in Chapter 9, should be followed in selecting plays for high school production. Universal appeal, characters with normal behavior, and precise language are qualities of the well-written play. Such minimum essentials should serve as guides in choosing plays in high school.

However, there is more than literary quality to be considered as a criterion in selecting a play. The high school teacher has a specific group of students who are to do the acting. They have certain abilities and interests. The audience will be drawn mainly from the high school area. Because of the nature of the community

—its size, location, industries, and natural resources—audiences there will have characteristic purposes, and the dramatic director must understand what these purposes are, and decide in what way they will contribute to the appreciation and understanding of the play. The dramatic facilities of different schools will vary from thoroughly modern theaters equipped with much material for building sets, and complete lighting, to a bare classroom with no curtain and no stage—perhaps not even a raised platform. Some schools will subsidize drama. The teacher will be expected to spend several thousand dollars on a single production, with no thought of whether or not box office receipts will cover expenses. In other schools, the entire cost of the play must be met through the ticket sales, and sometimes it is the custom to support athletics, music, or some other school activity with play proceeds. The newcomer into such a school may feel, naturally enough, that this situation ought not to be permitted to continue. Frequently a skilled teacher is able to make marked changes in such school customs, but what he finds in a given school usually has grown out of some particular problems and needs inherent in that situation, and marked change is often more difficult than one might suspect. The teacher usually must be satisfied, therefore, with slow, steady change rather than with sudden upheaval.

The teacher should select plays which will provide good training and enjoyment for his students, which can be produced with the facilities at hand, and which will be appreciated by the students in the school and the people in the community. The problem of play selection often may be used in teaching discussion (Chapter 14). Students will find this problem of immediate interest, and its solution will satisfy a real need. Working with the teacher, students can read and review plays; decide on whether or not they can be produced in their school; consider the cost of production, including royalty; evaluate drama as literature; and study the acceptability of various types of plays to people in the community. Boys and girls will soon learn where to find bibliographies of plays, become familiar with publishing houses, learn what is meant by production rights, and perhaps even carry on the correspondence to order the books and pay the royalties.

In such a project whole communities will learn that royalties are fair remuneration for time, effort, and money, invested by both author and publisher. They will refuse to consider such dishonest practices as changing the name of a play, refusing newspaper notices in order to mislead the public, keeping information from publishers, and thus escaping royalty payments.

By solving the problem of finding an appropriate play for their school, boys and girls will learn that a play is not a good play *per se,* but that it is a good play for them only if it fits the particular school and the particular community in which it is to be produced.

But the question of intrinsic quality immediately arises. If a play should be adapted to the tastes of a community, and those tastes are low, does that mean that the teacher should produce plays of poor literary quality? No, but he will not be able to get appreciation for plays too far above the heads of his audience. He should aim at advancing the taste of his public gradually, and must be satisfied to make each play slightly more challenging than the preceding one. A horse does not follow a carrot held so far ahead of him that he is unable to see it, and communities are not led to enjoy great dramatic literature by being shown materials so far beyond their appreciation that they cannot understand them. Such audiences will learn to accept better plays if they are given training in taste, because the most important test of great literature is that it has the quality of appealing to the many as well as to the critical few. Every community helps to make up that larger group, the many.

THE DIRECTOR'S PREPARATION

The director must understand the play and visualize its production. Every step in the preparation of a play will be simplified if the director has paved the way by careful study. Because this method is so important he will be wise to have the play selected early, in order to reserve time for thorough planning.

The Director Should Have the Full Meaning of the Play

All of the techniques for getting the complete meanings of material for reading aloud should be applied in getting the meaning of a play. The historical and geographical backgrounds, the life of the author, the meanings of the words, the significance of the literary form, explanations of all references and allusions, all must be clear to the director before he starts to plan how the play will look and sound in final production.

The Director Should Plan the Details of Movement and Stage Business

Even though many changes will be made in working out details in presentation there are advantages in having movement and stage business carefully planned, even before casting or rehearsing the play. Some directors draw diagrams of the scenes and use pins for characters, moving them as they would have them move on the stage. In this way principles of balance, variety, crossing, entrances, and exits are anticipated and considered apart from the confusion of early group meetings.

The Director Should Appoint Committees and Plan Their Duties

The director should have in mind all that must be accomplished before a play is ready for final production. In addition to casting and rehearsing, he must know what can be achieved in the way of setting and lighting, with the facilities at hand or with those that can be obtained; he should know whether costumes will be designed and made, rented, or borrowed from families in the community; he should be prepared to lead his group to accept simple everyday make-up, or to train them in details of complexion foundations, lining, false hair, and so on; and he should have a pretty fair idea of the most effective publicity that can be used and how the play is to be financed. After this preparation, the director is ready to direct the play as a class or community project.

GAINING CO-OPERATION

A successful play must be a co-operative affair. As has been said repeatedly in this book, the process of planning and preparing is usually more important and more fruitful in student learning than is the final performance. Advice, attributed to Andrew Carnegie, is apt in this connection. When asked how to be a good executive, his answer was, "Surround yourself with individuals who know more about the elements of your job than you do yourself." The speech teacher is so surrounded. There are students and faculty experts in manual arts who can build or remodel sets; home economics people who are prepared to help with costuming; students whose training in physics gives them the basis for understanding stage lighting; men's and women's physical education personnel who can help with dancing and other necessary physical performances; mathematics enthusiasts who know how to handle money and keep accounts and can deal with the problems of finances; students in English and journalism who will be glad to carry on correspondence and publicity; the department of music, which can help to provide and interpret musical backgrounds for the performance; and, finally, speakers who will interview, telephone, persuade, and act in the play. The wise director will make use of all of the available talent in the school and will give each participant full credit for his part in a successful enterprise. Few school projects can bring together so many helpers in school and community and generate so much genuine enthusiasm as can a dramatic production.

A big planning meeting is a good opening for the whole affair. At such a gathering the director must expect that much of what he has worked out will be modified or rejected altogether. At times during the discussion, when constructive ideas seem scarce, the director will be glad to have something definite to propose, even though his suggestion may not be accepted ultimately. The question of how to provide good entertainment with the facilities in and around a school is a problem for the whole community, and the methods considered in Chapter 14 should be employed to solve it satisfactorily.

CASTING THE PLAY

The best way to cast a play is by means of tryouts and with the help of a committee which, with the director, assumes the responsibility for choices of personnel. Before the tryouts, an effort should be made to help students understand the play and visualize the characters. The casting committee may wish to see that copies of the play are in the library for loan to students; they may wish to have the director give a talk on the meaning of the play, and describe the nature and importance of each character; and they may wish to bring in outside authorities for lectures and discussions. The fact is that no one can read or act well when he does not have the full meaning of what he is saying, and tryouts are satisfactory only when they result in a well-chosen cast.

The time and place for tryouts should be publicized well in advance. Announcements through the school paper, daily bulletins, assembly talks, and conversation will help to get complete information to every interested person. If there are students especially well suited to certain parts, it may be worth while to urge them personally to appear at tryouts.

When feasible, the tryouts should be held on the stage where the final production is to take place. This gives the committee the best chance to notice the comparative height, weight, coloring, age, and so on of the aspirants.

It is a good idea to have an information card filled out by each student who wishes to act. Such data as his name, telephone and street numbers, age, height, and weight can be filled in by the students, and the members of the casting committee can add whatever they think may help them in selecting an actor for each role. These cards should be kept in a file and used for future plays. It is helpful to have a record of the names of students who can play mature men or women, juvenile leads, children, or character parts, and so on, and, in addition, such a filing system encourages those who cannot be used at once to feel that they will be given consideration later.

Selected sections of dialogue should be read by the would-be actors. These sides can be typed or mimeographed and handed to students who come for tryouts. Each aspirant should have a short time to review and familiarize himself with the lines, even though he already has studied the play with reasonable thoroughness.

At first, the cast chosen should be tentative. The director and his committee should make it clear that final selection will depend on ability, co-operation, attendance at rehearsals, and so on. During this trial period the director should emphasize the importance of the right attitude toward the whole project. In a variety of ways he should help members of the cast who have minor roles to prepare as conscientiously as those students who are playing the major parts, and he should help the whole cast to see the need for team work, to master such difficult tasks as listening in character, and to put the welfare of the group ahead of personal interests.

As we already have explained in the earlier part of this chapter, in some plays the purpose can be served best by casting students in roles which will do most for them personally, while in others the purpose can be served best by casting them in roles which they can play most competently. Both procedures are quite legitimate; it is up to the director and his committee to make the choice in the light of their knowledge of the whole situation in which they are working.

REHEARSALS

As soon as the play has been cast and the working committees appointed, it is a good idea to have a meeting of all those who are to contribute in any way to the enterprise. The director may discuss the need for a unified production in which each individual has an important part. He may point out specific and concrete ways in which lighting can clarify the meaning of the play; he may show how a set can create the mood; he may emphasize the importance of music for this particular production; and he may show that every character, whether he has few or many lines, is vital to the success of the play.

After such a general presentation, the rehearsal schedule should be arranged and posted, and a copy given to each person who is supposed to attend. At the very outset, the director must make it clear that attendance is compulsory, and he must refuse to tolerate tardiness or absence. It is often wise to state the director's intention to replace an actor, even in the leading role, if the person assigned to the part fails to give full co-operation.

The rest of this first general meeting may then be given over to developing an appreciation of the play. There is seldom time to read the play in its entirety, or even as cut for performance. Probably it would not be desirable to do so if there were time. A successful method for coming to an understanding of the play is a co-operative one. The director begins by describing the opening scene; reading significant portions; asking the lighting expert to explain the relationship between the light changes and meaning;

asking the property man why a given article is important at one particular point in the play; inviting several characters to read together a bit of dialogue; warning the sound effects men to be on the alert for their cues and to try to decide just why a bell, the report of a gun, or a siren must be heard at the right second; and explaining how the music is related to specific scenes and speeches. In this way the entire play is considered, until the actors and production staff come to know the characters and the plot and begin to visualize the performance.

In the rehearsals which follow, interpretation, acting, movement, stage business, voice projection, memorization, and so on should be emphasized. Some teachers prefer to concentrate on one phase at a time, even though there is no way of isolating any single element. For example, the interpretation of Act I might be the focus of one rehearsal. At the next rehearsal, the task might be to block out the movement, paying particular attention to entrances and exits, and to training in bodily response. Emphasis at the next rehearsal might be on voice, articulation, and projection. It is usually good to work on meaning and action before insisting on memorization.

Directors who are successful work in a good many different ways. Some prefer to perfect Act I before moving on to Act II; others prefer to rehearse first one act and then another, to avoid monotony. All directors find it helpful to rehearse at special times scenes in which only a few characters are involved, in order to save other student actors from spending hours waiting for their scenes. Needless to say, there are times when all participants must be present together.

As early as possible, sets, lights, properties, music, sound effects, and costumes should be used in rehearsals. A boy or girl finds it difficult to move, stand, and sit in an Elizabethan costume, for example, unless he has practiced it many times; music really affects the actors, as it is supposed to do; and to handle an exquisite piece of porcelain is a different matter from handling a book which one imagines to be a vase. As the rehearsals progress, the director can make clear the relation of tempo to climax, the importance of emphasis and subordination, the methods of getting effective stage pictures, and the values of color, light, and form.

Frequent rehearsals should take place after the lines are completely memorized. Few high school students realize the importance of going over the material again and again until they have participated in several plays; then they feel the satisfaction which comes from working on subtle shadings in all the elements of the production.

The stage crew must have many opportunities to practice before the curtain goes up on the performance. They will derive great satisfaction from changing a set in 5 or 10 minutes, and from having every property exactly where it is supposed to be, but this perfection can be achieved only if each person has a specific job to do and has the chance to practice doing it many, many times.

THE STAGE SETTING

The purpose of the stage setting is to create a mood, to clarify the author's meaning, and to provide appropriate surroundings for the characters and the action. In high school, it is best to avoid complicated and elaborate staging, unless a group of students working in art, manual arts, and speech are motivated to do something very special. Usually this will not happen; students will be interested in working with the set of a particular play, but they will not have had technical training in staging. The need to make a certain deadline is too immediate to allow time for thorough background training in scene design and construction.

The play will have been selected with the available facilities in mind; generally the performance will be in the auditorium. This is not always true, however. Some schools have no auditorium, and some committees will be able to select or prepare a more appropriate location. Interesting performances have been given on the slope of a hill, on a porch, in a barn, on the school steps, in a city hall, in a home, on a river boat, or in the center of a classroom with the audience on every side. The point is that the imaginative director and his staff look about and make use of the best available facilities. A building with an appropriate door, or a leafy hedge in the open may be the background. But screens, flats, or drapes usually will stage the play. Doors and windows can be placed between screens, in flats, or arranged with drapes.

Scenes in general may be realistic or symbolic, depending on the play, the director, and what is available to work with. The realistic scene is practical and simple, and the audience members see an interior or exterior which remind them of those they see every day— walls, windows, stairs, curtains, pictures; or streets, houses, trees, walls, sky, clouds, and so on. Flats, screens, or drapes can serve as backgrounds for these, but usually flats are most satisfactory. A symbolic scene often can be arranged with drapes, and its distinguishing characteristic is that some emblem is used to represent the mood, the central idea, or some crisis in the play. For example, a single rocky cliff might represent the great obstacles which the characters are forced to face or overcome; stunted and twisted trees might suggest limited opportunities and abnormal influences; and delicate flowers, ferns, and fleecy clouds may conjure up the images of dainty carefree characters. Sometimes such symbols are painted on the background; sometimes on the stage floor; and sometimes thrown onto the background by lantern slides.

While background and design are important in successful staging, color also has a very significant function. Directors often turn to paintings for effective color schemes, because in them great artists have stirred up deep thoughts and strong moods. Psychologists have found definite relationships between specific colors and different emotions. Red produces feelings of irritation, yearning, hunger and distress; green suggests serenity, peace, and rest; yellow arouses emotions of happiness, joy, and cheer; black means sadness, gloom, and depression; purple portrays mystery, splendor, and majesty.

In the play, *I Remember Mama*, one director used a painting from Vermeer Van Delft as his color guide. In "The Cook," he found blue, green, tan, rust, white, gray, all softened to blend into a calm unity. "Mama" brought her family a feeling of security and the selected color scheme helped to create that impression. The director got his color effects in the background, the furniture, the drapes, the lights, the properties, and the costumes from Vermeer Van Delft's color scheme. He selected even the books and the neckties with the painting before him.

THE LIGHTING

The lighting of the play must be planned with the setting. Lighting serves three purposes: (1) It illuminates the stage so that the audience can see what is going on; (2) it tells whether the action is taking place in the daytime or at night; and (3) it helps to create mood, or atmosphere. Because lights affect color, it is important to experiment in order to make sure that the colors which the audience will see on the lighted stage are the ones which the director intends, and which give the desired effect. To put it mildly, it is disappointing to have the purple robes of royalty turn blue under blue light, and lush green meadows blacken under red light. Combinations of lights can solve many problems, but much experimentation must be carried on early enough in the rehearsal period to permit making necessary adjustments.

Whatever lighting is to be used in the play must be on a separate switch so that it can be handled independently of the house lights. Light on the stage should be so shaded that it will not disturb the audience. There was a time when a school bought footlights if it could buy only one type of lighting, but that is no longer true. The present-day director finds floods, spots, and borders more useful. He has discovered that footlights alone flatten features, and are not effective in providing sunlight through open doors or light from lamps or a fireplace or other natural sources; or for spotting important players in tense dramatic moments. Dimmers are very helpful in getting appropriate effects when gradual change in illumination is wanted, and, if they are not a part of the present high school equipment, they may be placed on a list for early purchase.

One of the best ways to work out the lighting of a play is to turn the lighting committee loose with all available equipment and give them time to experiment. The director should emphasize the need for keeping in mind the principle that all good lighting calls attention to the meaning of the play rather than to the lighting itself. Then, he should let the boys and girls discover how bright and dim lights, lights of various colors, and lights from many sources and directions can be employed to draw attention to characters, scenes, and moods in a play.

COSTUMING

The costume often takes a student out of himself and into the part he is playing. For this reason it must suit the character exactly and fit in with the rest of the play. If a girl is to portray an

Elizabethan lady, she should be dressed like one, even to detailed accessories such as shoes, hair ornaments, handkerchief, and rings. Women move, walk, and gesture in ways appropriate to their times. In addition to clarifying periods, characters, and attitudes, costumes may bring out relationships in the play. The color and cut of the villain's costume should contrast with those of the hero's. Tradition has trained audiences to accept blue for the heroine rather than red. Conservatism and modesty in attire bespeak the hero, and extravagance and ostentation the less worthy character.

The question arises immediately as to whether costumes should be: (1) Rented, (2) borrowed, or (3) designed and made in the school or community. It is clear that of these three methods, more training grows out of (3), and the results are usually more nearly what the director has visualized. Unless one can afford to pay high prices, rented costumes are often shabby and makeshift. Frequently they are not all of the same period, and the accessories are glaringly inaccurate. On the other hand, given adequate funds one can usually rent what he wants, but the sums necessary frequently are far beyond the high school budget. Borrowing costumes in the neighborhood is seldom satisfactory, if careful costuming is hoped for. If the play is a modern one, dresses and suits are likely to be recognized and to remind the audience of individuals in the community, and if it is a period play it is almost impossible to get consistency and harmony. The one sure way for a director to get exactly what he wants is to have it manufactured under his guidance. This method has the additional advantage of bringing together in a co-operative project departments in the school as well as groups of people in the community. If the home economics teacher will direct her students in the solving of the costume problem, and will enlist parents to help create what has been designed and sketched, a project in costuming can serve social purposes which go far beyond the production of a play.

The material used in costumes must appear to have proper quality and texture rather than really to have them. On the stage, outing flannel can be made to look like velvet or plush; unbleached muslin dyed and made up may look like linen; and sateen turned wrong side out appears more satiny than satin itself. Familiar, everyday materials should be draped and tried out under lights of varying brilliance and color. It will be very stimulating to adolescents and adults to use their creative genius on the costuming of a play. Such co-operative projects can build up a very valuable costume wardrobe.

MAKE-UP

The key to effective make-up is practice. When no more make-up is needed than that used by the girls every day, most students know how to apply that effectively. Student actors should be encouraged to avoid too much grease paint, especially when the auditorium is small and the players are appearing in straight rather than character parts.

It is the large auditorium and the acting of foreign or bizarre roles that cause difficulty. There are many kinds of grease paint and powder, which give satisfactory results if used with care, according to directions. More detailed information than that furnished with the products can be secured from books listed in the bibliography at the close of this chapter. Many teachers train large numbers of students in the use of make-up, by having them work in pairs. They may start with the simple process of applying cold cream to cleanse the face and remove all traces of make-up, and then rub on a base or foundation. The director may point out that different characters require distinct colors and shades, and then supervise the treatment of the eyes for youth, middle age, and old age, always emphasizing the fact that desired results are obtained only when the actor's natural features are given careful consideration. Lengthening or widening a face, increasing or decreasing the space between the eyes, lowering or raising the cheekbones, and narrowing or widening the mouth will be interesting problems for everyone. Students can work on making a young face look old and wrinkled, without making it look smeared and dirty. They can learn how to apply rouge, powder, and mascara. Some will enjoy making beards and wigs out of crepe hair, changing the shapes of noses with putty, adding scars and welts, and creating old hags by blocking out teeth. Dozens of suggestions on make-up will be found in the average library. The processes of making-up must be repeated, repeated, and repeated, if, in the short dressing time before the actual performance, all members of the cast are to be transformed into their respective roles effectively.

THE PROPERTIES

Properties and furniture must be collected, stored for the rehearsal and final production, and taken care of after the play is over. Directors often give credit to the property men for fine performances. It is important that a chair be placed correctly, that a book be on the table when it is needed, and that a cigarette lighter be one that works.

THE PROMPTER

Most dramatic directors appoint a prompter. Sometimes he is the same person who handles properties. The prompter must be present at every rehearsal. He follows not only the actors' lines but also all light and sound cues, and all the entrances and exits. He does not prompt too soon, and he does not wait too long before prompting; he knows the play.

THE BUSINESS MANAGER

The business manager usually carries the main responsibility for the financial success of the play. He advertises it throughout the school and community. If he is resourceful, he gets the students in speech classes to give persuasive talks before other classes, the general assembly, community clubs, and church groups. He asks the English teacher to help students write publicity for the school and local papers, and the art teacher to supervise the making of posters.

Tickets are usually printed in the school shops or by some student who has a printing press, and these are allotted to a number of student salesmen who are held strictly accountable for careful handling of them, and the reporting of receipts. The business manager keeps accounts, pays all bills authorized by the director, and hands in a careful account when the play is over.

THE FINAL PRODUCTION

Final performances frequently go off with more finish than the director has dared to hope for, but it is not safe to count too much on such good fortune. The play should be rehearsed thoroughly. Generally the teacher will find that the boys and girls are quite as eager as he is to have the performance a success, and, on the final night especially, will show gratifying co-operation.

The director will wish to see the final performance from the auditorium, but he should be back stage before the curtain goes up to make sure that actors, settings, properties, and lighting are all in readiness. He should show by his attitude that he feels confidence in his staff, and will leave them to manage their responsibilities. He makes sure that, after the performance, each contributor gets the credit due him.

THE CLEANUP

Many an otherwise successful performance has been partially ruined because of irritations in the school and community when borrowed furniture has not been returned promptly, costumes have been left in heaps on the floor, make-up has been smeared over desks in class rooms, bills have been left unpaid, properties have been lost, lamp bulbs have been broken and not replaced, and in general the theater has been left in disorder. The teacher should plan carefully to make the cleanup satisfactory, and he should let it be known that he is going to make a final inspection after the performance to see that everything has been taken care of properly. The cleanup committee must receive full credit with all the others who have contributed to the success of the play.

THE DIRECTOR'S PREPARATION

This chapter makes no claim to providing thorough training for a theater director. Anyone who wishes to specialize in drama as a part of a high school teaching load will be handicapped without college training in acting, directing, staging, costuming, lighting, and make-up. The surest way to get such training is to take courses which are correlated with laboratory work in actual productions. When that is not possible, much can be accomplished by reading, observing , and interviewing. The following bibliography will be helpful in this respect.

SELECTED BIBLIOGRAPHY

Andrews, Harry Lee, and Bruce Weirick, *Acting and Play Production.* New York: Longmans, Green & Co., Inc., 1925.

"A Suggested Outline for a Course of Study in Dramatic Arts in the Secondary School," *Educational Theatre Journal* (March, 1950), 2: 15–31. (Includes suggested units on radio, television, motion pictures.)

Benoliel, H. M., *Stage Make-up Made Easy.* Boston: Walter H. Baker Co., 1948.

Colvan, E. B., *Face the Footlights!* New York: Whittlesey House, 1940.

Dabney, Edith, and C. M. Wise, *A Book of Dramatic Costumes.* New York: Appleton-Century-Crofts, Inc., 1950.

Dean, Alexander, *Fundamentals of Play Directing.* New York: Rinehart & Company, Inc., 1941.

Dolman, John, *The Art of Play Production.* Rev. ed. New York: Harper & Brothers, 1948.

Johnson, Gertrude E., *Choosing a Play.* New York: The Century Company, 1920.

Liszt, Rudolph, *The Last Word in Make-up.* San Francisco: Banner Play Bureau, Inc., 1942.

Knickerbocker, Edwin Van B., *Short Plays.* New York: Henry Holt & Co., 1931.

Lees, C. Lowell, *A Primer of Acting.* New York: Prentice-Hall, Inc., 1940.

Mather, Charles Chambers, Alice Spaulding, Skillen Howard, and Hamilton Melita, *Behind the Footlights.* New York: Silver Burdett Company, 1935.

Ogden, Jess, and Jean Carter, *The Play Book.* New York: Harcourt, Brace & Co., 1937.

Ommanney, Katherine and Pierce C., *The Stage and the School.* Rev. ed. New York: Harper & Brothers, 1950.

Rasmussen, Carrie, *Teaching Speech in the Elementary School.* New York: The Ronald Press, 1950.

Robinson, Karl F., *Teaching Speech in the Secondary School.* New York: Longmans, Green & Co., Inc., 1951.

Ward, Winifred, *Creative Dramatics for Upper Grades in Junior High School.* New York: Appleton-Century-Crofts, Inc., 1939.

————, *Theater for Children.* Anchorage, Kentucky: The Children's Theatre Press, 1950.

CHAPTER 19

Radio, Television, Motion Pictures

INTRODUCTION

Most high school students today have been exposed to the idea that certain events in the history of communication have had a revolutionary effect on the ways in which mankind thinks, lives and learns. For example, the development of the alphabet is usually accounted an event of major importance in history, and the invention of the printing press, with its implications for recording and dispersing knowledge, is also celebrated. Our own century has witnessed revolutionary developments in communication which unquestionably will have a profound effect upon the course of civilization; yet our schools are only beginning the immensely important tasks of trying to evaluate the meaning of these developments; and of deciding how to help students to understand them, and, perhaps, to control them.

Today it is theoretically possible for the words of one man to reach the ears of every person in the world in approximately one-seventh of a second. Only a century and a half ago it took months for the news of President George Washington's election to be carried to the citizens of the United States alone. When General Douglas MacArthur spoke to a joint session of Congress on April 19, 1951, he reached an immediate audience of approximately 50,000,000 persons. To these persons came not only the sense of what the speaker was saying, but also the impression of the speaker's personality as revealed through his voice, and the television audience shared with the audience in the Capitol the effects of the speaker's visible action. These are facts which ought to stimulate the imagination of every teacher, and which ought to challenge every speech teacher with the realization that an immense force has been set loose in the world—a force which is technologically impersonal, and which will come to serve the purposes of mankind only to the extent that through education men may come to understand it, and use it efficiently for good ends.

Radio, television, and the motion picture are usually classified with newspapers and magazines as modes, or media, of mass communication. Radio, television, and motion pictures are not speech forms, in the sense that public speaking, reading aloud, and dramatics are speech forms. Rather, these media carry the forms in which our culture uses speech, modifying and adapting these forms to the particular medium involved. Because these media seem to have changed traditional speech forms, and because they are devices of immense significance for purposes of communication, speech teachers have approached the problem of organizing instruction in the speech of radio, television, and the motion picture from a number of different standpoints. The study of these media in the speech class has interested speech teachers in at least four rather specific ways which will be discussed in the following paragraphs.

Motivation Through Radio-Type Speaking

Radio-type speaking activities are common in the present day high school speech class. Such activities are usually developed not for the end of training students in radio speaking, per se, but as activities which may contribute to the general speech development of students. Radio-type speaking is interesting to the speech class for many reasons.

Speech teachers have found radio-type speaking highly motivating to students. Most high school students are active radio listeners. Their interest in speech forms within this medium is apt to be more highly developed than their interest in these same forms outside of the radio context. They are often attracted by the glamour of the radio industry; by the people who have made radio a profession; and by the technical side of radio, with its microphones, transmitters, and other electronic apparatus. Similarly, many high school students have a highly developed sense of form in radio speaking. The radio drama, newscast, or sports program seems to them a practical and useful speech activity because of their repeated experience with it. It is not surprising, therefore, that many speech teachers have found students highly interested in radio-type speech activities, and able to move ahead independently in the development of them.

It has become increasingly easy for the speech teacher to provide students with simple equipment with which radio-type speaking may be satisfactorily simulated in the speech class. Low cost public address systems are found today in most high schools. Recording equipment has become increasingly available. As we shall indicate later, such simple equipment is adequate to the dressing up of radio-type speaking for classroom purposes. Undoubtedly, high school students are motivated in part by a sheer love of gadgets. The interest thus generated may be put to good advantage by the alert speech teacher.

The radio format provides an efficient way of carrying out certain types of speaking activity, efficient in the sense that it permits a considerable amount of speaking practice, with a minimum of time devoted to preparation. For example, a radio drama can be made ready for a reasonably satisfying presentation in considerably less time than a play can be made ready for adequate presentation on the stage. Of course, the staged play offers certain types of valuable experience to the student which are not provided by the radio play. But, since many speech teachers like to include a large number of activities within the scope of a semester speech course, they find the use of radio-type speaking an efficient way of including dramatic activity.

Student Listening and Viewing Habits in Radio, Television, and Motion Pictures

For generations educators have understood the importance of the reading habits of children in their intellectual and emotional development. As a result, reading skills, reading habits, and taste in reading long have been among the most important goals of education. Now, quite suddenly, an analogous situation has developed with respect to the listening and viewing skills, habits, and tastes of students. For nearly all students, the radio, the motion picture, and television constitute important agencies of both recreation and learning. The skills and habits they bring to their use of these media constitute one of the crucial educational problems of our day. It is for this reason that teachers of speech have come increasingly to view the relationship of radio, television, and motion pictures to education, from the standpoint of the habits of listening and viewing demonstrated by students. One of the major tasks in education is helping students to understand the significance of the mass media of communication in our culture, helping them to appraise their own use of these media, and helping them to develop more useful habits of listening and viewing.

The Use of Radio Speaking as a Co-curricular Activity

The high school of today emphasizes the close relationship which ought to exist between the school and the community. In developing this relationship, radio has played an important role. Schools not only have brought radio and television programs into the classroom, but also have developed programs of their own, and by broadcasting these programs over local stations, have brought students and school activities closer to the community. In those schools using local broadcasting stations as outlets for student programs, the speech teacher properly may feel that such activities furnish important speech training.

Whether or not actual programs are broadcast by the students, many schools have developed radio workshops as student interest groups. In such workshops, students interested in drama, radio speaking, and radio announcing may combine these activities in the development of radio programs. These programs usually find a ready audience within the school.

Radio, Television, and Motion Picture Programs as Teaching Aids

The educational potentialities of the mass media have made them both a problem and a promise for our society. Speech teachers, as well as educators generally, have been interested in the possible uses of radio, television, and motion pictures as aids to the usual methods of classroom instruction. Today, teachers are finding available an increasing amount of recorded radio materials and educational motion pictures which pertain specifically to the problems of speech instruction.

The Scope of This Chapter

This chapter will consider radio, television, and the motion picture primarily from three different standpoints: (1) Radio-type speaking as a classroom activity; (2) educating the audience for radio, television, and motion pictures; and (3) the use of radio as a co-curricular activity. The use of radio programs and motion pictures as instructional aids is considered in the appendix, pages 543 to 550, and will not be developed further in this chapter.

Radio-Type Speaking as a Classroom Activity

We have already indicated that many speech teachers have found radio-type speaking a motivating activity for high school speech students. At the same time, it should be observed that the very aspects of radio-type speaking which motivate high school students may provide the speech teacher with a problem in keeping uppermost the specific objectives of speech training. Thus, high school students may be interested in radio speaking, not so much because they are interested in speaking, as because they are interested in the production aspects of the classroom radio show. They may be interested more in the electronic marvels represented by a tape recorder or in the development of sound effects as ornamentation for a radio play than in the quality of the speaking. Similarly, many high school students are attracted to radio by the glamour of the radio industry. As inveterate radio listeners, these students may have developed professional aspirations, and thus have come to look upon radio-type speaking as a form of pre-professional training, rather than as a means to the end of personal development in general speaking skills.

These considerations in no way invalidate the use of radio-type speaking as a classroom speech activity. Rather, they indicate the need for careful consideration by the speech teacher of the objectives for which the speech class is using radio activities, and planning which will assure the attainment of these objectives. The speech teacher may make the two sorts of discriminations discussed herein to keep a proper balance in classroom radio-type speaking.

Radio-type speaking is a means, not an end

The purpose of such activity is to increase the range of motivating speech activities available to the students. Thus the speech class will generally keep the production of classroom radio programs on a minimal basis. The emphasis will be on developing the best possible speaking, and then it will be on getting the program completed and evaluated.

How much stress should be placed on production problems in radio-type speaking as a classroom activity? As with so many problems in teaching, the answer must be a conditional one. If students are motivated to do a good job in their classroom speaking, they will want to make their programs as finished as possible in the time available. They may find that they can improve their performances by improving the quality of their writing, by discovering the ways in which a judicious use of music serves as a supplement to radio dramas, by becoming more skillful in balancing the voices of a discussion group with relation to the microphone, and by finding sound effects to supplement certain dramatic productions. In general, the control the teacher exerts over the emphasis to be given production of the classroom radio project will be in the direction of helping to decide the amount of time available for the preparation of a particular project—allowing sufficient time for a satisfying activity, but gauging this time allotment in terms of the total range of goals to be sought by the speech class.

Radio-type speaking extends student activity rather than developing programs with professional polish

In line with the instrumental nature of radio-type speaking as a classroom activity is the fact that few classroom activities should seek professional polish, even if one were to concede the possibility of attaining it. The classroom activity, which simulates the form of radio speaking, should be realistic enough to be satisfying to performers and listeners, but it should not consume hours of rehearsal in polishing a particular activity at the expense of curtailing other valuable activity. This statement does not discount the value to high school students of engaging in the preparation of radio programs in which every effort is made to develop the highest level of performance possible to the participants. In general, however, this search for the finished program will be more appropriate to the interests of a co-curricular radio group than to the speech classroom.

EQUIPMENT FOR CLASSROOM PRODUCTIONS

Though production considerations are only a means to some of the ends of the speech class, the speech teacher needs to plan carefully the techniques of achieving radio-type speaking which is satisfying to the participating students.

The speech teacher should survey the available equipment in his school and evaluate the possibilities for using it in developing radio-type speaking activity. He may also wish to work for the expansion of equipment which will increase the use of such activities. Five different situations regarding equipment may be distinguished, each of which will influence the actual planning of the speech teacher.

The School without Electronic Equipment

In some schools the speech teacher may find that neither recording nor public address equipment of any sort is available. Under such limitations, the radio-type speaking can be accomplished only in the presence of a classroom audience, using a mock or simulated microphone. High school students are often interested in dressing up a discussion, a newscast, or a radio drama with such a simulated equipment. Such a limitation on the possibilities for developing realism in radio activity, however, would seem a misfortune in this day and age.

The School with Portable Public Address Equipment

Many high schools have available a portable public address unit; a microphone and an amplifier may be placed in one classroom, and a loud speaker in another. Such equipment makes possible a considerable degree of realism in the preparation and presentation of radio programs in the speech classroom. By using a portable record player in connection with the microphone and amplifier, students may develop programs making use of music and recorded sound effects to increase the realism of their dramatic productions. The portable equipment is somewhat unsatisfactory because it must be set up and taken down each time it is used, a difficulty which may prove time consuming. However, if certain students in the class take over management of the equipment, the teacher may feel that its use does not detract materially from the efficiency of classroom operations.

The School with a Broadcasting Studio and Control Room [1]

An ideal situation for the speech teacher is provided by the school which has permanent public address equipment installed in a broadcasting studio. In some schools such equipment is centrally located, with loud-speakers, and microphones, in all classrooms. In other schools, such equipment has been developed to connect the studio with an adjoining speech classroom. Usually such permanent equipment will include an amplifier of sufficient size so that more than one microphone may be used simultaneously by the broadcasting group, and so that recorded materials, music and sound effects, may be fed directly into the amplifier. Such equipment is ideal; its use eliminates the time loss involved in setting up portable equipment, and it simplifies the attainment of reasonable realism for the programs. It is also ideal in that it often permits the development of programs in the speech class to be "broadcast" to the school at large, or to specific classes in the school. In one large high school, the speech classes prepared programs to be presented at intervals during the lunch hour, over a centrally located public address system which reached the school cafeteria. Student newscasts, record programs, and an occasional drama, not only enlivened the lunch hour but also provided a stimulating outlet for the energies of the speech students.

The School with Recording Equipment

Tape recording equipment has not only produced a considerable revolution in commercial radio production, but also offers great

---

[1] A description of the equipment and management of central sound systems in 12 high schools is presented in the pamphlet, *High School Radio Workshops in Cleveland*, Washington, D. C.: U. S. Office of Education, 1944.

possibilities for radio speaking in the speech classroom. With the use of such a machine, the students with radio-type programs for production can be sent to a room or an office other than the classroom to record their materials. Their program can then be played for the entire class, including the performers, at a later time. Even in schools with broadcasting studios, the teacher may wish to record the radio program, rather than broadcast it as a live program, in order to take advantage of the flexible scheduling permitted by the use of such recordings, and to permit the students making the broadcast to observe the effects of their efforts directly.

SPEECH SKILLS WHICH MAY BE SOUGHT THROUGH RADIO-TYPE SPEAKING

Nearly all forms of speaking may be placed within the radio format. Thus radio-type speaking need not be differentiated in its values from the objectives in public speaking, discussion, debate, reading aloud, storytelling, and drama. Nevertheless, this type of activity may have particular worth in the development of vocal skills, and thus may be used to good purpose by teachers seeking to emphasize such skills. Most high school students are aware of the importance of vocal skills in communication, more from their experience as radio listeners than from any other experiences in speech. As radio listeners they have become conscious of the ways in which personality is projected through voice, and of the significance of the various aspects of vocal production in communication. In using radio-type speaking, they will find their listeners tending toward increasingly rigorous demands for expressive, articulate speech, and if their efforts are recorded, they will have the opportunity for self criticism of their vocal skills. While students find a microphone motivating, they will also find it a severe critic of their voices, emphasizing their errors of pronunciation and their shortcomings in effective reading and speaking.

EDUCATING THE AUDIENCE FOR RADIO, TELEVISION, AND MOTION PICTURES

The curricular responsibility for developing better listening and viewing skills in high school students is one shared by many teachers.

Social studies teachers are often concerned with the listening habits of their students and with their evaluations of various news and news-commentary broadcasts. High school *Problems* courses often examine the mass media of communication in terms of the social issues raised by the programming policies of radio and television, and by the nature of the motion picture industry in our society. In other schools, a similar examination is made in English or speech classes. In many schools, teachers will want to plan together for the inclusion in the curriculum of appropriate opportunities for the study of radio, television, and the motion picture from the standpoint of the listener. The discussion which follows will indicate the variety of the possible approaches to the objective of listener education, without implying that all of the approaches can be, or ought to be, a part of every high school course in speech.

Correlation of Radio Speaking with the Listener's Education

In considering the mass media from the viewpoint of the audience, we are not implying that there is no relationship between the use of radio-type speaking in the classroom and the education of the radio audience. Actually, as students in the speech class prepare their own radio activities, they may, with adequate guidance, be developing their own skills and habits as listeners. For example, student-prepared radio programs often include pseudo-commercial advertising as transitional material. Such an inclusion provides an obvious opportunity for discussing the speech class' tastes in advertising, and perhaps for investigating the problems which have been faced by the radio industry in the use of radio as a medium of advertising. Similarly, the preparation by students of a newscast for the school audience immediately raises for them some of the problems faced by commercial radio in setting policy with regard to the purposes and nature of newscasts and news commentary. Students may discover by investigation that different broadcasting networks have developed different policies for the control of their news and commentary services, and they may wish to discuss the rationale of these policies and their values to the public. The teacher should consider the study of radio speaking and radio listening as interrelated.

Classroom Procedures in Audience Education

The following discussion will cover some of the approaches teachers have used in developing units of study in radio, television, and the motion picture. Two previous descriptions of radio listening activities have been included in this book: (1) An extensive description of the development of a radio listening project in connection with the general problem of developing skills of listening (pages 248 to 264); and (2) a description of the development of a radio listening club in connection with a project in the study of parliamentary law (page 287). The speech teacher will observe the great variety of relationships in which the education of the audience may be undertaken, and should not regard the proposals which follow as excluding the development of a unit in listening or viewing.

A useful basis for raising problems of listening or viewing with a high school class is provided by a survey of members' habits. Students may be asked to record the amount of time they spend in listening to the radio, viewing television, or attending motion pictures. They may be asked to list their preferences in radio and television programs and in motion pictures. They may be asked to report their habits in radio listening, indicating whether they give undivided or partial attention to radio programs.

The data gathered by such surveys can be analyzed by a student committee and presented to the entire class as a normative picture of the listening and viewing habits and preferences of the class. Such surveys, of course, are important only insofar as they provide a basis from which the class may develop real questions about (1) the values which radio, television, and the motion picture are supposed to have in our society; and (2) the values which the class members, as the audience, bring to their listening and viewing. Students will be interested in comparing their own habits and preferences with the habits and preferences of the American public generally.

Too often high school students discuss the role of radio, television, and the motion picture in American life, or criticize specific productions, within an aura of misinformation or lack of information about these media. The students' capacity to discuss intelligently the values in these media may be improved greatly by the development of information and historical perspective about the industry and the art form in question. The following illustration will indicate to some extent the information about a motion picture which might be profitably introduced in studying this medium from the standpoint of the audience. A similar program of historical and informational study might be undertaken with radio or television.

A teacher reports:

This class approached the study of the motion picture by viewing the film *Understanding Movies*.[2] On the basis of the material in this film, the techniques of directing, acting, photography, art and music, and editing were discussed.

The relationship of production techniques to the story was also considered. The class then viewed three different films selected from those available through a visual education service. These films included a documentary, a classroom teaching film, and a drama. Each of the films was evaluated in terms of its purpose, and its use of the various production techniques. The drama was evaluated also in terms of its story, and the values represented by the story. Standards for evaluation to be used in discussion were developed by the class, and included the following:

For the story:
  Does it distort life?
  Does it glorify unworthy goals in living?
  Is it a stereotyped, predictable plot?
  Does it give any insight into truth?
  Was it worth telling and worth seeing?

For casting and acting:
  Do the actors develop interesting characters, or simply exploit their own public personalities?
  Do the actors heighten and sharpen all possible meanings in the story?

For art and music:
  Do sound effects and music support and heighten the story or call attention to themselves?
  Is there evidence of imaginative taste in the selection of sound effects and music?

---

[2] A film prepared by a Committee of the National Council of Teachers of English and Teaching Film Custodians, 25 West 43rd St., N. Y., 18, N. Y.

For photography:
  Does it enhance the story rather than call attention to itself?
  Is there evidence of imagination and taste in the selection of camera
    themselves?

  Speeches of information were prepared and presented to the class,
covering: (1) Significant aspects in the history of motion pictures,
both as an art form and an industry; (2) types of screen plays;
and (3) objectives of different types of motion pictures.[3]
  Consideration of radio, television, and the motion picture from
the standpoint of the audience leads inevitably to the discussion
of the possible assistance of professional critics to the members of
the audience. The speech class may wish to become familiar with
various critics of these media, and to develop evaluations of the
possible services which they render to the public.
  Thus, for certain motion pictures, students might be asked to
compare the reviews given in one or more movie fan magazines
with the reviews from a number of periodicals, such as *Theatre
Arts, Time, Newsweek, Consumer Reports, The New Yorker,
The New York Times,* a local newspaper, and so on. The *Green
Sheet,* published by the National Board of Motion Picture Review,
ordinarily will be an important source of critical information about
motion pictures. Student investigations of various critical materials
might lead to discussions and reports, comparing the various methods
of criticism, the contents of criticism, the purposes various critics
seem to wish to accomplish, and the value of different types of
criticisms to the public.
  Critical information on radio and television programs might be
treated in the same way, although the literature of such criticism
is more limited than that devoted to the motion picture.
  High school students may find a challenging need for problem-
solving discussion by discovering and raising some of the important
social issues which have grown up relative to the place of radio,
television, and the motion picture in American life. Some high
school students will become familiar with certain issues through
their general reading. Others will discover such issues as they con-

----

  [3] There is an extensive literature on motion pictures which provides the
basis for much reporting and discussion by high school students. Some of
this is included in the bibliography at the end of this chapter.

sider the history of these various media, or as they read critical materials about various programs. Students may be able to formulate specific problems with relation to each of the media which will serve as the basis for further investigation by discussion groups— and ultimately as the basis for a public discussion. Such issues as the following may call for investigation and discussion:

For radio and television:
Why has radio (television) grown up under governmental licensing, while newspapers are not under direct governmental control?
Does radio (television) provide program materials desired by all groups of listeners in America?
What should be the purposes and responsibilities of radio (television) news services?
How do different news commentators treat the same news story? How do you account for these differences?
What are the differences in radio and television control in the United States and in Great Britain?

For the motion picture:
Are motion pictures censored? Should they be?
What view do the movies give of American life and American values?
Does the star system handicap the production of good movies?
How will television affect the future of the motion picture industry?
Is the public getting what it wants in motion pictures, or does it take what it gets?

The ultimate objective sought in all study of the various mass media from the standpoint of the audience, is to give high school students a basis for making: (1) More effective personal choices in their selection of radio, television, and motion picture fare; (2) a basis for forming attitudes on the functions these media might serve in American society; and (3) a basis for making more effective use of the programs attended, seen, and/or heard.

RADIO WORKSHOPS

We have already made repeated reference to the radio workshop as a co-curricular activity in many high schools. Such workshops are sometimes curricular in nature, operating either as a separate speech elective, or as an auxiliary of a speech class. More often, however, they take the form of a high school club, or interest group, which is closely analogous to such groups as dramatic and debate clubs.

The Workshop Correlates Many Valuable Educational Interests

One of the facts which has attracted many teachers to the radio workshop, is the way in which such an activity combines the efforts of numerous students, with a variety of interests. To the speech student, the workshop has an obvious appeal, offering as it does an outlet for his interests in drama, reading aloud, and various types of public speaking, debate, and discussion. To the aspiring writer, the workshop offers an outlet for his creative talent. The boy interested in electronics, or the management or building of equipment for the workshop will be attracted to the group. Music students, too, may be interested in the workshop which includes music broadcasts in its activity as well as incidental music in the development of radio drama.

The teacher directing a radio workshop may well be concerned with the possibilities offered by such an activity for broadening the range of interests and information of the participating students, who may be drawn to radio by specialized aptitudes, but who will there encounter and work with students with a different range of skills and information.

The Workshop May Find Many Real Audiences for its Productions

It is probable that much student speaking activity either reaches no audience at all, or reaches an audience with only nominal interest in it. Such a situation need not prevail so far as the activity of a radio workshop group is concerned. The directors of such workshops will need to examine carefully the possible outlets for programs prepared by the group, but although such opportunities may vary greatly from school to school, there are few schools in which it will prove impossible to gain the focus and stimulus offered by real audiences. The following paragraphs list some of the uses to which workshop programs may be put.

1. *Programs to be broadcast to the entire school from a central broadcasting studio*

We have already referred to the student broadcasts aimed at a lunch hour audience, as one possibility. In other schools, newscasts and special events programs dealing with school affairs are given recognition as an activity which fulfills many of the same functions as school newspapers. Thus, announcements of all-school events, the promotion of all-school activities, and the sharing of information about various school activities may be accomplished through radio programs reaching home room audiences.

2. *Programs for particular classes*

The radio workshop may find an outlet for its activities by preparing shows for particular classes in the school. Through consultation with classroom teachers, plans may be made for a documentary show in a social studies class, a drama based on a book being read in an English class, or an informational broadcast in one of the science classes. These programs may be recorded for presentation, if the problem of class schedules prevents the use of a live show.

3. *Radio plays to be included in a high school program of one-act plays*

In one high school, short radio plays, prepared by a workshop group, were given between one-act plays staged for an evening audience of parents and students. In this way the number of students taking part in the one-act play program was materially increased.

4. *Programs to be broadcast over local commercial stations*

Some metropolitan school systems operate educational broadcasting stations which offer a constant outlet for student talent in radio. Usually, however, the only actual radio outlet available to the schools is through local commercial stations which may offer some of their time to the schools as a part of their public service activity. Speech teachers should not undertake the preparation of programs for presentation to the public at large without considering carefully the responsibilities involved. There is a considerable difference between the level of radio programs which may be acceptable and useful for classroom purposes, and those which will be well received by an adult audience, listening to a commercial station. This is true despite the tolerance local adult audiences may have for the students who make no claims to professional capabilities. However, since the ostensible purpose of programs broadcast over commercial radio stations is to provide a public service, it follows that such programs should attain a considerable level of excellence if they are to fulfill that purpose.

If the radio workshop does accept the job of preparing programs for actual broadcast, it may fulfill its assignment more efficiently by considering carefully the relative difficulty involved in preparing different types of programs. Thus, programs involving talks by students; interviews of fellow students, faculty members, or other persons in the community; and student discussion groups are ordinarily relatively successful for public broadcast. In these programs the students face no involved problems of production. Radio dramas, on the other hand, can become painfully ineffective in a public broadcast. This is not to say that workshop groups cannot handle radio drama successfully for broadcast to the public; rather, it is to suggest that workshop groups ought to understand the difficulties of such programs before undertaking their preparation.

The Radio Workshop Can Find Many Sources for Programs

No narrow view should be taken of the program materials available to high school groups interested in radio. In dealing with such groups, the director may find it desirable to work with scripts already available in order to give students the motivation of early presentation of a number of programs. A part of the objective of the workshop, however, may well be to develop in students ingenuity in using the program materials available in the varied activities of their school and community. As students become familiar with the possibilities of documentary programs, interviews, on-the-spot news broadcasts, music programs, discussion programs, and radio drama, they may begin to see many possibilities for creating programs for their own. In one instance, students developed, through a series of interviews, the educational objectives of the various departments in their high school. In another school they developed programs describing the purposes and activities of various public service organizations in their community. In yet another school the workshop prepared a documentary on the history and activity of the student council, a program which was recorded for use in orienting new students to the school. Such programs are far from the student-produced variety show sometimes put together largely from pseudo-commercial advertising plus assorted nonsense. It has often been said that radio, together with the motion picture and television, can bring the world to the classroom. It is equally true that a student workshop group can take the class-room to the world, at least that part of the world which forms the particular school and community. This is a project with merit enough to challenge the attention of any speech teacher to the edu-cational possibilities of radio as a co-curricular activity.

SELECTED BIBLIOGRAPHY

Abbot, Waldo, *Handbook of Broadcasting.* New York: McGraw-Hill Book Co., 1941.

Anderson, Borghild F., "Are Good Radio Listeners Made?" *English Journal* (September, 1949), 38: 391–395.

Bendrick, Jeanne, *Television Works Like This.* New York: McGraw-Hill Book Co., 1949.

Callahan, Jennie V., *Radio Workshop for Children.* New York: Mc-Graw-Hill Book Co., 1948.

Chafee, Zachariah, Jr., *Government and Mass Communication.* Chicago: University of Chicago Press, 1947.

Child, Eleanor D., and Hardy R. Finch, "Motion Picture and Radio: An English Elective," *The Curriculum Journal* (October, 1939), 10: 253–257.

Dale, E., *How to Appreciate Motion Pictures.* New York: The Mac-millan Co., 1933.

Everson, George, *The Story of Television.* New York: W. W. Norton & Company, Inc., 1949.

Forman, H. J., *"Our Movie Made Children.* New York: The Macmillan Co., 1933.

Hellman, Edward, and Keith I. Tyler, "Radio and Speech Education," *Bulletin of Secondary School Principals* (November, 1945), 29: 131, pp. 98–116.

Herzberg, Max J., *Radio and English Teaching*, English Monograph #14. (Nat. Council of Teachers of English.) Appleton-Century, 1941.

Hill, F. E., and W. E. Williams, *Radio's Listening Groups.* New York: Columbia University Press, 1941.

Inglis, Ruth, *Freedom of the Movies.* Chicago: Commission on Freedom of the Press, University of Chicago Press, 1947.

Kaplan, Milton A., "The Radio Play as an Introduction to Drama," *English Journal* (January, 1950), 39: 23–26.

Lowdermith, R. R., *The School Radio Sound System.* Washington, D. C.: Federal Radio Education Commission, 1941.

Manvell, R., *Film.* Baltimore: Penguin Books, Inc., 1946.

Mullen, Sarah F., *How to Judge Motion Pictures.* New York: Scholastic Press, 1934.

Pease, Kent, "Hamden's Course in Appreciation of Movies and Radio," *Clearing House* (September, 1937), 12: 39–93.

Robinson, Karl F., and Stanley T. Donner, "Suggested Units in Radio for the Secondary School," *Quarterly Journal of Speech* (April, 1947), 33: 225–228.

Rotha, Paul, and R. Manvell, *Movie Parade, 1888–1949.* New York: Studio Publications, 1950.

Seldes, Gilbert V., *The Great Audience.* New York: The Viking Press, 1950.

Tallman, Marion L., "Teaching Discriminating Radio Listening," *English Journal* (October, 1948), 37: 408–412.

"The Motion Picture Industry," *Annals of the American Academy of Political and Social Science*, 254, 1947.

U. S. Office of Education. Radio-Script Lending Library. Washington, D. C. (Scripts lent upon request.)

Waples, Douglas, (ed.), *Print, Radio and Film in a Democracy.* Chicago: University of Chicago Press, 1941.

Whittaker, Charlotte, "Core Unit: Theatre, Movies, Radio, Television," *Clearing House* (September, 1949), 24: 21–25.

Woelfel, Norman, and Keith Tyler, *Radio and the School.* Yonkers, N. Y.: World Book Co., 1945.

CHAPTER 20

Speech Contests

INTRODUCTION

Everywhere in life competition is an incentive to better performance. While their parents and adult relatives and friends are running for office; improving breeds of livestock; working for promotions in factories, industries, and colleges; struggling to increase law practices; trying for leads in plays and operas; gathering support for grants or scholarships in order to do research; hustling to increase insurance sales; playing bridge; experimenting to perfect some new type of bomb ahead of other countries; or grooming themselves or a son or daughter for the most satisfactory marriage; boys and girls in high school are participating in contests in football, basketball, track, swimming, skiing, painting, stamp collecting, photography, story and essay writing, bird banding, rat eradication, milking, baking, canning, dressmaking, dancing, music, spelling, landscape gardening, arithmetic, oratory, reading, acting, debating, manual arts, and popularity! In practically every significant activity, human beings compete with each other for satisfactions, rewards, and prizes.

Few teachers will find themselves in schools where there is no organized competition in speech activities. In Chapter 2 we saw how contests in early Greece, Rome, and America originated in an effort to make speech training more functional and to bring it closer to man's needs. In the same chapter we traced the development of speech education in America and saw that the expansion

475

of the school program in all areas has brought with it an increase in the variety and amount of speech competition.

WHY CONTESTS DEVELOPED

Contests Furnish a Center for Community Social Life

In many communities, contests have served, in the past, and continue to serve, in the present, as foci for community social life. It is difficult for anyone reared in this period of modern transportation and communication to realize the significance of the community gathering of two hundred or even one hundred years ago. There were then no automobiles or planes, no radios, movies, telephones, television sets, or sound recordings. A trip of eight or ten miles required almost two hours. Therefore, communities had to rely upon their own activities for entertainment, which often took the form of some kind of competition. In warm weather, games, races, and stunts could be held in the open, but on long winter evenings which brought young and old together indoors, readers, actors, and speakers were much in demand.

"It was not that we *wished* to stay close to home," one oldster remarked after hearing a lengthy tirade on the present-day restlessness of parents and children who seem to come home only to eat and to sleep. "It was that the horses were too tired from work in the fields to take us to places of amusement. We were forced to get together within walking distance of our farms and amuse ourselves." The type of entertainment which became popular proved to be so interesting and so valuable, educationally, that it has continued in modified forms, down to the present time, and no doubt will extend into the indefinite future. New inventions have not replaced the old contests; they have helped to make them more effective.

Competition Motivates Extensive and Intensive Speech Learnings

The first speech contests were in debate and oratory but, as time went on, competitions in memorized and manuscript reading of stories, poems, and plays; extemporaneous speaking; discussion; play production; and radio speaking came into the picture. Each type of contest was adapted to serve the immediate needs of various groups of people. For example, farm boys spoke extemporaneously, read from the page, discussed, and debated, using topics relating to rural problems, while students in urban areas emphasized forms of speaking and reading more closely adapted to the problems of city life.

Because of the deep motivations inherent in competitive activities, boys and girls, in preparing for interschool contests, work much more intensively than they usually do in class performance. The fact that they represent their home, school, or community in competition with others gives each individual a responsibility which he takes very seriously. Instead of urging students to prepare more carefully, as is frequently necessary with class projects, the teacher often warns against overdoing in preparing for contests, and urges students to try several selections for reading, or several topics for debate and discussion, in order to avoid over-concentration on any one.

Meeting Students from Other Schools Widens the Range of Student Activities

Sometimes the benefits to students which result from visits to other schools and of entertaining representatives from other schools, are not considered of major importance. Yet, even more than the formal speaking activities of debating, declaiming, acting, or reading, the opportunity to attend assemblies in another school; to stay in hotels; to travel on busses, trains, and planes; to be guests in different homes; to go to dances in other communities; to talk to other teachers of speech; to accept criticisms from judges, are real life experiences of great potential educational value. Teachers who watch student behavior carefully are gratified at the many beneficial effects of interschool meetings. They notice that boys and girls gain confidence in their friendships with the opposite sex, and suddenly quiet little courtesies become a part of their regular social behavior. Students learn to open doors, carry luggage, help each other to put on coats, behave properly at table, and converse more fluently and naturally. Extemporaneous speaking is made use of outside of the formal contest situations. Students visit classes in the host school and are asked to "say a few words." They speak at banquets and at teas. They have experience in greeting hostesses, introducing others and being introduced by them, in moving from one group to another in conversation, and in saying good-bye and expressing appreciation. They come back to their own schools filled with enthusiasm and eager to repeat the experience. "There is no stopping them," parents and teachers say, because here are activities which are really meaningful to them. Therefore, these contests have survived and continue to increase in popularity.

Contests Give Extra Speaking Opportunities to Superior Students

The aim of every teacher is to keep all of her students working to capacity. Some students can accomplish many times as much as others and they should have an opportunity to do so. Contests challenge the gifted. All teachers have students who are bored and restless because they can complete regular assignments before the majority can do so. These talented youngsters can take on extra-curricular speech projects and work on them with genuine enthusiasm. There literally is no limit to the research which these students can carry on in the study of some well-chosen debate proposition. They will work long and faithfully in preparing to read literary material of high quality, to speak extemporaneously on problems of current interest, and to act in and stage plays for presentation before new audiences. They will develop the additional speech skills not needed before prejudiced home groups of parents and friends.

An eminent professor of geography, who had carried on much scholarly research, summarized the significance of speech contests to the superior student when he said, "The most thorough study I ever made of any question was in preparing for a debate on Philippine Independence. I started to work on it when I was third speaker on a high school debate team. I still feel that I made myself something of an authority on the problem, for from that day until this, I never see the announcement of a lecture or discussion on the topic that I do not try to attend; I never see an article in a newspaper or magazine on that subject that I do not try to read it; I never see the advertisement of a book on the subject or the listing of one in the card catalog that does not attract me; and, what is most important, my friends, students, and acquaintances, have always reacted to my comments on the Philippines as if they thought what I said was worth listening to. In later life, it is difficult to study many questions as thoroughly as a student investigates a debate proposition. Debating is a satisfying experience which students are fortunate to have." Many superior students echo these sentiments regarding the value of interclass and interschool speech competition.

Crowded Curricula Leave No Adequate Place for Speech Training

In many high schools the co-curricular speech program offers the only direct speech training available. It is difficult to make radical changes in the curriculum of any school. Year after year, the school program continues because a change means dropping some well-established subject or the shortening of class hours; either solution requires more effort than the average administrator is willing or able to make, so he turns to out-of-school hours and encourages speech training on the side. The history of desirable speech programs shows that in most schools they started as co-curricular activities and developed into curricular ones after they had proved themselves of prime worth.

TYPES OF CONTESTS

It is not possible to list or describe the numerous kinds of speech contests which are carried on as features of high school education in America. Most teachers will have opportunity to train students for contests in drama; in reading from memory, after thorough preparation and from a book, after limited preparation; in speaking extemporaneously and from memory, using both original or selected material; and in discussion and debate. Competition in the foregoing may take place directly before an audience or over the radio.

THE TEACHER MUST DEVELOP A PHILOSOPHY REGARDING CONTESTS

There is much discussion pro and con concerning the values of contests, and every speech teacher can profit by analyzing the favorable and adverse criticisms. It is important to determine which of the alleged weaknesses are inherent and which are due to shortcomings in the conduct of the contests. If the speech teacher is persuaded that competition is intrinsically wrong, and should be eradicated, then it is his duty, in our democratic society, to do what he can to get rid of not only high school speech contests but also all types of rivalry in our political, economic, religious, and social life. If, on the other hand, the speech teacher believes that common criticisms of contests concern the methods of conducting speech contests, he should focus his efforts on improving the attitudes toward, the training for, and the procedures in, organizing and judging the contests. It is the belief of the authors of this book that defending or attacking contests in toto is an unintelligent procedure for the teacher to adopt. Each school should evaluate the contests available to its students in relation to its own curriculum. For some schools, play and interpretative reading festivals may furnish a means of motivating extensive interest in speech activities better than do formal speaking contests. Another school may have developed more curricular speech activity than it can manage with the available staff and facilities without the added burden of such contests or festivals. In still other schools, a lagging interest in certain types of speech, as public speaking, discussion, and the like, may suggest the use of co-curricular contests to stimulate new interest in the neglected aspects of speech training.

In many schools the four major adverse criticisms of contests are being met and answered satisfactorily; they do not reflect inherent weaknesses in speech competition. The criticism that the emphasis in the speech contest is on winning rather than on speaking well often is heard. Those who make this charge cite instances where teachers have given boys and girls selections to deliver which have aggravated their particular speech difficulties. For example, a girl who is handicapped by babyish speech is given a selection in which a very young child is speaking, and the contestant capitalizes on the fault in her own speech. Or a boy with an unfortunately high pitched voice is assigned the role of a sissy in a play contest in which his experience further fixes his bad habit. Or a girl whose posture is unsatisfactory, who holds her head forward and slumps her shoulders, recites a monologue in which a tired-out old servant is characterized.

These critics also allege that students are trained to please certain judges, even though the coaches themselves do not approve of standards of speech set by the judges. For example, the teacher believes that Judge X likes complete characterization, or a great deal of action, or humorous facial expressions, and, therefore, he trains his students to please the judge, regardless of whether the delivery suits the material, the audience, or themselves.

Again these critics say that decisions are bought, not necessarily with money, but through influential friends, flattery, entertainment, high fees, or other types of bribery which take advantage of human frailties. There is no denying that all of these practices may be pursued on some occasions and by some unscrupulous people; unfortunately, there are a few dishonest teachers and a good many poor teachers. The solution, we believe, is to place contest activities in the hands of honest, competent teachers; the solution is not to discontinue the contests.

If the speech coach asks himself occasionally, "What is my purpose? What am I trying to accomplish?" he will never use any of the afore-mentioned objectionable procedures. If he is trying to train boys and girls to be more effective when they talk, he will not do anything to fix bad speech habits upon them by training them to please a judge rather than to speak well. Neither will he bribe a dishonest judge to render an unfair decision. Such meretricious practices are the rare exceptions rather than the rule. The teacher and the student who set out to win contests usually accomplish their purpose most effectively by developing superior speaking ability, which is the aim of all speech training.

Some critics say that contests place more emphasis on competition than on co-operation. The best way to form an opinion on the validity of this allegation is to observe many contests in many parts of the country and to do so with an open mind. One principal of a high school which was participating in speech contests for the first time, attended a meeting of principals and coaches to arrange for the season's competition. He was surprised to note that there was unanimous agreement on allowing the host school to choose the judges, on asking the teacher in another school to select materials for the readings from manuscript, on delegating the phrasing of the extemporaneous speaking topics to the coach in another school, and on having all schools contribute music to give variety and interest to the programs. He heard teachers name parents who were willing to transport and entertain contestants to reduce expenses, he heard coaches exchanging debate references which they had found particularly helpful, and, finally, he sat in on a closing dinner meeting which was attended by men and women who had become friends because they had found common interests and responsibilities. Upon his return from the meeting, he told his faculty that he considered speech contests an important means of encouraging friendly co-operation among high schools. In well planned speech contests, co-operation is much more obvious than competition.

Still other critics charge that most individual students are disappointed when they receive adverse criticisms and low ratings. This objection holds true in every project a student prepares, every talk he gives, every picture he paints, every theme he writes, every algebra problem he works, and every bird house he builds. He prefers to have his classmates and his teacher tell him that he has done well—very well. But the beginning teacher is warned against giving undeserved commendation. High school students are quick to recognize false praise and to feel insulted by it. Usually, they themselves are fairly good judges of where they rate, and they are perfectly willing to admit their weaknesses in order to obtain help in eliminating them. Most critic judges in tactful, definite, positive comments aim to give participants all possible assistance.

The final criticism is that many speech contests take place in artificial situations and with small audiences, sometimes only a judge and a coach or two. Tournaments are not always arranged in this way, but even if they were, would these objections justify the elimination of contests? Should not an effort be made to get larger and more typical audiences? Some speech contests attract such large audiences that, even though ten or fifteen programs are going on at once, all have minimum audiences of fifty. In some cities, high school contest speakers are scheduled to speak before both junior and senior assemblies, as well as before civic clubs and church groups. The solution to the problem of small audiences appears to be providing larger audiences rather than abandoning the contests.

On the issues raised by the critics of contests, the speech teacher must take a stand. The authors of this text believe in improving contests and not abolishing them, unless and until some more satisfactory form of co-curricular speech training develops to take their place. It is hoped that each speech teacher may profit from some of the evidence and argument herein presented in support of this view and will evolve his own philosophy regarding contests.

ORGANIZING SPEECH CONTESTS

In most states, there are very well organized speech (forensic) organizations which solicit membership, plan competitions, distribute materials, set up training institutes, secure judges, and provide awards. In some states 100 per cent of the high schools take part in speech contests of some sort. To direct contest work successfully anywhere presupposes a familiarity with local regulations, procedures, and programs.

Sometimes in preparation for the contests scheduled by the state association, the teacher wishes to hold preparatory, or preliminary competitions. These usually should be scheduled very early in the season. For example, all the interested students in two or more neighboring schools may get together for the purpose of working on the debate proposition. One teacher describes a Saturday meeting of this sort in a town where there is a teacher's college. Thirty students from each of two high schools got together with a class of prospective speech teachers. In the morning, with the help of their coaches, the students evaluated materials, authorities, and sources; discovered issues; and planned arguments. After that, they divided into teams of two, one representative from each school, and worked together until lunch time on cases that were to be presented in the afternoon. Lunch was a simple but pleasant potluck affair, served in the home economics room. Immediately following the lunch hour, fifteen debates were held in fifteen different rooms, with a prospective teacher or a coach in each room. Everyone did as well as he could with the training he had had, and received a critical evaluation. The day closed with a general assembly where significant matters growing out of the debates were brought up and discussed.

Similar meetings often are planned to give interested students experience in extemporaneous speaking and reading, oratory, or declamation. Students and faculty members get together after school or on Saturday, exchange materials, prepare readings and speeches, and present programs. Such procedures are more motivating and challenging than the regular after-class work periods and usually are worth the extra effort which they involve.

When there is no national, state, or local organization to plan contests, several schools may get together and organize a small association. It may be helpful to get from such organizations as the National Forensic League, or the State Speech Association sample constitutions and by-laws. These can be used as guides in organizing local leagues. They may help teachers to anticipate and solve problems. They frequently contain suggestions and regulations for conducting contests, which can be adapted to local conditions.

TRAINING STUDENTS FOR PARTICIPATION

Some people mistakenly think of contest speaking as different from speaking in other life situations; they look for special methods of training and distinctive styles of delivery. Such a point of view is most unfortunate. All of the principles of training in conversation in Chapter 12, for example, apply to the improvement of conversation in connection with speech tournaments as well. All of the suggestions for gathering and preparing materials for speaking, discussing, debating, reading, storytelling, and acting, in other sections of Part II and Part III of this text, should be applied in preparing for contests in these various forms of speech. This entire book is devoted to ways and means of training for and judging effective talk, in and out of high school. In every part, it applies to contests. The best coach is the teacher who understands best how to improve speech habits.

A committee of the Speech Association of America, in a report to the Commission on Secondary Schools of the North Central Association, recommends the following:

1. That co-curricular events be regarded as counterparts of curricular instruction.
2. That co-curricular events be integrated as closely as possible with class instruction.
3. That co-curricular speech activities be directed by a teacher whose qualifications are in every sense equal to those of persons teaching speech courses.

4. That the person directing co-curricular speech activities be given every right and privilege of other teachers, including the right to have the extra-class teaching counted as part of his program load.[1]

HELPING STUDENTS TO GET THE MOST OUT OF SPEECH CONTESTS

Speech teachers who accept positions where training for contests is part of their assignment are in honor bound to make every effort to see that students profit by their experiences in these activities. This obligation can be met in three ways.

Make Speech Training for Contests Worth While

If the speech teacher has mastered the principles of speech improvement and applies them in training boys and girls for contests and festivals as he would in training them for all other types of speaking, students will improve and always will be grateful for the training which they received regardless of whether they were rated first or last, A or C, by the judges.

Help Students to Make Use of the Judge's Reactions

The value of an expert judge is not that he is necessarily infallible, but that he is a competent critic, making honest, concrete appraisals of the speakers. He does not assert that there is only one right decision; he claims only to be a person of training and experience who has seen and heard many speakers, readers, and actors, and has noted how and why speech behavior fails or succeeds. Usually he talks over his reactions with contestants. He tries to make his criticisms constructive and helpful. He admits that his rating of a contestant is only his estimate, which should be taken for what it is worth, no more and no less. He makes clear that good judges may disagree, and he suggests to students that they can profit by getting other judgments, even by analyzing disagreements among judges.

Professor Ralph Nichols of the University of Minnesota received an interesting letter from a student contestant who had used one

---

[1] *Quarterly Journal of Speech*, "A Program of Speech Education," (October, 1951), Vol. 37, 3: 356.

judge's reactions as a judge's critique should be used. She began, "I just want you to know that your giving advice to eager speakers in the district is really worth the effort. Thanks to your emphasis on exposition, I managed to get a superior rating in the state contest. It's funny, but it had never occurred to me before that it would be possible to make up a story to illustrate a point. It's a lot more fun to talk in stories, too." After some very fine comments on what she considered the strong and weak points in the contest as conducted and a number of valuable constructive suggestions, she closed with, "Thanks again for your suggestions. They constitute most of the specific extemporaneous speech training I have had."

Helping Students to Profit from Trips

It is true that students will gain much from trips to tournaments, festivals, and contests, even if no specific preparation is made for meeting and conversing with other students, parents, and faculty members from other schools; or for registering at hotels; buying meals in restaurants or diners; riding in sleepers or on airplanes; or taking a street car or bus for the first time. It is also true that students can be directed to richer benefits if they are prepared carefully for what they are to do. When one considers that a typical ninth grader, six weeks before a tournament, wanted the teacher's advice on the best shirt to wear in giving his talk, it is clear that detailed preparation for a speech trip is the kind of project that teachers pray for. The student sees in it a need to make speech function effectively in a real and new life experience and he will prepare diligently in order to be successful and apply what he has learned, from the time he leaves home to the time he returns to tell his friends in detail about his trip.

SUMMARY

This chapter has aimed to show that contests have developed and survived to fill real community, school, and individual needs. It has emphasized the importance for speech teachers of a clear and well defined point of view regarding the values of competition in speech. It has reviewed the nature of training for contest or festival speaking. It has pointed out specific ways of helping students to profit by the comments of critic judges. Finally, it has urged making the interschool trips real-life projects, sufficiently significant to receive the direct, detailed attention of the successful teacher of speech.

SELECTED BIBLIOGRAPHIES

Abernathy, Elton, "The Criticism Against Speech Tournaments," *Quarterly Journal of Speech* (October, 1942), 28: 354–356.

"A Program of Speech Education" (prepared by a committee of the Speech Association of America for the Contest Committee of the North Central Association), *Quarterly Journal of Speech* (November, 1951), 37: 347–358.

Bavely, Ernest. *Drama Festivals and Contests.* Boston: Walter H. Baker Co., 1940.

Caldwell, Russell, "Building a Program of Extra-Curricular Speech in the High School," *Quarterly Journal of Speech* (October, 1936), 22: 397–400.

Ewbank, Henry L., "Speech Contests as Educational Techniques," *Quarterly Journal of Speech* (April, 1936), 22: 187–196.

Manning, George A., "A View of Speech Contests," *Bulletin of Secondary School Principals* (January, 1948), 32: 151, pp. 210–211.

Robinson, Karl F., *Teaching Speech in the Secondary School.* New York: Longmans, Green & Co., Inc., 1951, Chs. 19–22.

PART IV

Criticism and Evaluation

CHAPTER 21

The Criticism of
Classroom Speaking

W E HAVE suggested earlier that one of the major activities of the speech teacher is criticism. Inevitably, the speech teacher is plunged into the task of criticizing the speaking of a large number of persons, in a variety of circumstances. The fact that he is paid for such criticism suggests that he ought to display expertness of judgment, and expertness in knowing what to criticize and when to criticize.

Good speech teachers ought to approach this function of criticism with at least some feelings of trepidation, if not of downright alarm. To feel otherwise would imply a startling lack of understanding of the enormous complexity of the act of speaking, and of the pitfalls and possibilities of error which beset the path of any person who presumes to criticize the speech of another. Speech teachers may take warning by reflecting upon the general fate of critics in all walks of life, particularly the fate of the professional critics of drama and literature, who are apt to find their right to a livelihood, if not their right to live, periodically challenged by the persons whose work they evaluate. Speech teachers may take some comfort in the fact that their students are seldom either as attentive or as sensitive as the artists who bear the shock of professional criticism.

THE ROLE OF THE SPEECH TEACHER AS CRITIC

Of course, as a critic, the speech teacher fills a role somewhat different from that assumed by the professional critic of drama, literature, radio, or any of the allied forms of creative endeavor. Members of the latter group may differ among themselves as to their exact function, but they share a general belief that they are in the business of improving art forms by systematically encouraging the public to patronize the more reputable products, and by warning the public against the unworthy. Some critics, needless to say, regard the function of warning the public either as more entertaining or more necessary than the function of encouragement! Moreover, professional critics as a group are not above seizing upon the work of an unfortunate creative artist and exploiting it as a medium for demonstrating their own superior wit; they seem little worried about the feelings of those whose work they pillory. The professional critic who quipped, "Last night Mr. Blank played Hamlet; Hamlet lost," was not necessarily trying to encourage the actor to do better work, although he, might indirectly have produced this effect. He belonged rather to the school of criticism in which the role of the critic has been tersely defined as that of "delivering a clean blow, leaving the head standing."

The speech teacher's role as a critic is obviously very different from the role of the professional art and drama critic. His major objective always is to promote the growth of the student whose work he appraises. He automatically renounces all temptation to expand his own ego at the expense of the students with whom he works. Moreover, he tempers his judgment of the objective worth of a student's performance by remembering the needs and capacities of the student. Sometimes this combination of concern for the welfare of the student and evaluation of his performance leads to praising aspects of speaking which would not rate high on any absolute scale. Sometimes it counsels the substitution of kindly and judicious silence for possible condemnation. This action does not imply dishonesty on the part of the teacher-critic. While his ultimate goal is to bring each student to a valid, objective appraisal of his own capabilities, this is a long range goal, to be reached only by considered and accurate judgments of the personality needs of each student, at each stage of his development as a speaker. The good teacher knows very well that the quickest way to stifle improvement in the speaking of a high school student is to deny him all sense of satisfaction from his speaking; that students come to know themselves not from blunt, comprehensive, dogmatic, and uncomplimentary statements by critics—statements which arouse resentment rather than a desire for betterment—but by careful guidance in developing their judgment about the characteristics of good speech generally, and equally careful guidance in the path of self appraisal and understanding. As a critic, therefore, the speech teacher is confronted with the necessity for making two types of judgments: (1) Judgments about the personality needs and speech potentialities of the speaker, and (2) judgments about the absolute worth of a particular speaking performance. His criticism of any speaker is then what he thinks ought to be said in the light of these judgments. Since judgments about personal needs and abilities and judgments about the quality of speaking performances are both subject to considerable error, it becomes apparent that a competent teacher of speech is in need of extensive experience with young speakers and a recognition of his own fallibility.

We have stated earlier in this book that not all practice in speaking results in improved speech; some of it might better be left undone. We suggest here that not all criticism is helpful to students; some of it might better be left unsaid. A teacher with a keen sense of his own limitations is likely to avail himself occasionally of the right to be noncommittal.

Before setting forth certain positive suggestions concerning the speech teacher's task as critic, it is important to examine in greater detail the nature of the problems he faces. These problems, as we have already suggested, fall into three areas: (1) Those related to the judgment of the speaking performance, (2) those related to the needs of students, and (3) those related to the organization and phrasing of criticism. Let us consider these in turn.

PROBLEMS IN JUDGING SPEAKING PERFORMANCE

The Search for Standards

In the preceding chapters on the various aspects of speaking performance, action, voice, language, thought and attitude, we have set forth the usual goals sought through the high school speech curriculum. In a very real sense, the standards according to which a particular speaking performance is to be judged are established by the goal sought by the speaker. The standards of criticism are largely set by the purposes of the students who speak. Students who share in setting the goals of their speaking activities, and who feel personal involvement in a struggle to attain those goals, have already fixed the basis of the criticisms they wish to receive subsequent to their performance.

The speech teacher's problems in the field of criticism are greatly reduced if the performance has both a legitimate communicative purpose and a specific personal improvement goal for the speaker. Any purposeful activity creates its own standards of criticism in terms of the requirements of its purpose. Thus, a student who has as his purpose giving information to an audience, automatically faces the criterion implied in the question, Did the audience get the information?

While it is true that the purpose of an activity evolves its own critical standards, it is also true that critical standards held by the speech teacher relative to acts of speaking inevitably tend to shape the sort of purposes that may be set for speech improvement in his classroom. The teacher's notion of what constitutes good or poor speaking, his ideas concerning which matters are most important and which are trivial, will determine what type of speech class he will organize, and what sorts of speaking he will encourage. Therefore, one of the most significant self-inquiries any speech teacher can make is that which seeks to establish the sources and nature of the standards upon which he judges the worth of speaking performance. It is a question with philosophic overtones, and, therefore, not likely to be completely answered by any teacher in any finite period of time. Nevertheless, it is an inquiry in which most speech teachers engage, and ought to engage, most seriously and persistently.

The Dangerous Search for Absolutes

Teachers and others who have thought but little about the nature of speech always are powerfully intrigued by the search for absolute standards of rightness or wrongness which apply to all speaking

performances. The strength of the urge to discover such standards is understandable enough. Once a speech teacher has a set of
such standards, he can join the circle of comfortable and satisfied
teachers who know with certainty whether their students are performing well or poorly. The teacher of mathematics, unless overly
involved in Einstein's theories, feels little or no indecision when
confronted by a student's statement that 2 and 2 equal 5; the
chemistry teacher knows at least one critical comment to make
to the student who announces that the formula for water is HO_2.
Why should not the speech teacher be able to say with the assurance of the learned, "Johnny, you made several errors. During
your introduction, your left foot should have been in front of your
right; you should have gestured during the last sentence of your
second major topic; your conclusion should have been delivered
with a more orotund vocal quality; and please remember that the
phrase is 'different from,' not 'different than.' Now, try your
speech over, and get it right this time."

Obviously, a teacher with a well developed set of absolutes about
speech is in an enviable position compared with a colleague assailed
by doubts and uncertainties. He is spared much thought and worry.
He escapes the scorn students save for teachers who "don't know
what they want." And he revels in the praise of that large segment
of society which is eager to share quickly in the secret knowledge
and techniques that sell brushes or move the hearts of men. So
compelling are the pressures for setting standards of some sort,
that one suspects many speech teachers of paraphrasing Voltaire's
comment about God, and saying, "If there are no standards of right
and wrong in speaking, I shall have to invent some."

The Sources of Standards

While there are standards by which the worth of an act of
speaking can be judged, the speech teacher should not confuse
these with the more exact standards of mathematics or physics.
Moreover, the speech teacher should not be unaware of the tem-
porary or localized applicability of some of these standards. Speech
standards are not exact for the reason that the work of a specific
act of speaking varies from speaker to speaker, from situation to

situation, and from occasion to occasion. The speech which is appropriate, and thus effective, at a football banquet may fail dismally at a high school commencement. The verbal and vocal mannerisms appropriate, and hence effective, to a diminutive sophomore girl may be little short of startling if adopted by an older classmate of more formidable proportions.

One standard of good speech is its effectiveness. As Weaver and Borchers observe, "The speaker who, in the shortest time, can induce those whom he addresses to do willingly what he wants them to do is the best speaker." [1] Yet this very standard of effectiveness means that each act of speaking must be judged independently, and that its rightness or wrongness can be determined only in the context of the total situation in which occurs—the person speaking, the purpose for which he speaks, the occasion on which he speaks, and the audience to whom he speaks.

If the standards of good speaking must be related to a particular speaker and situation, they also must be appraised in the context of a particular culture or period of history. For example, we have come to see that the pronunciation of a word is right or wrong only to the extent that a group of people accept that pronunciation as right or wrong, and that the good, or preferred, pronunciation of a word may vary from one section of the country to another, or from one period of time to another. What is true of the pronunciation of words is true also of most of the other conventional aspects of the speech process, including usage of symbolic visible and vocal activity, and the like. Standards of good speaking, with respect to these conventions, derive from a particular culture, and are enduring or fleeting in proportion to the stability of the aspect of that culture which they represent. The speech class and the speech teacher should assist students to use forms which are not obtrusive or conspicuous in the immediate culture in which these students move, or in a broader society in which they may want to move. The speech class should also help students to evaluate these conventions for what they are, so that as speakers they may be spared the foolishness of regarding these transitory forms as permanent or universal necessities.

---

[1] Weaver, A. T. and Borchers, G. L., *Speech*. New York: Harcourt, Brace & Co., 1946, p. 20.

Empirical and Normative Judgments

At this point in our discussion it is possible to identify at least two relatively discrete sources for the judgments teachers make about the worth of acts of speaking. These two sources are based on different ways of looking at the value of speech, they result in different sorts of statements about speech, and they contribute in somewhat different ways to the development of speaking skills.

The first source of judgment is experience, and it gives rise to what we shall call empirical criticism. Empirical standards are derived from observation of the effectiveness of particular acts of speaking, in the actual situations in which they take place. Such judgments operate with the criterion of effect as a frame of reference, and seek to make statements interpreting the reasons for believing a speech to be appropriate or inappropriate to the actual circumstances in which it occurs. The teacher makes empirical judgments on the basis of his own reactions to an act of speaking, on the basis of his observations of the reactions of other auditors, and upon a basis of his own sensitivity to diverse factors in the situation of which the speaker did or did not seem aware. The teacher may make such statements as, "I couldn't accept your opinions very easily because you seemed to question their value yourself," or, "I wouldn't be surprised if your first statement about farmers irritated some members of your audience. Let's check on this, and, if it did happen, consider why it happened." Or, "You acted as though you had the most interesting subject in the world, and I believe that is one of the reasons I found your talk so interesting." Teachers should be careful always to help students realize that the sort of speaking which elicits a good response on one occasion may get a poor response on a different occasion. They also should stress those factors about the speech which made it successful, or otherwise, and which probably affect the success of speeches in most situations. Thus, a particular, or empirical judgment about the effect of a speaker's pleasantness of manner on a certain occasion may be the basis for a more general observation about the wide utility of pleasant attitudes in our society. The speaker may be told that not only was his pleasantness effective on this particular occasion, but that it probably will be effective on other occasions also.

It would be quite possible for speech teachers to limit themselves to empirical judgments about acts of speaking, to encourage their classes to do likewise, and still to teach their students to speak more effectively. The bulk of speech training is conducted in terms of pragmatic and empirical judgments, and a great part of its value lies in the sort of practical discipline it gives students in judging and meeting the varying problems in immediate and specific situations. Professor O'Neill has observed that one of the major values of speech training is that which accrues to it from its essential nature as "rhetoric on the hoof." A student comes face to face with the evidence of his own success or failure in achieving some goal in communication, and he sees his audience as an integral part of his future calculations about the nature of speech and speech situations.

However, it is not often that speech teachers limit themselves to such empirical judgments. Classroom speaking situations present the student with only a limited number of auditors and a limited number of speaking problems. Within the tradition of speech education and the experience of speech teachers are to be found criteria which may be applied to speech, without too much attention to immediate effectiveness. Teachers long have recognized the limitations of the standard of immediate effect in judging a speech. Quintilian, the pragmatic Roman, defined the orator as "a good man, skilled in speaking," and thus injected an element of ethical behavior into the criticism of speech. In our own day, most speech teachers would probably agree with Knower, that while "all good speech is effective, not all effective speech is good."

Over and beyond considerations of effect in the immediate situation, we make a good many judgments about the worth of an act of speaking based upon more or less stable norms or standards of behavior in the society in which our students must operate. Such judgments we shall call normative. Thus, the second source of our judgments lies in certain norms of society. One of the most important bodies of normative criteria, which is traditionally within the scope of the speech teacher's standards, is that furnished by logic. Arguments, by virtue of their form, are held to possess or lack internal validity. Moreover, according to logical standards, conclusions based upon evidence raise problems of the credibility of evidence, and of valid connections between and among various items of evidence. Speech teachers are seldom reluctant to appraise the validity of an argument in the light of their own study of logic, regardless of the effectiveness of the argument in the circumstance in which it was used. Such normative criticism looks toward the possible values to society of educating people to be careful in their use of evidence, and their statement of arguments. The development of critical thinking ability in students is not unrelated to the effective use of speech; in the classroom, at least, it often transcends questions about the immediate effectiveness of an act of speech. Thus a teacher may criticize a speech for some shortcoming in thinking which he detects, even though the audience generally is indifferent to the fault.

Other normative judgments enter into the criticism of speech from the area of ethics. "It is bad speaking to distort the facts of a case intentionally." "It is bad speaking to stir up hatreds and antagonisms among people intentionally in order to accomplish the speaker's objective." Judgments of this sort are clearly normative, and the ethical standards upon which they are based are relatively stable in our society. No speech teacher can avoid the application of the principles of honesty, fair-dealing, sincerity, courage, and the like in his criticism of speech behavior.

While normative judgments about matters of logic and matters of ethical behavior seem to possess stability and universality in our society, there are other obviously culturally-derived norms of speech which have less permanence and probably less significance, but which are not wholly without importance. Conventional English usage, at various cultural levels, sets up norms for language structure based upon the usage of society generally, or, in some cases, the "usage of the best educated." This latter norm long has been popular in schools, but it has become increasingly dubious as a standard to be applied to all speakers, in all situations. Standards of pronunciation are also based upon cultural norms and so, it would seem, are many of the phonetic characteristics of American speech, including patterns of inflection, emphasis, and rhythm.

Many of these cultural and conventional norms are exceedingly transient; others, less so. English and speech teachers have traditionally defended these norms, or at least some of them, as a part of our educational inheritance. Doubtless, this defense has slowed down change in language forms, and has helped students to avoid the stigma sometimes attached to non-standard speech by the un-thinking. However, insistence upon adherence to these norms be-comes foolish when transient standards are given a fictitious intrinsic worth, and are defended with greater fervor and anxiety than are the more stable norms of logic and ethics. Sometimes the defenders of language forms become so deeply committed to certain positions that they continue to battle for the enforcement of judgments about language which have ceased to represent the usage of any consider-able cultural group. The artificiality of so-called "standard speech" should warn teachers not to enlist under its false banner.

We have indicated that speech teachers use both empirical and normative criteria in criticizing speaking. The quest for, or urge to establish a single point of reference for criticism has led to much soul searching and not a little rationalization on the part of speech teachers—much of it designed to show that normative standards for speech are also empirically or pragmatically sound. The pull toward a pragmatic justification for all criticism is obvious enough in American society; it has been a reasonably consistent part of the entire tradition of criticism. Thus, teachers of speech and rhetoric long have sought to set up a pragmatic justification for asking stu-dents to acquire a working knowledge of the principles of logic. The student is asked to develop skill in reasoning not merely to be able to make more useful judgments of facts, or to be able to con-verse more easily with those who adhere to similar standards of discourse, but because, in some mysterious way, this skill improves one's effectiveness in speech. Similarly, it is interesting to note the pragmatic twist often given to simple, normative, ethical judgments; the debate coach's, "You made a misstatement of fact," becomes "Watch your statements of fact, or someone will catch you and make you look foolish."

The tendency of some teachers of speech to unify their criticism of acts of speaking around empirical judgments is balanced by the tendency of others to look increasingly for universal normative standards. An interesting example of this drive toward normative evaluation is found in some of the writing of teachers who have become interested in the field called "general semantics." Many of these teachers have assumed that language has only one legitimate function—promoting understanding among people—and that only language which meets rather severe tests of making sense should be cultivated in the speech classroom. Such teachers, if we are to judge from the emphasis in their writings, are interested in conforming mankind's use of speech to certain rather rigid concepts of the nature of good speaking. They are sharply critical of the sort of speech training which emphasizes the equipping of students to use speech effectively in the world in which they find themselves. Speech teachers, of course, ought to study the problems of the sort of norms for good speech which are to be established in their classroom, but, in so doing, they should not forget the unique practical results that have come from the speech training which stresses empirical judgments.

There is little or no evidence that a really comprehensive unification of normative and empirical criteria for the criticism of speaking is at hand. Speech teachers do not need to be too greatly alarmed about the use of criticism emanating from two very different sources. A good balance of the two sorts of criticism may be the soundest kind of program for the classroom. Moreover, both empirical and normative criticisms are apt to be strengthened through the frank recognition by the teacher and the students of the two different bases upon which criticism can be conducted, and of the uses and limitations of each.

The Problem of Personal Norms

One of the problems faced by the speech teacher in the application of criticism is the tendency to elevate his own personal preferences to the level of cultural standards held by all educated people, or even to the level of norms which ought to be universally observed. Thus a teacher may settle upon some standard of over-precise articulation as characteristic of cultivated speech, merely because it is either characteristic of the speech he himself uses, or of the speech he likes to hear. He then may classify as "slovenly articulation" the sort of conversational diction common to the high school community which he serves. He may go further and inform his students that "educated people don't speak the way you do," and perhaps expect them to take this judgment seriously despite the fact that many of the people admired and respected by these students do speak that way. The fact that teachers or scholars may even discover that the sort of speech they value is not only culturally sound, but also intrinsically valid, is illustrated by an interesting passage from an English scholar, H. C. Wyld:

> Everyone knows that there is a kind of English which is neither provincial nor vulgar, a type which most people would willingly speak if they could, and desire to speak if they do not. . . . I suggest that this is the best kind of English, not only because it is spoken by those often very properly called "the best people," but because it has two advantages that make it intrinsically superior to every other type of English speech— the extent to which it is current throughout the country, and the marked distinctiveness and clarity of its sound.[2]

Observe that Professor Wyld carried his argument beyond the usual justifications given for a standard English pronunciation, the fact that it is spoken by educated persons, and that it is spoken widely; and continues to the point of finding intrinsic clarity and distinctiveness in the type of English which he prefers. One might ask, clarity and distinctiveness for whom?

How is a speech teacher to avoid the confusing of his personal predilections with those standards of speech which are truly representative of the culture in which the student will live and work? It would seem to be sound advice that the teacher ought to become a good student of the speech of his own culture, including the speech of the community in which he teaches, of its adults and its children. He ought to relate his own personal standards to close and continuing observations of the preferences of other persons. He ought to seek the help of other persons, including the high school students with whom he works, in developing and checking his own judgments. And he ought to try constantly to create for himself and his students the common ground of a sensible, comprehensive view of the speech act, helping his students to understand why different types of speech are effective in different circumstances, rather than trying to get them to believe that there is one type of speech which is always and inevitably the best. Of course, there probably always will be lonely speech teachers who will seek martyrdom in becoming the last bulwark of defense for some failing phoneme or some pretty posture. Martyrdom is a vocation of dignity, but it is not to be confused with teaching.

---

[2] From "The Best English," S.P.E. Tract No. XXXIX, New York: Oxford University Press, cited in Claude Kantner and Robert W. West, *Phonetics*. New York: Harper & Brothers, p. 265.

SOME OTHER PROBLEMS IN SPEECH CRITICISM

The Problem of Part Versus Whole

It has become almost a psychological platitude to observe that the whole of any complex act (such as speaking) is more than the arithmetic sum of its parts. Nevertheless, this is a truth of considerable significance to the speech teacher. The fact that a speech can succeed, despite obvious shortcomings in many of its elements or fail despite the excellence of most of its aspects, deserves careful attention by all speech teachers. Seemingly, some speakers can achieve great success despite specific weaknesses in their voice, or action, or language, although, of course, there are limits beyond which these weaknesses become devastating to any sort of communication. Seemingly, too, there are great individual variations in the pattern of speech within which different persons effectively accomplish their purposes in communication. This sometimes tenuous and indeterminate relationship between the specific elements of speaking skill, and the total effectiveness of the speaker, tends to leave the speech teacher in an uncomfortable dilemma. The criticism of speaking, to be effective, must ordinarily be limited and specific. Yet how can the teacher be certain that the specific aspect of speech which he selects for praise or blame is actually significant in the total speech process of the student who is being criticized?

This seeming dilemma is capable of sensible resolution. What it implies is not that the speech teacher should be reduced to a state of guilty silence, but that he should select a specific aspect of the student's speech for comment, only after he has judged the student's speech in its totality, making tentative decisions as to which of this student's potentialities seem to be worthy of development, and which of his weaknesses might be eliminated to good effect. Each speech represents a unique problem in criticism, calling for a new judgment on the part of the critic as to the particular structure of success or failure which is represented by it.

Furthermore, the fact that the effect of any speech is total would seem to imply that ofttimes the most successful road to improved speech is found by helping a speaker develop his assets, rather than by turning his attention to the job of whittling away his liabilities. Frequently a speaker will present some notable deficiency which is not susceptible to modification, e.g., a lack of physical size or vigor. But this same student may have some potential source of power as a speaker, which, if developed, will make the deficiency seem relatively unimportant. The history of public speaking is filled with examples of such successful compensation. One thinks of the vocal limitations of Abraham Lincoln, whose ". . . thin, high-pitched voice, carrying nasal overtones, . . ." [3] did not prevent him from attaining enduring fame for eloquence.

The idea that the speech teacher should build on the strengths of speakers instead of dwelling on their weaknesses is not a universal precept. There are times when judgment dictates that a speaker should attempt to eliminate some conspicuous weakness; getting rid of the handicap may prove the quickest road to speech improvement. It is good advice, however, for the speech teacher to examine each student initially from the point of view of discovering his potential strengths. If he finds the direction along which the student has already made the greatest progress as a speaker, he may also find the path along which future development will proceed most efficiently.

A final suggestion may help some teachers in the process of reacting to a speech in its entirety instead of becoming preoccupied with particular aspects. Thonssen and Gilkinson, in the introduction to their text, *Basic Training in Speech*, suggest that a good critic ought to "Relax to the main purpose of the speaker. It is possible," they write, "for a . . . listener to become so interested in finding something to criticize that he fails to react in a normal way to the speaker." They suggest that a critic ought to try to listen to a classroom speech as he would listen in a non-classroom situation, allowing what is good or bad to come to his attention in a "normal way." [4]

This seems to be good advice, although it sometimes is difficult for the critic to follow. It requires of the speech teacher a unique capacity to accept each act of speaking to which he listens on its own merits—an ability that enables him to put aside preconceptions and prejudices as he becomes a member of the student's

---

[3] M. Berry, "Abraham Lincoln: His Development in the Skills," in *History of Public Address*. Vol. II. New York: McGraw-Hill Book Co., 1943, p. 853.

[4] Lester Thonssen and Howard Gilkinson, *Basic Training in Speech*. (Brief Edition) Boston: D. C. Heath & Co., 1949, p. 6.

audience. It demands that the speech teacher avoid the repetition of stereotyped criticism as he proceeds from one speaker to another. In short, it demands from the speech teacher a sort of revitalized receptiveness at the outset of each speaking act which he proposes to observe and appraise.

The Problem of the Easily Observed Versus the Significant

Not all aspects of a speaking performance may be observed with equal ease. Certain characteristics of a public speech are readily describable. Once problems of terminology have been solved, a group of critics may reach a reasonable consensus on such matters as a speaker's level of physical animation, his rate of speech, his use of pitch variation, and the like, although the critics may differ in their evaluation of the significance of what they observe in the speaker's effectiveness. There are other aspects of a public speech which are relatively difficult to identify or describe—the clarity or appropriateness of the speech structure, the relevance of the speaker's language to the meanings he intended to arouse, or the validity of a particular deduction. Matters such as these are observed, if at all, only as the product of active and vigorous analysis by an attentive critic.

Experienced speech teachers find it easy to acquire fluency and relative assurance in discussing many of the surface characteristics of speech, and as a result it may be that in their criticism they place undue emphasis upon details which are easily observed and talked about, while avoiding discussion of other matters more subtle and more difficult to bring to the attention of speakers. This is not to suggest that the mere fact that some aspect of speech is easily observed automatically makes it of less importance than some more obscure facet of the speech process. It is to say, however, that speech teachers must guard against the natural tendency to allow easily observed matters to predominate in their criticism.

Speech teachers ought to realize that the frequency with which they make particular comments about speaking will be taken by the students as some indication of the relative importance they attach to the various elements of the process. Thus, a high school teacher who makes more observations about "inadequate eye contact" in her class than about any other aspect of speaking, should not be surprised to find her students assuming that good eye contact is the most important principle of good speaking. And thus, a teacher who centers her criticism on surface aspects of the good speech process may distort the scale of values which her students use to judge speech.

There is no easy answer to the problem faced by the speech teacher in attaining balanced criticism of speech performance. Certainly, teachers need to practice self-criticism in this respect. They need to ask frequently if their criticisms of students reflect a balanced and mature view of the speech process, and if their criticisms are determined by observations which are most significant or by observations which are most convenient. Speech teachers need to realize that criticism is an active and an arduous process, and that the sort of criticism which flows easily from tongue or pen may well be compounded of phrases grown meaningless from overuse, rather than the product of vigorous and alert present judgment.

Summary

In discussing the criticism of speeches, we have observed that effective criticism is made possible by speech performances which are purposive in nature, and that the more specific the purpose of a performance, the more specific can be its criticism. A good speech assignment, therefore, reveals the nature and form of the criticism that is to follow. The teacher's judgments concerning the nature of good speech, however, shape his assignments as well as his criticism. Therefore, speech teachers need to examine the bases of their judgments about speech. Most teachers make two general types of judgments about speech—the pragmatic and the normative. Balanced criticism involves the use of both types. It is easier to maintain balance in criticism if one avoids confusing these two types and avoids altogether using personal norms. The good critic should be a student of speech in his own immediate social environment. He needs also to avoid the twin pitfalls of preoccupation with the elements of speech to the exclusion of its totality, and preoccupation with the easily observed to the exclusion of the more obscure but more significant.

CRITICISM AND THE NEEDS OF SCHOOL CHILDREN

The speech teacher's problems in criticism would be serious enough if they were related exclusively to the worth of a single, particular speaking performance. But, as we already have indicated, not all of his judgments, and perhaps not even all of his most important judgments, are related to the speech itself. As a teacher, the center of his attention always should be the child, himself, and the needs of the child, as a person as well as a speaker. It takes no special insight to realize that the truth of a criticism carries no fixed relationship to its teaching potential.

Children, or adults for that matter, seldom profit from criticism which arouses resentment or pain. All sorts of peculiar things may happen to an unpleasant or unwelcome comment to prevent its being registered in consciousness as an effective determinant of future behavior. For one thing, mankind seems to possess special capacity for forgetting disagreeable statements. Memory is selective; we tend to remember what we like to hear, and to forget what we do not care to hear. Forgetting is the active process of sublimating the unpleasant. Moreover, we not only possess ability to forget the unpleasant, we are skilled in distorting it. An accurate but distasteful comment may easily be converted by the auditor into an agreeable but inaccurate one. In this way the child who is criticized justifies his resentment of the critic, and changes the criticism into an obvious absurdity which merits no attention. It is reasonable to believe that whenever criticism arouses active disagreement in the person criticized, its possible benefit is slight indeed.

From the foregoing it is obvious that speech criticism which results in, or is subsequent to, a state of tension between teacher and pupil has little value in accomplishing the purposes of the speech class. The first task of every speech teacher is to build with his students that atmosphere of rapport which will permit the frankest and most honest sort of discussion of speech performance and needs. Until this spirit is in existence, much criticism, particularly of a negative character, ought to be avoided. It is to be feared that some speech teachers feel compelled to make searching criticisms of speaking from the first day of class, prompted no doubt by the oppressive realization that there is so little time available in which to present their accumulated wisdom to their students. An occasional vow of silence might be appropriate for such teachers; certainly the early weeks of a speech class ought to be a time of information-getting and rapport building on the part of the teacher. It is well to remember that a single criticism, sought after, accepted, and thought about by the student, is of more value than an endless flow of advice which is ignored or distorted.

To say that speech teachers ought to build rapport is to say little; to say how they can build rapport would be to say much, more indeed than is possible in this chapter, since such a problem opens up the whole field of human relations. Certain observations about rapport-building as it relates to the teacher as a critic are possible here, however.

First of all, it is obvious that students find praise less difficult to accept than blame, and there would seem little reason for a speech teacher to withhold praise or encouragement. The speech class is first and foremost one in which a variety of personality types and adjustment patterns may find success or, at least, some satisfaction. It is no place for the teacher whose ideas of "proper" behavior are rigidly fixed. At the same time, excessive devotion at the altar of positive criticism and permissive indulgence is apt to build neither rapport nor an intelligent view of the speech process. The teacher who praises indiscriminately and who offends the intelligence of some students in order to pamper the susceptibilities of others, can hardly hope to achieve a situation in which serious criticism will be taken seriously. The happy balance of accurate appraisal without distortion and encouragement without inaccuracy is to be sought after. This balance is one which is adjusted, however, not only to the total class, but also to individuals within the class. Thus all the students in the speech class share the personality need for approval and success, but they find satisfaction of such needs in a variety of ways. In other words, one child may have his need for approval fulfilled outside the speech class, e.g., in the approval of friends or parents. Another may be so insecure that his need for an extra ration of success or recognition becomes the key not only to much of his speech behavior, but also to the sort of approach which the teacher's criticism must take to be effective.

It is interesting to observe that students differ not only in their need for praise, or for success in speaking, but also in their sensitivity to certain aspects of their own speech. Thus, an adolescent girl may accept negative comment on the organization of her material, with the greatest of objectivity, and the highest resolve for improvement. Adverse public comment on her posture or her manner of walking, on the other hand, may evoke feelings of humiliation and resentment in her. These patterns which determine the differential sensitivity of individuals to criticism are common to our culture; e.g., a person's complexion is more personal than his English usage, and his clothing is more personal than the orderliness of his thoughts. These patterns are also related directly to the individual's experience. It requires a high order of awareness on the part of the teacher to appreciate the responses which his criticism is getting from an individual, an alertness to the fact that certain aspects of criticism are arousing unexpected emotionality.

The teacher who is building rapport attends to the personality needs of the members of his group. High school students are quick to concede the necessity for criticism, if the matter is discussed with them. They are quick to accept the need for balance in criticism, and for objectivity in reacting to adverse criticism. Ordinarily they will co-operate in building the sort of pattern of criticism most teachers would desire, provided their co-operation is sought. One of the early tasks of every speech teacher is to organize with his class the sort of discussion of criticism which will lead to setting a group pattern of permissiveness and objectivity with respect to an atmosphere in which criticism is sought as a key to self-help. There is no reason for indirection in such discussion, since here is a case in which the interests of teacher and students coincide. It should be explained that the development of desirable attitudes toward criticism, and social skill in the giving of criticism are objectives necessary not only to effective speech training, but also to social living in its own right.

THE TEACHER'S EGO

A final word may aid in understanding the speech teacher's role. Those who discuss the job of the teacher often dwell upon the child as a person, and sometimes seem to forget that teachers are people too; they are subject to personality needs, tensions, and frustrations of their own. The teacher's almost unlimited right of criticism provides him a unique opportunity for ego inflation. To the frustrated teacher or the teacher with marked inferiority feelings, the weapons of ridicule, sarcasm, or more subtle sadism may become the instruments of self-satisfaction. Speech teachers, particularly, need to be aware of the opportunities their jobs offer for self-inflation and self-justification. As critics they have the chance to expand their wit at the expense of unfortunate students, and if their wit be genuine it may win the applause of all save its victims. The critics are in a position to be dogmatic, domineering, ironical, or satirical, and to justify such attitudes as part of their professional duty. They would be less than human if they did not occasionally seek their own satisfaction. They are less than teachers if they do not derive their greatest personal satisfaction from the development of their students.

Summary

Knowing when to criticize is as important as knowing what to criticize. The speech teacher must judge constantly the readiness of a particular child for particular criticisms. Until rapport is established, negative criticism should be kept at an irreducible minimum, but there is no point at which the teacher can feel free of responsibility for judging the individual needs and patterns of readiness of members of the class.

One of the most important discussion topics for a speech class should be the objectives and methods of criticism. Student cooperation can be obtained, and ought to be sought in building attitude toward criticism and skills in criticism. Such attitudes and skills are tools of first importance to the speech class; they are also, *per se*, important social skills.

THE LANGUAGE OF CRITICISM

The third major problem faced by the teacher-critic is that of actually communicating his judgments and evaluations to the members of the class. In its broadest sense, this is a problem as big as the teaching of speech. But, more narrowly viewed, there are particular considerations which may shape the language of classroom criticism, and which profitably may be discussed here.

One of these considerations is the developing of an efficient critical vocabulary for use in a given speech class. One of the purely intellectual tasks of the speech class is the establishment of a common descriptive language to be used with reference to the speech process. The speech process is total, but it can be talked about intelligently only in terms of a variety of categorizing terms whose meanings become relatively common. Some of these terms are developed with relative ease, such as rate, pitch, volume, inflectional pattern, quality, and rhythm. These terms have reasonably objective referents, and are used by speech teachers with ease, a fact which should not blind the teacher to the need for developing their meanings rather carefully with high school students. An often neglected but ever valuable activity of the speech class is that of making objective or factual statements about particular speeches, without using judgment or value statements.

Other critical terms have less objective referents, and need to have meanings developed in the common experiences of particular classes. Terms such as "conversational delivery," "projection," "valid arguments," and "problem-solution organization" carry a variety of private meanings for persons with different backgrounds. A whole body of literature has grown up around the terms "impersonation" and "interpretation," and no small portion of the literature is a dispute over the meaning of these terms.

It is sound advice for the speech teacher to examine his own technical vocabulary, to develop lists of words he uses or plans to use, and to check frequently the commonality of meaning attached to these words by members of his class. Such checks often reveal that his critical comments have little or no communicative value.

Precisely because criticism involves a semantic problem, it is probable that the best criticism is limited in scope, or at least unified in its referent. Most speech teachers recognize the practical value of including both praise and suggestions for improvement in each criticism, but beyond this they should ordinarily avoid criticism which pretends or seeks to be comprehensive. A single idea for improvement, understood and acted upon, is of more value to the student than a wealth of suggestions that are only vaguely apprehended. The most valuable asset of the critic is the ability to cut through to the one or two specific aspects of a speech performance most vitally related to total effect or total value, and to center discussion upon these items. Of equal importance with the items most related to total effect are items most closely related to the speaker's personal concerns. It is a happy circumstance when these two types of items turn out to be identical, but their identity is not inevitable. An interesting device for unifying criticism in terms of the performer's concerns is to have the speaker, either prior to his performance or immediately after it, raise one or two questions which he would most like to have the class or the teacher discuss. Such a procedure seems to relate criticism directly to the speaker's goal, at least to the extent that the speaker is willing to have his goals discussed.

In pointing out the desirability of unified and limited criticism as opposed to comprehensive criticism, we are referring only to the practical critical activities of the fundamentals class. If the class carries on critical discussion of speech manuscripts, radio or convocation speeches, motion pictures or plays, the need for more comprehensive categories of criticism becomes obvious.

Summary

We have discussed the three major types of problems facing the speech teacher-critic: (1) Those related to criticizing a speaking performance, (2) those relating to criticizing a performer, and (3) those related to the language of criticism. With respect to the third of these problems, we observed that the speech teacher needs to build a common technical vocabulary with his class, and needs further to unify his criticism around a few items pertinent to the total value of a performance, or pertinent to the concerns of the performer.

We shall now consider a variety of characteristics of the class which is organized for efficient criticism.

ORGANIZING THE SPEECH CLASS FOR EFFICIENT CRITICISM

The Use of Oral and Written Criticism

A good balance between oral and written criticism will ordinarily characterize the high school speech class. Although concerned with the same materials, these two forms of criticism should be considered complementary rather than substitutes for one another. The oral discussion of speeches becomes an essential method not only of giving information to a particular speaker, but also of developing the common vocabulary, the speech goals, and the speech values for the class. It is, in short, the indispensable means by which the class organizes and makes effective its learning about speech. A portion of speech education, it is true, probably consists in the developing of reactive patterns in the nervous system, patterns which represent sub-verbal learning. But much of it consists of information and generalization about the activity-criticism goal setting basis already discussed in Chapter 4.

Oral criticism, however indispensable, is time consuming. The speech teacher seldom can devote an equal amount of class time to the discussion of the performances of all the students. Often oral criticism avoids singling out the faults of one speaker by basing itself upon some general principle, observable in five or six performances.

Written criticism gives the teacher the opportunity to personalize criticism in a way not always possible in oral discussion; to diversify criticism according to the varied goals of different individuals; and to balance up the critical attention paid various members of the class.

Some aids to written criticism

It is doubtful that any more versatile, useful, or generally satisfactory aid to written criticism has been developed than an unlined pad of grocery slips, permitting the simultaneous production of original and carbon copies of written comments. Our whole concept of criticism, that it ought to be individual in terms of each student and each performance and that it ought to be limited in terms of the number of aspects discussed, points to the desirability of a completely unregimented or flexible system of comment. Moreover, the use of carbon copies of criticism is an efficient way of maintaining a file of comments on each student. Such a file, if periodically reviewed, is an excellent aid to forming judgments concerning individual needs and individual progress. Students may use such slips in commenting on one another's work, and again, the carbon copies make possible the gathering of information on growth in the critical capacity displayed by various members of the class. The following is a typical grocery slip.

Grocery slip—an unstructured comment

> Jim
>
> I enjoyed your introduction. You have the report idea now—your little story not only caught our attention, but also it led right into the central portion of your speech.
>
> Do you pronounce "indisputable" correctly? Check it and let me know.

A form for a structured comment

Speaker's Name_____Critic's Name_____

Title_____Date_____

Compliments: _____

_____

_____

_____

_____

_____

Suggestions: _____

_____

_____

_____

_____

_____

Check lists; rating scales; profile charts

Any teacher whose fingers have been numbed by the writing of endless comments knows the attractions of a check list or rating scale. The possibility of turning out an erudite criticism by the simple device of marking a few X's here and there is undeniably attractive; moreover, students are generally impressed by the official and authoritative appearance of rating scales. A generation brought up on newspaper psychologists, guidance experts, and personnel managers is in no position to question the utility of a rating scale, particularly if the scale uses an excellent type body and carries a resounding title!

Scales, check lists, and profile charts have their legitimate uses, particularly in developing speech report forms, or in conducting research where data should be comparable for all members of a group, or should be comprehensive with regard to some phase of speech. For such uses, these forms are invaluable. Their use for classroom criticism is limited. In their stereotyped format, and their use of comprehensive divisions and sub-divisions, they violate the very spirit of individual criticism. In suggesting that these devices are of limited value as a critical instrument, we should not overlook their possible use as a teaching device. Co-operative development and use of a rating scale or check list by the members of the class has obvious advantages for teaching.

Three types of check lists and rating scales are included here as examples of these rating devices. Teachers and students may find them helpful as a point of departure for other check lists and scales as methods of evaluation. In a limited way they provide a picture of the strengths and weaknesses of a speaker. Often group consideration of a given form will make for understanding, and prevent meaningless and careless checking for the sake of doing something. Furthermore, developing these methods will help students to review the essentials of the speech process with the greatest value resulting from the making, rather than the using, of the scale, and the resulting variety which is brought to classroom procedure.

A "Profile Rating" for comprehensive observation

SPEECH RATING

NAME: _____GRADE: _____DATE: _____

Each of the items on this rating scale is important in speech. Your rating on each item is an evaluation of your performance as observed in the classroom.

A rating of 1 is inferior; 2, below average; 3, average; 4, above average; 5, superior.

	1	2	3	4	5
I. Is your speaking effective?					
II. Is your speech properly audible?					
III. Is your articulation precise?					
IV. Is your speech fluent?					
V. Is your speech pleasing to the listener?					
VI. Is your speech meaningful?					
VII. Do you appear poised and confident while speaking?					
VIII. How well do you use English?					
IX. Is your thinking and organization clear and definite?					
X. Do you participate effectively in classroom discussion?					

A check list for observing informal classroom speaking

Name_____Date_____Class_____

_____ 1. Class seemed to enjoy.

_____ 2. Attitude good.

_____ 3. Attitude antagonistic, sullen.

_____ 4. Seemed bored, disinterested.

_____ 5. Talked too softly to be easily heard.

_____ 6. Voice monotonous.

_____ 7. Voice fades out out at ends of sentences.

_____ 8. Mumbles or runs words together.

_____ 9. Lacks clear articulation.

_____ 10. Talks too fast.

_____ 11. Mispronounced common words.

_____ 12. Used a variety of vocal expression.

_____ 13. Had uncertain, hesitant manner.

_____ 14. Had good eye contact with audience.

_____ 15. Appeared alert and confident.

_____ 16. Standing posture poor.

_____ 17. Sitting posture poor.

_____ 18. Started speaking before getting attention of audience.

_____ 19. Left platform while still speaking.

_____ 20. Showed nervous fidgeting.

_____ 21. Used good gestures.

_____ 22. Lacked gestures.

_____ 23. Looked at floor, window, or ceiling.

_____ 24. Used good evidence.

_____ 25. Used good stories or concrete examples.

_____ 26. Material well organized.

Name _____ Date _____ Class _____

_____ 27. Appealed to interest of the audience.

_____ 28. Had no introduction—seemed to start in the middle.

_____ 29. Speech seemed incomplete—lacked conclusion.

_____ 30. Lacked knowledge of subject—not well prepared.

_____ 31. Used ideas and materials audience could not understand.

_____ 32. Interrupted other speaker.

_____ 33. Began too many sentences with "well," or "now."

_____ 34. Had a good vocabulary.

_____ 35. Used some words or phrases too often.

_____ 36. Used bad grammar.

_____ 37. Used too many big words.

_____ 38. Used interesting and colorful words.

_____ 39. Had clear, definite sentences.

_____ 40. Used too many slang expressions.

_____ 41. Used "uh" and "and uh" to excess.

_____ 42. Used rambling sentences which were hard to follow.

_____ 43. Contributed worthwhile, relevant material to discussion.

_____ 44. Contributions to discussion irrelevant—off the point.

_____ 45. Accepted responsibility.

_____ 46. Came prepared for work.

_____ 47. Impolite, unco-operative.

_____ 48. Failed to take part in discussion.

_____

Observer

Rating scale plus unstructured comment

SPEECH CRITICISM

Date_____

Speaker_____

Title_____

	Excellent	Good	Fair	Poor

1. Voice ....

2. Organization of material ....

3. Gesture and bodily movement......

4. Audience attention ....

5. Eye contact ....

6. Appearance and manner ....

7. Adaptation of subject matter to the audience ....

8. Comments and suggestions:

_____

_____

_____

_____

_____

Using Student Criticism

We have already suggested that criticism is a function of all members of the speech class. In an earlier chapter we pointed out that critical skill and listening skill are the natural reciprocals of speaking skill, and therefore the development of these skills is one of the basic goals of speech education. Efficient classroom criticism implies widespread use of student criticism. Some of the most significant truths about speech or language are illustrated only by the diversity of response a single performance will arouse in any representative groups of auditors. The recognition of these differences, and the explanation of their significance for the speaker, is one of the basic tasks of speech education. It is a task accomplished largely through the medium of student criticism.

Using Self-Criticism

Since all criticism aims, in part at least, at informing individuals of their own speaking characteristics and potentialities, one of the tests of the productivity of any speech class is its success in developing student ability in self-appraisal. At frequent intervals the teacher needs to gather the statements of students about their own speech needs and goals. Such statements often reveal a discouraging breakdown of communication between teacher and classmates on the one hand, and individual students on the other.

The Individual Conference

One cause of a breakdown in communication is doubtless the state of confused emotionality many students feel immediately subsequent to a speech, or, perhaps, whenever they are discussed by members of a social group. This suggests that the speech conference is one of the most significant and useful critical devices. Such conferences permit frank and open discussion of topics which could not be dealt with in class and which are too complex or emotional for treatment in writing. They permit opening the whole problem of self-appraisal, goal setting, out-of-class speech opportunities, and the like. Speech teachers, like other teachers, all too often call such conferences only with students whose grades are low or whose behavior is obnoxious. The conferences thus become forms of punishment, and are carried out at times when teacher-pupil rapport is low. Ideally, the conferences should be non-disciplinary, and should contribute to the creation of high rapport.

Summary

We have viewed the organization of efficient criticism as involving a balance of oral and written criticism, the use of aids to written criticism, the use of student criticism, of self-appraisal, and of individual conferences. Such activities in the speech class do not guarantee productive teaching, but they do at least make it more probable that criticism will be fruitful, or that the teacher will be aware of the shortcomings of critical communication among members of the class.

SELECTED BIBLIOGRAPHY

Bryan, A. I., and W. H. Wilkie, *The Bryan Wilkie Scale for Rating Public Speeches.* New York Psychological Corporation.

Ewing, William H., "Finding a Speaking-Listening Index," *Quarterly Journal of Speech* (October, 1945), 31: 348–370.

Johnson, Gertrude E. (ed.), *Studies in the Art of Interpretation.* New York: Appleton-Century-Crofts, Inc., 1940, pp. 229–246 (two selections on "Criticism," by W. B. Chamberlain and S. H. Clark, and by S. S. Curry).

Millson, William A. D., "Experimental Work in Audience Reaction," *Quarterly Journal of Speech* (February, 1932), 18: 13–30.

Robinson, Karl F., *Teaching Speech in the Secondary School.* New York: Longmans, Green & Co., 1951, pp. 138–148.

Thonssen, Lester, and Howard Gilkinson, *Basic Training in Speech. Brief Edition.* Boston: D. C. Heath & Company, 1949, 4–8.

CHAPTER 22

Measuring the Results of Instruction

INTRODUCTION

Many educators consider evaluation, or measurement, as both the beginning and the end of the teaching process. Prior to instruction the teacher evaluates his students for diagnostic purposes. He tries to determine their needs and potentialities, to guide him in planning their learning experiences. After instruction he evaluates them again. He wants to find out whether or not learning has taken place—whether or not his methods of instruction have been effective. He evaluates his students also to be able to tell them and their parents the facts about their achievement or lack of it.

For some types of classroom instruction, this procedure of diagnosis, instruction, and appraisal is easily carried out; each step in the process appears as a separate entity. Thus, students seeking to improve speed or comprehension in reading may start their work with a diagnostic reading examination, which will reveal the status of their reading skills. After instruction, they may take another form of the same test, the results of which will indicate their progress, or lack of progress.

While effective speech instruction also incorporates diagnosis, instruction, and appraisal, these processes seldom appear as discrete. Diagnosing a student's speaking needs and skills cannot be accomplished quickly or efficiently with standardized tests, although various such measuring instruments may aid in both diagnosis and appraisal. Diagnosis in speech is a continuous process of observation. Diagnosis starts with the beginning of instruction, as the teacher obtains test data on his students, and as he observes their speech behavior. For the speech teacher, diagnostic activity never is completed. As he observes his students in a great variety of speaking situations, he comes to know their needs better and better. Thus diagnosis and instruction in the speech class proceed hand in hand. The student's participation in speech activity is at once the basis of his instruction, and the basis of diagnostic evaluation. Classroom criticism, an essential aspect of speech instruction, always must be based upon observation and evaluation. And the appraisal of the results of instruction may rest ultimately upon this same type of observation.

THE SCOPE OF THIS CHAPTER

While the teaching of speech, as we have viewed it, is a continuous process of diagnosis, appraisal, and criticism, there may be advantage here in noting separately some considerations relative to the measurement of the results of instruction. We have already considered the diagnostic activities of the speech teacher, and the critical activities of the speech teacher, but the speech teacher faces two other practical tasks which require of him the best possible measurement of the outcomes of his instruction. These two tasks are listed below.

The Speech Teacher Must Measure the Effectiveness of His Instruction

As a control over his materials and procedures, he needs, as far as possible, to know whether or not his students are making progress, what sort of progress, and how much progress.

The Speech Teacher Ordinarily Must Grade His Students

The speech teacher faces the practical task of recording, by means of the grading system of the school, his judgment of the achievement of his students.

For the efficient discharge of the two foregoing tasks, the speech teacher finds it necessary to study the problems of measurement, in order to discover what practicable means are open to him for improving instruction and grading the work of his students.

THE MEASUREMENT PROBLEMS OF THE SPEECH TEACHER

Can the Objectives of Speech Instruction be Measured?

Many teachers think that measurement in education can be accomplished only through the use of tests, and they think that tests are exclusively paper-and-pencil instruments. Within such a frame of reference, a serious question arises as to whether or not the changes in behavior which are the ultimate goal of speech instruction actually can be measured at all. Certainly, no paper-and-pencil test of information, attitude, skill in applying data, and so on, can be regarded as a very exact measure of the speaking proficiency of any individual.[1] For this reason, teachers who think of measurement as necessarily involving the giving of tests and the recording of test scores, raise the question of whether tests actually measure the sort of achievement at which the teaching of speech is directed.

Actually, the measurement of speaking skills must be thought of in a much broader frame of reference than that of paper-and-pencil tests. It is a basic assumption in the field of measurement that the choice of methods must be determined by an examination of what is to be measured, rather than by a consideration of the sort of tests that are available. Thus, the speech teacher must begin thinking of his problems in measuring the outcome of special instruction not in terms of the sort of measuring instruments, or tests, with which he may have become familiar during his own schooling, but in terms of the sort of behavior changes he is hoping to induce with his teaching.

---

[1] Many speech teachers have worked at the problem of devising paper-and-pencil tests which would correlate with speaking proficiency. Some such tests have been developed which will predict reasonably well the speaking proficiency of groups of students. Perhaps the *Knower Speech Attitude Scale and Experience Inventory* is the best known of such instruments. (See F. H. Knower, "A Study of Speech Attitudes and Adjustments," *Speech Monographs* V, 1938.)

If the speech teacher begins his consideration of measurement problems from the standpoint of his goals, he is likely to conclude that no narrow testing program will accomplish much in speech instruction. Almost inevitably the speech teacher will conclude that his instruction is designed to serve such a variety of objectives that measuring them will require a great variety of testing methods. Some of the common objectives of speech tests, together with a description of testing procedures appropriate to each objective, will illustrate our point:

1. *The speech student should acquire information*

One of the objectives of the speech course is helping students to acquire information about speech and the speech process. This information is usually considered instrumental in nature; i.e., students do not seek information for the sake of information, but rather because the information is presumably helpful to them in understanding their own speech, and the speech of others. Knowledge helps students to talk intelligently with other persons about speech. However, since the acquisition of information is one of the objectives of the speech course, procedures appropriate to measuring the acquisition of information well may be used by the speech teacher. These tests usually will be of the paper-and-pencil sort; they will be prepared by the teacher and may be either of the objective or essay type.

2. *The speech student should develop understandings*

General concepts about speech, or understandings of speech, are important intellectual products of speech instruction. The student who studies speech in high school may be expected to develop such understandings as the following:

a. The ability to communicate effectively is essential to personality development, and to social adjustment.

b. There is no fixed form for effective speech. Effective speech fits the speaker, the audience, and the occasion.

c. We should respect the differences we find in the speech of persons from different sections of the country and from different social and economic backgrounds.

d. The ability to observe speech conventions (conventions of statement, organization, pronunciation, usage, and so on), contributes to the security with which a speaker meets social situations.

Understandings of this sort can be measured in a variety of ways. In paper-and-pencil tests, students may be asked to contribute illustrations of these understandings; or to state concepts which might be derived from the examination of an actual speech situation.

3. *The speech student frequently should modify his attitudes*

The speech course should produce changes in the attitudes of speakers toward speaking situations, themselves, and other persons. Attitude changes, like the acquisition of information and understandings, may be considered an instrumental objective for speech instruction, an objective which, if attained, will affect favorably the total speaking behavior of the student. Paper-and-pencil tests of attitude changes are available. For example, student attitudes toward the speaking situation might be measured as follows: On a somewhat subjective level, students may be asked to describe their feelings toward a particular speaking performance. On a more objective level, students may be given mimeographed lists of statements indicating the reactions a speaker might have to a speaking experience, and be asked to check those statements which agree with their own experience. Occasional use of tests of this sort may give the teacher an opportunity to secure evidence that students are actually changing their attitudes toward certain speaking situations.

4. *The speech student should improve his skills of criticism and listening*

The speech course should improve the student's habits of listening, and his skills in criticism. Measuring such audience skills would seem a particularly fruitful area in which speech teachers might develop more reliable methods of measuring the outcomes of instruction. Certain standardized tests designed to give relatively reliable measurements of certain aspects of listening skills already are available for use by speech teachers. Many teachers use informal tests, in which listeners are asked to reproduce in writing such items as the central proposition of a speech, and the main supporting arguments for it. From the data provided by such reports, a score can be determined which shows not only the success of the speaker in reaching his audience but also the success of each member of the audience as a listener.

The critical habits of students toward other speakers may be observed by the speech teacher. Such observation will provide little data for the measurement of changes in critical habits or critical content, unless the teacher adopts some precise method of noting the criticism offered by various students. Some speech teachers ask their students to prepare a series of written criticisms on speeches during the course of a term, and analyze the content of these critiques for evidence of changes in the critical habits of the students. Since criticisms gathered in this way always relate to different speeches, it is difficult for the teacher to be certain whether the changes noted represent actual modifications in the student's critical skills, or merely differences in his reactions to different speeches. Although little work has been done on this type of testing as yet, some teachers are securing the critical responses of students to recorded speech materials, both before and after a period of instruction, to see if changes are observable in the content of the criticisms.

5. *The speech student should acquire skills in specific speech elements*

The speech course seeks changes in the use of particular elements of speaking skill, skills of voice, bodily action, and language. Changes in a student's elementary performance skills ordinarily will be measured through direct observation by the teacher. Again, such observation will furnish data from which the teacher may appraise the results of his instruction only if he adopts some orderly method of recording his data. Sometimes observation will furnish rather specific evidence of change, or lack of change, in the speaker's use of a particular skill. For example, if a student has succeeded in eliminating some specific articulatory problem during the course of his speech work, the observation of this change may be made with considerable accuracy. Some other changes are observed with less certainty; e.g., changes in a student's level of implicit physical activity must be sensed by an observer, and will defy specific description.

Many speech teachers record their observational data on the speech behavior of their students on check lists, or analytical rating scales, of the type illustrated on pages 516 to 519 in Chapter 21. By filling in such rating scales or check lists over a period of time, the speech teacher will seem to have data indicating change, or lack of change, in the effectiveness with which students use various specific speaking skills. We must note, however, that the reliability of ratings on specific aspects of a speaking performance is open to serious question. Persons who listen to a speech performance tend to react to it as a whole. This is the normal pattern of response, and the one we should encourage in our classes. The reaction of the listener to the whole speech, however, tends to color the rating he will give to any particular aspect of it. Thus, the teacher who is pleased by a speech, generally, is pleased, almost indiscriminately, by the speaker's voice, physical action, and language. This tendency of the total judgment to influence judgments of the aspects, or elements, of a total performance is called the halo effect. Research has repeatedly demonstrated the presence of a halo effect in speech ratings.

Another serious problem confronts the teacher who depends upon his observational ratings of student performance as the basis for judging whether or not his students have made progress in attaining the outcomes sought by instruction. The teacher's optimism, or pessimism, may determine his expectations of improvement, and tend to color the ratings he gives a particular student. The teacher who expects improvement, will tend to feel that he is observing improvement. The teacher who fears that the student will not improve, may find his worst fears confirmed by his own observation. Teachers anxious to increase the reliability of their observations over the range of an instructional period, sometimes use before-and-after recordings of student performance to secure a basis for such a measurement. The student is asked to record a particular type of speaking performance before a period of instruction, and to record a similar type of performance after the period of instruction. If these recordings are then rated by persons who have no knowledge of which is the before recording, and which the after, the ratings may give a reliable index of the improvement, or lack of improvement. The use of several judges greatly increases the reliability of the composite ratings. Since a single speech is a very small sample of any student's speaking skill, such before-and-after ratings should not be taken too seriously as the measure of the improvement, or non-improvement of any given student, even though they may measure with considerable reliability the improvement or non-improvement of a group of students. Certain types of speech skills, especially vocal skills, skills of oral language, and skills of speech structure, can be measured through recordings, while other skills, notably those associated with visible action, are obviously beyond the reach of such recordings. Some teachers have used motion pictures to get at the visible skills, although the cost of such a method may be prohibitive for routine measurements.

6. *The speech course should increase skill in the integrated use of all speech processes*

The most important ultimate objective of speech training has traditionally been the development of speaking skills—an integration of all the part processes of speech into the total act of speaking. There is no paper-and-pencil test, or laboratory instrument known today which will measure, either directly or indirectly, the effectiveness of the total act of speech, or the sum of an individual's skills in speaking. For this reason, the most accurate measurement of the most significant outcome of speech instruction must be based upon the observation and evaluative judgment of an auditor, or group of auditors. After all, a speech teacher's grades on the general effectiveness of a series of speech performances may constitute the most direct and significant measurement of the outcomes of instruction. Here again, the optimism, or pessimism of the teacher may affect the trend of his ratings over a period of time. Although recordings of before-and-after speeches can never encompass the whole of speaking skill, they may give a large enough segment of it to be used as a basis for ratings in general effectiveness. Some teachers collect observational data on speech performances by keeping anecdotal records of the speaking performances of individuals in the class. If such notes are kept throughout the course, the teacher, by analyzing the changes in the nature of his records for particular students, may be able to make a valid judgment of the progress, or lack of progress.

While ratings of the general effectiveness of a speech, by its auditors, is the most common measurement of speaking skill, an indirect evaluation of the effectiveness of speaking is sometimes obtained by measuring the effects of the speaking upon the attitudes or knowledge of an audience. Thus a persuasive speech may be rated not in terms of how the listeners value it as a speech, but in terms of the amount of attitude change it produces in the audience. Although the measurement of some audience effects is an instructive sort of evaluation, both to student speakers and to their audience, such measurement is usually severely limited in the range of possible effects which it measures. Therefore, it is not to be considered an equivalent of the generalized judgment which a group of auditors might make about the effectiveness of an act of speaking. Moreover, the measurement of audience effect, in itself, has limited value for diagnosis.

Summary

We started with the question, "Can the results of speech instruction be measured?" The answer is a qualified "yes." If the speech teacher takes a broad view of the objectives of his instruction, and employs a variety of measuring instruments and methods, he will be able to accumulate much data relative to the achievement of his students at any point in their course. Whether these data are ever sufficient to encompass all of the essential skills of speaking, and whether these data are objective enough to give the speech teacher a clear and precise picture of the results of his instruction, are questions which must remain unanswered here; we are not quite sure how accurately the results of speech instruction really can be measured.

The measuring instruments and methods which may be used by the speech teacher include:

Paper and pencil tests

1. *Objective type or essay-type tests of information* (true-false tests, multiple choice tests, completion tests, and so on) which may be prepared by the speech teacher.

2. *Tests which may be prepared by the teacher to measure the acquisition of understandings about speech.* These may include essay-type or objective-type tests involving the application of understandings to specific examples, or the extrapolation of concepts about speech from descriptions of speech situations.

3. *Objective-type or essay-type tests designed to measure student attitudes toward the speaking situation, toward self, and toward other persons.*

4. *Tests of the content and scope of student speech criticism,* derived from essay or objective-type responses to a stimulus speech.

5. *Tests of listening comprehension,* based on the student's ability to reproduce the content or structure of an observed speech.

6. *Standardized tests of critical thinking, personal adjustment, personality, listening comprehension, reading skill or comprehension,* or other items of behavior which may be viewed by the teacher as important products of speech training, and for which tests exist.

Observational measures

1. *Accumulations of anecdotal reports on the speaking performances of students.*

2. *Accumulations of analytical rating scales.* In such reports, various aspects of speaking skill are rated at the time of the speaking performance.

3. *Accumulations of ratings on the general effectiveness of student performance in a series of speaking activities.*

4. *Anecdotal notations on changes in the amount and content of criticism offered by members of a speech class.*

5. *Comparative ratings of paired recordings, in which a specified type of speech performance is made by each student before and after periods of instruction.*

A word of caution may be necessary concerning measurement in the speech field. An experienced teacher viewing the variety of measuring instruments and methods referred to in the preceding list may be moved to observe, "These procedures are all very well, but if I used them, conscientiously and consistently, I would get very little work done other than giving, scoring, recording, and interpreting measurement data!" This point would be well taken. Measurement procedures are always designed to assist, rather than hamper, teaching. Every teacher, therefore, should use only those measurement procedures consistent with his instructional methods and objectives, and only those which he can find time to prepare, administer, interpret, and actually use for the betterment of his own teaching. Our purpose in viewing all of the means by which speech teachers may measure the outcomes of their instruction has not been to imply that the good speech teacher will use all of these measurements at all times, but rather to indicate the range of instruments and methods available to the resourceful and imaginative teacher.

THE PROBLEMS OF RELIABILITY AND VALIDITY IN OBSERVATIONS OF SPEECH BEHAVIOR

At several points in our discussion of the measuring instruments used by speech teachers, we have referred to the problems of reliability and validity. The two general criteria of good educational tests, reliability and validity, are familiar to most teachers today. It may be well, however, to summarize the problems involved in the application of these criteria.

The reliability of any measure refers to its quality of consistency. Since so many of the significant measures of speaking skills are obtained by observation, the speech teacher faces a serious problem of reliability. In general, the reliability of a teacher's observations can be no higher than the consistency he is able to maintain in the conditions which affect his judgment, e.g., the consistency with which he is able to maintain attention, and the consistency of his health and temperament. At best, therefore, observation by a single teacher is apt to have a very low degree of reliability. The problem of reliability in observations is met to some extent by two sorts of practices: (1) As a single teacher observes a large number of acts of speaking by a given student, the reliability of his average rating for all of these performances is apt to be considerably better than his reliability for any single observations; and (2) the reliability with which a single act of speaking is observed, or rated, may be greatly increased by using a number of observers, rather than a single observer. Many speech teachers, therefore, make it a point to use student ratings, as well as their own ratings, in arriving at a somewhat more reliable grade for a single speaking performance. Teachers may also periodically compare students' ratings with their own, to check on the extent to which the ratings tend to agree. This is not to say that any teacher should substitute the composite judgment of a group of high school students for his own grades. However, he well may use such ratings as supplementary to his own judgment.

The validity of any measure refers to its truth or accuracy. The question of validity is, Does the test actually measure what it purports to? A clock which tells time accurately has validity. A clock which is always 18 minutes slow is reliable, but not valid. In general, observations of speech behavior have a certain automatic validity. It is possible, of course, for an observer to delude himself by saying, "I am observing the total effectiveness of this student's speech," while, in reality, he is observing only some specific aspect of that skill, for example, the level of the speaker's vocabulary, or of adherence to correct usage. However, direct observation of complex behavior such as speech is apt to be a more valid measure of it than any indirect test can be. Indeed, about the only way in which the validity of indirect measures of speaking skill can be tested at the present time, is by seeing whether or not these measures correlate with the opinions of persons who observe and rate directly the skill in question.

Speech teachers rightly may feel at times that their observational measurements lack the reliability of the scores they obtain on paper-and-pencil tests of various sorts. They should not, however, succumb to the temptation to place more and more emphasis on paper-and-pencil tests and to distrust and discount their own observations. What the teacher's observations lack in objectivity, they make up in the significance of the factors which they measure. Knower says that, in the final analysis, "The evaluation of the student's achievement (in speech) becomes a matter for expert interpretation and a critical judgment. . . ." [2] At the present time the responsibility for measuring the outcomes of speech instruction rests squarely upon the mature judgment of the speech teacher. He may secure part-measurements and data from many sources, but he must correlate and interpret those data before he can give his final opinion that certain students have or have not improved their speaking.

A RATIONALE FOR GRADING SPEECH STUDENTS

All high school teachers are expected to grade the achievement of their students. This grade most frequently will take the form of a letter, a percentage, or a number grade, which places the stu-

---

[2] F. H. Knower, "What is a Speech Test," *Quarterly Journal of Speech* (December, 1944), 30: 492.

dent on a scale ranging from "superior" to "failing." The utility of the grading system needs little discussion here; it forms an important element in the basis upon which high school credits are given and scholastic honors awarded. It serves the general function of informing each student and his parents of his achievement level in each of his studies. The accumulated grade records of high school students furnish important evidence to their parents, their counselors, and their prospective employers. Nevertheless, the problem of assigning a grade as a summary of a high school student's achievement in speech is often a painful one, involving many complex considerations.

Setting a Standard for Evaluating Achievement

If a student is said to merit a mark of "superior" for his achievement in a speech course, just what meaning is to be attached to that mark? Is he superior as a speaker in comparison with other speakers in his class? Is he superior in the progress he has made in developing speaking skill during the course? Is he superior in the information and understandings about speech he has acquired, or in his critical and listening skills? Is he superior according to some postulated, or hypothetical absolute standard set by the teacher as a norm for superior students? The statement that a student is "superior" has no very definite meaning, unless we know the standard, or criterion upon which the rating is based.

At least three different standards for measuring achievement are used by speech teachers: (1) A hypothetical or absolute standard set by the teacher, or by a group of teachers; (2) a standard derived from the achievement level of the particular student group; and (3) a standard derived from the student's rate of progress. Each of these standards has merit in rating achievement, and, therefore, each should be considered carefully by the speech teacher.

The hypothetical or absolute standard

A speech teacher may decide, prior to teaching his class, that a "superior" speech student will be one who measures up to certain specified standards of superiority which are either envisaged or set forth by the teacher. Thus, the teacher may have decided that a certain body of information about speech should be known by the "superior" student, that certain understandings must be acquired by him, and that his speaking performances, and activity as a critic, must meet certain theoretical levels of superior effectiveness. The peculiar nature of the hypothetical standard may be understood by observing that the teacher using such a standard either may find no one in his class whose achievement is "superior," or, if the standard is low enough, may find many students achieving "superior" status.

The hypothetical standard for measuring achievement is not necessarily a purely arbitrary one. Sometimes groups of teachers working together will set up the objectives of a course of study in terms of the information and understandings which ought to be acquired by students. If their listing of those things which students ought to know is defensible in the light of the acknowledged purposes of education, and if it is reasonable in terms of the capabilities of high school students, it may serve as an effective point of departure for rating the achievement of individual speech students. While it may be fairly easy to set up hypothetical standards for speech information and understanding, it is clear that great difficulties attend the formulation of a hypothetical standard for speech performance. As we have already indicated, the rating of the effectiveness of a speaking performance is always an act of judgment, involving examination of the circumstances peculiar to the act of speaking. Hypothesizing a norm for a "superior" act of speaking, prior to the performance of the act, can be accomplished in only the most general terms.

While the hypothetical standard for speech performance is not wholly feasible, speech and English teachers in certain school systems are exchanging information reflecting their judgment of the qualities teachers ought to look for in "superior" or "inferior" speech. They do this by recording and rating samples of student speaking at various grade levels. Such recordings of "superior" or "inferior" samples probably should be regarded as setting standards for only certain parts of the total act of speaking, or perhaps for such elements as articulation, enunciation, pronunciation, correct usage, and so on. Standards of this sort do not reflect the totality upon which the speech teacher must judge the excellence of an act of speaking, and even these partial standards may have to be modified, to take into account the circumstances peculiar to the given samples.

The standard derived from the achievement level of the group

According to this standard, the achievement rating of any given student indicates his relative position in his class, or, perhaps, among all of the speech students in the school. High school students and their parents are interested in records which represent judgments of this sort. The standard is one which can be easily understood, and it describes the status of a student in a way which is meaningful to him as a member of a competitive society.

It is probable that the achievement level of a given class will influence the judgment of the teacher as to the quality of the speaking of any individual member. There are serious educational objections, however, to making average group performance the standard from which the speaking achievement of every individual is measured. Students who, for physiological or environmental reasons, suffer from severe speech handicaps profit very little by being compared constantly with their more favored fellow students; indeed, such comparisons often seem to contribute to the emotional disturbances of those who have special problems in their speaking.

The standard derived from measuring the student's rate of progress

Some teachers like to measure achievement in their classes by the amount of progress made by a student in ratio to his own present level of ability. Thus, they say, the student is competing neither with some hypothetical norm, which may be either too high or too low for his capabilities, nor with fellow students, whose average ability may be too high or too low to influence his learning in a desirable way. Rather, he is competing with himself, and is concentrating on that aspect of learning which is most significant for him—his own personal improvement. Speech teachers will recognize the fact that the self-performance standard for rating achievement is closely related to the goals of speech instruction, for, as we have said repeatedly, all speech instruction should accept each student on his own terms, take him at his present stage of development, and help him to make maximum improvement. Thus it is probable that all speech teachers use the standard of self-improvement to some extent in rating their students.

There are serious problems, nevertheless, in the rigorous application of such a standard. The standard implies that the speech teacher is able to judge (1) the present level of a student's abilities, and (2) his potential level. Judgments of this sort are tenuous at best. Students with excellent capabilities in speech may make very slow progress, either because they are already working near the maximum level of their capabilities, or because the sort of improvement made by a superior speaker may be subtly involved with his linguistic discriminations, and very hard to measure. Accordingly, no teacher can judge with any degree of accuracy the actual speaking potential of a given student, and, furthermore, there is no test which will measure it. Then too, a student with serious handicaps in speaking may seem to have much room for improvement, and, therefore, be expected to make rapid progress. Yet there is evidence indicating that students whose difficulties stem from excessive social fears make very slow progress in speech improvement, regardless of their present or potential ability level.

Moreover, persons who expect that school records will indicate to some extent the actual achievement level of students may justly observe that the record based on the standard of self-improvement is all but meaningless to those who know none of the facts about either the level at which the student started or the level at which he finished his study.

Summary

The foregoing discussion should suggest the desirability of the grading practice which is widely followed by experienced teachers of speech. Since no one standard will serve all needs, most teachers employ nearly all of the foregoing standards, sometimes separately and sometimes in combination. Thus the teacher may test the student's acquisition of information and understandings against a hypothetical standard, or according to the standard of group achievement, or by both. When both standards are used, the standard furnished by the achievement of the group will serve to influence the teacher's selection of a hypothetical standard. On the other hand, observations of speaking performance may be based on the standard of group achievement as modified by the standard of self-improvement. Some teachers will insist that one or the other standard forms the exclusive basis for their ratings, but both factors usually color the teacher's judgment.

NO SINGLE MEASURE OF ACHIEVEMENT IS VERY MEANINGFUL IN RATING THE WORK OF SPEECH STUDENTS

The foregoing discussion will serve to suggest that a single grade or numerical rating which purports to measure a student's achievement is all but meaningless, except to the person who issued the grade and the persons to whom he has personally explained it. For this reason, many speech teachers in their reports to parents may wish to use a system of reporting that is more elaborate than a grade card.

One suggested report form includes the following:

1. *A letter grade which represents the average of the student's achievement in moving toward all of the goals of the course*—acquiring information, understandings, skills of listening and criticism, and skills of speaking. This grade does not purport to be a statement of the student's speaking skill.

2. *A check list for rating the student's behavior on certain desirable characteristics of personality*, as:

    a. Respect for other persons.

    b. Respect for property.

    c. Reliability in carrying out assigned tasks, and so on.

3. *A rating scale to indicate the student's level of comparative achievement in various aspects of speaking in his age group.* In the case of handicapped students, this scale may be left blank, and comments extended in part (*f*) of the rating form (see page 519).

4. *A space for comments,* describing the individual's specific speech needs, and available lines of improvement.

Filling out such a report form requires considerable labor on the part of the teacher, and in many school systems the teacher's load already is so heavy that it is impossible to utilize such a complicated reporting method. It does, however, make possible the recording of data on achievement, in a form which is helpful to both the student and his parents, and informative to any other person seeking information from school records.

Summary

Every speech teacher should consider carefully the adequacy of his methods for measuring the results of his instruction. It is to his advantage to develop reliable and valid measures of the outcomes which he holds to be important. Only in this way can he check on the quality of his teaching and rate his students fairly and helpfully.

In measuring the results of instruction, the speech teacher ordinarily will use a number of methods and procedures. Paper-and-pencil tests and accumulated observations will furnish the data which, when integrated and interpreted by an expert in speech education, may represent fairly the achievement of the student. There are, however, serious problems which beset the teacher who seeks both reliable and valid measures. These problems are not insurmountable, but they preclude completely satisfactory measurement. The problem of reporting and recording student achievement in speech points to the inadequacy of any one standard and any single school grade as an accurate index of a student's work in the speech class. There is a real need for speech instructors who will bring new energy and imagination to the task of measuring speech skills.

SELECTED BIBLIOGRAPHY

Engelhardt, M. D., "How Teachers Can Improve Their Tests," *Chicago School Journal* (September, 1943), 25: 16–24.

Evans, Dina R., "Report of a Speech Survey in the 9A Grade," *Quarterly Journal of Speech* (February, 1938), 24: 83–90.

Knower, Franklin H., "Conducting a General Speech Survey," *Bulletin of Secondary School Principals* (January, 1948), 32: 208–209.

————, "What Is a Speech Test?" *Quarterly Journal of Speech* (December, 1944), 30: 485–493.

Monroe, Allan, "Testing Speech Performance," *Bulletin of Secondary School Principals* (November, 1945), 29: 133, pp. 156–165.

National Society for the Study of Education, 1946 Yearbook, XLV, *The Measurement of Understanding.* See Part I, "The Measurement of Understanding in the Expressional Arts."

Smith, Eugene R., and Ralph Tyler, *Appraising and Recording Student Progress.*   New York: Harper & Brothers, 1942.

Wrightstone, J. W., "Techniques for Measuring Newer Values in Education," *Journal of Educational Research* (March, 1942), 35: 517–524.

Appendix and Index

Appendix

I. TEACHING FILMS, AND FILM SOURCES

Until recently, few teaching films dealing directly with speech forms or processes were available. This situation is changing rapidly. The growing importance of speech education has led to increased production of teaching aids for this area, and the speech teacher of today will find an impressive array of films available for use in his classes.

Two lists follow: (1) A list of educational films useful for speech classes, and (2) a list of major producers and distributors of such films in the United States.

The lists do not purport to be comprehensive. Rather, they are presented to give the prospective speech teacher some indication of the range and sources of films available to support various aspects of speech training.

Speech teachers interested in getting up-to-date information on available films and film distributors will find a useful source in the *Educational Film Index*, published annually by the H. W. Wilson Company. Audio-visual aid departments, maintained by large city school systems, or by state universities, are also a particularly useful source of information and service.

II. FILM TITLES, LISTED TOPICALLY

Bodily Action	*No. of Distributor* [1]
1. *Speech: Function of Gestures,* 11 min.	46
2. *Speech: Platform Posture and Movement,* 11 min.	46
3. *Posture and Exercise,* 10 min.	12

Voice

1. *High Speed Motion Pictures of the Human Vocal Folds,* 20 min.	4

---

[1] Numbers refer to those in the list of distributors and producers under III (pages 545 to 547).

Language (Including Critical Thinking, Vocabulary, etc.)

Social Adjustment and Social Form

Speech Forms

III. DISTRIBUTORS AND PRODUCERS OF FILMS

1. American Telephone & Telegraph Co.
Information Dept.
Film & Display Division
195 Broadway
New York 7, New York

2. Bailey Films, Inc.
2044 N. Berendo
Hollywood 27, California

3. Bell and Howell
30 Rockefeller Plaza
New York 20, New York

4. Bell Telephone Laboratories
Murray Hill, New Jersey

5. Bray Studios
729 Seventh Avenue
New York 19, New York

6. British Information Service
30 Rockefeller Plaza
New York 20, New York

7. Cleveland Hearing & Speech Center

Western Reserve University
Cleveland, Ohio

8. Columbia Broadcasting System
485 Madison Avenue
New York, New York

9. Coronet Instructional Films
207 E. 37th Street
New York 16, New York

10. Eastin Pictures Co.
Putnam Bldg.
Davenport, Iowa

11. Edited Pictures System, Inc.
165 W. 46th Street
New York 19, New York

12. Encyclopaedia Britannica Films
1150 Wilmette Avenue
Wilmette, Illinois

13. United Film Service
1600 Broadway
New York, New York

14. General Electric
Room 1702B

570 Lexington Avenue
New York, New York

15. General Motors Corp.
Dept. of Public Relations
Film Distribution Section
3044 W. Grand Blvd.
Detroit 2, Michigan

16. International Film Bureau
Suite 1500
6 N. Michigan Avenue
Chicago 2, Illinois

17. Locke Films, Inc.
124 West South Street
Kalamazoo, Michigan

18. March of Time Forum Films
369 Lexington Avenue
New York 17, New York

19. McGraw-Hill Book Company
330 W. 42nd Street
New York, New York

20. Modern Talking Picture
Service
10 Rockefeller Plaza
New York 20, New York

21. Museum of Modern Art
11 W. 53rd Street
New York 19, New York

22. National Film Board of Canada
1270 Avenue of the Americas
New York, New York

23. National Safety Council
Chicago, Illinois

24. New York University
New York, New York

25. Ohio State University
Columbus 10, Ohio

26. Pennsylvania State College
State College, Pennsylvania

27. Radio Corporation of America
144 E. 24th Street
New York, New York

28. Rutgers University
Newark, New Jersey

29. Illinois State Normal
University
Normal, Illinois

30. State University of Iowa
Iowa City, Iowa

31. Teaching Film Custodians
25 West 43rd Street
New York 18, New York

32. U. S. Army
Army Rehabilitation Center
Washington, D. C.

33. University of Denver
Denver, Colorado

34. United World Films, Inc.
1445 Park Avenue
New York, New York

35. University of California at
Los Angeles
Los Angeles, California

36. University of Illinois
Division of Service for
Crippled Children
Urbana, Illinois

37. University of Michigan
Ann Arbor, Michigan

38. University of Minnesota
Minneapolis, Minnesota

39. University of Southern
California
Los Angeles, California

40. University of Wisconsin
Madison, Wisconsin

41. Veterans Administration
Visual Aids Service
Office of Public Relations
Washington 25, D. C.

42. Western Electric Co.
Motion Picture Bureau
195 Broadway
New York, New York

43. Westinghouse
Box 868–511 Wood St.
Pittsburgh 30, Pa.

Box 306 Fourth Ave.,
Pittsburgh, Pa.

44. Willow Distributing Co.
13 E. 37th Street
New York 16, New York

45. Yale University

Department of Theatre
New Haven, Connecticut

46. Young America Films, Inc.
18 E. 41st St.
New York 17, New York

IV. RECORDING MACHINES

The usefulness of sound recording machines for teaching speech has been recognized for many years, but only in the last decade has such equipment become generally available to the high school speech teacher. The development of magnetic recording processes, since the end of World War II, has made it possible for schools to secure low-cost recording equipment, simple enough to be operated efficiently by teachers or students after a few minutes of instruction, and yet capable of reproducing speech with reasonable fidelity. These recording machines have become the most frequently used and serviceable aid in the teaching of speech. Some of the uses to which they have been put are listed below.

1. For recording student speech as a preliminary to self-analysis of vocal characteristics—strengths and weaknesses.

2. For voice drills. Students seeking to establish certain vocal habits may drill with a recording machine, once their capacity to recognize and produce the desired voice objective has been established.

3. For recording classroom speeches, readings, discussions, debates. The recording may be used as a basis for critical discussion of the speaking activity in question.

4. For collecting a library of student speech performances. The recording machine gives each teacher the opportunity to build a library of speaking performances which illustrate the ways in which high school students handle particular assignments.

5. For bringing current speech materials taken from the radio before an entire class. Public speeches, discussion, or plays broadcast over the radio may be recorded for presentation to a speech class at its regular meeting time.

Types of Recording Equipment

Speech teachers may be interested in examining the various types of recording equipment available today. Two general types of recording machines are most commonly used.

Record cutters or embossers

Machines of this type include those which (1) record student speaking by cutting an acetate, or wax recording disk, or (2) record student speaking by embossing grooves on plastic disks or belts.

Magnetic recorders

The machines most commonly used are those which record on a plastic or paper tape, coated with magnetic oxides, or those which record on a steel or plated brass wire. Magnetic recording is also done on coated paper discs. The so-called "tape recorders" have become increasingly popular with speech teachers for a number of reasons: Recorded materials may be erased, and the tapes used over and over again, indefinitely; recorded materials may be edited by cutting out sections of tape, and splicing parts together; tapes which are broken accidentally may be quickly and easily mended; the recording operation is so simple that high school students may be instructed readily in the operation of the machine; and even the low-cost, portable recorders give a quality suitable for instruction in speech class. New models of magnetic recorders are constantly appearing, and the school contemplating the purchase of such equipment should seek the most recent information on available models.

The Cost of Recording Machines

Portable recording equipment is readily available today in the $100 to $200 price range. More durable machines, and machines giving more faithful reproduction, are available at prices from $200 to $1000.

V. SOME SOURCES OF RECORDING EQUIPMENT

1. Ampex Electric Corporation, Howard Avenue at Laurel, San Carlos, Calif.
2. Amplifier Corporation of America, 396–398 Broadway, New York 13, N. Y.
3. Ampro Corporation, 2835 Northwestern Ave., Chicago 18, Ill.
4. Bell Sound Systems, Inc., 555 Marion Rd., Columbus 7, Ohio
5. Berlant Associates, 4917 W. Jefferson Blvd., Los Angeles 6, Calif.
6. The Brush Development Co., 3405 Perkins Ave., Cleveland 4, Ohio.
7. Crestwood Recorder Corp., 624 West Adams St., Chicago 6, Ill.
8. Dictaphone Corporation, 420 Lexington Ave., New York, N. Y.
9. Eicor, Inc., 1501 Congress St., Chicago 7, Ill.
10. The General Industries Co., Elyria, Ohio
11. The Gray Mfg. Co., 16 Arbor St., Hartford 1, Conn.
12. Mark Simpson Mfg. Co., Inc., 32–28 49th St., Long Island City 3, N. Y.
13. Operadio Mfg. Co., St. Charles, Ill.
14. The Pentron Corp., Chicago 16, Ill.
15. Permoflux Corporation, 4900 West Grand Ave., Chicago 39, Ill.
16. Magnecord Inc., 360 North Michigan Ave., Chicago 1, Ill.
17. Presto Recording Corp., P.O. Box 500, Hackensack, N. J.
18. Revere Camera Co., 320 East 21st St., Chicago 16, Ill.

19. Sonar Radio Corp., 59 Myrtle Ave., Brooklyn 1, N. Y.
20. The Soundscriber Corp., 146 Munson St., New Haven 4, Conn.
21. The Stancil-Hoffman Corp., 1016 North Highland Ave., Hollywood 38, Calif.
22. Tapetone Mfg. Corp., Sales Office: Broadcasting Program Service, 23 W. 45th St., New York 19, N. Y.
23. Universal Electronics Sales Corp., 1500 Walnut St., Philadelphia 2, Pa.
24. Webster Electric Co., Racine, Wisc.
25. Wilcox-Gay Corp., Charlotte, Mich.

VI. RECORDED TEACHING AIDS AND THEIR SOURCES

The increasing availability of recorded speech materials suggests that speech teachers may find it both useful and practical to develop a "speech library." Recordings of public speeches, discussions, debates, readings, radio programs, and plays may be assembled by anyone who has recording equipment available. Such locally recorded materials may be supplemented by the recorded materials available commercially, or through audio-visual education services. Both sorts of materials may be used to supplement the teaching of nearly all aspects of speech. Such recordings may be used to illustrate facts and understandings about speech processes and forms, to stimulate the interest of students in various types of speaking, and to indicate for them the range of possible speech skills.

VII. SOME SOURCES OF RECORDED MATERIALS

The following companies, agencies, or educational institutions, have available recorded speech materials. Such materials are constantly being released, and speech teachers will need to follow information on the current releases of the major recording companies.[2]

1. Britam Agencies, Inc., 245 Fifth Ave., New York 16, N. Y.
2. Capitol Records, Inc., 250 W. 57th St., New York, N. Y.
3. Columbia Records, Inc., 799 Seventh Ave., New York, N. Y.
4. Dartmouth Recording Project, Department of Speech, Dartmouth College, Hanover, New Hampshire
5. Decca Records, Inc., 50 W. 57th St., New York, N. Y.
6. Linguaphone Institute, 92 RCA Building, New York 20, N. Y.
7. Lyrichord Discs, Inc., 464 W. 51st St., New York 19, N. Y.
8. The National Council of Teachers of English, 211 W. 68th St., Chicago 21, Ill.
9. RCA Victor Manufacturing Company, Camden, N. J.
10. Speech Arts Studio, Radio City, New York 20, N. Y.

---

[2] *The Quarterly Journal of Speech* and *The Speech Teacher* review newly released recorded speech materials.

Some recordings of interest to high school teachers

"I Can Hear It Now," Vols. I, II, Edward R. Murrow, narrator, Columbia.

"Poets Reading Their Own Works," The Harvard Vocarium Records, Harvard Record Service, Cambridge, Mass. (A series of recordings prepared by Associate Professor F. C. Packard, with such poets as Carl Sandberg, T. S. Eliot, Lennox Robinson, and Edith Sitwell.)

"The Appreciation of Poetry," Vol. I of Masterpieces of Literature, Columbia. (Recorded under the auspices of the National Council of Teachers of English.)

"Dartmouth Recording Project," Volumes I and II. (Readings of prose and poetry recorded by 20 teachers at the 1950 convention of the Speech Association of America.) Department of Speech, Dartmouth College, Hanover, N. H.

VIII. EXCHANGE SERVICES FOR TAPE RECORDINGS

Speech teachers will be interested in checking on the availability of "tape recordings" on an exchange basis through audio-visual education services. As an example of such services, the "Tapes for Teachers" project of the Extension Division, University of Minnesota, collects tape recordings of radio programs, and other materials which will be of interest to high school teachers, and which can be released to teachers. Teachers may select recordings of interest to them, and obtain these programs by sending in a roll of recording tape. The program desired is recorded on the teacher's tape, and returned for use in the classes. Such services seem likely to become increasingly available throughout the nation.

Index

551